Eau Claire Normal School students, 1916-17

Building Excellence:
University *of* Wisconsin-Eau Claire
1916-2016

by
Robert J. Gough and James W. Oberly

Maps by
Ezra J. Zeitler

THE DONNING COMPANY
PUBLISHERS

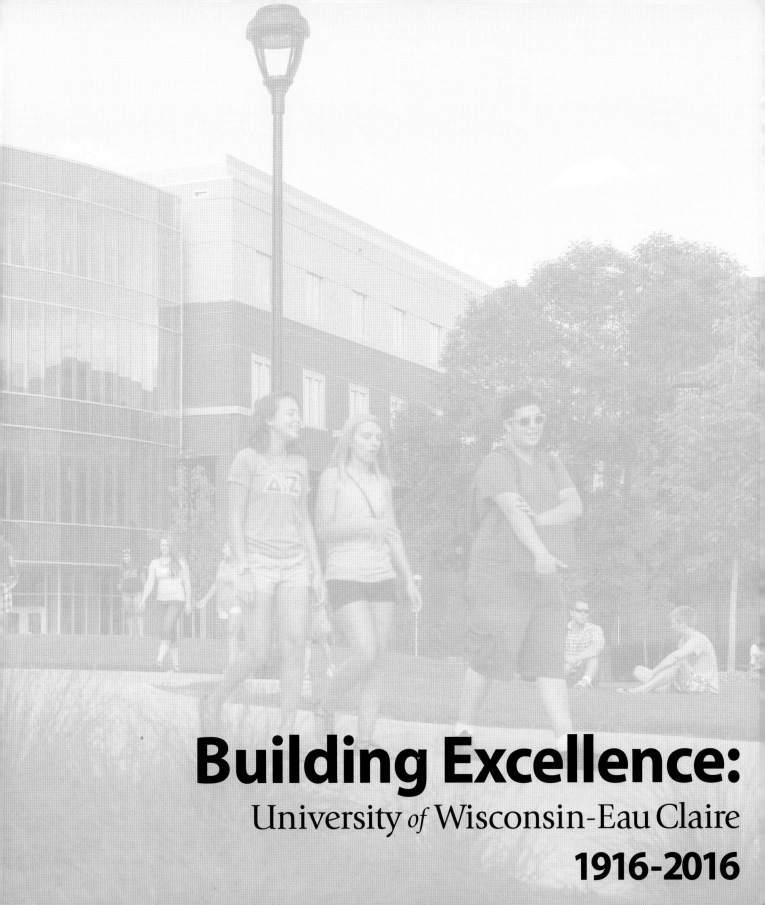

Building Excellence:
University *of* Wisconsin-Eau Claire
1916-2016

Robert J. Gough and James W. Oberly

Maps by
Ezra J. Zeitler

Copyright © 2016 by University of Wisconsin Eau Claire Foundation Inc.
P.O. Box 4004
Eau Claire, WI 54702-4004

All rights reserved, including the right to reproduce this work in any form whatsoever without permission in writing from University of Wisconsin Eau Claire Foundation Inc., except for brief passages in connection with a review.

Production by:
The Donning Company Publishers
184 Business Park Drive, Suite 206
Virginia Beach, VA 23462

Lex Cavanah, General Manager
Nathan Stufflebean, Production Supervisor
Anne Burns, Editor
Terry Epps, Graphic Designer
Dusti Merrill, Project Research Coordinator
Monika Ebertz, Imaging Artist
Katie Gardner, Marketing Advisor

Barry Haire, Project Director

Cataloging-in-Publication Data available from the Library of Congress

ISBN 978-1-68184-026-0

Printed in the United States of America

Contents

6	Preface by Foundation President Kimera Way
7	Foreword by Chancellor James C. Schmidt
8	Introduction
10	Chapter One—*In the Beginning: Eau Claire Builds a Normal School*
28	Chapter Two—*Institutional Struggles and Successes, 1916–41*
52	Chapter Three—*The Social and Academic World of Eau Claire State Students, 1916–41*
76	Chapter Four—*Building a State College During a Tumultuous Decade, 1941–52*
100	Chapter Five—*The College Leonard Haas Built, 1952–64*
130	Chapter Six—*The New University: Excellence and Growth, 1964–71*
164	Chapter Seven—*Pursuing Excellence Within a New State System, 1971–80*
194	Chapter Eight—*Conflicting Paths to Excellence, 1980–90*
218	Chapter Nine—*Redefining Excellence at the End of the Century*
240	Chapter Ten—*Measured Excellence in the New Century*
264	Acknowledgments
265	Bibliographical Note
268	Index
272	About the Authors

Preface

When we first started discussing plans for how to commemorate the University's Centennial, now a number of years ago, it was certain that a centerpiece of the celebration would be the story of our past. And who better to record the account of the spirit of this wonderful place than two of UW-Eau Claire's esteemed professors. Dr. Gough and Dr. Oberly committed to this project if they could write an honest and comprehensive record of our history as we look to enter our second century. They have more than exceeded our hopes and expectations.

The UW-Eau Claire Foundation is pleased and honored to publish this account of our past. We offer it in tribute to those who went before, paving the way for us today to "foster in one another creativity, critical insight, empathy and intellectual courage." Our hope is that readers find points of intersection with their own connection to the University while envisioning the future we all seek to create.

Here's to the University of Wisconsin-Eau Claire!

Kimera Way, President
UW-Eau Claire Foundation

100 YEARS OF excellence

Foreword

Anniversaries provide good opportunities for looking back and taking stock of how an institution has changed, what it has accomplished, and where it is headed. Bob Gough and Jim Oberly provide us with rich fodder for thoughtful reflection with their centennial history, *Building Excellence: University of Wisconsin–Eau Claire, 1916–2016*.

From 184 students in 1916, UW–Eau Claire has grown over the past one hundred years to almost 10,500 students. From its founding as a single-purpose school for aspiring teachers, it has expanded into a nationally recognized regional, master's level university with programs in nursing, business, and the liberal arts, as well as teacher preparation. From a single building in 1916, its campus has grown to twenty-eight structures on 333 acres with new facilities planned with public and private partners throughout the community.

As Gough and Oberly tell the story of this remarkable university, however, a pattern emerges across one hundred years of change: a consistent focus on providing for students from all backgrounds an education marked by excellence. While local, state, and national conditions change, the authors argue, campus leaders, staff, and faculty have always found new ways to deliver on this singular commitment to excellence.

The history of UW–Eau Claire shows we should expect the unexpected. World wars, social turmoil, economic recessions, changing demographics, academic mergers, and legislative changes from Madison and Washington all have left their mark and shaped the present and future for UW–Eau Claire. Many of the same questions we are asking today have been part of the continuing dialog of this university: What does it mean to be a Blugold? How do we assure both access and quality for our students? What does excellence mean for today and for tomorrow? Each generation has answered these questions in different ways, contributing to the many accomplishments this book outlines and strengthening our commitment to excellence. I am inspired by these stories and encouraged as the current generation of faculty, staff, and students continue to create our own responses to the questions of our times.

I invite all members of the Blugold family—alumni, friends, faculty, staff, and community members—to celebrate and learn from this history. Ours is a collaborative history, written with many partners and supporters. Together we take pride in UW–Eau Claire's one hundred years of achievement and look forward to a second century that continues our commitment to excellence.

James C. Schmidt
*Chancellor, University of
Wisconsin–Eau Claire*

**Chancellor
James Schmidt**

Schmidt was appointed chancellor in March 2013. He had been vice president for university advancement at Winona State University and executive director of the WSU Foundation.

Introduction

> But the wildest notion?—Enacted here—that not just
> the glittering sons of the rich, but the daughters
> and sons of farmers and mill hands might learn
> the art of how we learn, and how we pass it on.

The Poet Laureate of Wisconsin, University of Wisconsin–Eau Claire English professor Max Garland, read these lines from his poem "Dedicating a School by the River" in November 2013 at the inauguration of the university's seventh chancellor, James Schmidt. Garland was describing the spirit expressed in October 1916 at the dedication ceremony for the new Eau Claire State Normal School. Over the next one hundred years the normal school expanded in size and grew in scope, successively becoming the Eau Claire State Teachers College, the Wisconsin State College at Eau Claire, the Wisconsin State University–Eau Claire, and the University of Wisconsin–Eau Claire. As its roles and titles changed, however, the institution remained focused on its original goal: providing educational opportunities for students from the widest possible social and economic backgrounds.

As the university marks its centennial, this book will narrate how UW–Eau Claire achieved this goal. In part it is the story of an *institution*, with attention to presidents, regents, legislators, governors, donors, budgets, laws, committee reports, building construction, and so forth. It is also the story of *people*—students, faculty, administrators, community members in the region, and the people of Wisconsin more generally—and the ways in which their interactions shaped UW–Eau Claire. The university which exists today, as a result of these stories, is a special place, as this book will establish. But our narrative will also show that political events and social and economic developments in Wisconsin and throughout the United States affected the institution in ways similar to how they generally affected higher education throughout the nation during the past century.

The chapters that follow proceed roughly chronologically, with topical organization within them (chapters two and three together cover the 1916–40 period, congruent with the presidency of Harvey A. Schofield, and have topics distributed between the two chapters). Several themes emerge:

- For roughly the first third of the university's history, the institution's goal was survival. During the next third, it was dramatically transformed by unexpected expansion in multiple dimensions, made possible by increased financial support from the State of Wisconsin, and developed a focus on "excellence" in its programs. During the most recent third of its history, the university was outwardly stable and unchanging, while inwardly expanding excellence, in an environment of sharply decreasing state financial support and increasing influence from programs and policies of the national government.
- The leadership of presidents and chancellors has been central to shaping the institution, but their academic backgrounds, personalities, leadership styles, and visions have changed across time. Effective leadership in one era was different from that in another.
- As part of formal systems of post-secondary education, UW–Eau Claire has always been linked to other educational institutions in Wisconsin. This linkage has created a back-and-forth tug between centralized and local control and has also induced both cooperation and competition with other educational institutions.
- The profile of faculty members has changed from being exemplary elementary and secondary teachers, to being academics who had earned PhDs, to being scholars who engage in collaborative research with students.
- The explosion in enrollment during the second third of the university's history provided the basis for a more "collegiate" experience for students, at a time when they also received greater recognition of their personal and academic rights. Institutional oversight of students became more professional at the same time it had to adapt to changing attitudes and values of students.

- From its outset, UWEC enrolled students with backgrounds from a range of economic strata. The college was also in important ways a women's domain in its early years, but it became "masculinized" in the middle decades of the twentieth century. In the last decades of the century, it attracted growing numbers of students from underrepresented groups and international students, while at the same time its enrollment again became predominately female.
- As human knowledge expanded, and the mission of the university changed, the curriculum for students grew more elaborate and provided opportunities for more specialized study. The faculty, administration, and outside critics, however, always remained unsure about the seriousness of students.
- Members of the local community supported the university in its struggles to survive and expand and welcomed its positive financial, cultural, and entertainment impact, while seeking to insulate themselves from any restrictions or inconveniences the university might bring to their community.

The writing of the history of higher education in the United State has been based, to a great extent, on the experiences of the major research universities and prominent liberal arts colleges. In recent decades, the stories of women's colleges and historically black colleges and universities have edged their way into the overall account. Still absent from the narrative, however, is the story of institutions such as UW–Eau Claire which began as publically supported normal schools with the single purpose of teacher education. There are about 195 such colleges and universities in the United States in 2016, which enroll about 17 percent of students who attend four-year colleges and universities. About 10 percent of these institutions are still small "Baccalaureate Colleges," according to the classification of the Carnegie Foundation for the Advancement of Teaching. Another 15 percent of them have become "Research Universities" in the Carnegie scale. But the overwhelming majority of these former teacher-education institutions, including UW–Eau Claire, are what Carnegie calls "Master's Colleges and Universities" (which are part of a larger, loosely defined group often referred to as "regional comprehensive universities"). Their accomplishments need to be highlighted in the history of higher education in the United States.

Wisconsin's Most Beautiful Campus

With about 10,500 students, UW–Eau Claire is a bit larger than most "Master's Colleges and Universities," which have a median enrollment of about eight thousand. With a "Medium-sized," rather than a "Larger-sized," master's program, according to the Carnegie classification, UW–Eau Claire retains more of an undergraduate focus than most master's institutions. The quality of its undergraduate programs is also high: its admission's profile is categorized by Carnegie as "More Selective," which is a designation shared by less than 10 percent of former normal schools and only about 15 percent of all public four-year colleges and universities.

More importantly, returning to the poetry of Max Garland, UW–Eau Claire as its first priority in 2016 continues to teach its students that "it's by cultivating wonder/the commonwealth is fed."

IN THE BEGINNING:
Eau Claire Builds a Normal School

The existence today of the University of Wisconsin-Eau Claire is a consequence of one of the most important developments in nineteenth-century American history.

Beginning in the 1830s the "common school" movement introduced a widespread system of free public education. To staff the schools created by this movement, individual states established "normal" schools. In 1916 the Eau Claire State Normal School was one of the last such institutions to be established in the United States. Already by that time, though, in an era of economic transformation and political reform, many communities wanted their normal schools to expand their scope to include liberal arts education and, especially, professional training for occupations other than teaching. From its beginning Eau Claire Normal contained the seeds of what would become a multi-purpose regional university in the twenty-first century.

Public Schools and the Growth of West Central Wisconsin

Starting in the 1830s in Massachusetts, school reformers such as Horace Mann successfully advocated for an expanded, better-organized, and publically financed system of schools. The goals of these "common schools" were to assimilate the increasing number of non-British immigrants who were coming to the United States, teach them Protestant morality, and discipline them to become productive workers in a dynamic economy that was beginning to be transformed by industrialization. These schools needed teachers. Reformers in America looked to the model of Prussia, which had established in 1819 a state-supported system of teacher training institutions. In 1838, Massachusetts created three such "normal schools" (from the French *ecole normale*), with the expectation the localities in which they were located would donate buildings and their furnishings. Governor Edward Everitt emphasized the potential of these schools to be "an instrument of great good."

Public schools multiplied in number and enrollment and expanded westward as the United States grew during the nineteenth century. Between 1869 and 1899 the proportion of five to seventeen year olds who were enrolled in school increased from 57 percent to 72 percent; correspondingly, the number of teachers more than doubled. As Yankees migrated westward, New York, Pennsylvania, Michigan, and eventually Wisconsin followed the example of Massachusetts and established state normal schools to train some of these teachers. Even more than for occupations in agriculture, applied science, and engineering, post-secondary education expanded in late-nineteenth-century America to meet the demand for professionally trained teachers. Between 1866 and 1909, eight normal schools opened in Wisconsin alone. By 1900, there were about 140 such schools nationwide, enrolling 67 percent more students than they had a decade previously. In Wisconsin in 1900 there were 538 graduates from the normal schools.

In addition to providing staff, particularly for city and village elementary schools, normal schools offered educational and leadership opportunities for students, especially women, from social and

Eau Claire in 1906

By the early twentieth century an impressive central business district had emerged in post-lumber era Eau Claire. The four-story building at the center-left is the Masonic Temple (1898), now listed on the National Register of Historic Places and occupied by the Antiques Emporium. The Romanesque-Revival style building at center-right was the Ingram Block (1893), occupied in 1906 by the Orrin Ingram Lumber Company and other businesses and later the Middlefart Clinic. It is now the site of a parking lot. (L. E. Phillips Memorial Public Library photo collection, Chippewa Valley Museum)

economic groups which at that time could not expect to attend four-year degree-granting institutions. More so than their New England forebears, these midwestern normal schools were "people's colleges." They met the democratic demands of local citizens for schools where their children could complete high school or even a year or two of post-secondary study, without necessarily committing themselves to lifetime careers as teachers.

The decades at the beginning of the twentieth century were also ones of growth and change in West Central Wisconsin. In the wake of the collapse of the lumber boom in Wisconsin in the mid-1880s, civic leaders in Eau Claire labored to rebuild and rebrand the city's economy. An energetic booster claimed the city promised to be "the Poor Man's Paradise, the Capitalist's Opportunity, the Millionaire's Playground." Lumber-era enterprises, such as Phoenix Manufacturing and McDonough Manufacturing, found new markets in the western United States for their sawmill equipment. Businesses linked to new directions in the national economy, most importantly the Gillette Safety Tire Company, built manufacturing plants in the city. A handsome Carnegie library, constructed in 1905, embodied the cultural aspirations of the community. Enrollment at Eau Claire High School doubled between 1899 and 1907 to 560 pupils. Three trunk railroads connected Eau Claire to Milwaukee, Chicago, and the Twin Cities, and an interurban electric trolley took passengers back and forth to Chippewa Falls, a city of eight thousand about fifteen miles to the north. Eau Claire itself was a city of 17,500 in 1900, and the number of residents in Eau Claire and adjacent counties had increased to 181,000 from 154,000 in 1890. Boosters wanted to further diversify the city's economy, strengthen it as the focus of its geographical region, and improve the education of its children by getting a state normal school located in Eau Claire. They started their labors in earnest in 1893.

A Normal School for Eau Claire

Repeated efforts by Eau Claire normal school advocates were at first unsuccessful but improved markedly in 1908 when there was a change in membership of the board of regents which governed all the state normal schools. Eight of the ten regents appointed by the governor represented the interests of the schools located in their community (and actually participated in their administration). There were also two at-large regents, and when a vacancy occurred in 1908 civic leaders in Eau Claire organized a mass meeting to nominate a candidate who would push to establish another normal in their city. Governor James Davidson appointed their choice, Emmet Horan, a partner in McDonough Manufacturing. Horan's lobbying, in conjunction with the efforts of Senator John Thomas from Chippewa County, was successful, and in 1909 the legislature designated Eau Claire as the site for a ninth normal school. The legislation made it clear, though, that the City of Eau Claire "without cost to the state, shall furnish a suitable site" for the school.

On July 27 a committee of regents visited a dozen potential sites in a caravan of "fast racing automobiles," only one of which held up for the entire tour. Three sites emerged as top candidates: on the West Side, ten acres on the peninsula surrounded by Half-Moon Lake (what is now Carson Park), owned by Eugene Shaw; in the Third Ward, a seven-acre lot near the junction of Little Niagara Creek and the Chippewa River, owned by the Park Company; and, on the East Side Hill, a large tract owned by J. C. Barland. (Eventually, another East Side Hill site, thirty-five acres adjacent to Forest Hill cemetery owned by lumberman John S. Owen, which the committee had not visited in July, also attracted consideration.)

The subsequent heated debate in the newspapers and at a public meeting on January 31, 1910, regarding which site was preferable brought out class and neighborhood divisions within Eau Claire. Supporters of the Third Ward location emphasized it adjoined "the best residential section of the city," while supporters of the West Side site, in particular, emphasized it would be more accessible to the "laboring people" who should be the natural constituency of a normal school. The Park Company wanted $7,000 from the city for its land, critics pointed out, while Eugene Shaw offered to donate his. The predominant opinion at the January 31 meeting, observed by three regents, was in favor of the West Side location. At their February meeting, however, the board of regents selected the Park Company's site. Its natural beauty, the supposed favorable quality of its soils for construction, and its proximity to the city's streetcar system apparently persuaded the regents, while they were concerned about the lack of existing infrastructure at the Half Moon Lake site.

It was now the responsibility of the city to acquire the designated property, a process further complicated by the regents' insistence on securing a twelve-acre site rather than the seven-acre lot they had originally identified. David Drummond, representing the Park Company, was a hard bargainer with the city fathers, insisting on $12,000 for their twelve acres. The Park Company rejected the city's counteroffer of $9,000 and Horan warned that Eau Claire was in danger of losing the normal school if it did not promptly meet the regents' requirements. The *Eau Claire Leader* finally openly explained the underlying issue: lumberman Henry C. Putnam, the principal owner of the Park Company, was hinting he intended to donate to the city undeveloped land "of much value" that adjoined the normal school site (perhaps a reference to land Putnam had actually *already* donated, which today is Putnam Park, or perhaps to other property). Therefore, "why not pass over what seems an excessive amount asked for the twelve acres," the editors concluded. The city commissioners finally acceded to the $12,000 price tag (comparable to about $300,000 in 2016), and the Park Company agreed to substitute land abutting Park Avenue in place of less-desirable, lower-lying acreage. A few months later, during a controversy about changing the city's form of government, a critic of the existing system claimed the commissioners had "stood by and saw the city butchered for the sake of a few money grubbers and never entered a protest." The newspaper's editor indignantly denied "most emphatically" this implication of "graft in the selection of the Normal school site" and called on everyone "to look up and not down and have 'Enthusiasm for Eau Claire.'"

The resolution of the controversy over site selection secured for the normal school a beautiful natural location on a bend in the Chippewa just beneath the river's bluffs. The location enabled it to eventually promote itself as "Wisconsin's most beautiful campus." This original location, however, also contained limitations, as subsequent chapters will discuss. Soil conditions proved to be unfavorable, rather than ideal, for future building projects. Even when the Third Ward became fully developed during the interwar years and was built up to the edge of the school's campus, it could not provide sufficient affordable rental housing for students. Furthermore, this valuable residential land to its east, the river to its north, and the bluffs to its west and south blocked future expansion of the campus, as critics had brought out during the controversy in 1910.

Getting the Normal School Built

Supporters of the new normal still had to overcome several hurdles before the school eventually opened in 1916. "Eau Claire must leave no loophole for others to successfully oppose our getting the new normal school," the local newspaper warned early in 1911, "and the matter had better be pushed to the finish at the present time." The historic 1911 session of the Wisconsin legislature adopted numerous Progressive reforms, including an income tax, designed to increase political democracy, extend economic regulation, and provide greater social opportunities for state residents. Additionally, during this session the legislature found time to consider proposals that affected the incipient Eau Claire Normal School. In the aftermath of the death of James Stout, the legislature thought about taking over the existing Stout Institute in Menomonie, twenty-five miles to the west of Eau Claire, which educated manual training and domestic science teachers. For reasons of efficiency, Senator Timothy Burke of Green Bay advocated combining it with the new normal school. Other proposals called for building a new normal in Green Bay, Rhinelander, or Antigo in place of or in addition to Eau Claire. Rumors that quickly circulated in Madison that the site selected for the Eau Claire campus was swampy encouraged these second thoughts among legislators. Another mass meeting in Eau Claire, on March 22, expressed public support for going ahead with building in Eau Claire, and local civic leaders and their legislators eventually deflected the proposals that favored other sites in the state. Before adjourning, the legislature made a small appropriation which was spent during the 1911–13 biennium for site preparation and architectural planning for the normal in Eau Claire.

There was another push in 1913 to get funding for the construction of a building. Twenty-six citizens, including Horan, Orrin Ingram, and Owen, published a twelve-page pamphlet, *Eau Claire State Normal School: Why the Normal School Should Be Constructed Now*. A group of fifty, with representatives from as far away from Eau Claire as Black River Falls and Rice Lake, traveled by special railroad train coach to Madison to lobby in person for the building project. In their efforts, the business community was joined by the Eau Claire Socialist party, which endorsed building the normal school as beneficial to "workers' children." These efforts were successful. The legislature appropriated $225,000, in three yearly installments, for normal school construction in Eau Claire.

Beginning in the summer of 1914, the Hoeppner-Bartlett Company of Eau Claire built a 100,000-square-foot school building, with two floors and a full basement, on the site that had been selected in 1911. Prominent Milwaukee architects Henry Van Ryn and Gerrit Jacob DeGelleke designed the structure, which contained an auditorium, library, gymnasium, and cafeteria in addition to offices and classrooms.

Eau Claire County Training School, c. 1909

Commonly referred to as the County Normal, the training school was located at 746 Second Avenue across the street from the county courthouse.

EAU CLAIRE STATE NORMAL SCHOOL

Old Main, c. 1916

Old Main at the time of construction, before landscaping.

Van Ryn and DeGelleke were prolific architects of public school and normal school buildings. In 2016 thirteen of their surviving structures in Wisconsin are listed on the National Register of Historic Places. Their building in Eau Claire clearly echoes a design they did a decade previously for the first building at La Crosse State Normal. There were squabbles that threatened to delay the construction of their Eau Claire building: the Wisconsin Federation of Labor protested to the regents that the contractor was not observing prevailing standards regarding maximum work hours, and an Eau Claire businessman complained to the governor the contractor was using wood from out of state. The regents skillfully deflected these problems and the building was completed in September 1916. "Old Main" essentially would be the only building on the Eau Claire campus for the next thirty-five years.

The Expansion of Education in the Progressive Era

While the normal school project was gradually coming to fruition between 1909 and 1916, other opportunities developed in Eau Claire for post-secondary education. In response to a 1908 law which for the first time required at least six weeks of formal training for a beginning teacher, the normal school regents established summer programs, including one at Eau Claire starting in 1910. Through an arrangement with River Falls Normal, Eau Claire summer students received credit toward normal school diplomas. Delos Kinsman from Whitewater Normal (who had drafted for the legislature the 1911 income tax law) was president of the 1916 summer session at Eau Claire, which enrolled 234 students, about half of them high school graduates. Future students could start their studies in this summer program and transfer their credits when Eau Claire Normal opened.

In addition, beginning in 1905 Eau Claire County operated a training school for rural teachers, which had been authorized by 1899 legislation. One of twenty-seven such schools around the state by 1912, this Eau Claire County Normal School offered a two-year program for students with an eighth-grade education and a one-year program for high school graduates. Over one hundred students registered at the county normal in the fall of 1915. During these years, still another stream of teachers came from the high school in nearby Chippewa Falls, which in 1912 set up its own program to train teachers for country classrooms.

Library, 1917
This room housed the college's library for over forty years. All the rooms in Old Main originally had the wood floors shown by this photograph.

The University of Wisconsin also expanded its presence in Eau Claire. Under the leadership of Charles R. Van Hise, appointed president in 1904, the university pushed the "Wisconsin Idea" to offer its services to every citizen in every corner of the state. In 1908 a reinvigorated University Extension Division began to offer an extensive program of courses, credit and non-credit, both by correspondence and at sites around the state. In 1913 it initiated a division in Eau Claire headed by Joseph W. T. Ames, from the normal school faculty at River Falls where he also had been high school principal and president of the People's Lecture Course Association. Ames's staff included an instructor in engineering and a field organizer, who immediately set out to establish courses in subjects such as electrical work, shop mathematics, drafting, and gas engines.

Furthermore, in response to another of piece of landmark state legislation of 1911, the City of Eau Claire established a Board of Industrial Education which in 1912 opened a trade school with classes in subjects such as mechanical drawing and telegraphy. At first, the focus of this "vocation school" was "continuing education" for fourteen to eighteen year olds who had left the "regular" high school and joined the labor force. In time, however, as it evolved into what in the twenty-first century is Chippewa Valley Technical College, it began to offer post-secondary programs, diplomas, and eventually two-year degrees.

Overall, local interest and state enablement expanded educational opportunities in the Progressive Era in Eau Claire. This development meant from the outset there would be competition for the new normal school, both from other providers of teacher education and from providers of post-secondary education for occupations other than teaching. It also meant the normal school would have to develop cooperative relationships, especially regarding curriculum duplication and transfer credits, with these other institutions already present in the city, especially the University of Wisconsin.

What Should be Taught at the New Normal School?

During the seven years between the authorization and the opening of Eau Claire Normal there was a sometimes-contentious statewide conversation about defining the purpose of normal schools. The programs Eau Claire eventually adopted reflected these controversies, which would continue to affect the subsequent history of the school.

Following a general curriculum adopted by the regents in 1892, with subsequent modifications, Wisconsin normals offered one-, two-, and four-year programs. The one-year program was designed to prepare rural teachers and did not require high school graduation. The two-year and four-year programs were designed primarily for prospective city and village grade school teachers and required high school graduation and eighth-grade graduation, respectively. These programs varied only in length and did not focus on preparing teachers to teach different grade levels or different subjects. As high school graduation became more common, starting with Oshkosh in 1911 the normals began requiring it for admission. Admissions offices, however, were never successful in establishing a pattern of required high school courses—e.g., two years of math, three years of English, and so forth.

In the early twentieth century, the normal schools also began to expand their offerings to provide teachers for the "special subjects"—agriculture, home economics, physical education, etc.—Wisconsin high schools were rapidly adding to their curricula. In 1913, for example, Whitewater became the second normal in the United States to offer a business education program. Not everyone agreed these programs should be taught in the normal schools. Critics argued students could never learn to teach such "practical" subjects in any classroom and collaborative work/study and apprenticeship programs were preferable.

In addition, starting in 1907 the normal schools began to press for legislative authorization to expand the length of their programs and begin preparing high school teachers in academic subjects. These proposals met with fierce resistance from Van Hise, who felt aspiring high school teachers should transfer to the university after two years at the normal schools, which he felt were not staffed or equipped to offer full college educations. Some normal schools began expanding their programs to prepare high school teachers, however, and finally in 1914 the regents went ahead and formally authorized their schools to offer three-year, post-secondary programs to prepare high school teachers. By this time, about one-third of the teachers of "regular" high school subjects in Wisconsin, mostly in smaller high schools, were normal school graduates; about one-third had graduated from the University of Wisconsin; and about one-third came from other four-year colleges.

Also controversial were proposals for the normal schools to offer programs in areas other than teacher education, which could be completed by transfer to a four-year college. Presidents of normal schools in locations distant from Madison, particularly at Superior, sought to boost enrollments by satisfying demands that local high school graduates receive their first two years of college education closer to home. Some faculty members who taught academic subjects thought by offering such a "college course" their institution would gain prestige. Most school principals, superintendents, teacher education professionals, and other schoolmen, however, opposed the addition of such programs to the normal school curriculum. They feared it would dilute the schools' focus on teacher education and lessen their own influence. The principal of New Richmond High School told the 1914 meeting of the Northwest Teachers Association, an annual professional conference in Eau Claire, "The College Course has no business in the Normal School." It was an expensive duplication of work done by the university, he said, and it encouraged "social events" and athletic activities inappropriate for future teachers. Novice teachers, he felt, graduated with "no idea whatever that it was wrong to attend dances lasting until two or three in the morning on school nights."

For his part, Van Hise seems to have calculated that the University of Wisconsin could deflect the normal schools' push to offer four-year programs for high school teachers if it acceded to their wishes regarding two-year "college courses." Consequently, following legislative authorization, the normal school regents went ahead in 1911 and established such programs. The *Eau Claire Leader* endorsed this decision as a "move to democratize the state educational institutions and bring them near the themes and home lives of the people." By 1913, all of the normals except River Falls had college courses, which together attracted almost 250 students, about 6 percent of overall enrollment. It would take decades, however, to resolve squabbles about transfer credit to the university for work done by students in the normal schools.

In 1914 an outside investigation and full-length report with policy recommendations addressed these questions regarding the focus of the normal schools in Wisconsin. The State Board of Public Affairs, a 1911 creation of the legislature designed to promote "efficiency" by conducting surveys of Wisconsin government and society, commissioned A. N. Farmer, of the Bureau of Municipal Research in New York, to do this work. His resulting study was very much in the tradition of Progressive Era fact-filled and lengthy "surveys" of social and political problems. (The Bureau of Municipal Research completed a similar report the following year for the University of Wisconsin, which was even more critical in tone and controversial than was its survey of the normal schools.) Farmer's report emphasized the normal schools "should frame their courses with no other end in view than that of fitting students to teach in the public schools." College courses were not "wholesome" and should be abolished. The normals, rather, should focus on preparing elementary-level teachers. The report grudgingly acknowledged they could offer courses for teachers of high school and special subjects, if the courses were kept "practical." More instruction was needed in subjects such as penmanship, while subjects such as trigonometry and foreign languages should be eliminated. Most students enrolling in the normal schools could not benefit from such instruction, the report felt, because they were too young and "woefully weak in the fundamentals of the common branches" of learning. High school graduation, therefore, needed to become a requirement for normal school admission. The report also felt teaching in the normal schools was "inexcusably poor" because faculty "selected chiefly on the basis of their academic attainments" were too "academic, bookish, and far above the heads of the pupils in the class."

The press trumpeted, if implemented, Farmer's recommendations to eliminate duplication by the normal schools of work that should be done in high schools and the university, and to adopt other "efficiencies," would reduce the state's appropriation to the normal schools by 10 percent. The regents were careful not to make an unqualified endorsement of the report, but they did move immediately to drop the college course at three normals, eliminate instruction in Latin everywhere except at La Crosse, and abolish all classes with fewer than ten students. The regents' secretary emphasized to the Northwest Teachers Association meeting in the fall that the normal schools were "vocational" institutions, not "colleges." But regardless, in 1915 Governor Emanuel L. Philipp, more conservative and fiscally tight than his Progressive predecessors, used information from the Farmer survey to attack the supposedly low academic standards and incompetent faculty of the normal schools.

When it finally opened in 1916, the programs offered by the Eau Claire State Normal School were a product of this changing and contentious educational environment in Wisconsin. Reflecting a policy of differentiation established by the regents in 1914, the new normal designated specific courses of study for students intending to teach at different levels: a one-year program for country school teachers; two-year programs for teachers in grades one through four and grades five through eight, respectively; and a three-year program for high school teachers. The same subject, such as American History, would be taught in separate courses for students in different programs. Eau Claire Normal also set up separate programs for potential grade school and high school principals. "This school is in fact primarily vocational," stated the "Platform" in an early school *Bulletin*. "We are a teacher-centered school, not a college." Despite the recommendation of the Farmer survey, however, a two-year "college course" was part of Eau Claire's curriculum from the beginning, and the first *Bulletin* emphasized the "University of Wisconsin gives credit for this work." Latin and German were also part of the curriculum.

The *Bulletin* ensured prospective students, of course, that the "quality of work" in all these courses "will be equal to that of the best colleges and universities." Indeed, at a time when 20 percent of the enrollees in Wisconsin normals were not high school graduates, there was no provision for secondary-level instruction at Eau Claire Normal. From the outset high school graduation was the expected admissions requirement. Exceptions were allowed for some experienced teachers and those who could pass an entrance examination, but even in the early years only a handful of students enrolled each year without a high school diploma.

No "special subjects" were offered in 1916 at Eau Claire in contrast, for example, to the programs in physical education at La Crosse and agricultural education at River Falls, the existing normal schools closest to Eau Claire. Although administrators in later years felt this void held down enrollments, the absence of an identification of the school with a particular special subject made Eau Claire unique among its peers in the state and eventually contributed to the development of the institution's strong liberal arts orientation. Offering a college course and only post-secondary instruction from the outset set Eau Claire Normal apart from its sister normals and in the long run became sources of academic strength.

Staffing the New Normal School

Early in 1916, as construction of Old Main progressed, the need was to find a founding president for the new normal school, who in turn would choose the initial faculty. Regent Horan received nineteen applications (that the "resident regent" managed the search process was indicative of the direct involvement he had in the school). The high quality of the applicants suggested the still-to-be completed school promised to be a strong institution. Eventually at least five of the group would become heads of normal schools.

Public discussion in state newspapers identified the leading candidates as Kinsman, who was already head of the summer normal school in Eau Claire; Ames, who had led University Extension in the city; Frank Hyer, director of teacher education at Stevens Point Normal; and A. M. Royce, who held a similar position at Superior Normal. Also in the mix were W. N. McIver, the Oshkosh school superintendent who previously had held the same position in Eau Claire; S. B. Tobey, the Wausau superintendent (both McIver and Tobey would eventually be presidents of the Wisconsin Education Association); and J. E. Williams from the faculty at Superior Normal. Among the additional applicants was nationally known scholar Oliver Dickerson, then teaching at Winona State Normal School in Minnesota. Unfortunately for Dickerson, the regents decided to limit their consideration to applicants from Wisconsin, a decision which also eliminated the school superintendent at Blue Island, Illinois, and the vice president of the normal school at Valley City, North Dakota, who were not among the eight finalists interviewed by the board. The board's final choice was a dark horse: Harvey A. Schofield, principal of St. Paul Central High School in Minnesota, whose Wisconsin nativity evidently qualified him for consideration.

Harvey A. Schofield

Schofield was president of the Eau Claire State Normal School and Eau Claire State Teachers College from 1916 to 1941.

The regents did not give the reasons for their choice (Regent President Theodore Kronshage casually reported that at the completion of the search he destroyed all relevant materials!), but apparently Schofield's connections to northwestern Wisconsin influenced their decision making. The *Eau Claire Leader* reported he "was well known in the community." The superintendent at Chippewa Falls told the paper Schofield was "well and favorably known throughout the part of Wisconsin that is naturally tributary to Eau Claire." Laura Sutherland, a teacher at Eau Claire High School who soon joined the normal school faculty for a long tenure, later recalled he was the "best known" schoolman in the region. Perhaps even more important, his reputation among schoolmen was of "a man who has a great deal of human in him."

Schofield was a native of Augusta, a community about thirty miles east of Eau Claire. In March 1895, more than a year before he graduated from high school, Schofield passed an exam to teach in the country schools in Eau Claire County (if he began teaching immediately, that

Original Faculty of Eau Claire Normal School

may explain why he did not graduate from high school until he was nineteen). In the typical manner of a turn-of-the-century schoolman, Schofield proceeded to advance his career by alternating short teaching and, eventually, administrative assignments at progressively larger schools with periods of post-secondary education for himself. During these years, he graduated from the University of Wisconsin in 1904 (see sidebar on Schofield as a Badger athlete). When he was selected for the Eau Claire presidency, he was in his fourth year at St. Paul, following three years as principal of two different high schools in Superior. He would remain at Eau Claire until 1940 and would be the dominant figure of the first twenty-five years of the new institution's history.

As Schofield said publically just after his appointment, it was a "rare opportunity" for a school administrator to be able to "select his own faculty." By September, he had engaged the seventeen initial faculty members. Sutherland later identified "youth" as the quality Schofield was looking for in his new hires. Indeed, six of the seventeen were young enough they taught at Eau Claire for at least twenty years (which, in some cases, Schofield came to regret) before retiring, as did several additional persons—including Sutherland herself—hired in next few years after 1916. The youngest member of the first faculty was twenty-four-year-old geography teacher George Simpson, who was also designated as football and basketball coach and whose appointment received national attention. Simpson, after two years of coaching experience at Eau Claire High School, had returned to the University of Wisconsin where he was a lineman on the 1915 football team and president of the senior class of 1916.

Eugene McPhee, a later protégé of Schofield's, said the president preferred to hire public school superintendents, with backgrounds like his own. Indeed, the initial *Bulletin* emphasized the faculty included "several of the most successful superintendents of the state." Among the founding faculty with experience in educational administration were biology teacher Merritt Pope, the thirty-three-year-old president of Mayville State Normal School in North Dakota; forty-three-year-old psychology and pedagogy teacher William A. Clark, who was president of the Lincoln County Training School for teachers in Wisconsin; thirty-eight-year-old manual training teacher Arthur J. Fox, who was teaching at Madison Central High School and had previously been superintendent at Willow Lakes, South Dakota; and thirty-six-year-old English teacher Edgar Doudna, who had been teaching since he was sixteen and was superintendent at Richland Center when he completed his BA at the University of Wisconsin in 1916.

The Mystery of Harvey Schofield, Athlete

Authoritarian towards his faculty and puritanical towards his students, Harvey Schofield appears in the twenty-first century as having had a stern and rigid personality. During his youthful career as an athlete, however, which the 1933 *Periscope* admitted was "not commonly known," he may have skirted player eligibility rules. This behavior showed there was a worldly aspect in his background, at the least, and also probably influenced his policies towards athletics as president of Eau Claire State.

Schofield played football and basketball during his two years at Stevens Point Normal School and was captain of the 1900 football team. (The UW–SP athletic *Media Guide* also identifies him as that year's coach.) In March 1901 he played with the Stevens Point Athletics, which participated in the national AAU basketball tournament in Chicago. The Athletics advanced to the semifinals before forfeiting over a scheduling dispute with the tournament organizers.

After serving as a grade school principal for a year at Wausau, Schofield enrolled as a junior at the University of Wisconsin. He was a lineman on the football team in the fall of 1902 and played basketball the following spring. Since he was a returning letterman, it is surprising Schofield was not mentioned in pre-season and early-season newspaper reports on the 1903 Badger football team. Perhaps this was because in early September he was hired as the coach at Stevens Point Normal, over one hundred miles from Madison. There were also newspaper reports he officiated high school football games in the Stevens Point area. Presumably he was paid for this work, which would have made him ineligible to participate in collegiate sports. (Interestingly, when Schofield was named to an all-time Stevens Point team in 1934 and on other occasions when he returned to the city, he was always identified as a former player and never as a coach.)

Schofield did eventually return to the UW football team and in early November the press reported him as practicing at fullback. He played in three important Big Nine games later in the month. His lost fumble, alas, was the key play in the Badger's loss at Ann Arbor on November 14. After the season, Schofield earned a second "W" letter, which was given to men "who had played through at least one half of the championship games." In the spring of 1904, he captained the UW basketball team, which lost a controversial and roughly played game at Nebraska for a mythical "championship of the West" which ended in a general brawl among players and spectators.

On July 18, 1904, the *Janesville Daily Gazette* ran an exclusive front-page article headlined "Professional or Amateur Player—Harvey Schofield of the University Football Team May Be a Professional." The article alleged that "it is commonly admitted" Schofield had been playing professional sports "for years" and had been actively recruited by the UW for his athletic abilities. At the beginning of the 1903 football season, when the Badgers played against Wisconsin college teams which might have recognized him, Schofield was said to have used the *nom de sport* of John Harvey. The *Daily Gazette* further reported John Harvey/Harvey Schofield was now playing baseball with the Milwaukee Brewers of the American Association.

There is some corroboration for the *Daily Gazette*'s claims. In early October 1903 a mysterious "Harvey," first name not given, "who tried for tackle last year" was reported as having just come out for football and begun practicing at fullback for the Badgers. Once "Harvey Schofield" began to play in November, there is no further mention of this "Harvey." Furthermore, a Jack Harvey, a promising third baseman with the Racine semi-pro team, signed a professional contract with the Brewers on July 16, 1904 (although he did not play in the American Association that year). Press reports identified this Harvey as a UW graduate.

The *Daily Gazette*, however, clearly erred in claiming that Schofield intended to play football for the UW in the fall of 1904—he had used up his four years of eligibility and had graduated in June. Furthermore, there was a John L. Harvey who played shortstop on the UW baseball squad and had graduated in 1900 who quite likely was the actual prospect signed by the Brewers in July 1904. In any event, Harvey Schofield remained in Madison for 1904–05 as history teacher and football coach at Madison High School.

College football was at the center of a national tempest in the fall of 1905. Amid charges of corruption and brutality, the sport came close to being abolished. In a multi-part series of muckraking articles in *Collier's*, Schofield's former Badger teammate Edward S. Jordan exposed the underside of football in the Big Nine. "Victory in the West today," he wrote, "depended upon the ability of the colleges to sustain men by devious means." Jordan devoted an entire article to corruption in the UW program—"victory is dearer to Wisconsin than her honor." He named a half-dozen players who, with the collaboration of coaches, faculty representatives, and student managers, had received improper financial benefits or should have been academically ineligible to play sports. Schofield, however, was not mentioned by name.

1917 Football Team

President Schofield is at the left of the front row.

By the time Schofield was a senior in 1903, UW President Van Hise had become alarmed about reports of athletic recruiting abuses and tried to obtain cooperation among the Big Nine institutions to restrict the prominence of athletics. In the scandal-saturated atmosphere of 1905, the faculty, led by historian Frederick Jackson Turner, went further and voted to suspend football for two years. Students and alumni mounted a defense of big-time sports, though, and the regents ultimately adopted a compromise, which only deemphasized football for a few years. Similarly, on the national level, the intervention of President Theodore Roosevelt eventually led to the establishment of the National Collegiate Athletic Association, which soon functioned to legitimize rather than restrict professionalized collegiate sports.

It is impossible to determine definitively Schofield's degree of culpability, if any, in the abuses in the UW sports program between 1902 and 1904. It also needs to be recognized that as an undergraduate he was more than a dumb jock: as both a junior and a senior Schofield was a member of the Athenaen Society, the oldest literary group on campus, which Turner himself had reinvigorated when he had been a student in the early 1880s.

Schofield remained interested in sports throughout his life and regularly attended Eau Claire State and Badger games. He coached the faculty team in its annual basketball game against students and played baseball for the Kiwanis against other service clubs. In 1928, he earned recognition in *Who's Who in American Sports*. Having been tarnished in an eligibility scandal himself, he was perhaps sympathetic towards George Simpson, who was targeted in the national press in 1915 for playing Badger football when he was allegedly a professional, and therefore inclined to appoint Simpson to the initial Eau Claire faculty. His experience in Madison almost surely disposed Schofield to stand up for the Eau Claire Normal football players who were ruled ineligible by the conference midway in the 1920 season and to allow a forfeit to go to River Falls Normal rather than pull them from the line-up.

More importantly, having seen big-time sports firsthand, Schofield kept limits on his school's athletic program, brushing aside suggestions the normal school conference be enlarged beyond Wisconsin and post-season games be allowed. In general, exposure to questionable practices as a young man may have contributed to Schofield's paternalistic determination in later years to protect the students in his college from the vices of sloth, alcohol, gambling, and sexual suggestiveness.

Edgar Doudna and Lester R. Cruetz

Doudna (English) and Creutz (History and Economics) were members of the original faculty. Typical of ambitious schoolmen in the early twentieth century, they soon left Eau Claire Normal for school superintendencies—Doudna (shown at center) at Wisconsin Rapids and Creutz (shown at right) at Monroe.

As the city newspaper noted, most of these men had been brought up on farms, which also may have made them attractive to Schofield, a farm boy himself. Faculty members with a rural background included Benjamin W. Bridgman, who was hired by Schofield to teach physics and chemistry. Bridgman had also been a school superintendent at Phillips from 1904 to 1906. But he perhaps also had the strongest academic background of any of the initial Eau Claire faculty: he had earned an MA in physics from the University of Wisconsin and had taught for seven years at Westminster College in western Pennsylvania, where he also served for a year as acting president.

Schofield felt that "the most important position that I have to fill and the one which will make or break the school" was that of director of teacher education. His choice was Charles J. Brewer, the superintendent at Chippewa Falls, who became in effect Schofield's right-hand man. Brewer had been an outspoken advocate for establishing a normal school at Eau Claire and was among the group that traveled to Madison in March 1913 to lobby for the building appropriation for it. Like Schofield, he had begun teaching in Pierce County country schools while still in his teens. He advanced to administrative positions at Ellsworth and New Richmond before coming to Chippewa Falls in 1912, where he set up that school's teacher education program.

In his educational style Brewer was an example of an "administrative Progressive," who emphasized the importance of efficiently organized, centrally directed schools with curricula differentiated to pupils' needs and abilities (who were somewhat different from "pedagogical Progressives," like John Dewey, who emphasized schools should be oriented to pupils' interests with hands-on curricula built on children's experiences). As the Chippewa Falls superintendent he had issued eighteen "rules" for his teachers emphasizing their responsibilities for maintaining strict "order and discipline" in their rooms and keeping "neat and accurate records . . . entirely in ink." Teachers should allow neither "pupils nor themselves to waste the time set apart for study and work," Brewer insisted and would lose one-half day's pay for any "absence from teachers' meetings." As Sutherland later explained delicately, "It is not clear to what extent he valued courses requiring scholarship beyond the immediate needs of the children" the normal school graduates would have to teach. In any event, having Brewer on the faculty gave Eau Claire Normal immediate respect throughout West Central Wisconsin. More specifically, it cemented a close relationship in both recruiting and placement between the new normal and the Chippewa Falls schools, which lasted for at least a decade. The initial *Bulletin* stressed that "special arrangements will be made to accommodate students living in Chippewa Falls," including no scheduled eight o'clock classes and discounted trolley fares.

To the extent he relied on public school administrators to staff his faculty, Schofield narrowed his pool almost exclusively to men. The initial faculty at Eau Claire was indeed more male than at any of the normal schools except Superior. At a point in time when there was a widespread belief that more men should enter the overwhelmingly female occupation of teaching, perhaps Schofield meant for the composition of the Eau Claire faculty to provide a relatively masculine tone for the new school and to encourage the enrollment of male students. Encouraging male enrollment was certainly the governing board's goal. Kronshage had written in 1914 that equalizing the salaries of male and female teachers in the normal schools would be "fatal" to this objective.

Schofield, however, did appoint nine women to the seventeen positions of the initial faculty. This group included long-time faculty member Hilda Belle Oxby, who would be the school's first foreign language teacher. Among the English teaching staff was Honora Frawley, daughter of the principal of Eau Claire High School and member of a leading local family. The domestic science teacher, Zelma Monroe, had academic credentials almost as impressive as Bridgman's: she had bachelor's degrees from both Wellesley College and Illinois Wesleyan College and was teaching at Pacific University when she was offered the position at Eau Claire.

In addition to these appointments, Schofield hired four women to staff the model school, with pupils in grades one through eight, which was part of the new normal school. One of them, Katherine Thomas, would remain part of the faculty for thirty years. As sites for educational experimentation, model schools were prominent features of pedagogical Progressivism, especially associated with Dewey's work beginning in the 1890s at the University of Chicago Laboratory School. But as a place for nascent teachers to gain experience, model schools had been part of normal schools since the first one was established at Trenton State Normal School in New Jersey in 1855, and they were embraced by traditional educators such as Schofield and Brewer as much as they were by pedagogical Progressives. By educating children from the city, the model school

Fifth/Sixth Grade Classroom, Campus School, 1921

When Loura Ives married and left teaching, President Schofield hired Fannie Hunn in the fall of 1921 to teach the fifth/sixth grade class in the Campus School. Hunn continued to teach in the school until 1951.

at Eau Claire also helped to connect campus and community, not in the least by picking up educational expenses for school-age children that otherwise would have been borne by Eau Claire taxpayers.

The First Textbooks

From its establishment, Eau Claire State Normal School, like its sister schools in the state, provided a textbook in each course for its students paid for by their fees, a policy that continues in the twenty-first century as the "textbook rental system." Farmer's survey had found faculty members at the existing normals considered the policy "abominable," and during the following decades evaluators, accreditors, faculty, and students would repeatedly criticize it. Administrators always kept the policy in place, however, citing its economic advantages for students. Although Schofield asked his faculty about what texts they wanted to use, the system also allowed presidents to keep for themselves some degree of control over course content. In any event, the policy contributed to the textbook-centered instructional style characterizing most courses at Eau Claire for many years.

When analyzed today, the textbook choices of Schofield and his new faculty reveal something about what Eau Claire Normal's initial body of students learned—or were exposed to at least. Schofield hired Lester Creutz, superintendent at Beaver Dam, to teach history and social science courses. Creutz's subsequent involvement in patriotic associations, his selection as superintendent at Monroe and later at Janesville, and his election as president of the Wisconsin Association of City Superintendents suggest he was a man of conventional social and political views. The textbooks he used in 1916–17, however, were up-to-date syntheses by authors who were both eminent scholars and activists in Progressive reform movements.

Creutz's economics students used *Economics*, a textbook by Scott Nearing and Frank D. Watson. (The copy in the stacks of McIntyre Library in 2016, with student marginalia in pencil, was probably part of the original textbook rental library.) Nearing was a brilliant and prolific young economist on the faculty of the Wharton School of the University of Pennsylvania. Although the textbook Creutz used was not particularly provocative, in his other work Nearing had developed a strongly Progressive, if not radical, critique of American society. In *The New Education* in 1915 he also advocated for pedagogical Progressivism. "The schoolmaster," Nearing believed, "has laid aside the birch, the three "R's", the categorical imperative, and a host of other instruments invented by ancient pedagogical inquisitors [in order] to reshape the schools in the interests of childhood." He also became an advocate of "The New Economics" (originated by University of Wisconsin economist Richard T. Ely), which told Americans they did not have to be "prostrate before the throne of 'competition,' 'individual initiative,' 'private property,' or some other pseudo-god." It was these sorts of ideas that led the Penn trustees, in a *cause celebre,* to dismiss Nearing from the faculty in 1915. In 1921, President Edward A. Birge, more conservative than his predecessor Van Hise, would ban him from speaking on the University of Wisconsin campus.

For his courses in ancient, medieval, and modern history, Creutz adopted *Outlines of European History* by James Harvey Robinson, James Henry Brested, and Charles A. Beard. All three authors would later be presidents of the American Historical Association, and in 1916 they were the leading academic proponents of the "New History," which sought to extend the study of the past beyond politics to include technological, social, and intellectual developments. In his address on assuming the presidency of the American Historical Association, the University of Chicago's Brested—the most distinguished historian of the ancient Near East of his generation—scolded his predecessors for their "incredible lack of imagination" in limiting the scope of their investigations to public events. Beard, for his part, had recently shocked conventional-thinking Americans by arguing that the authors of the United States Constitution had acted, not as timeless heroes guided by God's voice, but in the interests of an economic class to which most of them belonged. Creutz also used a textbook by Beard, coauthored with his wife Mary Ritter Beard, in his American government course. Barely a year after Eau Claire students were first exposed to his ideas, Beard resigned his position in a confrontation with the Columbia University trustees over academic freedom. Robinson, who particularly emphasized that the study of history should be for the improvement of the present, soon followed him from Columbia to the New School for Social Research.

In his course in American history for students in the grammar course (for students preparing to teach grades five through eight) Creutz used David Saville Muzzey's *An American History*. Robinson wrote the preface for this 1911 textbook by his Barnard College colleague in which he explained an "unmistakable" purpose of studying history was "to explain prevailing conditions and institutions by showing how they have come about." For his part, Muzzey brazenly told readers of *An American History*, "The greatest danger to our republic to-day is the corruption of the government by the money power." However, he felt in 1911 there was "a wonderful awakening . . . of reform sentiment," particularly evident in Wisconsin and associated with policies advocated by US Senator Robert M. La Follette.

The orientation and staffing of Eau Claire Normal to a degree reflected narrow and local perspectives. In their history and social science textbooks, however, its first students encountered challenging interpretations of ongoing national and state public issues, explained to them by the most eminent scholars of the day.

Eau Claire State Normal Opens

On September 18, 1916, a beautiful early fall day in Wisconsin which was clear and cool with high temperatures in the fifties, 158 students reported for the first day of classes at Eau Claire State Normal School (186 would eventually officially enroll). Almost half came from the city of Eau Claire. The college course and the high school teaching course each attracted about 15 percent of them, about 20 percent enrolled in the grammar course and 35 percent in the primary course, and about 20 percent chose the rural course, with a handful taking in the principals' course or enrolling as special students. Those who

The Normal School's First Students, 1916-17

The initial gender imbalance at Eau Claire Normal is evident from this photograph.

George Simpson

Geography teacher George Simpson was a member of the original faculty. He also coached basketball for one season and football from 1920 through 1924. In addition, he became well known around the state as a busy sports official and as an officer in the Wisconsin National Guard, activities in which he involved Eau Claire State students.

Simpson played football at Oshkosh Normal, the University of Wisconsin, and semi-pro teams in Wisconsin in the early 1920s. As a coach at Eau Claire High School from 1912 to 1914 and subsequently at the normal school, he was also energetic in organizing and publicizing interscholastic athletic tournaments and naming all-state teams. By the late 1920s, he was in charge of scholastic football, basketball, and track officiating for the Northwestern Wisconsin Officials Association and encouraged Eau Claire students to qualify to work at games and meets. As a track official himself, he judged the javelin throw at Big Ten and NCAA Championships and was head judge of field events at the 1932 Big Ten meet.

In the 1930s, Simpson became one of the top collegiate football officials in the Midwest. Like many good officials, he had run afoul of the rules as a player—ejected for roughness, for example, from a 1923 semi-pro game—and learned from the experience how to manage a game. By the late 1930s, he was working as many as ten Big Ten contests, in addition to several Marquette games, in a season. One of his final assignments, on October 18, 1941, at Minneapolis, was the undefeated Gophers' 39-0 thumping of Pittsburgh, which contributed to their number one ranking in the Associated Press poll at the end of the season. When President Robert Hutchins eliminated football at the University of Chicago, Simpson defended the sport. He felt football built "Americanism" and was equal "in value [to] any academic subject." Football coaches, he believed, made the best teachers.

Simpson was involved in his share of *contremps*. A pattern of disputed calls favoring the visitors and confusion about the operation of the clock at the end of what was ruled a tie game produced widespread booing from the crowd at the 1933 Minnesota–Purdue game. The *Wisconsin State Journal* commented sarcastically, "It's easy to see offside, why not call it if you are getting about $50 and expenses to do it." In its reporting about the controversy, however, the *Spectator* emphasized Simpson's integrity had not been questioned. The following year, a controversial call by Simpson was instrumental in Illinois's 14-3 win over Northwestern. Instant replay was not available, of course, but when celluloid film of the game was developed, it showed Simpson had incorrectly nullified a long Northwestern run which would have set up a touchdown, which would have given the Wildcats the lead at that point of the game. It was actually an Illinois player, rather than a Northwestern player, who was offside on the play.

Simpson's other avocation was the military. He took leave from Eau Claire Normal to serve with the US Army in Europe during World War I, separating from active duty in the grade of captain. During the interwar years he was an officer in the 128th Infantry Regiment, a Wisconsin National Guard unit. He commanded its Eau Claire-based Company B in 1923; was promoted to lieutenant colonel in 1934; attended the Command and General Staff School at Fort Leavenworth, Kansas, in 1936; and served as acting chief of staff of the 128th's parent Thirty-second Infantry Division in the fall of 1939. Simpson also served a term as president of the Wisconsin Reserve Officers Association.

During the interwar years Simpson was an avid promoter of the Citizens Military Training Camp movement, which provided an opportunity for young men to earn an army officer's commission by attending four summer camps of about four weeks each. Eleven students from Eau Claire Normal, for example, attended the 1926 CMTC camp at Fort Snelling, Minnesota, with Major Simpson. These summer assignments provided Simpson an opportunity to combine his avocations: at Camp Custer, Michigan, in 1924 he coached a team of Wisconsin trainees, including Eau Claire Normal quarterback Red Carroll, against teams from other midwestern states.

Simpson, along with several Eau Claire State Teachers College students who were enlisted men in the 128th Infantry, was called to active duty in October 1940. As part of the Thirty-second Infantry Division, of which Simpson was now assistant chief of staff for intelligence, the 128th spent over a year training at Camp Beauregard, Louisiana. In September 1941 Simpson was assigned command of the division's 125th Infantry Regiment, a Michigan National Guard unit, and was promoted to colonel in December. He wrote to Purdue football coach Allen Elward seeking recommendations for junior officers for his regiment, expressing his "belief that good athletes who have military knowledge make, on average, much better line officers" than others.

The Thirty-second Infantry deployed to New Guinea in September 1942 where it engaged in fierce and costly combat. Simpson and the 125th Infantry, however, had been detached from the division before it left Louisiana as part of a general army reorganization. Instead of the New Guinea jungles, the 125th moved to California in 1942 and was assigned to the Western Defense Command, which protected defense facilities and garrisoned training installations. Simpson sought an overseas combat position, but subsequently spent the rest of the war in assignments in the United States.

Simpson's legacy is very evident at UWEC in the twenty-first century. The outdoor track and football practice facility on the upper campus was named for him in 1969. His younger son and namesake, who attended Eau Claire State and played football in the early 1940s, left $6.3 million to the university (the basis of which had been the inheritance of his mother, Marie Stannard, who before marriage had been a student of his father at both Eau Claire High School and at the normal school). An initial $2 million came in 2003, and the remainder in 2011 upon the death of his widow, movie actress Denise Darcel.

The College Club, 1917

These young men and women were enrolled in the program, which existed from the origination of Eau Claire Normal, for students intending to transfer to four-year colleges.

intended to teach in Wisconsin paid a $5 per semester fee; others paid $14. If they were not living with their family, they needed to budget about $5 per week for room and board. (In 2016 terms, room/board/tuition/fees totaled about $4,000 per year.) President Schofield assembled the student body at 9 am in the school auditorium, the first of thousands of such meetings he would conduct there. He summoned the eighteen young men among the enrollees to sit immediately in front of him in the first row, where Coach Simpson, who was sitting with the other faculty members on the stage behind Schofield, could evaluate their numbers and suitability for athletics. In no-nonsense fashion, the president then explained policies and sent the students to their first classes.

The formal dedication of the new normal school occurred a month later. As the climax of decades of boosterism, the city's Civic and Commerce Association organized the event and enlisted householders in the school's neighborhood to decorate their homes as part of the festivities. The organizers encouraged widespread participation—the event was explicitly not a "dress-up affair"—and the auditorium in Old Main (now the Schofield Hall auditorium) was almost full on October 19, 1916.

The dedicatory speeches by dignitaries reflected some of the tensions underneath the founding of the new normal. Charles P. Cary, the irascible State Superintendent of Public Instruction, added fuel to the conflict between schoolmen and President Van Hise by alleging that many of his University of Wisconsin students did not know the multiplication tables (the kind of "fundamental" learning well-prepared normal school graduates, like those to be forthcoming from Eau Claire, would instill in their pupils, Cary implied). The scope envisioned for the new school was also a bit ambiguous. Regent President Kronshage emphasized that "normal schools are primarily vocational schools" for teachers, which also certainly reflected Cary's perspective. In his somewhat rambling remarks, however, Governor Philipp implied the normals were actually part of an educational system which included rural, grade, and high schools and the university (towards all of which Philipp, facing reelection in a few weeks, positioned himself as a great champion).

Whatever their implications, the remarks of the dignitaries launched Eau Claire Normal with high anticipation. Kronshage emphasized that "the normal schools have been charged with the performance of the most vital and fundamental function of our government"—providing the troops for "the American schoolhouse, the fortress of American liberty." In more down-to-earth fashion, Philipp reminded students that their new school "has been built by the fathers and mothers and other interested taxpayers in order that you, the young sons and daughters of the commonwealth, might have better educational service."

Getting a normal school operating in Eau Claire took almost a quarter century of effort by different groups of people. Civic leaders sought to gain the economic benefits of a state institution in their community; middle-class and working-class citizens wanted an inexpensive "people's college" to provide upwards mobility opportunities; parents wanted post-secondary education that would keep their children close to home; schoolmen wanted further elaboration, with increased opportunities for themselves, of the system of public education. Their efforts were part of an almost century-long educational expansion in the United States, but also came to fruition during the flowering of Progressivism in Wisconsin. The new school would have to live up to great expectations.

1916-41
Institutional Struggles and Successes

Eau Claire State Normal School faced a series of ordeals during its first quarter century. Some of them could have been anticipated in 1916.

Between 1916 and 1941, for instance, the components of post-secondary education in Wisconsin continued to fight among themselves. Financial support by the state was usually inadequate. Whether Eau Claire State should confine itself to teacher education, or offer other programs, was incessantly debated. In addition, national and international events unanticipated in 1916—wars and economic disaster—posed challenges to the institution. Several times its very existence was in doubt. During these years, President Harvey Schofield managed Eau Claire State with authoritarian paternalism. He kept the institution's focus on teacher education, while accommodating some of the voices in the community that wanted it to become something different. Eau Claire State did not blossom during these years, but it survived, and seeds were planted for future growth.

Lieutenant Arthur Olson

At the instigation of George Simpson, a memorial to Olson was dedicated at the school assembly on April 6, 1921.

World War I and Eau Claire State Normal School

During the new normal school's second semester in operation, the United States entered World War I. About twenty-five students, as well as geography teacher George Simpson (see sidebar in chapter one), joined the military. One of them, Army Lieutenant Arthur M. Olson, was killed in action in France. The disruption associated with the war was no doubt responsible for a 13 percent dip in the enrollment in the fall of 1918 compared to the previous year. Eau Claire had been approved for a Student Army Corps Training program, but it was the only Wisconsin normal not to have enrolled SATC students by the end of the war on November 11, 1918. The consequent shortage of potential basketball players in the spring of 1918 tempered the coach's usually optimistic pre-season evaluation. Omer Loop admitted, "If we win half the games we will be doing well." (His team went 0-9.)

Eau Claire Normal avoided serious entanglement with the major problems that disrupted American society during and immediately after World War I. Elsewhere in the state, and particularly at the University of Wisconsin, the presence of a significant German American population and the anti-war position of US Senator Robert M. LaFollette resulted in

Liberty and Justice for All

World War I patriotism was evident when pupils in the Campus School performed this pageant on February 11, 1918, in the Old Main auditorium. History professor Lester Creutz wrote the script, and student teachers from Eau Claire Normal helped the pupils mount the production.

inflammatory public controversies. At Eau Claire Normal, President Schofield, chair of the Patriotic Program Committee of the Eau Claire County Council of Defense, kept the school calmly but firmly in support of the war effort by instituting non-controversial measures such as meatless Tuesdays in the school cafeteria. Instruction in the German language was discontinued, but there was no ideological purge of the faculty, as occurred at other institutions.

The school also dodged the devastation of the 1918–19 flu pandemic. Perhaps 500,000 Americans died during the pandemic, but there was "little Illness" reported at Eau Claire Normal. As a precautionary measure, the school closed for nine weeks during the fall of 1918, and a nurse screened students when the school reopened to ensure they did not bring the flu back with them to Eau Claire. At the end of the 1918–19 school year, Schofield reassured the assembled students, "The war and the influenza tried to annihilate the school this year, but we are lustier than ever."

Enrollment rapidly rebounded after the war, reaching five hundred by the fall of 1922. Over one-third of these students were males, who constituted a majority of enrollees in the college course which prepared students to transfer to finish their degrees. The state encouraged this enrollment boost by providing stipends to veterans who sought public secondary or post-secondary education, the most generous such program in the United States. These veterans qualified for payments of $30 a month for up to four years. About twenty-five veterans enrolled in the fall of 1919, and the 1920 *Periscope* featured a group picture of thirteen of "Our Bonus Boys."

State Politics and the First Attempt to Close Eau Claire Normal

Progressives returned to political power in Wisconsin after World War I. But increased funding for post-secondary education was not one of their priorities. Indeed, Governor John J. Blaine was reelected in 1922 by campaigning as the "Economy Governor." The focus of the 1923 legislative session returned to the perennial topic in Wisconsin politics: the state income tax. Blaine proposed to increase income tax revenue (by reducing the personal property tax credit to the income tax) and use it to reduce property taxes by having the income tax pay for some educational expenses. This tax-credit measure would generally have favored rural taxpayers, and it met with sharp opposition. A stalemate developed in the legislature, and by the end of the year it had passed no appropriation bill for the state normal schools. Eau Claire State had to limp through the 1923–25 biennium with stopgap funding at the levels of the previous biennium. The nine new faculty positions, athletic field, and model school playground Schofield had expected never materialized. He became so discouraged that in an unusual public criticism of officials, Schofield explained, ". . . legislative support had not been good," and he was considering leaving Eau Claire to become superintendent at Superior, an appointment he ultimately declined.

The legislature in 1923 also considered a proposal to close Eau Claire Normal. Assemblyman J. D. Miller from Dunn County, chair of the Assembly Education Committee, argued Wisconsin had too many normal schools, with too high a faculty-student ratio, which produced an oversupply of teachers. He proposed turning Eau Claire Normal over to the City of Eau Claire for use as a high school and, he hoped, as a campus for a two-year junior college. Schofield rejoined that there was "a lively demand" for Eau Claire graduates and history teacher Joseph Ames ascribed Miller's proposal to jealousy on the part of other normals. Schofield and Regent Peter J. Smith organized community protests, and a delegation from the city and surrounding area took a petition with "thousands of signatures" to Madison for the bill's hearing on May 17 before the legislature's Joint Education Committee. At the hearing, Schofield refuted statistics about oversupply of teachers presented by C. J. Anderson, the assistant state

Class Day, 1920

During the 1920s, the north side of Old Main—facing the Chippewa River—was the common site for formal and informal gatherings of students.

superintendent of public instruction, and argued his school's costs were the third-lowest per student in the normal school system. Eventually Miller's proposal was overwhelmingly rejected by voice vote when it came to the floor of the assembly.

Repurposing Wisconsin Normal Schools

During the legislative debates in 1923, the question of Eau Claire Normal's existence was intertwined with the issue of the continuation of the college course in the normal schools. Most Wisconsin schoolmen, bolstered by recommendations in a 1920 report published by the Carnegie Foundation, wanted their normal schools to return to being single-purpose teacher-training institutions. College courses, they felt, diverted scarce resources in a normal school from teacher training by "dissipating its energy" and tempting students to abandon teacher training. Left unsaid was the fact college courses made schoolmen seem like second-class academicians within their own institutions. In 1922 the regents agreed. "It was the deliberate judgment of the Board of Regents of Normal Schools," they reported, "after ten years' trial of such local and personal interests, that the increasing numbers of students in college courses . . . were in direct and harmful conflict with the paramount teacher-training function of the normal schools." The regents slated the college course to end after July 1923.

Local interests, especially from Milwaukee, resisted this decree and sought to have it reversed by the legislature in 1923. An exchange of obscenities and punches between William Kittle, secretary to the regents, and Assemblyman F. P. Peterson of Milwaukee, in a public corridor in the capitol, failed to resolve the issue. (Perhaps Peterson was in a hurry to get to the assembly chamber to vote on a bill passed the same day that outlawed immorality in automobiles.) The Wisconsin Senate finally voted down the proposal to retain college programs.

For the next twenty-five years, the regents, and Regent President Edward Dempsey in particular, stressed the primacy of teacher education in the normal schools. The board's position was, "The Normal Schools . . . should make no attempt, in any way, to encourage non-professional students either through arrangement of courses, evaluation of credits, recommendations, or other means at their disposal." The normal schools now had singleness of purpose, but it was achieved at the cost of narrowing their public support.

The legislature in 1923 also failed to enact a proposal for a junior college system in Wisconsin, such as was suggested by Assemblyman Miller. There were various suggestions that these two-year college-preparatory institutions would be freestanding, would be part of the University of Wisconsin, or would be part of the local public school system. The State Board of Education, a relatively toothless oversight body created in 1915 to coordinate educational programs at all levels in the state, advocated for junior colleges. However, the board was unpopular with all of the agencies it sought to corral—faculty in the normal schools, in particular, opposed its attempts to increase their teaching loads and class sizes in the name of "efficiency"—and it was legislated out of existence in April 1923. (Its demise may have motivated its friends to seek revenge by supporting the proposal to eliminate Eau Claire Normal.)

In any event, without a junior college system in the state and a central coordinating body to check them, normal schools like Eau Claire quietly continued to operate two-year transfer programs for students who wanted them, despite the position of the regents. In an article entitled "Normal Losing College Work Means Little," an Eau Claire newspaper reported an unnamed "local citizen who is interested in education" (surely Schofield) explained "there is very little change in the studies offered" and "two years at a smaller school is a fine preparation for university." For over a decade, Schofield carefully accommodated pressure from the Eau Claire community to provide opportunities for college education while remaining on close terms with Regent President Dempsey, a fellow Democrat who appreciated his frugality as an administrator. For example, in 1933 Dempsey relied on Schofield to recommend Archie Hurst to him as the regent from Eau Claire to succeed Smith.

Fewer students interested in transferring, as well as more veterans concluding their subsidized studies, contributed to a system-wide enrollment decline in the mid-1920s. At Eau Claire State, only

Charles J. Brewer

Brewer was the director of teacher education from 1916 to 1938 and also served terms as president of the Northwestern Wisconsin Teachers Association and the Wisconsin Education Association

346 students enrolled in 1927, down 31 percent from 1922. Ever vigilant for "efficiencies," as part of a proposed comprehensive set of changes in state spending, a special legislative committee early in 1927 recommended closing three state normals, specifically including Eau Claire.

Defenders of the normal schools counterattacked. Regent Smith declared, "Wisconsin is not ready for a Mussolini," implying the three-member commission proposed by a legislative committee to govern all higher education in the state would be undemocratic. In a short book, President H. A. Brown of Oshkosh Normal marshaled statistics to support an argument the normals were cost efficient and their enrollments would likely rebound. At Eau Claire, Schofield reassured the students their school was not in danger and again rallied support from community members by suggesting if the normal school closed they might find a state school for delinquent girls would replace it. Charles Brewer was dispatched to Chippewa Falls, where he had been school superintendent, and told the local newspaper, "[T]he Junior College proposed by the bill does not offer a single advantage that is not offered under the present arrangement." Its program, he stressed, "will have no money value whatever" to students from Chippewa Falls who might attend. Subsequently, the *Chippewa Herald-Telegram* editorially supported Brewer's position. The city's mayor joined a delegation to Madison led by Schofield, which presented a "violent protest" to the Joint Finance Committee on June 29. By a 63-32 vote, the assembly rejected the closure proposal on July 13.

As Brown had predicted, enrollments in all Wisconsin normals rebounded in the late 1920s. Eau Claire grew from 346 enrollees in 1927 to 539 in 1930, the largest percentage increase among the normals. At the end of the decade, the regents reassured doubters about the demand for teachers by reporting that in the previous ten years 87 percent of graduates statewide—and 83 percent at Eau Claire—had secured placements as teachers, comparing favorably to a national rate of 85 percent. The expanding programs of the teachers colleges produced 42 percent of the new teachers in Wisconsin high schools in the fall of 1929, compared to only 19 percent from the University of Wisconsin.

From Normal School to College

During the 1920s, as part of a nationwide effort by normal schools to put themselves on a more equal footing with existing colleges, Wisconsin normal schools transformed themselves into teachers colleges and began offering four-year degree-granting programs. Schofield was a supporter of this movement. He told the 1921 meeting of the Northwest Teachers Association that providing students with "adequate knowledge of subject matter, a knowledge of the latest class room methods, together with scientific measurement of results is utterly impossible in the two or three years we have them in our charge." Left unsaid was the fact enrolling students for a longer period would, of course, help compensate for enrollments lost by dropping the college course. In general, schoolmen endorsed the change with reservations: the expanded coursework in longer programs should be devoted to "professional" rather than "academic" subjects. The *Wisconsin Journal of Education* editorialized the normal schools must not "give their students a training which will make them dissatisfied with elementary teaching."

The regents committed the system to change at their July 1922 meeting and at the same time dropped the college course. Eau Claire State added a four-year course for high school teachers in the fall of 1923

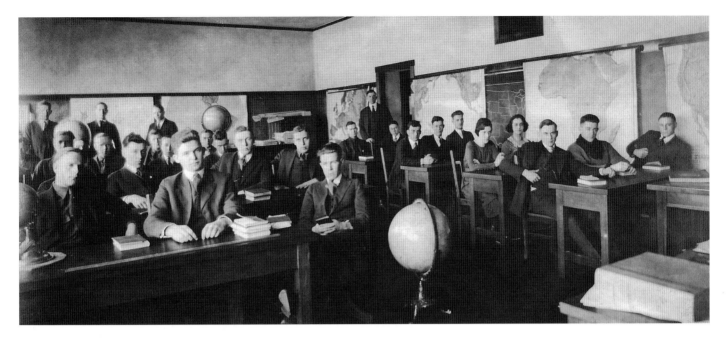

Geography Class, 1927

and dropped the corresponding three-year course in 1927. In 1928, it added three-year courses in both the "primary" and "upper grades" courses and dropped the corresponding two-year courses in 1934. Having received legislative approval, in 1927 all the normal schools restyled themselves as teachers colleges. Eau Claire State Teachers College now offered bachelor of education degrees to students who completed four-year programs.

Conrad Patzer, Brewer's counterpart at Milwaukee State, explained the intellectual underpinnings of these new teachers colleges. He emphasized they did not provide "reviews" of the content taught in elementary grades, they did not focus on teaching pedagogical "methods" as if they were a bag of tricks, and they were not "academically" focused colleges. He believed, rather, they were "institutions of collegiate grade affording a professionalized course of a college level." Because they were designed to prepare future teachers, he explained, "the courses in history offered by the teachers colleges," for example, "differ greatly from the courses offered by the liberal arts colleges" even if they bore the same title. As Edgar Doudna, a member of the original faculty at Eau Claire State who succeeded the pugnacious Kittle as secretary to the regents in 1928, later wrote, "There is a difference in the attitude toward subject matter by teachers whose preparation is wholly academic and those whose education, training, abilities, and interests are directed toward the problems facing teachers in elementary and secondary schools."

With the needs of the small high schools in West Central Wisconsin in mind, Eau Claire graduates had to be ready to teach several different subjects. After the four-year course was in place after 1927, however, there was a greater degree of specialization in their programs. They selected one of five thirty-credit majors—history, social science, physical science, English, or math—and a twenty-credit minor. Thirty additional credits of their program were in professional courses. Overall, they needed 128 credits for graduation. For students in the elementary-grade courses, the addition of a third year to their programs allowed for twenty-four additional credits in electives and a six-credit required "Survey of Civilization." They continued to take twenty-six credits of professional courses.

The shift from being a "school" to being a "college" was gradual and not without problems. Two-year programs for elementary teachers and the one-year for rural teachers remained in place until 1934, and not until 1936 did the number of graduates receiving degrees exceed the number receiving diplomas. The three-year diploma courses for elementary teachers and the two-year diploma course for rural teachers

INSTITUTIONAL STRUGGLES AND SUCCESSES

continued even after the college initiated four-year degree programs in 1935 for elementary teachers and in 1939 for rural teachers. With such a mix of students on campus, the *Spectator* posed the question in the fall of 1927, "What Are We Now, Teachers' College or Normal School?"

There also were implications beyond academics in the change from school to college. Toward the end of the 1927–28 academic year, the *Spectator* editorialized that teachers colleges "should make [their students] finished men and women." For the *Spectator* this meant instituting lectures on manners, but for others it meant developing a "collegiate" social life (as seen in chapter three). In sum, as a result of maneuvering by the regents and legislators during the 1920s, the college course was formally removed from the curriculum at Eau Claire State, but the identity of the college remained unresolved.

1924 Commencement

Until 1941, commencement was conducted in the auditorium of Old Main.

Finding a Place in Wisconsin's Higher Education World

After the reorganizations of the mid-1920s, Eau Claire State continued to co-exist with the county normals as suppliers of rural teachers (chapter one). Direct competition finally ended in 1930 when Eau Claire County Normal closed, giving a boost to Eau Claire State. Schofield tried to maintain a good relationship with the county normals; he ensured Eau Claire State gave full credit for all transfer work from them. But relations with the county normal presidents and county superintendents remained touchy. County superintendents, in particular, insisted they control placement of Eau Claire State students in rural schools under their jurisdiction.

Territorial rivalries also affected Schofield's relationships with his fellow state teachers college presidents. Each of the colleges had defined "territories" and it was considered improper to enroll—and certainly to recruit—students from outside the prescribed territory. Presidents were quick to defend their territorial boundaries if they thought their colleagues were poaching. In 1937, for example, President Jesse Ames of River Falls State objected to what he thought was improper recruiting in his territory by Eau Claire football coach Willis Zorn.

Indeed, conflicts abounded among the members of the Wisconsin State Teachers College Conference from its founding in 1913. Eau Claire State had to forfeit football games in 1920 as a result of player-eligibility violations. Revised rules in 1924 mandated, among other requirements, athletes successfully complete fourteen credits during the previous semester, required "migrants" to sit out a semester, and provided for rosters to be sent in advance to opposing schools for review. Problems continued, however. As a result of violations, Superior State in 1930 and Stevens Point State in 1935 were temporarily expelled from the conference. Stevens Point acknowledged using ineligible players in its 47-0 victory over Eau Claire in 1941, but rather meanly did not offer to forfeit because the game did not count in the conference standings.

Eau Claire State's most difficult external relationship, however, continued to be with the University of Wisconsin. Eau Claire State's *Bulletin* insisted that "credits from Teachers Colleges are accepted on exactly the same basis as those from any collegiate institution" for students transferring to the university. Officials at Madison, however, adopted specific course requirements for some of their programs, generally did not give credit for professional education courses taken by transfer students not majoring in teacher education, would not count credits from county normals accepted by Eau Claire State when evaluating graduate admissions, and in general remained skeptical of the quality of academic work at Eau Claire State. To accommodate the University of Wisconsin, Eau Claire revised its curriculum in 1935 to move professional education courses out of the first two years of students' programs. It was unable, however, to convince the UW that economic geography was a science course. It was also embarrassing to Eau Claire State in 1939 when the university found out the college's five-credit general chemistry course for which it was giving transfer credit did not have a laboratory component. The rather lame rejoinder from Arthur Fox, Eau Claire's registrar, blamed overcrowding and explained that chemistry teacher Frank Ackerman's "demonstrations" were "almost realistic enough" to be considered labs. To Schofield, Fox emphasized, "If we could just get the survey courses ironed out, without having to pretend to include actual laboratory work, it seems to me that our difficulties with the University would be pretty well taken care of." By this time, Schofield had lost patience. "I am sick and tired of kowtowing to the University Staff," he exploded.

Especially problematic were the procedures for certifying Eau Claire State graduates as high school teachers. To receive accreditation, which was highly sought after by city high schools, the North Central Association of Colleges and Secondary Schools required high schools employ graduates of *colleges* it had accredited; alone among the Wisconsin teachers colleges, Eau Claire State did not achieve such accreditation during the interwar period (chapter three). To allow Eau Claire State students to qualify for teaching positions, therefore, the NCA's Commission on Secondary Schools in Wisconsin, a joint body of the university and the Department of Public Instruction (DPI), agreed Eau Claire degrees would be considered "equivalent" to those of an accredited college after a satisfactory review by the commission of the graduate's credentials. Almost all graduates were approved, but the process was tedious and humiliating and occasionally a transcript was questioned. University staff "are getting into everything and are trying to do work that they are not qualified to handle," Schofield fumed.

Schofield may have feared the teachers colleges were getting squeezed between the university and DPI. University President Glenn Frank adopted a policy of *rapprochement* with schoolmen, especially by the appointment of Frank Holt, a seasoned public school administrator, as registrar in 1927. The university relaxed its admissions requirements by lowering the number of required academic units, as schoolmen wanted, and in 1932 abandoned its own inspection and accreditation of high schools, leaving that responsibility to DPI. Secretary Doudna expressed fear about the results of this accommodation when he warned Regent President Dempsey in 1940 that "some one wants to get us—and when I say 'us' I mean you and me." He specifically identified collusion between Superintendent of Public Instruction John Callahan and C. J. Anderson, Callahan's former assistant who had become education dean at the university and who, it should be recalled, had testified to the legislature in 1923 in favor of closing Eau Claire State.

There were fears similar to Doudna's at Eau Claire State. Registrar Fox felt too many school administrators had begun to take the side of the university because they had done graduate study there, and Schofield pulled out of participation in Holt's efforts to implement a statewide testing regime for high school seniors which could be used for guidance and placement purposes. When the issue of restoring a statewide higher education oversight board arose again in the late 1930s, the president's solution was for "a tie-up of all of the state teacher training agencies with the state department of public instruction," an alignment that would strengthen the normal schools in their continuing battle with the university by peeling away DPI from Bascom Hall. Callahan, by contrast, favored creating a governing board with unified authority over all higher education in the state. Doudna chose to run against him on this issue in the spring election in 1941 and lost.

The College and the Great Depression

State financing for Eau Claire State improved in the late 1920s. The legislature in 1929 adopted a salary scale for faculty giving them every third summer off from teaching and a year off at half pay after five years to study for an advanced degree. In 1931, by law faculty received the protection of tenure after two years of service. Beginning in 1929, however, the Great Depression created challenges greater than the college had faced in its first thirteen years. Faculty, students, and the institution itself had to "make due" to survive the next decade as the United States struggled through the worst economic reversal of the twentieth century.

As jobs became scarce during the early years of the Depression, college enrollment increased nationwide, especially in inexpensive, close-to-home institutions like the Wisconsin teachers colleges. Eau Claire enrolled 672 students in the fall of 1932, up from 450 in 1929. About 60 percent of these students had to earn at least part of the money necessary for them to attend college.

Eau Claire State's ability to serve these students was impaired. Only weeks after requesting a 4 percent increase in the state colleges' budget for 1931–33, the regents accepted without protest Governor Phillip LaFollette's proposal for a 7 percent reduction. As the state's finances worsened further as the national economy collapsed during 1932, Regent President Dempsey was not sympathetic to teachers protesting salary cuts—they had to realize, he felt, the "vast fortunes" they thought could be taxed to keep up their salaries had been lost by the Depression. The regents made "temporary" cuts in salaries for the 1932–33 academic year. "I remember how Dorothy Armstrong cried and cried . . . when President Schofield came back from the board meeting and told us" about the cuts because it upset her marriage plans, recalled a co-worker of Armstrong's on the classified staff. At an April assembly, students heard Lotus Coffman, the president of the University of Minnesota, blame "insurance companies, bankers, and industrialists" for pushing budget cuts in education.

After his election in the fall of 1932, Democratic Governor Albert Schmedeman presented a budget for the next biennium with an 18 percent cut for the teachers colleges. The *Spectator* editorialized, "Reduce extravagance in government, yes, but don't deny to the youth their only hope—education." Dempsey and Secretary Doudna, however, again accepted the cuts without protest, which the Republican *Wisconsin State Journal* ascribed to their partisan desire to support Schmedeman. (The *New York Times* reported Doudna as under consideration for a high-level appointment in the incoming Roosevelt administration in Washington.) For 1933–34, consequently, the regents implemented a graduated salary cut for faculty, starting at 17.5 percent for those with the highest salaries. Doudna lashed out at the "stupidity and greed of those who have pretended to control our financial system" and explained teachers understood "recovery" of their salaries "when and if it comes will be slow and inequitable." In fact, they would not receive their full salaries again until the fall of 1937.

At Eau Claire State this regime of salary "waivers" meant that in 1936 chemistry teacher Benjamin Bridgman, one of the original faculty who at $4,000 in 1929 was in the highest-paid group of teachers, actually received $3,300. French teacher Elizabeth Ayer, less experienced and a woman, went from $2,600 to $2,210. It needs to be recognized, however, that prices fell about 19 percent between 1929 and 1936, mitigating the loss in salary, and teachers at Eau Claire State were at least paid regularly throughout the Depression, unlike the situation in many public school districts around the country. The size of the faculty was not reduced either, although the regents discontinued the practice of giving teachers every third summer off.

As public schools retrenched (there were 2.4 percent fewer teachers in the United States in 1933 than there had been in 1931), Eau Claire State graduates found it difficult to locate teaching positions. Only about one-third of 1934 graduates found jobs, the lowest percentage among the state teachers colleges. Given such bleak prospects, student opinion in the *Spectator* began to question why students at state teachers colleges could not prepare for other occupations. A 1935 survey of students found only half of them really intended to teach. The legislature again considered a proposal in 1935 to revive the two-year college course in the state colleges as part of a consolidation of the teachers colleges into the University of Wisconsin.

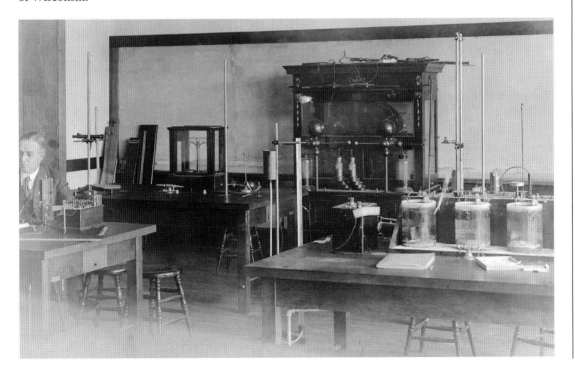

Physics Lab, 1920s

Physics and chemistry professor Benjamin W. Bridgman's research interest was the melting point of tungsten. His 1906 bachelor's thesis at the University of Wisconsin was entitled "High Temperature Measurements Using Platinum Thermometers."

There was a specific threat to Eau Claire State in 1937. With "little or no opposition" on April 21, the legislature's Joint Finance Committee, citing the oversupply of teachers, approved a bill to close the college and turn its property over to the University of Wisconsin, which would operate a two-year junior college as part of its extension program. Similar proposals had been made for teachers colleges in other states, and reportedly this one was "highly favored by some" of the Eau Claire community. This group wanted a more prominent University of Wisconsin presence in the city and desired the existing campus, which they saw as bothersome, moved away from the Third Ward, perhaps to the town of Hallie between Eau Claire and Chippewa Falls. In statements and at public meetings Schofield, Brewer, and Fox decried the measure, pointing out students in the new junior college would be restricted to transferring to the University of Wisconsin. The Eau Claire State Alumni Association denounced the proposal, and four hundred students signed a protest petition. Less than a week after its introduction, the bill's sponsor agreed to withdraw it in return for an unspecified "reorganization" of the Eau Claire State administration and a study of "realignments" by a joint committee of university and state teachers college regents. Neither condition led to any substantive changes. Eau Claire State survived for a third time.

New Sources of Support during the Depression Decade

Federal government programs, heretofore unimportant to Eau Claire State, were vital in helping the college and its students survive the Great Depression. As a consequence, students and college employees gradually began to become more directly attached to the national government. For instance, in the fall of 1933, the Civil Works Administration put unemployed men to work on "campus beautification" projects. A Public Works Administration project in the spring and summer of 1935, which employed as many as forty men at one time, improved landscaping around the campus. Beginning in the fall of 1935 various Works Progress Administration (WPA) programs paid about $35,000 towards such undertakings as repairing the roof, repainting the interior, and installing new classroom cabinets in Old Main; constructing a running track, bleachers, and a lighting system for the athletic field; dredging Little Niagara Creek behind Old Main and building two bridges to span it; and constructing a small garage with a second floor which could be used for band practice. The *Spectator* editorialized that these projects had "greatly improved" the campus.

Financial assistance to students also came directly from the federal government for the first time. The Federal Emergency Relief Administration (FERA) provided $2,403 to seventy-three students during the spring 1934 semester. Schofield selected the recipients on the basis of "need" and "character," and in a foreshadowing of later mandates, he had to maintain a gender balance among them in proportion to enrollment. The program expanded during the following academic year to pay a total of $9,359 to about 150 students. These students assisted in the library, worked as janitors, helped teachers grade papers, and trimmed shrubs and cut grass, among other responsibilities. A survey in the fall of 1934 found about 25 percent of the student body worked in FERA jobs, about 30 percent had other employment, and parents or relatives supported about 45 percent.

While accepting their necessity, Americans were uneasy about this and the other public assistance programs of FERA and the agencies that succeeded it, and this uneasiness was evident at Eau Claire State. The editors of the *Spectator* repeatedly denounced the program, alleging "in all cases the most needy were not served first" and many assistance recipients were "chiselers" who brazenly drove automobiles while claiming to be in need. Schofield issued a public warning to FERA-assisted students about "loafing." The president, however, also emphasized the importance of continuing the program. "Many students are already wondering what they will do another year without this aid," he wrote to FERA officials in February 1935. "They will probably have to quit school."

Students continued to receive needed assistance after the end of FERA's two-year statutory existence. In the summer of 1935 the newly organized National Youth Administration (NYA), part of the WPA, began to award financial aid to students as part of a comprehensive program of assistance to young people. In each of the next two academic years, about 250 students at Eau Claire State worked for the

NYA. The editors of the *Spectator* came around to endorsing the program in the fall of 1935. Beginning in 1936 these students could earn their stipends through off-campus work. They found jobs in the public schools, in the city library, at the YMCA, with the Boy Scouts, and in other non-profit organizations in the community. A larger proportion of students receiving NYA assistance worked off campus at Eau Claire than at any other Wisconsin teachers college. In the late 1930s, the NYA trimmed its financial aid to college students, but 150–200 Eau Claire students still continued to work under the program at twenty-five cents per hour between 1937 and 1942.

Erna Buchholz, Librarian

Erna G. Buchholz was a faculty member at UW–Eau Claire longer than even President Leonard Haas. Allowing for his 1946 study leave at the University of Minnesota and his 1971–73 assignment to UW System administration, Haas had a tenure of forty-one years. Buchholz was a campus fixture in the library for over forty-two years, from January 1920 to May 1962.

Buchholz was born in Fall Creek on October 22, 1897. Early in the twentieth century her family moved to Eau Claire, where her father operated a clothing store. Buchholz graduated from Eau Claire High School at the mid-winter commencement in February 1917 as salutatorian of her class. She immediately enrolled in the high school course at the new normal school. She graduated in January 1920 and straightway became the school's assistant librarian. President Schofield named her chief librarian in 1930.

The library had a central role in the life of Eau Claire State. Its expansion demonstrated the academic growth of the college: the library's book collection grew from an initial four thousand (selected by Schofield), to twelve thousand by the time Buchholz took charge, to over sixty thousand by 1960. Students also used it daily for between-class studying and to complete collateral reading assignments, which supplemented textbooks in most courses (chapter three). There was no other space for students in Old Main, at least not until the student lounge opened in 1940, except for occasional use of the auditorium balcony. For their part, since they had no offices, faculty members retreated to the library when another teacher taught in "their" room. Buchholz interacted regularly with a greater proportion of the college's population than did any other person. In recognition of her contributions to Eau Claire State, the 1956 *Periscope* was dedicated to her. In 1977 she received the Alumni Distinguished Service Award.

More readily than some of the teaching faculty, Buchholz used summers to take course work to strengthen her academic qualifications. She earned a BA from Ripon College in 1926 and a BS in library science from the University of Denver in 1944. When Eau Claire State began offering library science courses in 1947, which led to the introduction of a minor in library science in 1956, Buchholz taught in the program.

As an undergraduate, Buchholz was active in the Kodowapas Camp Fire (chapter three) and was its president for the fall of 1919. During the 1920s, she was the faculty advisor to the YWCA group. Buchholz was also active in community affairs. Most importantly, she was a founding member (along with Hilda B. Oxby) in 1922 of the Eau Claire Business and Professional Women's Club and later served as its president.

As President Davies began to expand the role of the faculty, Buchholz took on her share of responsibility. During World War II, she served on the Faculty Defense Committee. Most importantly, she became chair in 1948 of the Library and Collections Committee. This committee allocated funds for book purchases among the divisions into which Davies organized the college's departments (chapter four). It also managed the collections—books, furniture, photographs, drawings, *objects d'art*—which the college began to acquire by donation beginning in 1940. Using these materials, during the early 1950s Buchholz curated exhibits in the library for the public on the history of the Chippewa Valley.

During the late 1950s, Buchholz chaired the Library Planning Committee, which outlined the new library building for Eau Claire State. As Davies and Haas had done to get ideas for the College Center (chapter five), she traveled extensively to view academic libraries around the United States. Fittingly, Buchholz turned the first shovelful of earth at the groundbreaking ceremony for the new building on May 20, 1959. The completion of the new library was both a significant academic enhancement for the college and a personal triumph for Erna Buchholz. In his dedicatory remarks in October 1960, Director Eugene McPhee emphasized the centrality of libraries to academic institutions and recommitted the State of Wisconsin to providing widely accessible public higher education (chapter five). But he also gently teased Buchholz by including in his remarks fond recollections of his days as a student at Eau Claire State when she had repeatedly warned him to whisper in the library, and he impishly answered he did not know how. For Buchholz, it simply was the "greatest day of my life."

Erna Buchholtz Supervising the Library, 1940s

State programs also assisted students. Beginning in 1935, Legislative Scholarships covered fees for two categories of students; the highest-ranking one to three graduates from each high school, depending on its size; and students with financial need and leadership qualities from the top half of their graduating classes who were chosen by the college presidents, in proportion to the college's enrollment. In 1939, forty-six students (6 percent of enrollment) received such scholarships. A few students (six in 1939) received rehabilitation scholarships from the Wisconsin Board of Vocational Education or veterans' assistance from the state adjutant general. The college itself employed about a dozen students as "student assistants." In 1935 the legislature also initiated an Unemployment Relief Student Loan Fund; by the end of the spring semester Schofield had approved ninety of 120 applications for loans of up to $60, to be paid back within two years of graduation. Altogether, in 1939 about 12 percent of students received financial assistance apart from the NYA.

The College at the End of the 1930s

Government assistance enabled students to attend Eau Claire State who otherwise would not have enrolled or dropped out. After dropping from 637 in 1932 to 509 in 1937, overall enrollment surged to a record 735 in 1939. There was a similar pattern for the summer session, which enrolled almost exclusively in-service teachers. From a low of 296 in 1932, summer session enrollment increased to 495 in 1940. Supporting this enrollment trend was an improving job market for teachers. Economic growth in the United States averaged 7 percent annually between 1933 and 1940, and per capita output in 1940 was greater than it had been in 1929. Consequently school boards began to hire more freely. Nationwide there were 4 percent more teachers in 1939 than there had been in 1933. Among the Eau Claire State graduates of 1940, 81 percent immediately found teaching jobs (and another 12 percent went on to graduate study or into the army).

Enrollment also increased for another reason. In 1937, the regents officially recognized what had long existed in practice at Eau Claire when they created a "non-professional" category for students not interested in public school teaching. Beginning in 1937, the *Bulletin* labeled these students' first two years of study as "junior college" work, applicable to professions other than teaching. Almost 25 percent of Eau Claire undergraduates enrolled in this category in the fall of 1940. Referring to both professional and non-professional students, the administration explained now "the first two years in all courses will be made up of liberal arts subjects."

Despite this rosier outlook in the late 1930s, Schofield could not relax. New problems for Eau Claire State originated from Madison. The election of 1938 ended four years of Progressive administration and put Republicans back in power. Perceiving a threat from Communists, the new governor, Julius P. Heil, wanted students with "obnoxious minds" banned from the teachers colleges. The regents managed to deflect this demand, but they could not prevent a 10 percent budget cut for the 1939–41 biennium. Regent President Dempsey warned Schofield that the increased enrollment in the fall of 1939 had to be managed by "a heavier teaching load by our present faculties." The regents eventually had to slash faculty salaries above $1,800 by an across-the-board 6 percent for the spring semester of 1940 and 4.5 percent for 1940–41.

This cut in state support provoked the regents, for the first time, to limit access to the colleges by imposing enrollment caps. At a regents meeting in which Doudna refused to make eye contact with the governor, Heil in rambling remarks claimed the regents should cut the number of faculty rather than reduce their salaries. He suggested, in implicit contrast to the regents, "I want the girl paid enough so she can be a good, clean mother when she decides to marry [and] I don't want the girls walking the streets at night to be the lure of vultures." While discrete in public, Schofield was privately contemptuous of Heil, comparing him to the buffoonish Andy in the popular radio program *Amos n' Andy*. "Our troubles are due, largely," he wrote, "to a Governor who has no idea of what is right and what isn't in state government."

Campus Management During the Schofield Era

President Schofield ruled Eau Claire State as a benign monarch. For the first twenty-five years of the college's existence, like most heads of teachers colleges around the United States in this era, he personally directed all activities beyond immediate classroom instruction and asked for little assistance and tolerated little interference in his domain. "He was the supreme being," his secretary, Jerry Wing, later recalled almost blasphemously.

There was no system of faculty governance during the Schofield years. "He rather ruled his faculty with an iron hand," Wing recollected. Neither state law nor Schofield's practice gave the faculty any role in budget, staffing, or curriculum decisions. For instance, while the faculty at the University of Wisconsin developed the scheme for their salary waivers during the 1930s, the faculty of the state teachers colleges had no say in how their pay was cut. Eau Claire State faculty members did essentially clerical work at registration, while Schofield and Brewer did any substantive advising. Where faculty committees existed, they had responsibilities such as pouring tea at the annual September party for students hosted by the faculty. In a document he apparently prepared in the late 1930s for his own use, Schofield listed in column format the pros and cons of "faculty participation in policy." The point which seemed to weigh most heavily was one of the "cons:" faculty participation "would be discouraging to aggressive personalities in the administration."

Schofield was occupied with details such as ordering paint to redecorate a classroom because the college had few other staff. Besides the faculty, in 1940 the college employed only four clerks, two janitors, an engineer to maintain the furnace, an assistant engineer/janitor, and a few cafeteria workers. When there was heavy snowfall, the janitors came in at 2 am to shovel the sidewalks. They received no overtime pay but rather "just worked extra hours in those days," explained Leonard Haas, who was a student in the early 1930s and later became the college's president.

Faculty Christmas Party at the Home of Frances and Harvey Schofield, 1935

The entire faculty socialized together regularly during the Schofield era.

In addition to Brewer, a few members of the faculty had reduced teaching responsibilities because they performed administrative tasks at Schofield's pleasure. Schofield created the post of registrar in 1926 and assigned the job to Arthur Fox. Fox was the most pedagogically progressive of the original faculty—in response to a question from the *Spectator* in 1940 he endorsed the views presented to a Northwestern Wisconsin Education Association meeting by Stanford's Paul Hanna, a leading progressive, and argued there was too much emphasis on academics in the public schools. After an apparent falling-out with Fox, perhaps over educational philosophy, Schofield replaced him with George Hillier in 1929. "Oh my, he was handsome," Wing recalled, and Hillier became intimately involved with the daughter of a prominent community member. When he learned about the relationship, Schofield, with the concurrence of Regent Hurst, dismissed Hillier from the faculty during the summer of 1934.

James R. Wallin, one of the first faculty members to have a PhD, came from the University of Montana to replace Hillier as an economics and civics teacher and registrar. Perhaps insecure, Fox referred to Wallin as "The Doctor" and in 1939 warned Schofield that as a result of a summer tour of other colleges "he will have filled up on crazy ideas." Fox urged the president to "put the quietus on that gang" and reappoint him as registrar. Schofield agreed, and two weeks before the college opened, Fox moved back into the registrar's office and Wallin learned he had been assigned to teach the history of education, "which I am sure you will enjoy," Schofield told him unctuously. The *Spectator* was led to believe the regents were responsible for the change and welcomed Fox's return editorially.

As part of the small beginnings of administrative machinery in the college, history teacher Vine Miller served as dean of women from 1925 to 1939. She worked arduously to find housing and part-time jobs for women students. Laura Sutherland, an Eau Claire native who joined the Campus School faculty from Waukesha High School in 1921 and later taught history in the college, administered the NYA program for women students and succeeded Miller as dean of women. Monroe Milliren was Sutherland's counterpart for men in the NYA administration, and he became the college's first dean of men in 1939. Previously a chemistry teacher, Frank Ackerman had informally helped male students to find housing and employment.

Schofield's most important assistant was his director of teacher education. Charles Brewer served as principal of the Campus School, taught educational methods courses in the fall semester, and traveled extensively during the spring to visit teachers who were Eau Claire State alumni and find placements for new graduates. He commanded respect from people at all levels: his fellow schoolmen elected him president of the Wisconsin Education Association in 1931, and a misbehaving Campus School student received a lifetime memory from "a balding little man who wore square-toed, ankle-high laced shoes" who dealt "with the situation with a flat switch, which he drew from inside his jacket." Once Eau Claire State began to grant degrees, questions about Brewer's educational qualifications were resolved by his receipt of an honorary bachelor of education degree from River Falls State in 1928. However, by the late 1930s he was well into his seventies and he finally retired in 1938.

Brewer's successor was Eugene McPhee. After earning a diploma from Eau Claire Normal, McPhee was the superintendent at Winter for a decade before he received a bachelor's degree in 1931. He then served as superintendent at Elk Mound for a year before Schofield brought him back to campus as principal of the junior high school within the Campus School. McPhee had Schofield's confidence: the president summoned him for a conference at Bayfield when he was formulating a response to Fox's proposal to displace Wallin.

Laura Sutherland

As history teacher, dean of women, mentor of Leonard Haas, president of the Wisconsin Council of the Social Studies, and in other ways, Sutherland was the most influential woman on the faculty during the first half of the college's history. In a tribute at the time of her death in 1964, the local newspaper said, "She got the best out of her students with a unique combination of determination and kindness."

Having tagged him as Brewer's replacement, Schofield assigned McPhee to the job in 1938 without considering any other possibilities and gave him a salary second only to his own. Local schoolmen who wanted the job protested to the regents. Doudna, who felt McPhee was "a nice young chap" but unqualified, questioned Schofield's authority to decide unilaterally. Regent President Dempsey, however, chose not to intervene directly. As the director of teacher education, McPhee continued in the tradition of Brewer as a staunch critic of pedagogical progressivism. However, he expanded opportunities for student teachers, in what he thought was a more realistic direction, by locating placements outside the Campus School at Elk Mound High School and later in the Eau Claire city schools and at Black and McKinley country schools northeast of Eau Claire.

Harvey Schofield's Faculty

President Schofield personally selected faculty members without input from others. When he received a late resignation in August 1939, Schofield informed the office staff but enjoined them to keep the news confidential. "I have too many local complications," he wrote, "and want to settle this my own way." He was proud that he did not permit community influence into faculty personnel decisions (or listen to alumni when evaluating the performance of coaches). Beginning with the original faculty, the names of most potential teachers came to Schofield from the Yates and the Clark-Brewer teaching placement agencies, and he often traveled to the agencies' offices in Chicago to interview applicants. It was at such an interview in 1925 that Schofield asked Vine Miller, who would eventually teach history at Eau Claire State for over thirty years, to remove her hat so he could ensure she did not have bobbed hair.

The primary characteristic Schofield was looking for in a faculty member was "personality." "As you know," he told a placement agency, "personality counts with me very strongly." He only grudgingly acknowledged the increasing importance of formal qualifications. "I could fill this faculty up with PhDs at less salaries than I am paying today," he wrote in response to an unfavorable evaluation by accreditors in 1928, but, "I would also have a faculty that probably would not be more than one-half as efficient as the one I have now." "Efficiency" was in large part measured by "cooperation" with the president. Overall, Schofield wanted his faculty to be a "family," with him as its paternalistic head. "I do not want any person who is developing crabbiness in any way," he emphasized. "We always have a sufficient number of those on our faculty."

Schofield's faculty appointments took on multiple responsibilities. Arthur Murray taught English for over twenty years and authored a high school textbook. A former newspaperman, he advised the *Spectator* and the *Periscope* and assisted in preparing the college's catalogs and other printed materials. Temperamentally a conservative—in response to a question from the *Spectator* about equal rights, he explained that women "cannot lower themselves to do the things men have to do"—he helped Schofield mold the college's public persona. When he came to Eau Claire State in 1930, Roy Judd was the first faculty member to have a PhD. His new course offerings expanded the curricula in physics and mathematics. Beginning in 1932, he also advised the student Radio Club, which developed on-campus facilities enabling college programs to be broadcast over local radio station WEAU. After she became Eau Claire State's sole music teacher in 1924, Clara May Ward initiated the school's first orchestra and revitalized struggling vocal music groups. During the 1930s, her A Cappella Choir used the broadcasting technology installed by Judd's students and also toured extensively, presenting a 1939 concert at the White House. Amy Kjentvet Delsrude, a choir member, had fond memories for the rest of her life of having tea with Eleanor Roosevelt. The first lady wrote publically that she had enjoyed "a most enjoyable hour of music" from the choir.

In addition to working with student organizations, during the interwar period faculty members had to be flexible about what they taught. For example, in 1929 Hillier's appointment as registrar set off a chain reaction. Sutherland took over Hillier's social studies teaching methods course; Charles Donaldson, who had taught education and psychology since 1921, moved into Sutherland's modern history course; and Coach Willis Zorn was assigned to Hillier's US history course.

Hilda Belle Oxby was a close friend of Ward's and one of Schofield's initial appointees in 1916. She taught for almost forty years and had particularly broad intellectual interests and teaching responsibilities. Hired to teach German and Latin, most of her classroom work was in Spanish and English. She also developed an interest in international affairs, earned an MA degree in that subject from Columbia University, and attended the Williams College Institute of Politics for several summers between 1927 and 1932. She spent the summers of 1934 and 1937 traveling on her own in Europe. She also visited the Caribbean, Canada, Mexico, and the Andean region. These experiences were the basis for numerous presentations to community groups in Eau Claire and shifted the focus of her teaching from written language skills to foreign culture appreciation. A forceful and independent woman, Oxby proudly recounted in later years an incident when Schofield called on her to reprimand women students for having rolled down their stockings at a school dance. She told Schofield she would "as soon as he walked over to some of the women teachers dressed in similar style and did the same . . . He didn't." In general, the college's male leadership did not intimidate her. "I used to stand up to them," she recalled of Eau Claire State's presidents. "I never felt I was working *under* them. I was working *with* them."

Not all of Schofield's selections for the faculty worked out positively. He blamed a placement agency for a run of disappointments in the late 1930s. "The three people that I have hired from you in the past three years have in general been 'lemons,'" he complained. However, his preference for single-handed selection could also have been problematic. For the late opening in English in the fall of 1939 that he deliberately kept confidential, Schofield appointed Claiborn Hill without an interview, apparently in the belief his reported PhD from the University of Oxford would impress accreditors. Hill proved to be

Mabel Chipman and the Business of a College

Through the administrations of three presidents, Mabel Chipman carefully managed the day-to-day business operations of Eau Claire State, which became increasingly complex during her thirty-two years of service. She brought to her job a combination of skills from the education and business worlds.

Chipman graduated in 1916 at age sixteen from Redgranite High School, about fifty miles east of Oshkosh. She then completed a three-year diploma course in 1919 at Oshkosh Normal and taught mathematics, economics, social problems, and bookkeeping for the next ten years at high schools in Winneconne, Cadott, Thorp, and Redgranite. From 1930 to 1932, she studied at the University of Wisconsin and earned a bachelor's degree in finance and a master's degree in commerce with an emphasis in accounting.

Jobs were scarce for everyone in 1932, and the feeling was often men deserved first crack at those that were available. Chipman sought the security of a civil service position and passed the examination for junior accountant on May 28, 1932. Her job search, however, was discouraging. When she applied for an assistant deputy assessor of incomes position, she was told the Wisconsin Tax Commission employed "men only for this work."

Her break came the following summer, ironically as a result of the Depression-era prejudice against women in paid labor. Frances Jagoditsh had worked at Eau Claire State since its opening in President Schofield's office in a position classified as auditor (like Chipman, she had previously been a teacher, at New London). "He had come to know her so well," Leonard Haas later related, that after Schofield's wife, Dorothy, died in 1932, "he felt the need for this companionship, so he married" Jagoditsh in July 1933. There seems to have been no question that the new Mrs. Schofield would resign her position. There now was an opening for Chipman. Although her academic qualifications were better than some members of the faculty, and she had more teaching experience than others, she accepted a position classified as accounting clerk. "She proved to be a very efficient woman," Haas recalled, "and soon took charge in that office."

Chipman's duties were varied. In the 1930s and 1940s, she later recalled, "[W]henever a student cut his finger, he had to come to our office" on the second floor of Old Main "to get a bandage." Most importantly, she had the responsibility for collecting fees, purchasing supplies, disbursing the payroll and student loan funds, preparing reports, administering staff benefits, and keeping accounting records. She also supervised the other clerical workers at the college. The presence of the army air force training unit during 1943–44 (chapter four) was "quite an event" for Chipman, as she found herself responsible for purchasing the food to feed the hungry trainees and completing exacting federal government reporting forms. During the war she also maintained a scrapbook of newspaper clippings and other materials documenting the military service of Eau Claire State faculty and students. After the war, she worked closely with President Davies in preparing the college's biennial budget requests. In 1956 her position was reclassified to business manager. The 1957 *Periscope* recognized her with a special salute.

Like Erna Buchholz and Hilda B. Oxby, Mabel Chipman was active in community affairs. She was a member of the Eau Claire Business and Professional Women's Club and in 1949 was elected its president and served as recording secretary of its state organization. She also belonged to the Eau Claire Women's Club and sat on that group's board.

Chipman retired in 1965. "The more business-like education becomes," she believed, "the better education itself will be."

"a cracker-jack teacher," according to Schofield, but he abused alcohol and ran up debts and his Oxford PhD proved to be fictitious. A year after his termination at Eau Claire in 1940, Hill was in jail in New York City for fraud and larceny.

Like most academic administrators, Schofield wished he had more power to terminate unsatisfactory faculty members. Even before tenure rights legally protected them in 1931, he complained, "[I]t is difficult to fire teachers even for more serious offenses than just not going to school." Schofield was not without some power. In 1927 he discharged Katherine Ryan, Brewer's assistant in the Campus School, because of her epilepsy. As previously stated, he sacked Hillier in 1934 for his personal behavior. In 1940, health concerns led him to induce the retirement of math teacher Blanche James, one of the original faculty members. Schofield fibbed by telling her students had complained about her teaching to the regents. In a private letter accompanying her formal retirement letter to Schofield, James bitterly asserted she was still healthy, there was only a "misunderstanding" about her late submission of grades, and retirement would impoverish her. In what appears to have been a carefully worded article that included no statement by Schofield, the *Spectator* reported "surprise" by James's friends and former students at her retirement.

Student Affairs During the Interwar Years

> At Assembly he's fond of presiding,
> For our sins everyone of us chiding,
> In his office he sits,
> And O.K.'s our permits—
> For our school he does the deciding.

As this limerick in the 1929 *Periscope* highlighted, Harvey Schofield tolerated little interference with his management of student affairs. He felt it was demeaning to institutional authority for Eau Claire State to actively recruit students—"there is too much drumming up of students to enter schools." After students enrolled, the president paid little heed to their parents. In response to a mother's complaint about inedible food served to her daughters in the college cafeteria, Schofield asserted, "[T]here may be something wrong with your children" because he had heard no other objections. An intermittent student council was established in 1924, but organized student government ceased in 1930 because, in Sutherland's opinion, it was "not given sufficient responsibility" by Schofield. "[T]here wasn't really anything effective" regarding student government "during the time when I was a student here in '32 to '35," Leonard Haas later recalled. Schofield's promise in the spring of 1938 that the college would again have a student council in the fall did not come to fruition.

Schofield also held students to strict standards of behavior. Late arrivals in the morning had to see him personally before being admitted to class, inappropriately dressed women were sent home to change their clothes, and misbehaving students were publically shamed in the daily assemblies. In response to student supplications, the president did sporadically allow rooms in Old Main to serve as student lounges, but he squabbled with male students, in particular, about behavior in their "rest room." Smoking, gambling, and furniture damage led to its periodical "padlocking." There were also problems with between-class use of the balcony in the auditorium where, according to an irreverent newssheet, students were "brushing up" their "technique." For their part, students were unhappy about Schofield's increasingly strict enforcement of attendance policies at daily assemblies.

Schofield's leadership style of authoritarian paternalism was effective, however, because he maintained the respect of both students and faculty. The students recognized he was "very generous and very soft hearted," even to the extent of giving them personal loans. The president "to me represents the spirit of our school: democratic to the core," wrote an alumnus in 1925, who felt it had been a great "privilege to have come under the influence of . . . his personality as the spirit of our school." Schofield also had a subtle sense of humor. The annual monarchical-like celebrations of his birthday, for instance, in school assemblies and at faculty dinners, had a gently self-mocking quality.

A more cooperative and less confrontational relationship between students and the administration began to develop at the end of the 1930s. After becoming dean of women in 1939, Sutherland prepared a report on student government (the first "institutional study" in the college's history). Conrad Patzer, who had argued that teachers colleges were distinctive because they taught "democracy" through campus life and not as an academic subject as in a liberal arts college, influenced her thinking. Prompted by Sutherland's report, in the fall of 1940 Schofield designated a large classroom on the first floor of Old Main, across from the auditorium, as a student union. The Student Life Committee, consisting of elected students and faculty appointed by the president, managed the union as well as supervised college dances and "conduct in the hallways." Schofield himself donated a piano for use in the student union. This student union was only a measured step toward allowing more autonomous student behavior. In an article entitled "Student Life Opens New Student Lounge," the *Spectator* reported the new Student Life Committee had banned "lounging" in the new lounge. The committee, however, was an important step forward in the development of student self-government.

Town–Gown Relations during the Schofield Era

There were many positive aspects to relations between the college and the Eau Claire community during the interwar years. President Schofield worked diligently to remind community members of the economic value to them of Eau Claire State. He also personally participated in organizations and activities that brought him into contact with community leaders. His involvement with the World War I County Patriotism Committee, for example, led to a large contingent of normal school students participating in the city's Memorial Day parades during and after the war. In 1919 Schofield also blended the college's lecture and entertainment series, established in 1917, with the Kiwanis Club's musical and lyceum series. This initiative was short lived, but it foreshadowed by almost twenty-five years the college-community cooperation behind the establishment of Artist and Forum series (chapter four). There were also parallel ways in which community members became involved with Eau Claire State. The Campus School "was found to be a very attractive place for people in the city," Leonard Haas later recalled, and the pupils when grown "still like to identify themselves" with the college. Several local businesses also responded to Schofield's ad-hoc appeal and helped finance the A Cappella Choir's 1939 tour to the East.

Choir Trip, 1939

The choir's 1939 eastern tour, in a bus sponsored by businesses in the community and decorated with college insignia, was a great adventure for its participants.

Town–gown relations were not always smooth. For one thing, Eau Claire State's location proved problematic. Schofield's scheme in the mid-1920s to build an athletic field to the east of Old Main, along Park Avenue at approximately where Centennial Hall is now located, was blocked by influential Judge James Wickham, who felt his home on the southeast corner of Park and McKinley Avenue would be devalued. Conveniently, Wickham owned fourteen acres south of Old Main, across Little Niagara Creek, which he sold to the regents in 1926 as an alternative location for a football field and running track. Regent Smith's pronouncement that Eau Claire State "now has all the land it will require for all time" was inaccurate, however, and resistance to the college's further expansion by community members would continue to be a problem, as became evident in the 1937 closure controversy.

Map 2.1

Eau Claire normal campus, mid 1920s

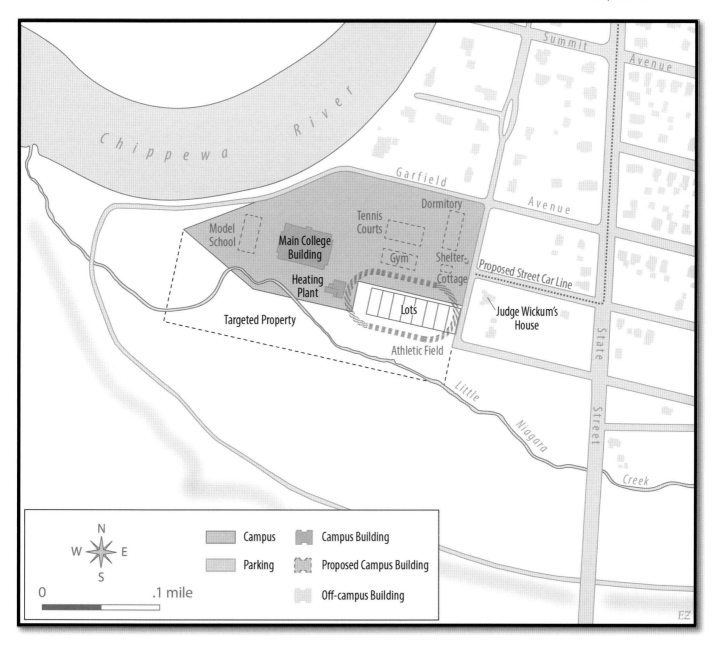

Basketball Game, Gymnasium, Old Main, 1940s

Athletic facilities in Old Main were cramped for both athletes and spectators, affecting the quality of play and the level of community interest in college sports.

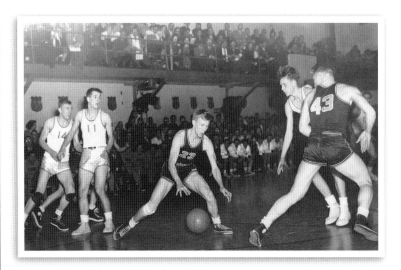

After construction of the football field in 1929, the college shared the facility with the local high school. This arrangement reciprocated the policy of the college playing its basketball games after 1925 in Eau Claire Senior High School's new building in downtown Eau Claire. This practice could be seen as an example of college-community cooperation. But playing its ill-attended basketball games at a gym distant from campus did not foster identity or school spirit at Eau Claire State, which the *Spectator* felt was much lacking during the interwar years. Similarly, the *Spectator* blamed the college's isolated location for the lack of community turnout at football games. Besides college and high school students, paid attendance averaged 535 per game in the fall of 1939. In general, during the 1930s the college was overshadowed in the community by the high school, which had a more impressive building and a much larger enrollment—over twice as many students graduated from Eau Claire Senior High in 1941 than did from Eau Claire State.

While not ignoring the community, Schofield repeatedly emphasized that the college was a "state," not a local, institution. He "didn't want to be told by people out in town how to run the college," explained Josephine Schneider, the wife of a faculty member and later a college librarian. The president did not develop a close relationship with the Eau Claire public schools, a problem McPhee had to work to correct after he became director of teacher education. While active himself at the First Methodist Church, Schofield did not encourage local congregations to have a presence on campus. Except for the Junior Prom and athletic matches, he did not allow community members to attend campus events. As Sutherland later conceded, by the late 1930s "contact with the city and area was not always good." Enrollment reflected this tepid relationship. While the boost in registration in the late 1930s was encouraging, overall enrollment at Eau Claire increased just 14 percent between 1933 and 1939, compared to 27 percent among the teachers colleges as a whole (which was almost exactly the corresponding percentage increase in high school graduates in the state).

Improvements in Facilities and Equipment

President Schofield's goal was to make Eau Claire State a "modern," "live," and "up-to-date" place. The new athletic facilities in the late 1920s and the WPA improvements in the 1930s helped advance that goal. As much as possible, the president also introduced new technology. The normal school bought a "moving picture machine" in 1919. A radio operated by Bridgman was able to pick up a broadcast from Great Britain for the first time in 1923. By the late 1930s radio broadcasts could be made from campus. In November 1939 students in daily assembly listened to a visiting lecturer explain the potential of the new medium of television.

Schofield, however, did not realize his hopes for major campus improvements. In the fifteen years following the completion of Old Main, the regents and the legislature authorized building projects at each of the eight other teachers colleges, climaxing with a $332,500 gymnasium at Milwaukee. Then in 1933, the regents designated new campus school buildings at Eau Claire and La Crosse as their highest priority projects. But just at the moment when it was Eau Claire's turn for a new building, the Great

Depression ended state appropriations for construction at the teachers colleges. Schofield, however, continued to press for a second building at Eau Claire: "I feel that there is no school with more need of additional space than Eau Claire," he emphasized to Doudna. Oxby later defended Schofield's efforts: it was "not true he had been lax in getting buildings," she felt.

Towards the end of the decade, the regents turned to the WPA to finance their construction projects. Schofield was disappointed when in August of 1938 federal authorities approved the proposal for La Crosse's campus school, but rejected that for Eau Claire. A few months later, Regent President Dempsey dashed Schofield's inquiry about the possibility of the college acquiring the large home on the northwest corner of State Street and Garfield Avenue, which the president eyed because of the recent death of its occupant, Mary Dulany, widow of lumber baron Daniel Dulany. The Wisconsin teachers colleges, Dempsey felt, were too small to have separate student unions or libraries, possible uses for the Dulany property. The 735 students who enrolled at Eau Claire in the fall of 1939, therefore, had essentially the same physical facilities as had their 184 predecessors in 1916. When she moved to Eau Claire as the wife of a newly appointed faculty member in 1930, Josephine Schneider was shocked to find worse facilities at Wisconsin's teachers colleges than she was familiar with in her native South Carolina, one of the poorest states in the nation. Wisconsin was a low-tax state during the interwar years, and its public facilities consequently suffered.

Aerial View of Eau Claire State, 1939

By the end of the Schofield era, the campus included athletic fields south of Little Niagara Creek, but planned development east of Old Main had stalled. Putnam Park stands out dramatically in this photograph, which also shows the space south of the top of the bluff was still farmland.

The Schofield Era Comes to a Close

Illness plagued President Schofield during the late 1930s, and he was absent from campus for extended periods. Finally, citing health concerns, he announced his retirement to the regents on April 15, 1940. For reasons unclear today, this action was not made public until October. Schofield, therefore, was still in charge of the college for the fall semester; when he retreated to Bayfield in late August to escape the hay fever season in Eau Claire, as had become his practice, he appointed Monroe Milliren as acting president.

Milliren was one of a dozen applicants to replace Schofield. The regents received strong letters of support for him from school principals and superintendents in the Eau Claire area. Milliren's colleague George Simpson, however, was also intensely interested in the position. "It's a job I want very much" and "have pointed at . . . for years," he beseeched Regent President Dempsey. A flood of letters endorsing his candidacy came from elected officials, local businessmen, and the Eau Claire alumni association. "I am being deluged with letters from Eau Claire on behalf of Simpson," Dempsey bemoaned. At the regents' office in Madison, however, Simpson's former Eau Claire Normal colleague and University of Wisconsin classmate Edgar Doudna strongly believed presidents should be Wisconsin men with public school administrative experience. "It would be nothing short of tragic," Doudna felt, "to have George Simpson take the presidency." Eventually Dempsey reported, "Several letters which I have received from Eau Claire indicate that it would be a mistake to elect a local man," and Milliren and Simpson both dropped from consideration.

In searching for Schofield's successor, the regents largely narrowed their focus to Wisconsin school superintendents. Dempsey and Regent Smith were very interested in William C. Hansen, superintendent at Stoughton. As a result of the sudden death in late September of President E. T. Smith of Stevens Point State, however, Hansen was slotted to fill that position. Superintendent Everett C. Hirsch of Wausau withdrew from consideration for the Eau Claire job. Schofield was negative about other possibilities. By early November Regent Smith felt that "my first choice" was Superintendent William R. Davies of Superior. However, Regent Jay Grim, another member of the Search Committee, made a trip to Superior and got negative feedback about Davies from public school teachers. Rumors also reached Madison about Davies's health, while Dempsey touted the candidacy of Ernest Thedings from the faculty at Oshkosh State.

Davies favorably impressed Dempsey in an interview at Oshkosh on November 22, however, and the regent president decided, "[W]e can take a chance on his health." With that information, Doudna consulted with John Callahan, the state superintendent of public instruction and another member of the Search Committee, and concluded, "[I]t seems to me we might just as well settle upon him." The regents officially announced Davies's appointment at their meeting during the first week of December. In general, the decisive factors in his selection appear to have been a predisposition to pick a Wisconsin schoolman and the weight given to the favorable opinion towards Davies by Eau Claire Regent Peter Smith.

There was a quick transition from Schofield to Davies as president, which was effective on January 1, 1941. Fox wrote to Davies immediately after his appointment, congratulating him because "we should have a Wisconsin man, and also an experienced school man." Schofield invited Davies to come to Eau Claire, where he addressed a student assembly on December 18. According to Sutherland, he impressed the students as friendly, but firm in his convictions. In his own farewell remarks, Schofield explained, "My philosophy of life has been to talk the language and appreciate the lives of the common people." The *Spectator* editorially expressed its appreciation for his leadership by proposing the newly opened student union be named the "Harvey Schofield Memorial." Milliren's daughter Jane, who was a member of the Student Life Committee, ironically organized a retirement banquet on December 12. Leonard Haas, a recent graduate now teaching in Wausau, gave the principal address.

Davies's background was a bit different from that of Schofield and Brewer. He had received a liberal arts education, earning his BA from Ripon College in 1915 with majors in mathematics and philosophy.

He then embarked on a career in public school administration while earning a master's degree in education from the University of Wisconsin. After a series of career-enhancing moves, he came to Superior as superintendent in 1931. There he was a mild pedagogical Progressive, emphasizing to his teachers, for example, that classrooms should be "laboratories" not lecture halls. Davies served in the US Army during World War I and participated in the reserves during the 1920s. This experience had made him interested in international affairs and skeptical of military solutions to world problems. He was proud to have been president of the Wisconsin American Legion Schoolmasters and to have served on the Americanism Committee of the Superior American Legion post. In 1935, however, he had urged his principals in Superior to organize Armistice Day programs "stressing the futility and wastefulness of war" and honoring people who "live for a cause" as well as those who die.

In general, Davies did not outwardly reject the ideas of the world of Wisconsin schoolmen to which he belonged. This world emphasized that hiring should be from within a small circle of like-minded individuals and there should be a distinctive course content for students preparing to teach in contrast to those preparing for other occupations. It believed the unique purposes of American public schools—to create citizens in a democracy—meant other institutions, including the colleges and universities some of their students would eventually attend, could not assess them. Davies was prepared to broaden this world and would work to do so at Eau Claire during the next twenty years.

At the end of the 1930s there was a buoyant mood in the United States. An Indian summer in Wisconsin, which had its warmest November until late in the century, followed the beginning of war in Europe in September 1939. In parallel fashion, socially and economically the end of the decade was a period of relaxation and optimism before the state's residents would feel the dislocations of war. The ravages of the Great Depression had ended, and advertisements filled the Eau Claire newspapers for consumer products that were affordable because wages were rising and wartime inflation had not yet set in. In respect to popular culture, late 1939 and early 1940 was the most fertile period of the studio era in Hollywood. Between late August and mid-January the studios released *The Wizard of Oz, Mr. Smith Goes to Washington, Ninotchka, Gone with the Wind*, and *The Grapes of Wrath*. In the sports world, in March 1940 plucky Seabiscuit—whose upset of regal War Admiral in 1938 encapsulated the populist determination of the country in response to the Depression—ended his career by dramatically winning the $100,000 Santa Anita Handicap. As the 1940s began, streamlined features of modern design increasingly infused the objects of material culture used by Americans; they were nowhere better seen than by Eau Claire residents when the Chicago & North Western Railroad's *400* train stopped twice daily en route between Chicago and St. Paul. Modern design especially imbued the appearance of the 1939–40 New York World's Fair, at which Eau Claire State's A Cappella Choir performed. The fair optimistically projected "a world of tomorrow" shaped by modern technology. This was the world into which President Davies wanted to lead Eau Claire State.

1916-41
The Social and Academic World of Eau Claire State Students

Aerial View of Old Main and Third Ward, late 1920s

New development during the 1920s along Roosevelt and McKinley Avenues, still unlandscaped when this photograph was taken, in what had been Driving Park, constrained the possibility of expansion towards the east by the college.

The small enrollment and limited facilities of Eau Claire State during its first quarter century meant the faculty and students, for better or for worse, had close personal relationships with one another.

Working with the abilities and the resources they had, they slowly built more academically challenging programs supported by co-curricular activities that engaged student interests. The students were for the most part conventional in their attitudes, but they were not immune from national influences. They respected President Schofield, but in 1941 welcomed his successor, William R. Davies, who wanted to integrate Eau Claire State even further into the world beyond the public schools of West Central Wisconsin.

The Students of Eau Claire State, 1916–41

During the interwar period, Eau Claire State students were practical minded and had a utilitarian approach to their education. Eugene McPhee, a student in the 1920s and a faculty member in the 1930s, later explained they were "very serious" and saw the college as a "stepping stone from factory and farm work to the professions." "It cost me plenty to get here," wrote a freshman in 1931, "and I intend to get my money's worth . . . I have certain aims in my heart, and . . . a college education is the first step towards them." What this attitude meant was that, as a student told the *Spectator* in 1929, "although we come to college, we aren't here to get an education" but rather vocational training. The *Spectator*'s reporting found students specifically chose Eau Claire State because of its location close to their homes, its relatively low costs, its athletic programs, and friends who were already enrolled.

The college predominately served students from its surrounding "district." In 1940 50 percent of students came from Eau Claire County (an increase from 43 percent in 1930) and 40 percent from adjacent counties (an increase from 38 percent in 1930). Students also tended to stick close to home after graduation. For instance, information available one year after graduation for about 75 percent of the class of 1937 shows fifty-six were working or going to school in Eau Claire or adjacent counties and only thirty-two elsewhere. The pattern is even more evident among the editors of the *Periscope* from 1917 through 1934: the 1938 yearbook reported fourteen out of nineteen were still living in Eau Claire or adjacent counties. Despite the problems caused by the Great Depression, there were opportunities for graduating students to remain close to home because the district around Eau Claire was growing slowly but steadily. Its population increased about 20 percent between 1920 and 1940, close to the statewide rate of growth. The district remained predominately rural in 1940 when only about 20 percent of its population was urban, compared to 38 percent of the state's population outside of Milwaukee.

During the interwar period, most students (64 percent according to a 1933 *Spectator* survey) lived at home and commuted to campus daily, staying from 8 am to 4 pm. As automobile ownership became more common during the 1920s, some students began to carpool to campus. Another *Spectator* report in 1933 found sixty-two cars in the campus parking lot (probably including a few that were faculty operated), and 125 students indicated on a 1935 survey they came to campus by car. For instance, Norman Olson, who attended Eau Claire State from 1938 to 1940 and would later serve as dean of the School of Business in the 1960s, drove several other students from Chippewa Falls to campus daily in his Model A Ford. Other students came from outlying communities such as Colfax and Mondovi in publically subsidized school buses, which made for exciting travel on snowy mornings. Students from out of town who preferred to walk to their classes found rooms, with or without board, in private homes near campus. When Eau Claire Normal opened, a locally published magazine told its readers, "The biggest thing you can do just now is to provide homes for the Normal students." This practice would benefit city residents: "People who are busy complaining about the hicostalivin would do well to consider . . . renting a room or two," they were told. The 1935 survey reported about 27 percent of students were roomers and another 10 percent had "light housekeeping" facilities.

Supervision of Student Life During the 1920s and 1930s

Eau Claire State's strict *in loco parentis* policy governed off-campus student behavior during the interwar years. It "fit in perfectly with the period when there was no active student government," Leonard Haas explained. Regulations for 1927–28, for instance, specified, "Men and women students may not room in the same house," and they mandated a 10 pm weeknight curfew for women. Revisions in 1940 made it clear that so-called "brothers" could not be entertained in women's rooms. The regulations also imposed requirements on householders who rented to students, which created ongoing friction among students, householders, and the deans of men and women. Householders, for instance, twice a week had to provide hot water for baths and make a first-floor parlor available in the evening to female students "for entertaining gentlemen callers."

President Schofield admitted he grew increasingly "puritanical" during the 1930s. On the basis of an article he had read in *Life*, Schofield objected in 1938 when the Eau Claire State Theater showed the controversial documentary *The Birth of a Baby*. He ranted against the dangers of taverns and "as a college president" told the brewing industry trade association he was worried about the welfare of "young ladies . . . standing up to the bar drinking high-balls with the men." Schofield also cooperated with Edgar Doudna, the regents' secretary who was a prominent Congregationalist layman in Madison and a prohibitionist, and slated traveling speakers from the Women's Christian Temperance League as part of the daily assembly programs. Schofield's attitudes affected students even more directly when in late 1937 he banned "barroom forms" of dancing at college events (see sidebar).

Some students acquiesced in the regulation of their private lives by the president and his deans. A student columnist in the *Spectator* in 1929, for instance, refuted criticism from the leftish *Nation* directed towards normal school students who were expected to "toe the mark" and argued instead that students *should* conform to "accepted practices." McPhee later explained students at teachers colleges "were supposed to be more on the conformist side." But both McPhee and John Schofield, the president's son who was a student during the late 1930s, admitted "everyone" regularly drank alcohol at "holes in the wall," even during Prohibition. A non-scientific in-class survey of students in 1931 found 80 percent had drank during the previous six months, and a *Spectator* survey in 1939 found 60 percent of students were "drinkers." Referring to his fellow students during the mid-1930s, Haas later carefully admitted, "There was the exercise of some freedoms in terms of their sexual life." In general, students carved out their own self-regulated social sphere, which was neither hedonistic nor strictly controlled by college officials. As the *Spectator* editorialized in 1938, it was a fact most college students drank alcohol; the real problem was some drank "too much" and specifically drunken women could "lose their reputation" because "men will talk." Similarly, Schofield believed his students generally exercised self-control in drinking alcohol because they knew when they became schoolteachers they could not indulge, at least publically.

Harvey Schofield as DJ

A 1937 episode provoked by a popular dance step, the "Big Apple," demonstrated the extent of President Schofield's "puritanism" and the limited effectiveness it had against the popular culture young Americans came to embrace by the 1930s.

The "Big Apple" had its origins in the "ring shout" performed by African American slaves in the early nineteenth century. The Roxy Theater in New York presented the dance commercially to white audiences in a successful show, which ran for three weeks in September 1937. It was quickly adapted into the routines of Whitey's Lindy Hoppers, a popular performance group based at the Savoy Ballroom in Harlem. It soon became a wildly popular dance craze around the country. To cultural conservatives, however, its physical expressiveness was too suggestive: Bosley Crowther denounced it in the *New York Times* (Crowther ended his career thirty years later with a famous excoriation of another cultural milestone, the film *Bonnie and Clyde*). Other Americans, especially if they appreciated African American culture, were more tolerant. Eleanor Roosevelt publically approved it for dancing at the White House.

In a move that attracted statewide notice, on December 8 Harvey Schofield banned the performance of the "Big Apple" and related steps such as the "Praise Allah" at dances at Eau Claire State. He characterized them as "barroom forms" of dancing and insisted on greater "formality" at future events.

Schofield was perceptive about the potentially subversive quality of the "Big Apple." On the following Sunday night, Mae West was the guest on NBC's top-rated radio program, *The Chase & Sanborn Hour*. She played Eve in a Garden of Eden sketch. Referring to Forbidden Fruit, she told the Serpent to "Get me a big one. I feel like doin' a big apple." (In another sketch later in the broadcast, she told the randy dummy Charley McCarthy that he was "all wood and a yard long" before inviting him "to come home with me now" and "lay in my woodpile.") The studio audience roared its appreciation of the *double entendre*.

Other Americans, however, were not amused. In Wisconsin, Regents Secretary Doudna led the protests about the program which came from women's organizations, church officials, civic groups, and schoolmen. "I want my dirt left in burlesque theaters and not on the radio," he was widely quoted as telling Chase & Sanborn. In Washington, Congressman Donald O'Toole of New York called for a congressional investigation. The Federal Communications Commission found the program "vulgar and indecent." Consequently, Chase & Sanborn issued a groveling apology and NBC indefinitely banned West from its networks.

In Wisconsin, Schofield found himself ridiculed by the *Manitowoc Herald-Times* as a "so-called educator" whose proscription of the "Big Apple" was actually counterproductive and an expression of "pseudo-morality." Nothing about the ban ever appeared in the *Spectator*, so apparently it was quickly dropped or ignored. In sum, the episode showed that by the late 1930s even conventionally minded Eau Claire State students were not immune from the commercially driven popular culture, with music at its forefront, which was spreading infectiously among American youth to the dismay of their elders. By the 1960s the problems for students and administrators posed by this cultural conflict would far exceed the shock caused by a few suggestive words on the radio in 1937.

Socio-economic Characteristics of Students at Eau Claire State

President Schofield and other spokesmen for Eau Claire State emphasized the modest socio-economic backgrounds of the college's students, especially in contrast to those at the University of Wisconsin. "[P]eople who really had funding" during the 1930s "would probably go to the University at Madison or perhaps to a private institution" rather than Eau Claire, recalled Leonard Haas. Supporters of the college argued it deserved public support because it provided these students with upwards mobility prospects, in the spirit of the "people's colleges" discussed in chapter one.

TABLE 3.1
FAMILY SOCIO-ECONOMIC STATUS, GRADUATES OF EAU CLAIRE STATE TEACHERS COLLEGE, 1921-41

OCCUPATION	1921	1931	1941	U.S.1940 (approx.)
Farm Sector				
Farm Operator	42.2%	37.0%	40.5%	11.0%
Farm Manager		1.7		
Farm Laborer			4.3	7.0
Non-Farm Sector				
Business Class				
Higher White Collar				
Professional	4.8	7.6	3.4	7.0
Major Proprietor/Manager/Official	2.4	8.4	4.3	
Lower White Collar				8.0
Petty Proprietor/Manager/Official	16.9	16.9	11.2	
Semi-Professional	4.8	0.8	1.7	1.0
Clerical/Sales	8.4	7.6	8.6	17.0
Working Class				
Artisan	2.4	2.5	0.8	
Foreman	1.2	1.7	0.8	
				11.0
Blue Collar				
Skilled	1.2	5.9	8.6	
Semi-Skilled/Operatives	6.0	2.5	5.2	14.0
Unskilled/Laborers	3.6	5.0	4.3	7.0
Service	4.8	2.5	3.4	15.0
Police/Fire			2.6	1.0
N=	83	119	116	
Occupation="None" (1920,30) or blank (1940)	12	9	12	
Student located but not parents		8	1	
Student and parents both not located	7	5	5	
Parents' occupation omitted		1	n.a.	
Ambiguous identification of student	1	1		
Illegible/Faded/Torn Enumeration Sheet	2	1		
TOTAL STUDENTS GRADUATING	105	144	134	

Table 3.1

Table 3.1 shows the family socio-economic status of the graduating classes of 1921, 1931, and 1941. The occupation of the head of the student's household (usually his or her father) determined the student's family socio-economic status (except in a few cases where the students themselves were married and obviously self-supporting). The occupations were those given on the manuscript United States Census for 1920, 1930, and 1940.

The cost of attending Eau Claire State during the interwar years, however, was not insignificant, even though no "tuition" was charged to students who declared their intention to become a teacher. In 1928, the *Spectator* estimated "fixed costs" for students from Eau Claire were $65 per year, for students commuting from Chippewa Falls were $135, and for out-of-town students living in Eau Claire were $315. The newspaper favorably contrasted these figures to an estimate of $600 to attend the University of Wisconsin. That same year, a report apparently prepared by faculty member Arthur Fox estimated "yearly expenses" for all students at about $400; presumably, this report incorporated clothing (estimated at $90 per year for women in 1940), recreation, and other expenses not considered by the *Spectator*. By 1940, at Eau Claire State the "incidental" fee (which included book and laboratory fees), the student activity fee, and the student health fee totaled $27 per semester. The college *Bulletin* explained that students who needed room and board in Eau Claire should also expect to spend about $170–260 for the academic year. Taking into account clothing and other items, it would appear total expenses for out-of-town students were at least $450 (close to $8,000 in 2016 dollars). About 60 percent of students at this time depended on paid labor or financial aid to meet at least some of these expenses or earned room and board in return for housekeeping or childcare services.

Did these costs prevent students from lower socio-economic backgrounds from attending Eau Claire State, in spite of what officials said were the opportunities the college offered? The best answer to this question seems to be "not entirely." Students from a wide variety of socio-economic backgrounds attended the college, although not unexpectedly in imperfect proportion to their weight in the overall population (Table 3.1).

The family socio-economic status of Eau Claire State students was only moderately skewed towards relatively privileged backgrounds. Schofield was about right when he wrote in 1937 that 75 percent of the students came from the "middle or poorer classes." Teaching, rather than medicine or law, was the most common occupation in the professional category, and grocery store operators were much more common among proprietors than factory owners. Befitting the rural character of the district around Eau Claire, farm operators most frequently headed the families of graduates—about 40 percent at each point in time—during the college's first quarter century. Interestingly, five graduates in 1940—4 percent of the total—had parents who were farm laborers. The emergence of this group, which had not been represented at all among 1920 or 1930 graduates, is part of an overall shift during the Great Depression decade towards more plebian socio-economic status among students.

This shift reversed the pattern of the 1920s. During that decade, college students around the country increasingly came from families with business and, especially, professional backgrounds. There was a similar shift among Eau Claire State students between 1921 and 1931: the percentage coming from professional and higher proprietor/manager families increased significantly. This trend reversed itself, however, during the Depression decade when the percentage of students with working-class backgrounds increased from 19 to 26 percent (30 percent if farm labor is included). Correspondingly, the percentage of students from the lower white-collar category, while remaining significant, dropped across the entire 1920–40 period from 30 percent to 22 percent.

The family socio-economic status of Eau Claire students was a bit more plebian than that of the other Wisconsin teachers colleges. Data gathered in 1931 showed Eau Claire State had the lowest percentage of students with fathers who were proprietors of any of the nine teachers colleges and had the next-to-highest percentage of students who were at least partially self-supporting. Eau Claire and its sister teachers colleges also stood in contrast to the University of Wisconsin: a 1930 report identified 16 percent of the freshmen at Madison as having professional parents (compared to 8 percent at Eau Claire), only 10 percent as having parents who were farmers, and 16 percent as having parents who were from the working class (compared to 39 percent and 20 percent, respectively, at Eau Claire). UW officials at that time also estimated only about a third of their students were self-supporting, in contrast to more than half at Eau Claire.

Student Ethno-religious Backgrounds

Similar to their varied socio-economic backgrounds, Eau Claire State students came from a spectrum of religious backgrounds. As would be expected given the predominant Norwegian and German ancestry of the district around Eau Claire, about 35 percent of the students were Lutherans. More than 10 percent were members of Grace Lutheran Church, the English language Norwegian Lutheran congregation in Eau Claire. Methodists, Congregationalists, Presbyterians, and Baptists, in succession, had the next largest representation among Protestants. Catholics were 15–20 percent of the student body. In contrast to their larger presence at the University of Wisconsin, there were only a handful of Jews at Eau Claire State. Few students did not have a religious preference, and only one or two stated they were atheists.

Students tended to be native born and from families long resident in the United States. Of the 325 enrollees during 1920–21 about whom data can be found, only 1 percent was foreign born and 39 percent had a foreign-born parent. Statewide in Wisconsin in 1920, 7 percent of twenty to twenty-four year olds were foreign born and 49 percent had a foreign-born parent.

At Eau Claire State, Catholic students and those from immigrant families sometimes felt insecure. While the proportion of Catholic students at Eau Claire was similar to that at Madison, at the University of Wisconsin they were the largest single denomination, perhaps providing more security. In any event, when the Ku Klux Klan was resurgent in the early 1920s and targeted Catholics and immigrants as un-American, the regents allowed Klan klaverns to meet in normal school buildings at the discretion of school presidents and local regents. Schofield, to be sure, was always careful about religion—when hiring faculty, he stressed he was non-discriminatory (although Katherine Thomas and Katherine Ryan were apparently the only Catholics he ever hired) and there is no record the Klan or a similar group ever met on the Eau Claire campus. There were periodic expressions of dissatisfaction, however, by Catholic students. For instance, a letter to the *Spectator* in 1932 deplored the anti-Catholicism which supposedly had determined recent campus elections. Later in the decade, the mother of eight children who had attended the college complained to Regent President Edward Dempsey about "plenty of bigotry" on campus, allegedly encouraged by Schofield and Charles Brewer "who saw that Protestants and the children of Masons would receive first awards in any thing." She particularly attacked Clara May Ward as a "black protestant" who delighted in forcing Catholic students in the A Cappella Choir to sing Protestant church hymns. However, Dempsey—himself a Catholic—believed in general the Wisconsin teachers colleges did not discriminate against Catholic students or teachers.

Eau Claire Students and Partisan Politics

Permissive about personal behavior while seeking respectability and vocational advancement, Eau Claire State students like most undergraduates around the country generally held conservative political and economic views, although this pattern weakened somewhat during the 1930s in response to national events and the changing socio-economic backgrounds of the students (Table 3.2).

A few weeks after classes began at Eau Claire Normal, a presidential straw poll strongly favored the reelection of President Woodrow Wilson, a Democrat. That result is somewhat surprising because voters in Eau Claire County and each of the surrounding counties, as well as the state as a whole, clearly favored Republican challenger Charles Evans Hughes. Perhaps the students, at an age when their partisan preferences had not yet become as set as those of their parents, showed deference to Wilson as the incumbent, as they also did by voting to retain Governor Emmanuel Philipp (a Stalwart Republican) and US Senator Robert LaFollette (a Progressive Republican), both incumbents.

Again in 1924, student opinion bucked statewide and local trends and strongly supported the reelection of a Republican, Calvin Coolidge. This result was all the more remarkable because the students rejected LaFollette, who ran on a third-party ticket as a Progressive and, for example, was the clear student preference at River Falls Normal. In its analysis of the Eau Claire poll, the *Spectator* pointed out that even students from the country, where LaFollette's support was generally strongest, preferred Coolidge. Deference may have again played a role, but there were also clear ideological differences

TABLE 3.2
STUDENT PARTISAN PREFERENCES 1916-36
1916 (N=120)   Wilson (Dem.)= 72%   Hughes (Rep.)=27%   Hanley (Proh.)=2%
1920 (N=17)   Harding (Rep.)=71%   Cox (Dem.)=29%
1924 (N=359, incl. 15 faculty)   Coolidge (Rep.)=57%   LaFollette (Prog.)=32%   Davis (Dem.)=12%
1928 (N=104)   Hoover (Rep.)=78%   Smith (Dem.)=22%%
1936 (N=321)   Roosevelt (Dem.)=50%   Landon (Rep.)=50%

among the three candidates in 1924, and Eau Claire students, like college students around the country, chose the most conservative candidate. They continued to show their support for the status quo in 1928 by overwhelmingly endorsing Republican Herbert Hoover, who after the election Laura Sutherland pronounced was the "greatest American today."

In 1936, President Franklin D. Roosevelt was reelected with over 60 percent of the vote in Eau Claire County and a greater percentage statewide. Despite the fact that about 40 percent of Eau Claire State students received financial assistance from the National Youth Administration (chapter two), they evenly split their votes between Roosevelt and Republican Alf Landon. The *Spectator* reported there was widespread "surprise" about Roosevelt's overwhelming victory, which suggested the temper of campus before the election was not enthusiastically pro-Democrat. Nationwide, student support swung towards the Democrats in 1936, especially at public institutions. Roosevelt was the clear choice, for instance, at the University of Wisconsin, Oshkosh State, and Milwaukee State. For their part, students at Eau Claire State were less conservative by 1936 than they had been during the 1920s, to be sure, but they still tended to come from slightly above-average socio-economic backgrounds, have native-born parents, and have bourgeois aspirations, which disposed them to support Republicans. Certainly, none of the student strikes or other protest activities associated with groups such as the Communist-tinged American Student Union, which occurred at Milwaukee State and elsewhere across the country during the 1930s, happened at Eau Claire State.

What Was on the Minds of Students During the 1930s?

As their voting behavior indicated, conservative attitudes remained strong among students during the 1930s. The college experience at Eau Claire, however, enabled them to become aware of contemporary problems. Daily assembly programs were often pedestrian, undoubtedly, with presentations by magicians, yodelers, temperance enthusiasts, and automobile insurance agents extolling driving safety. When scheduling one speaker, Schofield admitted she had not said anything significant at a previous presentation, but "she was rather interesting to look at, and that may help out, especially with the men." Some assemblies, however, exposed the students to serious ideas. For instance, in 1931 the distinguished University of Wisconsin sociologist Edward Ross explained the need of government aid for farmers. The presentation in 1941 by Rabbi Harry Margolis from St. Paul on "Crucial Moments in Jewish History" was informative to the nearly all-Christian student body. Assembly programs such as those in 1935 by the Utica Jubilee Singers and in 1940 by Dorothy Maynor, the African American soprano fresh from a sensational New York debut at Town Hall, added a degree of appreciation for racial diversity to the students' college experience. The

Clara Mae Ward and Dorothy Maynor, 1940

Reviewing her sold-out New York debut at Town Hall on November 19, 1939, Ollin Downes wrote in the New York Times *that Maynor's voice was "phenomenal for its range, character, and varied expressive resources."*

A Cappella Choir also advanced this goal by sponsoring a recital at the city auditorium in the fall of 1939 by contralto Marian Anderson, touring after her celebrated concert the previous Easter at the Lincoln Memorial.

For its part, the *Spectator* was carefully censored, as were collegiate publications across the country, and devoted most of its space to banal reports of student activities and calls for greater school "spirit" and stricter Lenten observance. Occasionally, it challenged the status quo. In December 1934, the newspaper criticized discrimination by an Eau Claire hotel towards the African American cast of a traveling production of *Green Pastures*. In 1936, in line with collegiate student opinion in general, the student newspaper took a strong position against compulsory participation in the Reserve Officers Training Corps.

In addition, new faculty members brought fresh ideas to Eau Claire State. Samuel Davenport, who taught speech and directed Strut and Fret, the college's theater group (until his academic credentials were found to be bogus), in 1934 authored a one-act play, *I Am a Jew*, which was performed around the state and alerted students to growing anti-Semitism in Europe. Beginning in 1930 John Schneider (whose PhD from the University of Wisconsin was genuine) taught history and sociology and came, in Haas's opinion, "very close to expressing basic socialist values." Schneider incorporated a critique of racism into his sociology courses and eventually—as the only "acknowledged" Democrat on the faculty—was instrumental in establishing a Young Democrat Club. He must have been proud of the *Spectator*'s 1939 endorsement of the need to recognize an adequate standard of living, collective bargaining, the best possible health care, the rights of minorities, and other principles of "security" as new "human rights." In this instance, the *Spectator* editors anticipated—and in regards to minority rights, exceeded—the program President Roosevelt would eloquently outline in his 1944 State of the Union message.

New faculty who came to Eau Claire State during the 1930s with advanced academic degrees and relatively cosmopolitan backgrounds were to some extent objects of curiosity. The curiosity itself suggested a degree of provincialism existed on campus, but at the same it also meant students were open to learning from the newcomers. Shortly after their arrival in the fall of 1930, Schneider and physicist Roy Judd described for *Spectator* readers the process of studying for a PhD. A year later Marie Heuer, who taught in the Campus School for one year, discussed campus life at Harvard University, where she had recently earned an MA in comparative literature. Richard Hibbard, who was born in Canada and had lived for six years in Greece where his father had been a YMCA secretary, related "his experiences in foreign lands" to the *Spectator* when he was an undergraduate in 1928.

In particular, students were not "isolated" from awareness of the growing international tensions that led to the outbreak of World War II in 1939. Hilda B. Oxby and other faculty members regularly reported to the campus on their summer visits to Europe. Secretary Doudna traveled through Germany in the summer of 1936, and he came to Eau Claire in November and made presentations in four classes about current conditions. "Assembly Speaker Raps Nazi Regime" was the *Spectator*'s description of one of the increasingly numerous assemblies at the end of the decade that focused on international events. The *Spectator* also regularly sought out faculty members for interviews about the world situation. In January 1938, when it came to a vote in the House of Representatives, the campus paper editorially opposed the Ludlow Amendment to the US Constitution, perhaps the hallmark of 1930s "isolationism," which would have required a popular referendum to ratify a congressional declaration of war and had 68 percent popular support according to the Gallup Poll.

In general, while opposed to the country's involvement in war (although in a May 1938 plebiscite they only narrowly favored an "isolationist" to a "collective security" policy), students did not have their heads in the sand. They were skeptical, rather, of the populist idealism behind schemes such as the Ludlow Amendment, as they also were of fighting an idealistic war for democracy. For the 1938 *Periscope*, none of the ten students questioned agreed Americans should fight "to preserve world democracy;" such language was only "the sales talk of land and property-hungry egoists," wrote one student. The following year, a *Spectator* editorial asserted, "International idealism at this moment appears to be somewhat akin to asininity." In a similar non-idealistic spirit, in 1940 the *Spectator* evaluated the newly adopted military draft from the perspective of its readers and felt it unnecessarily disrupted the careers of young men just getting established.

Student Activities and Sports During the 1920s and 1930s

During the interwar years, students expressed their special interests and talents through numerous campus organizations. Literary societies had been a major feature of nineteenth-century American campus life (President Schofield was a member of Athenean during his years in Madison), but they became less attractive to collegians by the 1920s and efforts to establish them at Eau Claire faltered. As an alternative, clubs with pseudo-Indian names linked to the Camp Fire movement for women were active for a few years into the 1920s (see sidebar). Debate and musical organizations, also present from the founding of the school, were more permanent and played an increasingly important role in campus life (discussed in chapters four and two, respectively). They were joined by the 1930s by honorary societies, subject-discipline clubs, denominational groups, and other organizations. Apparently in response to a new federal requirement to collect tax on paid admissions to public events, in 1940 Schofield identified fifteen organizations with formal constitutions, in addition to musical groups. These groups sponsored events such as late-afternoon teas and talks by faculty members and took on the responsibility for presenting some assembly programs for the entire college.

Beginning with the normal school's first year, students produced a yearbook, the *Periscope*, which pictured the graduates and documented the year's events. With the help of Schofield cajoling subscriptions from students at an assembly, a student newspaper, the *Spectator*, began publication in 1923. During the interwar years, it appeared bi-weekly, and beginning in 1935 it featured syndicated articles from the Collegiate Press, which served somewhat to broaden student perspectives.

President Schofield was hostile towards fraternities, considering them undemocratic. Despite an appeal by fraternity brothers for public support, he seems to have been tolerant towards the perpetrators of a 1923 incident in which seven members of the Fox Fraternity were tarred and feathered in Old Main by antagonistic non-members. As a substitute for fraternities, "honorary" societies took on some fraternity-like characteristics and became important on campus. Crusaders, established in 1921, and De Chatillon, established in 1927, sponsored all-male "smokers" and dances. A 1938 student gossip sheet coyly predicted, "Without a doubt, several new alliances will be made on the De Chatillon sleigh-ride party this P.M." Membership in these groups was based on scholarship, high "morality," leadership in campus organizations, athletic participation, and promotion of school spirit. Initiation into the Crusaders during the 1930s, at least, involved fraternity-like hazing. In 1935, at Laura Sutherland's initiative, a similar organization for women, Amphyctyon, was organized with the goal "to enliven interest in other school activities." In 1940, Lyla Flager, who taught home economics and a variety of other subjects from 1918 to 1952, was responsible for establishing Sigma Gamma Zeta, an organization for older women which presaged "non-traditional student" groups in the late twentieth century. (Flager herself was a divorcee.)

The oldest student group was a campus chapter of the YWCA, organized early in 1917, which remained active throughout the interwar years. It does not seem to have focused on Bible study, benevolent work, or other religious activities. Rather, it sponsored a mother-daughter banquet and an all-girl prom, in which women cross-dressed and acted as escorts for other women, and supervised the "girls' rest room" in Old Main. At a time when the college had few resources to supervise off-campus life, the YWCA stepped in and held a fall tea for landlords, student renters, and local pastors.

Beginning in 1929, the Junior Prom was the major social event of the spring semester. It survived the financial stringencies of the Great Depression, and in 1940 two hundred couples paid $1.50 ($25 in 2016) and danced to music by Arch Adrian and His Orchestra from Fond du Lac. By this time, the prom had moved from the gymnasium in Old Main to the city auditorium on Barstow Street. It was one of the few college events open to community members. Without a student government, much less student affairs

Camp Fires Along the Chippewa

> In the sacred halls of learning
> In the hall of Eau Claire Normal
> Met the cheerful Kodowapas
> Gay and happy Kodowapas

This doggerel, following the form of Henry Wadsworth Longfellow's "Song of Hiawatha" (1855), accompanied the photograph in the 1923 *Periscope* of fourteen women in pseudo-Indian garb who belonged to Kodowapa Camp Fire. Kodowapa and another Camp Fire, Benis-ah-Nepay, were active organizations from the outset of Eau Claire Normal, designed to train Guardians of the Fire who, when they left Eau Claire, would organize and lead Camp Fires in communities where they settled. Why did the student members of these groups choose to "play Indian?"

The Camp Fire movement, which started in 1910, was spreading rapidly when Eau Claire Normal was established. Its emphasis on outdoor pursuits, handicrafts, and health-building activities was in part a romantic reaction against "modernization" and the urbanization and industrialization with which it was associated. Furthermore, as with the contemporaneous Boy Scout movement for males, the rituals associated with Camp Fire paralleled for young people the distinctive bonding practices of popular adult organizations such as the Improved Order of Red Men.

The inspiration for Camp Fire ritual was the "Noble Savage" idea of American Indians which dated from the eighteenth century and remained popular with whites into the twentieth century. In particular, Camp Fire rituals latently made the domestic role of women seem to be a natural given by emphasizing the female association with earth, nature, and family nurturing. Especially during the groups' first few years, the members of the Camp Fires at Eau Claire Normal adopted pseudo-Indian names for themselves, dressed as Native Americans, and performed "ceremonial dances" at their meetings.

However, as seems to have been the case in Camp Fires nationwide, students at Eau Claire State also shaped their groups along the lines they wanted. Social activities, outings to the movies, and community service work became the most important features of Eau Claire Camp Fires by the early 1920s. The closest their members came to outdoor camping was a week at a cabin on Lake Chetek. Benis-ah-Nepay folded in 1920 and after 1923 Kodowapas abandoned Indian dress for their *Periscope* photographs. Indeed, it is not clear whether the allusion to "Song of Hiawatha" in 1923 was intended to invoke dignity for the Kodowapa Camp Fire or to mock a poem whose literary reputation was already in decline and which Kodowapas had perhaps had to memorize unwillingly in the sixth grade.

In December 1923 Kodowapa became affiliated with the Girl Scouts and thereafter was referred to by the *Spectator* and *Periscope* as a "club" rather than a "camp fire." It took on responsibility for presenting short plays during daily assembly—none of which had Indian themes—and supervising the girls "rest room," as well as continuing to hold teas and suppers. During 1925–26, Kodowapa became an "honorary" society with selective membership, explicitly parallel to the Crusaders. As Eau Claire State became more "collegiate," however, and male students moved into more leadership roles, female honorary societies do not seem to have thrived, and Kodowapa last appeared in the 1928 *Periscope*.

Even the approximation of life on a modern college campus that developed at Eau Claire State by the mid-1920s undermined the possibility that the Camp Fire movement could recapture for young white women an "authenticity" still supposedly possessed in the early twentieth century by Native Americans.

Benis-ah-Nepay Camp Fire, 1918

Christmas Dance Hosted by the YWCA, 1929

President Schofield preferred the dance steps of these couples to contemporary fads such as the Big Apple, although he was probably concerned about the skirt length of the woman in the center. The site of this dance was the gym in Old Main, which was a multi-purpose venue during the interwar years.

Young Women's Christian Association, 1931

The 1931 Periscope needed five photographs like this to encompass the entire YWCA group, the largest student organization. Another page of informal photographs showed the members "unlaxing."

62 CHAPTER THREE

professionals on the college staff, junior-class students themselves took on the responsibilities of renting and decorating the venue, hiring the band, providing refreshments, and managing finances so as to at least break even.

Athletics provided opportunities for students as participants and spectators. Beginning in 1928, Willis Zorn coached the men's basketball and football teams (in addition to teaching four classes). At the time of his appointment, the *Spectator* characterized him as "a real gentleman—the Alonzo A. [*sic*] Stagg type of man," referring to the highly respected coach for whom Zorn played at the University of Chicago. On the court at Eau Claire, Zorn had the most success with the basketball teams that shared the Wisconsin Intercollegiate Athletic Conference championships in 1938 and in 1939. "The biggest thrill I had was going to the [N]ational [Association of Intercollegiate Athletics] tournament at Kansas City," where the team lost to eventual champion Southwestern of Kansas, remembered Chick Kolsad, a forward on the 1938 team. By 1940 male students also participated in intercollegiate baseball, track, tennis, and hockey, although the schedules in these sports were limited and ad hoc. Only track had a conference championship. Beginning in 1923, lettermen were recognized by the formation of the E Club, which sponsored banquets and other events.

The Woman's Athletic Association was established in 1923, reflecting the idea that healthy exercise was part of being a "new woman" in the 1920s, and a basketball team from Eau Claire Normal played against Eau Claire High School in 1926. The focus of women's athletics, however, was on intramural activities and informal "play days" with other colleges. In the late 1930s, the WAA sponsored tournaments in deck-tennis, ping-pong, intramural basketball, and other sports. Women accumulated points for recognition by the WAA for *participation* in these activities. Along with teaching required physical education classes, Rosemary Royce, who had an MA from the University of Iowa, was faculty advisor of the WAA from 1937 to 1941. As at most American colleges, the goals of women's athletics were the development of fitness, morality, cooperation, and self-confidence, in contrast to the alleged over-exertion and hyper-competiveness of male intercollegiate sports.

Athletics and social life came together in Homecoming festivities, which began in 1924. The first celebration "did not prove a huge success," the *Periscope* admitted, but the event quickly became larger and more popular. The 1927 festivities included a Friday morning pep assembly; an evening bonfire followed by a snake dance into the central business district, where there was "college night" at the State Theater; a Saturday afternoon football match against Stout Institute; and an evening banquet followed by a dance in the gym in Old Main.

In sum, student organizations grew parallel to the gradual academic expansion of Eau Claire State during its first quarter century. They were held back, however, by the small mass of students enrolled in the college; the fact that none of them lived on campus; the need for a large percentage of students to commit their time outside of class to paid work; and the limited assistance student activities could receive from the faculty, who had little expertise in the programs they were assigned to advise and limited time to give to them on top of their teaching schedules. The repeated calls of

Women's Sports, 1930

The 1930 Periscope *identified the principles underlying women's sports during the 1920s and 1930s.*

Football, 1929

The Periscope *admitted Eau Claire State's line was "hopeless" and its backfield was "slow," resulting in an 18-0 loss to River Falls State in the conference opener on October 5, 1929.*

President Schofield and writers in the *Spectator* for more school "spirit" suggested student engagement with Eau Claire Normal was limited. "Something is radically wrong with our school spirit," the *Spectator* concluded in 1926, when only fifty of 350 students attended a party sponsored by the Crusaders. "Our social life was very limited," Leonard Haas recalled of his days as a student in the mid-1930s. "Generally the campus was dark after 4:30 pm."

Eau Claire State Students and Gender Roles

By the early twentieth century in the United States, schoolteachers—and the normal schools that trained them—were predominately female. Normal schools, therefore, provided opportunities for women at a time when many occupations were closed to them and created a sisterly environment in which women could flourish. These were characteristic features of the early decades of Eau Claire Normal, but they gradually eroded as the institution became more self-consciously a "college."

The masculine presence at Eau Claire increased as time passed. Originally there were only a handful of men in the student body (chapter one). During the 1920s, men made up about one quarter of the graduates. By the late 1930s, two-thirds of new students were men, as were over a third of the graduates in 1940. Nationwide, college enrollment became increasingly male during the 1930s. Specifically at Eau Claire State, as a larger proportion of students chose to major in secondary rather than elementary education, as male graduates of the Depression years often successfully found non-teaching jobs, and as the college formally recognized a category of "non-professional" students who intended to earn a bachelor's degree elsewhere, the college became more attractive to men.

Campus life also took on a more masculine tone. During the 1920s, an ex-servicemen club, a club of Citizen's Military Training Corps veterans, and eventually a Stephen Decatur club offered fellowship for male students with military interests. Armistice Day assemblies celebrated the wartime contributions of students from Eau Claire Normal. For Armistice Day in 1931, the American Legion organized a program in which National Guard units faced off against one another on opposite sides of Little Niagara Creek in a sham battle.

Geography teacher George Simpson actively promoted these activities and also recruited students for the National Guard unit he commanded (chapter two). During the 1930s, Simpson also regularly led extended automobile trips during summers and school recesses by male students to different parts of the United States, with academic credit optional. President Schofield's son, John, fondly remembered his trip with Simpson to New Orleans in May 1931, in which he rode in the rumble seat of a Model A Ford. Simpson was "a man's man," John Schofield recalled; his sister, Betty Lou, said he preferred boys as students and only "put up with girls." Overall, the college faculty shifted from 50 percent male in 1916 to about 60 percent male by 1940.

As campus demographics shifted, and as Eau Claire State slowly moved away from being a normal school, the roles of women students changed. For one thing, they occupied a smaller proportion of campus leadership positions: in 1925, 1926, and 1927 taken together, women held 57 percent of offices in the seven co-educational organizations with information presented in the *Periscope,* while by 1939 and 1940, taken together, they held only 48 percent of offices in ten co-educational organizations. There was an even more dramatic change in who was the senior editor of the *Periscope*: it was always a woman between 1917 and 1922, but only half the time between 1923 and 1928 and only once between 1929 and 1934.

A stereotypically feminine world also increasingly enveloped women students. For instance, in 1932 the *Spectator* introduced "Beauty School," a syndicated feature by Helena Rubenstein. When surveying student-reading habits later that year, the paper emphasized, "The periodicals [in the library] most popular with the girls are those concerned with home-making and the latest fashions in clothes." A "Popularity Queen" began to be elected along with queens for Homecoming and Junior Prom. Beginning in 1936, the campus YWCA sponsored a style show with women students as models. In 1938 and 1939 these shows were held in the Old Main auditorium and were featured in the *Periscope* (which pictured women wearing stylish pajamas!). The growing objectification of women was clearly displayed in the 1939 *Periscope,* which included a ten-page spread entitled "Beauty on Campus," consisting of soft-focus studio photographs of the eight women whose beauty the editors thought represented that of the women of Eau Claire State.

The "Collegiate" Environment at an ex-Normal School

The changing position of women on campus was part of Eau Claire State becoming a "college." President Schofield and the faculty insisted the academic programs of the institution were such that it deserved recognition as a "college" (chapter two). In the 1920s, however, undergraduates "were inclined to be more like high school students in outlook and conduct," a local newspaper learned from librarian Ferne Thompson, who was "frequently troubled by problems of discipline." Perhaps students with behavioral problems tended to attend Eau Claire State because the principal of Eau Claire High School believed in 1928 that "the immature high school graduate is better off in a small college, near his own home." But gradually students accepted the idea they were attending a college and shifted their behavior and mannerisms to become "collegiate," following the lead of their counterparts throughout the United States.

A distinctive "collegiate" style emerged among American undergraduates in the 1920s, popularized by the success of F. Scott Fitzgerald's *The Far Side of Paradise*. Male students were self-assured young men who wore flannel pants and sports coats, rather than suits; enjoyed the pleasures of the moment with coeds at fraternity parties; and cultivated reputations for disdaining study beyond what was necessary to maintain a gentleman's C average. Their female counterparts by the 1930s embraced a carefully casual clothing style of saddle shoes, tweed jackets, and "sloppy joe" sweaters; flaunted a "peppy" manner which promised sexual pleasures (but which usually led to intercourse only after men produced an engagement ring); and studied home economics rather than art history or English literature as their mothers did. Recognition of their beauty and popularity depended on securing dates to the Junior Prom or Homecoming game with the "big men on campus" who exemplified the lifestyle of the male collegian.

Not all American college students, certainly not the ones with the socio-economic backgrounds and occupational aspirations of those enrolled in institutions like Eau Claire State, fully conformed to these ideal types. But in the public imagination, at least, they were the "college man" and "college woman."

An approximation of the idealized college man and woman gradually emerged at Eau Claire State. As early as 1926, the *Periscope* identified and pictured "Honor" graduates. At first this designation seems to have been "scholastic," and actual grade point averages sometimes accompanied photographs of the honored students. Beginning in 1933, these specially designated graduates were labeled "leading seniors" chosen on the basis of "promise of future usefulness" and starting in 1936 became "outstanding seniors" chosen for "character, scholarship, and leadership." The choice of these honor graduates remained in the hands of the faculty (about which students repeatedly objected), but in this way Junior Prom queens, football players, and Crusader presidents became exemplars for the Eau Claire student body.

Starting in 1929 and becoming more prominent in the 1930s, illustrations in the *Periscope* pictured the campus as a haunt of collegiate-like students. These photographs showed men and women casually but carefully dressed in slacks, sweaters, and fitted skirts walking arm in arm on Putnam Drive, chatting in groups under trees in Putnam Park adjacent to campus, and sitting on the stone bridges which crossed Little Niagara. The 1937 edition featured a couple "sitting on a romantic promontory overlooking the lordly Chippewa" and the 1940 edition explained a pictured bridge over Little Niagara was "a popular place for college lovers." The somewhat conflicted message appears to have been that alongside the prominence given in the *Bulletin* and other publications to "modern" equipment and "up-to-date" teaching methods, what made Eau Claire State a real "college" were the bucolic surroundings and the neo-Gothic building by which the *Periscope* framed its pictures of students.

A practice began in 1927 by which seniors took responsibility to provide a "collegiate initiation" for new students. A section of the *Periscope* explained this new program and included pictures of the officers of the 1927–28 "underclassmen;" the male president and treasurer proudly faced the camera to highlight their "E" sweaters. Already by 1931 the *Spectator* characterized as "traditional" the green bennies worn by freshmen as part of this initiation. Across the country, the popular media represented the public singing of college songs as a major feature of undergraduate life. At Eau Claire State in the late 1930s the revival of the singing of "Eau Claire Normal," the school song written in 1920 by Cora Bartlett and Ellen Charles, furthered the development of collegiate spirit. So did the introduction of the term "Blugold" for athletic teams in 1935.

During the 1930s the *Periscope* increasingly emphasized the history and traditions of Eau Claire State. For the twentieth anniversary in 1936, the yearbook provided collegiate *dignitas* for the institution with a fifteen-page spread on its history. When necessary, it also invented history for the still-young college. The 1938 *Periscope* provided an essay on the "historical background of Little Niagara Creek." The bluff above the entrance of Little Niagara into the Chippewa, it was said, was "without a doubt" the boundary between Ojibway and Sioux territory delineated by the Treaty of Prairie du Chien of 1825. The yearbook wanted this event recognized as "one of the traditions of the college." It soon became enmeshed with the story, represented in a large WPA-sponsored painting by Clarence Peters that hung in the college library, that the Sioux and Ojibway had traditionally parleyed under a tree near the mouth of the Little Niagara that came to be known as the Council Oak. Interestingly, one of the campus Camp Fire groups held rituals at the mouth of the Little Niagara; however, there is no specific evidence in the documentary record or in Ojibway oral history to confirm the campus had been a site of inter-tribal meetings. What is certain is by the end of its first quarter century, Eau Claire State wanted to elevate its collegiate status by representing itself as part of a long historical tradition.

Council Oak

The Council Oak played an important role in the efforts of the college to develop its identity during the 1930s.

Student–faculty Interaction During the Schofield Era

The small size of Eau Claire State before 1940 encouraged close interaction between students and faculty—in daily assemblies, in classrooms, in student organizations, and in the hallways of Old Main. "The faculty and the students worked together," Hilda Oxby recalled. "Some of us weren't that much older than the students, and so it was easy to take part in the social affairs." Faculty members regularly entertained groups of students, such as members of organizations they advised, in their homes. When John Schneider arrived on campus in 1930, he was struck by this "spirit of democracy" he found in the college. Schofield's concept of the college as a "family" was apt: the *Spectator*'s reporting of school absences for minor illnesses, weekend recreational trips, and other routine activities reflected the close personal interest faculty and students had in one another. The family atmosphere of the college was reinforced daily by the homey aromas from the cafeteria whiffing through Old Main.

Like in any family, relationships between students and faculty were sometimes frayed. The gentle mocking of faculty foibles by the *Spectator* and the *Periscope* occasionally had an edge. At a fictitious faculty meeting to consider allowing women students to smoke, for instance, the *Periscope* had Simpson concerned only with, "How will it affect the C.M.T.C.? If girls smoke, won't it injure the army and navy in some way?" In an article on "Faculty Faux Passes," the *Spectator* reported long-time pedagogy teacher Charles Donaldson had been unable to deliver a recent lecture on the principles of teaching because he had forgotten his notes. The newspaper was certainly serious when it editorialized in 1935 in favor of mandatory retirement for teachers to make way for "younger men and women." On another point regarding student-faculty relations, the *Spectator* also repeatedly objected to the faculty practice of bucking the serving line in the cafeteria, arguing it was "undemocratic."

Cafeteria in Old Main, 1922

Crowded together in the small cafeteria, faculty, college students, and Campus School students shared aspects of a "family."

The most frequent and regular interaction among faculty and students, of course, was in the classroom. While there was some individual variation, in the 1930s the typical student was in class for sixteen hours per week, and the typical faculty member taught for fifteen hours per week. Enrollments fluctuated (chapter two), but during the 1930s the faculty/student ratio was around twenty to one, similar to what it would be in the early twenty-first century. Since the faculty taught more courses during the 1930s, the typical class size at that time was twenty to twenty-two students, compared to thirty to thirty-five students in the early twenty-first century. The size of the classrooms in Old Main, furthermore, precluded large lecture courses with one hundred plus students, which were common in introductory courses at that time at the University of Wisconsin. There was no way for a student at Eau Claire in 1940 to be an anonymous seat holder in the back corner of a classroom. In 1936 the *Spectator* editorially defended the quality of "small colleges," such as Eau Claire State, because they provided the advantages of "close personal contact" between students and faculty.

What was this relationship supposed to produce? Ideally, students learned more than just points of subject matter content they would pass on to their own students. The relationship of a college teacher to a student "is not a process of exposing the student mind to a lot of scholarly material," Registrar Fox wrote in 1940, "but is a process of directing the student mind to a living experience in the subject field." How was this goal achieved? For one thing, teaching was not confined to the classroom. George Simpson took his physical and economic geography classes on field trips to observe landforms and business-environment interactions, and John Schneider's Cooperative Marketing students observed on-site operations of co-ops in the region. Guest speakers, such as Secretary Doudna relating his European travel experiences, also brought a variety of viewpoints and methods of presentation into classrooms.

Field Trip, probably in Economic Geography, 1920s

George Simpson frequently took his geography classes on field trips. As this photograph shows, he also encouraged out-of-class bonding among Eau Claire State male students.

The day-to-day method of teaching, however, was generally the "recitation." The 1914 Farmer report (chapter one) provided detailed descriptions of typical recitations in Wisconsin normal schools at that time. Farmer lauded recitations in which students asked questions, gave reports, debated controversial topics, or solved problems at the blackboard. He disdained classes in which the teacher lectured or called on students to answer questions orally based on assigned readings. In the terminology of the late-twentieth century, Farmer favored "active learning" which provided to the students, in Fox's words, "engagement" with the subject. Many faculty members, however, felt they needed to use class time to explain basic points to underprepared students. "[T]hey'd lecture, and we'd take notes" was all a student from the late 1930s had to say about instructional techniques when asked in 2013.

Student ideas about good teaching did not always align with those of Farmer and Fox. Some chose courses on the basis of the teacher's reputation as "hard" or "easy." The personality of the teacher, especially if it was considered eccentric, attracted other students. If the teacher could make the subject "interesting," often by connecting it to current events, it would appeal to other students. At least in their later memories, some students—particularly those who were more academically inclined—admired rigorous teachers. No teacher was more respected than Laura Sutherland. "Many students attended her class with great fear and trembling," recalled Gerry Wing, "but . . . when they came back as graduates they admired her very much." Leonard Haas admired her because "she would just sit behind her desk and fold her hands, and then in conversation sometimes bring the students into . . . this wonderful outflow of the stream of history."

A Closer Look at Teaching Practices

Surviving course materials provide some idea of the variety of classroom practices employed by two Eau Claire State social studies teachers during the 1930s and early 1940s.

John Schneider joined the faculty in 1930 with a PhD from the University of Wisconsin. As his wife, Josephine, later emphasized, Schneider was burdened every semester with multiple course preparations. He regularly taught Greek and Roman history, the area of his graduate preparation, but most of his teaching effort went into sociology. He also developed a course on cooperatives which, although required by the state for nascent social studies teachers, was "a thorn in the flesh of private business," and constant complaints about it from local businessmen distracted Schneider from his teaching. In the spring semester of 1936, for instance, he taught two sections of J206: Cooperative Marketing; two sections of J205: Social Problems; and one section each of D201: Roman Civilization and D105b: Modern History (sixteen credit hours in total). One hundred sixty-four students enrolled in these courses. Schneider made an effort, though, to try to know each of them—in his grade book he recorded the occupation of each of their fathers.

Schneider was a popular teacher in and out of the classroom. By all accounts, however, his teaching was not well organized. "I wouldn't view him as an exceptional teacher," admitted future Eau Claire professor Marshall Wick, who took a course with Schneider as an undergraduate in which "I'm not sure I learned all that much about sociology." If the surviving scribbled lists in pencil of three or four points on a torn sheet of paper are indicative of his lesson plans, Schneider's reputation for absent-mindedness and off-the-cuff rambling in class was probably justified. Almost certainly he was the unnamed subject of a mocking two-page essay in the 1932 *Periscope*.

In his Social Problems course, in particular, Schneider emphasized student reports. Each student presented between one and four reports on topics such as "social legislation in Germany" and "local safety programs," based on "parallel readings" from assigned books in the college library. Schneider carefully recorded the number of pages—between 500 and 1,800—read by each student. Students submitted their reports on these topics to Schneider on a standard form; whether they also presented them orally in class is uncertain. On the report form, among other queries, Schneider anticipated the students' role as future teachers and asked them to prepare questions which would show "whether or not the person questioned had read the material."

In addition to assigning student reports, Schneider administered a dozen in-class quizzes and hour exams in Social Problems. He gave fewer such tests in his history courses and only two or three in Cooperative Marketing. Schneider's hour exams consisted of a half dozen of what in the early twenty-first century would be categorized as "identification" or "short answer" questions, which often referenced specific chapters from the textbook. Students wrote three or four-sentence answers to straightforward questions such as "What is the mirrored self?" and "Give some [of] the more hopeless features of conditions of Russia before the Revolution of 1917." Josephine Schneider, while arguing her husband gave rigorous instruction, allowed that he did not require students to write out-of-class papers because he did not have time to grade them. Examples of ten-book bibliographies prepared by students in preparation for term papers in Schneider's Latin American History course in the spring of 1948 did survive, which suggest he did sometimes assign papers.

In regards to final grades, Schneider was stingy with "A"s but failed few students. In his Social Problems sections in 1936, on the scale in use in 2016, his grades averaged 2.85, which was certainly higher than the norm in the college in the 1930s. He believed personal circumstances could affect a student's grade: a student related years later that, after learning from her in confidence about another student's ill mother, Schneider compensated for that student's problems by raising her final course grade.

Beginning in 1941 Leonard Haas, a protégé of Sutherland, was a colleague of Schneider. A "leading senior" with the highest GPA in the class of 1935, Haas had earned an MA in European history from the University of Wisconsin in 1938 and then taught at Wausau High School. His classroom practices both resembled and differed from those of Schneider.

In contrast to Schneider, Haas taught tightly organized courses carefully divided into units and subunits, if the materials surviving from four courses he taught in the early 1940s are representative of his practices. Haas prepared detailed outlines of course content, which in some cases he distributed to students. If the outlines for his courses in US history reflected what was actually taught, the courses were more comprehensive than comparable introductory courses in the early twenty-first century. Like Schneider, Haas sometimes required student reports on individually assigned topics, presented to him on 4 x 6 index cards. More so than Schneider, though, Haas appears to have presented formal lectures to his classes. In Recent American History during the 1944 summer session, there were twenty-three lectures with titles such as "The Sense of Well-Being" in the late nineteenth century. Haas usually required out-of-class writing by his students. In Colonial American History in the fall of 1944, students wrote a six- to twelve-page paper, with at least five sources, chosen from a list of topics prepared by Haas. The topics all related to "economic and social life in the colonies" and were probably deliberately meant by Haas to complement the political and military topics which dominated his lectures. In his exams, Haas used objective questions more than Schneider. Although his unit exams sometimes included an essay question and/or identifications, his final exams apparently always consisted of multiple choice, true-false, and matching items. Haas had retained copies of exams given in the introductory history courses at the University of Wisconsin during 1937–38, when he had been a teaching assistant, and while he followed the common practice in these courses of distributing to students detailed outlines and bibliographies, he did not adopt their practice of essay examinations.

Academic Standards at Eau Claire State

How strong academically was Eau Claire State during its first quarter century? There were conflicting contemporary opinions. Schofield defended the quality of the education at his college as equal or superior to that at the University of Wisconsin. As proof, he emphasized the subsequent attainments of graduates as teachers and in other occupations and their success as transfer students and as graduate students at the university. A pleased former student told Registrar Fox in 1927 that at Eau Claire Normal he had taken "the subjects right in line with journalism, and when I transferred, I became, within one week, a junior with full University standing." The *Spectator* prominently reported such anecdotes. On the other hand, public opinion in general, and faculty opinion at the University of Wisconsin specifically, patronized normal schools, including Eau Claire (chapter two). Some Eau Claire students shared this opinion. Teaching at Eau Claire State was "more on a high school level than a college level," the *Spectator* editorialized in 1933. In the mid-1950s a successful alumnus wrote to the then-president commending the improvement in the academic program of the college since he had been a student twenty years previously, when "most students spoke rather apologetically for attending 'Minneycreek.'" Schofield's daughter later recalled what she learned as an Eau Claire State student during the late 1930s seemed comparable to what her grandchildren were learning in high school in the 1980s. It was "sort of a continuation of like, high school," a 1942 graduate later recalled.

Assessment of college education was as difficult and controversial in the early twentieth century as it is in the early twenty-first century. For a few years around 1920, the regents tried to formally assess the quality of their school by sending a committee to Eau Claire to orally examine seniors, in a manner similar to that of pre-Vatican II Catholic bishops examining candidates for Confirmation, but they soon dropped that ritual. Today it is impossible to assess definitively the quality of education at Eau Claire State during the interwar years, but a retrospective look at several academic measurements provides some idea about the strengths and limitations of the college at that time.

How well prepared for college were Eau Claire State students? As was discussed in chapter one, from its outset Eau Claire Normal required high school graduation for admission; beginning in 1926 these graduates needed to have taken fifteen units "distributed over the various fields of High School subjects." Starting in 1935, they needed sixteen units, at least ten of which had to be in academic subjects. Although a bit less strict about mathematics, these requirements were similar to those at the time at the University of Wisconsin. But unlike the situation at Madison, Eau Claire State's academic unit requirements did not apply to graduates in the upper 50 percent of their high school class. In any event, the typical first-year student who entered Eau Claire State in the fall of 1936 came from the seventieth percentile of his or her high school class and in the fall of 1940 came from the seventy-fifth percentile. They were not much different, therefore, from their counterparts at the University of Wisconsin at that time or at UW–Eau Claire in the early twenty-first century.

Standardized testing of college-bound students began in the United States during the 1930s. As registrar of the University of Wisconsin, Frank Holt led the development of a statewide testing program for high school students to establish their post-secondary niche. The median score of Eau Claire State students on the Henmon-Nelson mental ability test given to high school seniors in 1938 placed them twenty-fourth out of twenty-eight among Wisconsin colleges. In any event, Schofield was skeptical of the benefits of such testing and admitted he "made very little use" of Holt's data. Schofield's response in 1939 when the academic records of a potential transfer student arrived in his office was indicative of his opinion of testing and also showed the growing insularity of Wisconsin schoolmen. "I am at a total loss to interpret this slip," he wrote back to the student's previous college, referring to the report of the student's Scholastic Aptitude Test scores. "What English 574 means I haven't the slightest idea," he confessed.

President Schofield opposed the adoption of stricter admission requirements for the Wisconsin teachers colleges. In 1932 he criticized a proposal from the system-wide faculty organization, which was never adopted, that students from the lowest 10 percent of their high school classes be excluded. "[I]t is only fair," Schofield believed, "that a high school graduate be given a chance in college to succeed or fail." Later in the decade, when the regents considered raising admission and retention standards, Schofield was skeptical. He identified fourteen specific students at Eau Claire who had recently failed at least three courses during their freshman year but eventually graduated. "All I want to do is sit down with a boy or girl and talk with them for ten minutes," Schofield pleaded, "and I will be able to tell you if they will be a success in school or not."

Nationwide, however, the oversupply of teachers in the 1930s led teachers colleges to restrict enrollment. Finally in 1940, in response to budget cuts (chapter two), the regents adopted a policy of "selective admission" for the Wisconsin teachers colleges. Students in the lowest 25 percent of their high school classes and with low scores on the American Council Psychology Examination were not supposed to be allowed to enroll as freshmen. Eau Claire State granted only twelve admission exceptions for freshmen that fall, half of whom did not return for the spring semester. The new policy was probably partially responsible for an almost 50 percent drop in the size of the freshmen class at Eau Claire State in 1940 compared to 1939 and for a slightly higher median high school rank of these freshmen compared to 1935. Fox described to the absent Schofield in late September 1940 that there was a new "seriousness" in the student body because of the new "scholastic" standards. Subsequently, as a result of their first-year work, only about 15 percent of freshmen who entered that fall were "dropped," compared to over 20 percent of the 1939 cohort. The new admissions standards aligned the teachers colleges more closely to the University of Wisconsin, which during the 1930s had strongly discouraged enrollment by weaker students, especially as determined by tests. At the same time, in the early 1940s the university responded to pressure from schoolmen and adjusted its admission standards to resemble those of the teachers colleges by allowing freshmen to present fewer academic units in high school courses—only six for students in the top 10 percent of their high school class.

In any event, how much students know when they *enter* a college is not a direct measure of its quality, as critics in the twenty-first century of *U.S. News & World Report*-like rankings often point out. What is more important is how much students know when then *graduate*. Already in the early 1920s William Kittle, the regents' secretary, had argued largely on the basis of tests of "mental age" that normal school students were as capable as university students. His criticism of the normal schools, rather, was they did not academically challenge their students to the extent of their capabilities. Hilda Oxby echoed Kittle's point in a short piece in the *Spectator* arguing for more student "scholarship." Some changes in academic policies at Eau Claire in the late 1920s and 1930s followed Kittle's recommendations for strengthening the normal schools. Beginning in 1928, students took only sixteen credits per semester, instead of the twenty that was common when Kittle wrote, and they were required to have a 2.00 GPA in order to graduate. If the examples discussed earlier of Haas's courses are representative, Eau Claire State also began to put more emphasis on "content" into its courses, as Kittle recommended. The college ignored other recommendations: textbook rental was "fatal to scholarship and high standards," Kittle believed, but it remained in place at Eau Claire State. Kittle also believed faculty-student relations were too close, which led to "coddling" of students, but Schofield and his faculty saw this dimension of their college as a *strength*, not a problem.

Kittle believed mid-1920s academic standards were higher at the University of Wisconsin compared to the state normal schools because ten times as many students were "dropped" from colleges than from normal schools, and students were ten times more likely to transfer from colleges to the normals than vice versa. He presented no data to support these claims. However, Elizabeth Hoyt Ayer, the French teacher at Eau Claire from 1920 to 1948, implicitly agreed with him in 1925 when she argued that small schools like Eau Claire Normal allowed students to "find themselves," in contrast to the University of Wisconsin where "you must either come up to the requirements or leave, and there is no middle ground."

To investigate Kittle's claims, one can retroactively try to establish what in the twenty-first century are called "attrition rates" and "graduation rates" for Eau Claire State during the interwar years. Each year from 1933 to 1937, first-year students entering degree programs had about a 25 percent to about a 45 percent chance of graduating four years later. (Graduation rates were higher for students in two-year and three-year diploma programs.) These graduation rates appear to have been similar to those at other American colleges, including the University of Wisconsin, during this time period. Besides correcting the misunderstanding of educational "reformers" in the twenty-first century that there was a "golden age" when it was common for college students, once enrolled, to easily complete their degree program in four years, what do these figures mean? The answer is uncertain. A high attrition rate could have meant a college had rigorous academic standards and did not tolerate slackers. Alternatively, it could have meant the college was not doing a good job of engaging and motivating its students.

Beginning in the late 1930s Eau Claire State became more self-conscious about encouraging student success. A once-a-week series of freshmen orientation lectures began during the fall of 1939. Citing the impact of the "selective admissions" policy, in the fall of 1940 Schofield told the faculty that "we are using the first few days to acquaint the freshmen with the many changes that their new status as college students entail." Welcoming lectures, aptitude testing, group singing, entertainment, advising, registration, dinners at local churches, and tours of Eau Claire filled the first two days on campus (the highlight of this program in 1941 was certainly the bus tour to the new city sewage treatment plant). In 1941 the college administration began to assign specific faculty members as advisors to each first-year student. Even as assistance programs developed further in later years, however, high rates of student failure and withdrawal continued to concern the faculty and administration.

Outside Evaluation of the College

During the interwar years, external organizations used formal procedures to assess the quality of the education offered by Eau Claire State. President Schofield, at least, did not believe these assessments fairly reflected the goals of the college, and his successor, President Davies, used other means to evaluate how well the college was doing its job.

Shortly after it became a college in 1927, the American Association of Teachers Colleges, a nationwide organization linked to the National Education Association, accredited Eau Claire State. Throughout the 1930s, the AATC's annual confidential reports, based on data submitted to it by its members, showed Eau Claire State placed in the broad middle of teachers colleges nationwide. These data and periodic visitations by AATC inspectors highlighted lingering issues with the academic qualifications of the Eau Claire faculty (a common problem at Wisconsin teachers colleges) and the level of spending per student (a consequence of state budget policies discussed in chapter two). "No deficiency noted" was the conclusion of the 1932 reaccreditation report, but in 1935 the AATC formally noted a deficiency in "preparation of faculty." This issue was cleared up by 1938, but the accreditors were now concerned about the lack of student health services. They gave the college three years to correct this deficiency or be dropped from the AATC. Schofield studied the situation at other Wisconsin teachers colleges and in the fall of 1938 added a nurse, Alice Matz, to the college staff and provided limited medical care for students, paid for by a new student health fee. The AATC reaccredited Eau Claire State in 1941 with "no warnings attached."

It was more difficult for Eau Claire State to earn recognition from the regional higher education accreditation agency. In 1928 the college was not approved in the teachers college category by the North Central Association of Colleges and Secondary Schools; Oshkosh State and La Crosse State were among the dozen institutions that were successful applicants that year, joining about fifty other teachers colleges approved by the NCA since 1918 (Milwaukee State more ambitiously applied in the college category and was rejected in 1928). Schofield accepted the NCA's decision with good grace; he admitted to Melvin Hagerty, dean of the College of Education at the University of Minnesota who did the on-site inspection of Eau Claire for the NCA, that the "scholastic preparation of our faculty" was the weakest feature of his college. A year later, as the result of its own inspection, the University of Illinois also found shortcomings at Eau Claire State. It awarded the college a "B" grade for the first two years of its program, which allowed full credit for undergraduate transfer work, but only a "C" for the last two years of its program, which meant Illinois would accept only .75 percent of transfer students' credits and would require graduate students from Eau Claire to do an additional year of work for an MA.

Schofield became more antagonistic towards the NCA during the 1930s. By 1938, he was "quite disgusted" with the 1928 NCA inspection; Schofield said nothing about the deficiencies it had found in the faculty and instead blamed the NCA's decision not to accredit his college on a faulty evaluation of library and equipment resources. Doudna's outspoken views in the 1930s probably influenced Schofield's attitudes. The regents' secretary denounced the NCA's "dictatorial power" as comparable to that of the "grotesque . . . hoodlum" Huey Long, controversial governor and United States senator from Louisiana.

Schofield agreed. "I would like to see it voted out of Wisconsin schools," he wrote. In the fall of 1938, a faculty committee considered the possibility of reapplying for accreditation, but as was the case with the work of most faculty committees during the Schofield era, nothing seems to have come of it.

The goal of the Eau Claire State faculty during the interwar years was to open the minds of practical-minded students who came to them from families in which higher education had not been the norm. They wanted these students to become better-informed citizens who, in turn, would model for their own pupils an appreciation for learning. They focused their efforts on face-to-face instruction in introductory-level courses which, according to Farmer's 1914 survey, was what Wisconsin normal school students needed most. The faculty had limited expertise for teaching advanced courses—their teaching load was heavy, they had no time or resources to pursue scholarship, their academic credentials for the most part were limited, and they often had to teach subjects for which they had little academic preparation. By 1939, 63 percent of them had advanced degrees, but this percentage still lagged the system-wide figure of 73 percent. "It was a faculty that was becoming old," Haas later admitted. Of the nine teachers colleges in Wisconsin, in 1940 only Eau Claire had never been accredited by the NCA (although some colleges had gained and lost accreditation).

In 1941 the college's new president, William R. Davies, wanted to learn about the public perception of the quality of Eau Claire State. He initiated a survey of eighty school superintendents in the Eau Claire area. His digest of their opinions was Eau Claire State was doing a good job in preparing its graduates in educational methods and an adequate job preparing them academically (Davies concluded only the University of Wisconsin seemed to be more highly regarded). But his conclusion was the superintendents he had surveyed believed Eau Claire graduates seriously lacked "cultural" attributes such as travel experiences and appreciation of art and music. This evaluation was similar to the judgment about teachers college students nationwide that Ester Marion Nelson had made in 1939, based on visits to fifty-seven colleges including Eau Claire State. Davies recommended the college enhance its new "selective admission" policies by giving more attention to the "personality" of applicants, provide better advising to students once they enrolled, and "insist on a still higher plane of academic achievement" by them as college students. He put his greatest emphasis on the college providing more extensive "substitute experiences" to make up cultural deficiencies—guest speakers and performers, trips to museums and cultural events in the Twin Cities, faculty-student discussion groups, etc. This report displayed a degree of self-criticism which had not previously existed in the college's history. It also clearly identified specific areas for upgrading. Davies certainly felt the education provided by Eau Claire State could be improved. He wanted this revamped education to be holistic and not measured simply by improvement in standardized test scores or lengthier reading and writing requirements in advanced courses.

Commencement, June 1941

Left to right: Silas Evans, president of Ripon College; Harvey A. Schofield; William R. Davies.

For President Davies, commencement on June 5, 1941, was a memorable occasion. He had allowed a vote by the graduating class, and they chose to hold the event outdoors on the lawn north of Old Main, overlooking the Chippewa River. June 5 was a brilliant early summer day in Wisconsin and the river sparkled with the sun's reflection (the guest speaker later facetiously explained to Davies that at a subsequent engagement his sunburned nose aroused suspicions he had been drinking alcohol in Eau Claire). Davies was proud of what he had accomplished in his first few months as president and was confident for the future of the college. He had won the respect of the students, who felt that among other things he had given purpose to the usually tedious daily assemblies by instituting the singing of the "Star Spangled Banner." The college had rebounded from its mid-1930s lows—a record number of students had attended the Junior Prom on May 16, Eau Claire State would award the greatest number of diplomas and degrees in its history on June 5, and essentially all graduates would find employment. Silas Evans, the president of Davies's *alma mater*, Ripon College, had come to Eau Claire to honor Davies by delivering the commencement address. Harvey Schofield, returning to campus for the last time before his death a few weeks later, joined Davies and Evans in the academic procession. Although Davies was not aware of it in June 1941, his confidence about getting greater public support for Eau Claire State became more likely the following year when his college roommate Orland Loomis, a Progressive, ousted Schofield's *bête noire*, Julius Heil, from the governor's office in Madison.

Just as the Great Depression smashed Schofield's plans in 1929 for expanding the college by construction of a second building, Davies's honeymoon would not last. World War II would soon bring an even greater upheaval to Eau Claire State than did the Great Depression.

1941-52
Building a State College During a Tumultuous Decade

> In his first months as president of Eau Claire State, William R. Davies quickly focused his energy on several dimensions of the college he felt needed improvement.

He had some modest success with these efforts, although national events would soon postpone for more than a decade the achievement of his larger goals.

To overcome the college's sense of isolation from the community (chapter three), Davies quickly began speaking to civic groups and joining organizations such as Rotary and became a member of the First Congregational Church. He also dealt more tactfully than had President Schofield with recommendations and complaints from community members. For instance, he suggested to a representative of the Constitutional Educational League that eliminating the social conditions denying employment to young people would be more effective at maintaining social harmony than would anti-Communist witch hunting. He also gently pointed out to a local pastor affronted by the sex references and the "vulgar climax" in the college's production of *Kiss and Tell*, which had just completed a hugely successful run on Broadway, that the play was a satire.

On campus, Davies urged his faculty to develop better relationships with high schools by regular visits and to recruit promising students they identified in the schools. He initiated a formal external review of the college's outcomes (the survey of superintendents discussed in the previous chapter) and ordered internal reevaluations of the curriculum by faculty members. He also tried to ramp up pressure to get construction started on a second campus building.

Faculty Tea in Old Main Library, 1940s

President Davies is fourth from the left.

World War II quickly overshadowed these initiatives and created a new set of challenges and opportunities for the college. The untimely death of Davies's former college roommate Orland Loomis a few weeks after his election in 1942 dispelled any idea the governor's office in Madison might begin to show favoritism towards Eau Claire State. As a result, Davies and his administrators needed a decade of hard work to transform the college beyond what it had been in 1941. By 1952, however, the president was pleased the campus finally included a second building, the academic quality of the college had qualified it for accreditation by the North Central Association, and the college had become a state college offering liberal arts programs.

Financial Issues in 1941

Marshaling support from students, alumni, and the Eau Claire community, Davies tried valiantly in 1941 to obtain financing for the long-delayed second building on campus. He was unsuccessful, at least in part due to a lack of support from Regent President Edward Dempsey. Dempsey criticized the proposals from Eau Claire, which mentioned the need for a gymnasium, a library, a separate Campus School building, and a dormitory, as unfocused and overly ambitious. He took the opportunity to remind Davies that he wanted the focus of the college to remain on teacher education. The regents, Dempsey wrote, will not "compromise on the emphasis that must be placed on teacher training." Dempsey also wanted to remain the exclusive point of contact between the teachers colleges and the legislature and did not appreciate *ex parte* lobbying by Eau Claire interests. Specifically, as the legislature prepared the 1941–43 budget, he wanted to emphasize enhancing the teachers colleges' operating rather than capital budgets.

The ever-shrewd Dempsey was successful in his plans. He got the Joint Finance Committee to increase funding for the teachers colleges by about 2.5 percent above the level Governor Julius Heil proposed in his executive budget, even as the committee was cutting the overall state budget. The salary "waivers" for faculty and staff instituted in 1940 (chapter two) could be dropped. The legislature, however, approved no building program for the teachers colleges. Undaunted, Davies continued to press during the fall of 1941 for another building for Eau Claire, even as shortages of materials stopped all state construction projects. In a strongly worded letter to the Eau Claire-area member of the assembly, he justified the need for a separate building for the Campus School by explaining grade school children could not understand the "adult behavior" they observed around them from college students.

War Comes to Eau Claire State

World War II affected Eau Claire State much more than had the previous world war or the Great Depression. The impact began in the fall of 1940 when mobilization of the National Guard took from campus five students of the 105th Cavalry Regiment and four students of the 128th Infantry Regiment. During the academic year, geography teacher George Simpson and Director of Teacher Education Eugene McPhee were also called to active duty as officers. On October 16 over eighty male students registered for the draft, and they began to be inducted in 1941. Consequently enrollment dropped by half from the fall of 1940 to the fall of 1943. Only sixty men enrolled in the fall of 1943, and the Blugolds did not field a football team that year. Female enrollment also fell as young women found jobs in burgeoning wartime industries in the Chippewa Valley. The *Spectator* felt it necessary to argue that attending college in wartime could be patriotic. In December 1942 Regent Secretary Edgar Doudna sent an ominous message to Eau Claire and the other teachers colleges: "Your enrollment has dropped 40%, yet you haven't noticeably decreased your teaching staff and operating costs; how can you justify asking for practically the same appropriations for the next biennium as for the current biennium?"

To meet the implied threat in Doudna's letter, Davies worked tirelessly to give the "full and complete support" of the college to the war effort. James Wallin, who continued to play an important role on the faculty even after his ouster as registrar by President Schofield (chapter two), headed the committee which coordinated the college's war efforts and promoted a message of wartime unity and sacrifice.

The theme of the 1942 *Periscope* was "One Nation, Indivisible" and the 1943 yearbook featured a fifteen-page spread on the "American Way of Life." Like other Americans, faculty and students stepped up and donated blood, rolled Red Cross bandages, and bought war bonds. In a rare example of cooperation with the University of Wisconsin, Eau Claire State faculty taught UW extension courses on war issues to adults. In the spring of 1942, students participated in a one-credit "Forum on Present-Day Problems." Davies departed from the pre-war practice by teachers college presidents to treat President Frank Baker of Milwaukee State as a pariah because of his leftist political views, advocacy of Progressive education, and ambitions to introduce liberal arts programs to his campus and invited him to address an assembly. Baker explained to the students the war would increase "respect for the common man," "government planning," and other social and economic goals.

Davies also tried to have the college contribute to the war effort by maintaining as much as possible its traditional role of preparing teachers, the need for which increased because of wartime personnel diversions. The college worked with county superintendents, in particular, to offer courses needed for women to become certified as supervisors and to offer "refresher" instruction for teachers who had been absent from a classroom in recent years. Bill Zorn organized clinics for local high school coaches unable to attend statewide meetings in Madison because of wartime transportation shortages. The summer session adopted timely themes such as "And Gladly Teach the Ways of Peace" and by 1944 its enrollment had rebounded to where it had been in 1938 and 1939. The 1944 summer session also included special "pre-induction" courses in trigonometry and physics for recent high school graduates. As was common throughout the country, the college also tried to "accelerate" students through its programs, such as allowing full-time teaching on emergency certificates to count for credit as student teaching. The college also said accelerating graduation was the reason for reorganizing the academic calendar, beginning in the fall of 1942, into three twelve-week "quarters" and two six-week summer sessions, instead of two eighteen-week semesters and one six-week summer session (to the extent that acceleration was successful, of course, it only reduced enrollments further).

Eau Claire State also helped train manpower needed for the war effort. Beginning in the fall of 1940, Zorn organized a Civilian Pilot Training Program, one of about seven hundred around the country, under the sponsorship of the Civil Aeronautics Administration and with the participation of a local flying school. In its first ten-week program, about a dozen students including a woman, began to learn to fly. In the spring, six of the men were accepted for naval flight training. After the declaration of war on December 8, 1941, many Eau Claire State students also enrolled in army and navy programs that allowed them to continue their schooling for a semester or a year before beginning active duty. It was also Zorn's responsibility to coordinate these programs in his capacity as dean of men, which began in the fall of 1941.

Eau Claire State took justifiable pride in the military service performed by its faculty and students. The 1944 *Periscope* recognized over five hundred of them by name. The class of 1945 sponsored a memorial program on May 1, 1945, "to make the students of Eau Claire State forever conscious of the supreme sacrifice made by those alumni who have given their lives in World War II." Seventeen individuals were honored that day, and eventually twenty-three names were inscribed on a memorial plaque in Old Main.

301st College Training Detachment

Eau Claire State made its greatest direct contribution to the war effort by hosting an US Army Air Force training detachment. This program made a small but tangible contribution to the war endeavor, had a positive impact on the college, and demonstrated how a teachers college could show the unexpected resilience and usefulness that characterized American higher education in general during the war years.

Throughout 1942 the US Army Air Forces (AAF) sought to protect its supply of highly qualified young men and especially keep them out of the hands of the US Navy and Marine Corps by allowing them to enlist and remain in school or their jobs until called to active duty. By early 1943 there was growing public concern about this stockpiling. The other armed services wanted their share of the best manpower. The War Manpower Commission and local draft boards felt they were being outmaneuvered, and citizens complained about thirty-five-year-old married men being drafted while twenty-year olds remained in college as part of the US Air Corps Enlisted Reserve. AAF Commanding General Harold Arnold's solution was to absorb this troublesome and inchoate pool of enlisted reservists into a college training program. After basic training, these newly activated airmen would spend about five months on college campuses until openings became available for them in pre-flight training.

With enrollments in a tailspin, and Doudna's threat no doubt in his mind, President Davies applied for Eau Claire State to be the site of a military training program. Two army officers inspected the campus in January, and on February 6 the War Manpower Commission's Joint Committee for the Selection of Non-Federal Educational Institutions announced the college was one of seven sites in Wisconsin approved for an AAF College Training Program. Nationwide, about 150 colleges and universities took part in the program. They were disproportionately small private colleges and teachers colleges; President Franklin Roosevelt insisted on the inclusion of these institutions in wartime military programs and the AAF CTP did not require the engineering or other technical facilities many other army and navy programs needed. A cohort of three hundred men, fresh from basic training at Jefferson Barracks in Missouri, began to arrive at Eau Claire State on March 11 and was billeted in former Civilian Conservation Corps barracks hastily relocated to the lawn next to Old Main. These troops constituted the 301st College Training Detachment. This was the first of a dozen cohorts, totaling more than one thousand men, which each trained for about fifteen weeks at Eau Claire State. The last group graduated on May 19, 1944, after which the program ended nationwide because the backlog of men awaiting pre-flight training had been erased.

The college provided the trainees with instruction in English, history, mathematics, geography, and physics. Davies scrambled to find an additional half-dozen faculty to staff these courses, turning to high school teachers and underemployed faculty at other teachers colleges. These faculty members, according to history teacher Leonard Haas, were taken aback when ordered "to have lesson plans ready on Monday morning . . . for that week for their courses, [which] were checked by military personnel." Zorn directed

301st AAF Detachment Drill, 1943

The view is to the east, towards Park Avenue. On the right is the Colonial Revival-style home (1926) of Judge James Wickham, who had blocked campus expansion in his direction during the 1920s (chapter two). On the left is the French Provincial-style home (1940) of Lewis E. Phillips, whose Presto Industries profited from armament manufacturing during World War II and who would become a major benefactor of the college in the 1960s (chapter six).

daily physical training. The cadets received ten hours of flight instruction, of an orientation nature, from civilian contractors at the small airstrip at the top of the bluff south of the college on what became known as Putnam Heights. (The airstrip was upgraded with $10,000 in contributions from businessmen in the community.) A small cadre, commanded for most of the 301st's existence by Captain William Rodenberg, a Harvard Law School graduate, provided military training, mostly in close-order drill and ceremonies.

Campus life changed with the arrival of the 301st. "[M]y, the girls were delighted," recalled Gerry Wing, Davies's secretary. These women students mixed with trainees at weekly dances at the city auditorium and the YMCA sponsored by the United Service Organization. "The girls loved it," Wing reported. Laura Sutherland, in her capacity as dean of women, was not as pleased. She tightened up curfews and required women students to maintain an hour-by-hour log of their daily activities. Sutherland candidly admitted to Davies that housemothers enforced college rules only about 50 percent of the time. However, the social problems evident nationwide because of wartime turmoil did not significantly affect Eau Claire. "Disciplinary problems at this detachment have not been serious," the 301st's official history reported. Only one trainee was court-martialed and none had a run-in with the civil authorities.

AAF officials at the national level did not emphasize the academic dimension of the program. They repeatedly shifted its stated goals and altered its curriculum, while insisting 99 percent of trainees pass academically. The faculty at Eau Claire, however, ably taught the trainees in their program. Results survive for six psychometrically sophisticated tests administered by the AAF, which measured trainees academically at the end of their course against the results of a diagnostic test they had taken prior to the course. On five of the six administrations, Eau Claire State scored in the highest quintile of programs in the AAF's Western Flying Training Command. It would seem the strengths of the faculty—background at all grade levels, experience in teaching students of different ability levels, flexibility with assignment to new subjects on short notice—made them a good fit for this program. Regent President Dempsey congratulated Davies when the regents learned AAF inspectors had given Eau Claire State "a very high rank." Geography scores were particularly high, and Henry Kolka, who started at the college by teaching geography in the AAF program, remained on the faculty for forty years. Several trainees returned to Eau Claire State as students after the war, and the college awarded all trainees up to seventeen academic credits.

For Eau Claire State, the AAF training program, in Haas's words, "was a great thing." It showed the college was able to handle a program which, on just a month's notice, almost doubled its enrollment and required its faculty to teach a new curriculum. "We know that some of the professors had classes at hours that only farmers would claim in caring for a good dairy herd," acknowledged a local newspaper. The program also increased faculty morale, connected the college in a positive way with the surrounding community, and prepared it for the postwar influx of students who had been servicemen, like those in the 301st College Training Detachment.

While You Were Away

To be sure, President Davies was frustrated by the diversion of resources to the war effort, such as by hosting the 301st Detachment, but the hostilities in some ways also encouraged the college to move in directions he wanted.

With a view towards updating instruction, Davies directed the faculty to reevaluate the college's curriculum during his first year as president. Three of these reports survive. Samuel Davenport critiqued freshman English. He argued the course should teach "*modernized* English," rather than prescriptive grammar, and students should have to do only "*voluntary* reading" inspired by the teacher. Someone with a different perspective prepared a new model syllabus for freshman English, which specified six syntax errors would "disqualify" a five hundred-word essay. This person also outlined a proposed succession of English, speech, and literature courses that should comprise a "junior college English" sequence. Davenport left the college late in 1941 (just before a double check by Davies of all faculty qualifications revealed his fraudulent academic credentials), and Thelma Hruza (with a recently minted genuine PhD from George Peabody College for Teachers) replaced him as director of dramatics and also taught English and psychology. In her report, Hruza proposed expanding the dramatics program to make teachers of music, art, speech, and physical education "better prepared to pass on to students a richer outlook on life." (Hruza later implemented these ideas at the University of Wisconsin Medical School in the 1950s as a pioneer in the field in psychodrama). Their impact at the time appears to have been limited, but these reports show Davies wanted to reexamine what Eau Claire State was doing, and he expected and trusted the faculty to do the reexamination.

During the war years Davies also tried to improve the cultural profile of Eau Claire State students, which his survey of area school superintendents had found deficient (chapter three). At his initiative, early in 1942 Hilda Oxby teamed with several prominent figures in the community, including attorney Francis Wilcox and arts-patron Florence Larkin, to establish a lecture series which would give students, in Haas's words, a "more metropolitan character." Given the ongoing world war, Davies particularly wanted this Chippewa Valley Forum to address world affairs—hence the selection of Oxby, the most internationally traveled member of the faculty, to be on the planning committee. During its first season, the forum's speakers included Maurice Hindus, a popular lecturer and prolific author whose sympathetic views towards the Soviet Union made him a controversial figure.

Davies tried to bring a global perspective to the college in other ways. He was active in the World Citizenship Movement and worked during the war years with the Institute of International Education on possible postwar exchange programs with students and faculty in Central and South America. Davies's commencement address at Cameron High School in 1945 was "Old World—New World—One World." For the postwar world, he foresaw a "world federation" in which "all men are brothers." When peace returned, Oxby led the college's first study-abroad program, which went to Mexico in the summer of 1950.

An important step toward raising the academic profile of the college occurred in May 1943. After a site visit by its national secretary, Kappa Delta Pi, which recognized high-achieving students in teacher education, established a campus chapter, the first nationally affiliated scholastic honorary society at Eau Claire State. Laura Sutherland was primarily responsible for this accomplishment, an outgrowth of her work with Amphictyon (chapter three) and she became the group's faculty "counselor." During the war years the chapter held monthly meetings where it elected new members, presented awards to outstanding students, and listened to presentations by faculty and guest speakers. Reflecting Davies's interests, the program planned for 1944–45 included a four-part series of faculty presentations on "world education."

In a muted way, during the war student life also continued to develop the "collegiate" character identified in the previous chapter as emerging in the late 1930s. The 1942 *Periscope* included a pictorial feature "College is Fun" which included the ubiquitous photos of students lounging on the stone bridges across Little Niagara Creek. Marking a departure from Harvey Schofield's policy, that yearbook also recognized for the first time a social sorority on campus, Sigma Phi Kappa. The chapter initiated new members each fall with publically humiliating "Hell Week" activities in downtown Eau Claire. The 1944 *Periscope* reported pledges had to wear black stockings and "submit to other forms of de-glamorization."

New Faculty in the Early 1940s

A combination of leaves for military service, retirements, resignations to work in private industry, and deaths gave Davies an unusual opportunity to recruit new faculty to Eau Claire State during the early 1940s. In seeking new teachers, the president moved away from Schofield's reliance on teacher-placement agencies. Instead he contacted academic departments and placement bureaus in midwestern universities, sought recommendations from the network of school superintendents to which he had previously belonged, recruited at meetings of the American Association of Colleges for Teacher Education, and directly approached high school and teachers college instructors who had been recommended to him.

He explained, "I am interested in finding a young man who is human and who would fit into the scheme of things in a teachers college" and has successful high school teaching experience.

Davies's most significant appointment, in the fall of 1941, was based on personal recommendations. On August 12, Monroe Milliren, the long-time teacher of mechanical drawing and other subjects and also dean of men in 1940, died suddenly of complications from appendicitis. Sutherland and John Schneider pressed Davies to replace him with Leonard Haas, a star pupil who had graduated from Eau Claire State in 1935 and was presently teaching social studies at Wausau High School (chapter three). Davies had met Haas when the latter had given a eulogy at Harvey Schofield's funeral a few weeks previously. Listening to his faculty more than Schofield would have, Davies reshuffled teaching schedules, moved Zorn to be dean of men, created a faculty position in American history and government, and offered the new job to Haas. "I was particularly anxious to have him," Davies explained apologetically to the principal of Wausau High School, "because I wanted some one who had the background of the college here at Eau Claire." Haas's ethnicity also helped Davies to cultivate better relations with Eau Claire Mayor Donald Barnes, who was pressuring him to appoint Norwegian Americans to the faculty. Drawing on Haas's background in organizing a guidance program at Wausau High, Davies put him on the faculty committee tasked to implement the president's new program to improve academic advising at Eau Claire State. Haas also became the first president of the campus chapter of Kappa Delta Pi, which often met in his home.

When Eugene McPhee left for military service, Norman Bailey, who had been hired in 1940 to teach English and rural education, became acting director of teaching training and placement. His ambitious manner rankled some of his colleagues, and during the summer of 1944 when, in Haas's words, "he was becoming involved in some pursuits that I guess could be called immoral, at least at the time"—homosexual behavior—Davies dismissed Bailey and he and his wife hastily departed Eau Claire. The president by now shared Sutherland and Schneider's opinion of Haas's abilities, and Davies asked him to fill the director's post until McPhee returned. Haas began an administrative career which would last until he retired as chancellor of UW–Eau Claire in 1980.

In 1942 Floyd Krause replaced the retiring Frank Ackerman, who had taught chemistry since 1919. Over the next thirty-five years, Davies and Haas relied on Krause as the key person in the development of the college's chemistry department and the science program in general. A shorter-term appointment, but one that fit with Davies's international emphasis, was Graham Lawton in geography, to fill in while George Simpson served in the army. After studying in Great Britain, Lawton was delayed in his return to his native Australia by the outbreak of war in the Pacific in December 1941 and was available to teach for a year at Eau Claire State. Upon the retirement in 1941 of Benjamin Bridgman, a member of the original faculty, William A. Calder, an astronomer with a PhD from Harvard University, came to Eau Claire State from Knox College. He left, however, for Carleton College to become an associate professor in 1943 and would have a long career at Agnes Scott College after the war—Davies was not always able to retain the most able faculty members he was able to recruit.

The death in November 1942 of Charles Donaldson, who had taught psychology since 1921 and coached the college's debate team, and the resignation in 1944 of Hruza, who had been handling the drama program, provided Davies an opportunity to give greater emphasis to speech, debate, and dramatics. "It is strange that this president who had been a high school, public school administrator until 1941," Haas later remarked, "had the ability at a time of great shortage to pick out what would be probably two of the finest people in the field of speech . . . and to retain them." Earl Kjer moved to the college from Eau Claire High School to direct dramatics in 1943 and Grace Walsh, who had taught at Chippewa Falls High School throughout the 1930s, was called from University High School in Madison to coach the debate team in 1944. Davies "just said: Build a program," Walsh later related. Kjer's program, as Laura Sutherland later explained, was not focused on developing professional actors, or even high school drama teachers, but rather on having student players "experience appreciation of character and human relations." In the decades after the war, "the shining light of the institution, insofar as co-curricular activities were concerned," Haas believed, was "in these areas." In 1947 Eau Claire State became the first teachers college accepted for membership in the National Collegiate Players and the debate squad soon participated in competitions at the national level. (The first topic for Walsh's squad was "Should F.D.R. or Dewey be elected in November?"—Eau Claire State students, at any rate, bucked the national trend as they had in the 1930s [chapter three] and preferred Thomas Dewey by a 111–105 margin).

Grace Walsh and the Forensics Squad at the 1948 Iowa State Teachers College (now Northern Iowa University) Debate Tournament

Walsh taught speech from 1944 to 1980. She coached eleven individual state forensics champions. When she died in 2000, she earned praise from US Senator Russ Feingold, who had participated in a summer program she directed.

During the war years Davies also established the basis for the music program, which would become one of the strengths of the college by the 1960s and 1970s. In 1944 he added a faculty position in instrumental music. He searched widely geographically and appointed Robert Gantner from Hays High School in Kansas, who had no previous connection with Wisconsin but "was a dreamer" with "visions." With the idea in his mind of introducing an academic minor in music as soon as possible, Davies told Gantner, "You're going to build the Music Department." Gantner quickly reached beyond the college and organized the Chippewa Valley Symphony, both to strengthen campus–community ties and to augment the meager number of student players he found at Eau Claire State. When Hilda Mae Ward retired immediately after the war, Davies again turned to Kansas and found Caldwell Johnson to replace her to direct campus vocal groups. At this time, Davies also hired Kathleen Olson to teach music education; this had previously been a part-time position.

Caldwell Johnson in Class

Johnson taught vocal music at UWEC for twenty-four years beginning in 1946. The UW-Eau Claire Alumni Association made him an honorary alumnus in 1994.

By his appointments in music, Davies began to change the faculty in ways that in later decades would become more general in the college, and sometimes problematic. In music performance programs, for instance, male faculty replaced the almost entirely female instructional staff of Eau Claire State's first thirty years. At the same time, music education became an increasingly separate domain with women faculty, which continued when Charlotte Hubert replaced Olson in 1952. Before the end of the 1950s, as seen in chapter five, tensions emerged between teacher-education and other members of the college faculty.

Davies was less successful during the war years in finding leadership for student publications than he was with speech, drama, and music. Arthur L. Murray, who had been the advisor to the *Periscope* and the *Spectator*, retired in 1943 after twenty-five years on the English faculty, and Davies sought a replacement whose "views on life are sane and wholesome." Short-term faculty members advised student publications until Lee Hench's arrival in 1949, and the *Spectator* and the *Periscope* lacked direction. As a result, the 1946 *Periscope* was a slim paperbound volume.

Administration of the Wartime College

President Davies kept a firm hand on the helm of the college, but he began to distribute authority more than had President Schofield. He continued Schofield's number-two man, Arthur Fox, as registrar and gave him the additional title of dean of instruction. "The students didn't like him too well," Gerry Wing admitted, "because he was a little bit caustic at times." (The *Periscope* presented a story in which Fox ended a discussion with Charles Donaldson by telling him, "Please shut the door from the outside.") According to Haas, however, Davies also "was willing to start to pass some of the responsibility on" to Fox and involve him in personnel and curricular decisions. In addition, Davies attempted to give faculty members more responsibility and make them feel like they were stakeholders in the college.

Davies sought out the opinions of the faculty before making decisions. For instance, early in his administration he solicited suggestions about what "activities" should be located in the second campus building, if and when it was constructed. By the fall of 1944, the faculty also clearly had a role in determining the college's calendar. Faculty committees—twenty-seven formally existed by 1944—also began to play a greater role. After soliciting suggestions from the faculty, early in 1943 Davies organized an administrative council of about ten faculty members which at first chiefly served to represent the college to public officials and the community (financed by an assessment on the faculty of .005 of all salaries), but after the war became something of an executive committee. In 1943 Davies reported the college had a Faculty Curriculum Committee, chaired by Fox, which "is responsible for a continuous and progressive study of the courses of study" and made recommendations to him. Even more important was the Student Personnel Committee, which by 1944–45 was making recommendations about what English placement exam to administer, what activities to include in freshmen week, and what class attendance policy to enact. Regarding use of the student union, for instance, the committee felt "card playing should be limited to the latter portion of the day."

In early 1945 Davies also set up the Area Advisory Committee, which would continue to function until 1973. Its first chair was Glen Rork, head of the Eau Claire electric utility Northern States Power Company. The committee's thirty members, twenty-five of whom came from communities in the college's "service area" outside of Eau Claire, met on campus twice a year for briefings by administrators and opportunities to attend cultural and athletic events. For this committee Davies selected people like bankers, judges, and newspaper editors whose roles would be that of "a spokesman" for their communities towards the college and "a contact and liaison" who would promote the college locally, especially by recruiting promising students. Over time, Davies also increasingly called on members of this committee to lobby the governor and legislators for favored programs. Erwin Homstad, for instance, was "Mr. Black River Falls" where he owned the hotel, the bank, and other enterprises and was "a hardworking Republican." "If we needed something," Haas remembered, "Davies simply called Homstad: Can you do something for us? . . . Homstad would get busy . . . and often save programs for us."

Planning for the Postwar College

Even as he struggled to solidify the college's existing programs while adapting to the needs of World War II, President Davies was thinking about the future. He wrote repeatedly to state and national elected officials, especially encouraging them to adopt internationalist policies and create programs that would assist higher education. His own planning for the future of Eau Claire State focused on the introduction of a four-year liberal arts program and the construction of additional facilities to accommodate an anticipated growth in enrollment. His long-range goal, as he told alumni at their annual banquet in 1942, was for Eau Claire State "to perpetuate the American ideal of equal educational opportunities for every boy and girl."

"We began to look at ourselves and find that we were a liberal arts type of institution," Leonard Haas recalled about the war years. This realization arose from two facts: first, expansion possibilities in teacher education were limited because Eau Claire State did not offer any "special subject" (chapter one); and second, influential elements in the Eau Claire community continued to press for their city to have public higher education other than for teacher training. In 1945 Area Committee chair Rork wrote to businessman Earl Hale, the leading advocate of establishing in Eau Claire a branch of the University of Wisconsin, explaining he, too, favored the development of a "widely-known, well-established and complete four-year degree institution" in the city, just not as part of the university. (Rork emphasized to Davies that this transformed institution should be called "Western Wisconsin University" and have a big-time athletic program.)

Immediately after the war a new mission statement for the college, probably drafted by Haas, stated teacher training would still remain its "chief function," but it would take on additional responsibilities to provide "pre-professional training" for students who would transfer and provide four-year liberal arts programs to "develop the capacities of individuals to specifically meet the needs of our community." "If we were able to extend our undergraduate general education to include the liberal arts degree it would improve our reputation in higher education," Dean Fox further explained. "Best of all it would equip us to do [a] much more superior job of training teachers." Because of the college's existing strengths in liberal arts subjects, Davies and Haas believed offering four-year programs would require little or no additional resources.

The newly appointed regent from Eau Claire, William D. McIntyre, who replaced Peter Smith in 1945, encouraged these ambitions. Haas later recalled a dinner party at which McIntyre, his immediate neighbor in the Third Ward, became "very wrapped up in the fact that we ought to have regional institutions serving with a broad background of the liberal arts." The Area Committee endorsed adding a liberal arts program to the curriculum. The Eau Claire State Alumni Association, which Bailey had revitalized before his unfortunate departure, likewise backed the proposal. In sum, while most of its sister institutions hesitated, Eau Claire State was in the forefront of the transformation of the Wisconsin teachers colleges into liberal arts institutions.

William D. McIntyre and Wendell Willkie, March 1944

McIntyre was a prominent Republican whose political connections benefitted the state colleges while he was a regent from 1945 to 1965. In this photograph he is conferring with Wendell Willkie, the 1940 Republican nominee for US president. Willkie was a candidate in the April 1944 presidential primary in Wisconsin. His poor performance ended his campaign. (Wisconsin Historical Society)

Davies pushed during the war years to add specific programs into Eau Claire State's curriculum. Early in 1942 he opened discussions with Luther Hospital in Eau Claire about developing a cooperative program that would give students a health education degree and a registered nurse credential; it would take decades to develop, but this initiative marked the beginning of what led to the School of Nursing in the 1960s. After hiring Kjer and Walsh, Davies also advocated for adding a speech major to Eau Claire State's program. The proposal received Dempsey's endorsement and eventually came to fruition after the war, but as an "academic" rather than a "special subject." Furthermore, when Milwaukee State and Superior State tried to protect their existing music education programs by blocking the addition of a music major at Eau Claire State, Davies outmaneuvered them by setting up *minors* in vocal and instrumental music, which when taken together provided students with certification for positions as high school music teachers. Finally, in 1951 the regents approved teaching and liberal arts majors in music. Sensing a demand from high schools in West Central Wisconsin, Davies also wanted to add a major in business education; in an important procedural precedent, the faculty voted in January 1946 to approve allocating a position to this area.

With these new opportunities for students, Davies expected a surge in enrollment after the war. In the fall of 1946, the increasingly significant administrative council planned for an enrollment of higher than one thousand for the following year.

Additional students needed additional facilities and construction required state financing. The prospects for this development improved in Madison when Davies's old friend Orland Loomis, who died before taking office as governor, was conveniently succeeded in 1943 by Regent President Dempsey's old friend Walter Goodland. Indeed, the operating budgets of the teachers colleges perhaps did better than expected during the 1943–45 biennium. No new construction, however, was possible during the war because of material shortages. Still, in the face of opposition from the *Milwaukee Journal*—which felt the teachers colleges were already overbuilt and had campuses that should be transformed into junior colleges—and skepticism from Dempsey, Davies continued to marshal community support and lobby regents, legislators, and the state architect to add another building to his college after the war.

He was eventually successful. Dempsey's comprehensive postwar plan for the teachers colleges gave first priority to Eau Claire for building construction. In the fall of 1944 Goodland was elected governor in his own right, and with the state coffers bulging as a result of wartime prosperity, he proposed an ambitious postwar state building program of $23.2 million. The Democratic and Progressive minorities in the legislature supported him, but he had to scold and harangue his fellow Republicans to eventually approve $16.5 million. Of this, $3.15 million went to the teachers colleges, whose regents designated $435,000 of it for Eau Claire, the second-largest appropriation in the system trailing only Milwaukee. After fifteen years of effort, Eau Claire State was now closer to getting a second building, but it still had to decide its purpose and location and secure the release of the funds for actual construction. As Haas would later point out, it was ironic that eighty-two-year-old Goodland, the oldest person ever to serve as a governor in the United States, was the individual most responsible for improved postwar educational programs for the youth of Wisconsin.

From Servicemen to Students

When he proposed his building plan in 1945, Governor Goodland, referring specifically to teachers colleges, said that "we owe a definite responsibility" to the "young men and women" returning from the battlefield who now expected to receive "the advantages of higher education." Most Americans agreed. The Serviceman's Readjustment Act of 1944 (the "GI Bill") provided almost $15 billion of federal government aid to more than two million veterans who attended college. Undergraduate enrollment nationwide more than doubled between 1944 and 1948. The consequences of this program were significant: opportunities for young people to attend college grew; the involvement of the federal government in higher education increased; colleges and universities became more flexible in accommodating hordes of older, often less-academically prepared, and vocationally oriented students;

campus facilities expanded enormously; the representation in popular media of veterans as students made college life more comprehensible to large numbers of Americans; and the idea took hold that higher education had a major role to play in creating democratic citizenship in the United States.

The benefits of the GI Bill, however, have sometimes been overstated. They went overwhelmingly to just white men. Most of the beneficiaries would have gone to college anyway. At pre-war rates of college graduation (based on the number of high school graduates four years previously), about 2,050,000 Americans would have received bachelor's degrees between 1942 and 1951; actually, with the boost of the GI Bill, about 2,300,000 graduated.

Charles B. Woodson Jr. and the Racial Integration of Eau Claire State

Charles B. Woodson Jr. was probably the first African American student at Eau Claire State. His life story, although incomplete in 2016, is fascinating in itself and touches on several aspects of the history of the college.

Woodson was born in Nebraska on August 17, 1923. His family soon moved back to be among extended kin in the area around Horton, Kansas, then a city of approximately four thousand about seventy-five miles northwest of Kansas City, where Charles B. Woodson Sr. farmed. Woodson Sr.'s father, Aaron, almost certainly was an ex-slave who had moved from Tennessee to the Horton area sometime between 1882 and 1891 as part of the post-Reconstruction era migration from the South to Kansas of "exodusters." Aaron's daughter Cassie later wrote that the motivation for moving his family was to obtain a good education for his children in the then racially integrated schools in Kansas. Charles Jr. grew up around Horton during the interwar years as part of a small African American community—about 150 blacks lived in the city in 1920. In June 1942 Charles Jr. graduated from Horton High School, which was then racially integrated, and was academically in the middle third of his class. While in high school, he earned money working as a school janitor through a program sponsored by the National Youth Administration (chapter three).

After working as a field hand in the wheat fields of western Kansas, in October 1942 Woodson enlisted in the US Army Signal Corps at Fort Leavenworth, Kansas. According to his 2011 obituary, he was trained as a radio technician and achieved the rank of technician fifth grade (equivalent to corporal) in the US Army Air Force. This was an unusual accomplishment, as most African Americans during the war were limited to duties as privates in the quartermaster and other service branches of the army.

It is unclear today what Woodson did following discharge in 1946. However, it is known he traveled to East Asia, because he was a passenger on the USAT *General Mason M. Patrick* when it arrived at Seattle from Yokohama on August 2, 1949.

A few weeks later, Woodson enrolled at Eau Claire State. No doubt he wanted to use his veteran's educational benefits, but what brought him to Eau Claire, a city with just seven blacks among over thirty thousand residents in 1950, is a puzzle. Although he had played football at Horton High School, there is no indication of his involvement with athletics at Eau Claire State. Whatever his reason for enrollment, his records show in his two years at Eau Claire State, Chuck Woodson—as he was now known—was an excellent student. His classmates also recognized his abilities: a small picture of him as part of a montage in the 1951 *Periscope* shows him at a typewriter at work on a paper and has the label "Quiet, genius at work." He belonged to the International Relations Club which, much in line with President Davies's thinking and his goals for the college, sought to "develop understanding and promote action relative to international affairs." Woodson was the club's vice president during 1950–51.

Reflecting his international orientation, Chuck Woodson transferred in 1951 to Mexico City College (MCC). This English language college had an interesting history between 1940 and the early 1960s. Refugee European scholars and American professors fleeing McCarthyism largely staffed it. For students, it attracted a combination of bohemians, frugal-minded veterans, and sunshine-seeking partiers. A feature in *Ebony* in June 1955 identified, from the college's own mission statement, why it especially appealed to African Americans. MCC students were "modest patriots, but internationally-minded ones, who will look for the likenesses which link them to their fellow men rather than for apparent unlikenesses" such as "race . . . which separate them." About twenty-five of its 475 students in 1955 were African Americans.

Chuck Woodson probably first learned about MCC while he was at Eau Claire State. Another Eau Claire student, Ray Hetchler, attended MCC for a quarter and returned in early 1950 to report he had "fun," despite "heavy" reading assignments and a "heavy" diet which he had to take at his lodgings because of the dangers for gringos of eating at restaurants. Another Eau Claire State student, Dan Saylor, had preceded Hetchler to MCC.

Whatever the reason he went to MCC, Woodson graduated from the college with a bachelor's degree in economics in 1953. According to his obituary, he also earned an MA degree from MCC, and he was indeed identified as an economics student in a photograph that accompanied the *Ebony* article in 1955. His obituary said he remained in Mexico and engaged in business ventures including an English language school. He returned to the United States sometime before 1995 and died in Kansas City in 2011. Reflecting his military service, Woodson was buried in the National Cemetery at Fort Leavenworth, Kansas. His accomplishments certainly made his grandfather Aaron proud and confirmed Aaron's decision to relocate his family to Kansas in the 1880s.

Student Housing in Old Main Gym, 1946

The enrollment surge was greater than expected in the fall of 1946, and some male students temporarily found themselves in barracks-like accommodations in the gym on the ground level of Old Main.

Eau Claire State followed these nationwide patterns. In the fall of 1946, enrollment more than doubled from the previous year to 787, including 325 veterans. Admissions were halted in late August, but 550 first-time students still enrolled. Despite the work of a veterans counseling staff of five, throughout the year registration was understandably chaotic. Most students registered in pre-professional and liberal arts programs, over one hundred in pre-engineering alone. Davies scrambled to hire adjunct faculty to staff additional course sections for these students. "We anticipated an overflow, but not this many," he told Douda. The three AAF barracks on the lawn next to Old Main housed male students, and four more temporary structures joined them in 1947 as a student union and classrooms. The college provided twenty-four married men and their families with shabby housing on Birch Street in apartments with only oil-fired space heaters. The president projected enrollment would grow to 1,100 the following year and eventually peak in 1950. He told students at the opening of the academic year, "Eau Claire State is coming into its own."

The postwar boom was surprisingly brief. Enrollment fell in 1947 and again in 1948. The size of the sophomore class in 1947 was only 54 percent of the size of the freshman class in 1946, the lowest retention rate among the Wisconsin teachers colleges. Subsequently, enrollment temporarily rebounded. However, only half of the freshmen who entered in 1950 returned in the fall of 1951, and overall enrollment fell back to where it had been in 1939. Davies correspondingly had to trim the size of the faculty for the fall of 1951 (he was helped by being able to dismiss English teacher Paul Smith, who witlessly registered at a hotel in St. Paul with one of his students listed as his wife).

All of the teachers colleges in the state lagged behind the University of Wisconsin in boosting enrollment after the war. In 1946, enrollment in the teachers colleges was only 8 percent higher than it had been in 1940, compared to 63 percent higher at the UW. Even at its postwar peak in 1949 enrollment in teachers colleges was up only 20 percent from 1940, compared to a 56 percent gain at the university. McPhee, who resumed the directorship of teacher education in 1946, later acknowledged the teachers colleges "did little" for veterans and as a result engendered hostility from officials in Madison.

The postwar influx of students, however brief and short of expectations it was, unquestionably changed the character of Eau Claire State. By the fall of 1949, only half of the students were enrolled in teacher education programs. The proportion which came from Eau Claire and adjacent counties had dropped to about 80 percent, and a handful of international students had enrolled. Over 60 percent of the student body, even 50 percent of those who were not veterans, was male, in contrast to the period before the war. For a few decades at mid-century, Eau Claire State was "masculinized." The changing composition of the student body also affected the traditional-aged students who were still the majority of the student body. "All we'd known were college kids," recalled a female student from the late 1940s and early 1950s. Veterans "were married and had a baby . . . That was a real shocker . . . They'd say such grown-up things."

Administrative Reorganization at the State and Local Levels

In part as a result of unexpectedly disappointing postwar enrollments, a series of interconnected events produced new leadership in Madison for the state teachers colleges. These changes led to leadership changes at Eau Claire State, which eventually contributed to the achievement of President Davies's goals for the college.

As has already been mentioned, William D. McIntyre, an Eau Claire businessman whose children attended the Campus School and who was a fellow member with Davies of the First Congregational Church, replaced Peter Smith as regent in 1945. McIntyre, a prominent Republican, was a good fit for the board, since with the demise of the Progressives (Smith's party) the GOP swept the state elections in 1946 and would hold near-hegemonic sway for the next decade. McIntyre also favored transforming Eau Claire State into a liberal arts institution; the regents moved towards that position when Dempsey, long an advocate for sticking to a teacher-education focus, resigned in October 1946. As recently as the previous March, in a spirited exchange with President Jim Dan Hill of Superior State, Dempsey had denounced liberal arts instruction in the teachers colleges as "unconstitutional," while Hill countered that it would assist veterans. Dempsey's replacement as regent president was George Sundquist from Superior, who rejected the contention that liberal arts programs would attract students away from elementary education programs where they were desperately needed immediately after the war.

Secretary Doudna departed soon after Dempsey's resignation. Hill and Sundquist maneuvered legislators to curtail a proposed salary increase for the regents' secretary, and Doudna indignantly announced his retirement in June 1947, letting known publically his dissatisfaction with the "woodchopper" faction of the regents, including McIntyre, which favored adding liberal arts programs. McIntyre was a member of the committee which subsequently redefined Doudna's position more broadly as chief administrative officer and educational advisor to the board. The choice for this new position, retitled as a directorship, was Eugene McPhee, who had been McIntyre's neighbor and close friend in Eau Claire during the 1930s. Director McPhee soon became the central figure in the state teachers colleges and a thorn in the side of the University of Wisconsin for his success at promoting them at the expense of the UW.

McIntyre became regent president in 1950 and continued to work effectively with McPhee, a fellow Republican. "[B]oth knew how to handle the legislator[s] in the bars," Haas explained. But Haas believed, unlike Dempsey who he said showed favoritism to Oshkosh, McIntyre and McPhee did not give undue preference to Eau Claire.

McPhee's departure led to administrative changes at Eau Claire State. Lester Emans, who came to Eau Claire in 1946 from the Lakewood Elementary School in Maple Bluff to replace Katherine Thomas as principal of the Campus School, became director of teacher education and placement. With different titles, Emans headed the college's teacher education program for the next two decades; his election as president of the Wisconsin Education Association in 1949 was a recognition of his standing in the profession. A few months after Emans's appointment, in July 1948 Haas became dean of instruction and registrar. By at least 1944, Davies had identified Haas as Fox's successor when the later retired; after

Haas stepped aside as director of teacher education when McPhee returned to that post in the summer of 1946, he studied full time for two quarters towards a PhD at the University of Minnesota and then spent a year and a half as an understudy to Fox. Also in 1948, Sutherland decided to give up her position as dean of women and return to full-time teaching. As her successor Davies appointed Stella Pedersen, a former colleague of Haas at Wausau High School who was dean of women at Winona State Teachers College. With a master's degree in guidance, Pedersen was the first professional in student personnel on the staff. Eau Claire State had, therefore, "a complete new lineup," in Haas's words, "with a president who . . . has finally gotten over the interruption of the war and [had] plans . . . sufficiently ready to make the progress that was coming."

A Championship Season on the Gridiron

A highlight of the postwar years on campus was the football team's 1948 Wisconsin State College Conference championship. This achievement took on extra significance because, for the first time since 1933, football competition in the conference was statewide and not broken down by division.

Except for a previous WSCC championship by George Simpson's 1922 team, which played an abbreviated two-game conference schedule, the Blugolds had not fared well on the football field. In the five seasons previous to 1948 they had gone 2–16–6 in conference play (there had been a wartime hiatus from 1943 to 1945). But a new era began in 1947 with the arrival of a new coach, Ade Olson, a 1926 graduate of Eau Claire Normal. Olson had coached successfully at Eau Claire Senior High School since 1929, winning the 1933 state championship with an undefeated team. By 1948, at the college, he had put together a squad largely of returning war veterans, including Link Walker, Earl Perkins, Warren Chamberlain, Frank Lowry, Sam Young, Ade Washburn, Dick Emmanuel, Herb Kohls, Cliff Washburn, and Warren Buckli.

Boosted by early-season wins over Stout and Stevens Point, the Blugolds travelled to La Crosse on October 9 as Homecoming opponents. Their defense stopped the favored Eagles three times inside the five-yard line, Perkins ran for two touchdowns, and the Blugolds emerged with a 27–0 victory and tied for first place in the conference. Five days later they met co-leader Milwaukee State on Thursday night at Carson Park in a game scheduled to coincide with the annual Northwest Wisconsin Education Association meeting in Eau Claire. In a tight defensive battle—there were only sixteen first downs by both teams together in the game—the Blugolds again emerged victorious, 13–6. The key play was a last-second, forty-yard touchdown pass at the end of the first half from Jim Simon, a freshman who had just come into the game, to speedy Bob Funk, who had been sidelined by injuries until this game.

Eau Claire and River Falls, both undefeated in the conference, met in River Falls the following week. The Blugolds earned a dramatic come-from-behind 13–7 win when Bob "Pinky" Schaaf broke loose in the fourth quarter for a fifty-one-yard touchdown run. A subsequent loss to Superior still left Eau Claire—at 5–1—the sole champion of the WSCC and, including a win over Winona State Teachers College, the team finished 6–1 overall.

Olson coached for eight more years, finishing his career in 1956 with a 7–1 season and another conference championship. His overall record as a college coach was 42–34–3. "It was a terrific competitive spirit that made Olson a great football coach," concluded long-time Eau Claire sports journalist Ron Buckli. "Sportsmanship was his trademark—but he still was a terrible loser." The addition to the Eugene R. McPhee Physical Education Center on upper campus was named in his memory following his death in 1988.

Link Walker, the quarterback in 1948 in Olson's single-wing offense, returned to Eau Claire as an assistant in 1962 and became head coach in 1968. Over the next nineteen seasons, his teams went 104–85–3 and won two conference championships. He and Olson are members of the Blugold Hall of Fame, and their plaques and those of other honorees are proudly displayed in 2016 in the McPhee Center.

Ade Olson, Coach of the 1948 Blugold Football Team

Postwar Challenges

In addition to managing unpredictable enrollments, Davies's new team faced several other challenges in the immediate postwar years. They were disappointed by the failure of officials in Madison, citing high postwar construction costs, to follow through on the legislature's 1945 building program. "[A]lthough millions of dollars have been available since 1943," the *Wisconsin State Journal* reported in 1947, "not a single important permanent structure has been added to the state government's physical plant." Measured by square feet per student, Eau Claire continued to operate with about 60 percent of the average space in the teachers college system and less than half the space at Whitewater and Platteville. Because of these "inadequate facilities," according to a local magazine, "[t]he headline high school students have given Eau Claire State but scant attention . . . when deciding where to continue their education."

Davies pushed indefatigably, but unsuccessfully, with legislators and the public to obtain the release of funds for building construction at Eau Claire and for additional appropriations. All the state teachers colleges had need for more space, but the problem was most acute at Eau Claire because the timing of the building cycle (chapter two) had left it without new construction for over thirty years. Perhaps because of this great need, the number, location, and purpose of proposed buildings remained in flux. The 1949 *Catalog*, for instance, included a map of a future campus with a library building on Garfield Avenue and a gym on Roosevelt Avenue, both east of Old Main, and an interconnected auditorium, student union, and Campus School building on Park Avenue between Garfield and Roosevelt. Other proposals included dormitories and a natatorium.

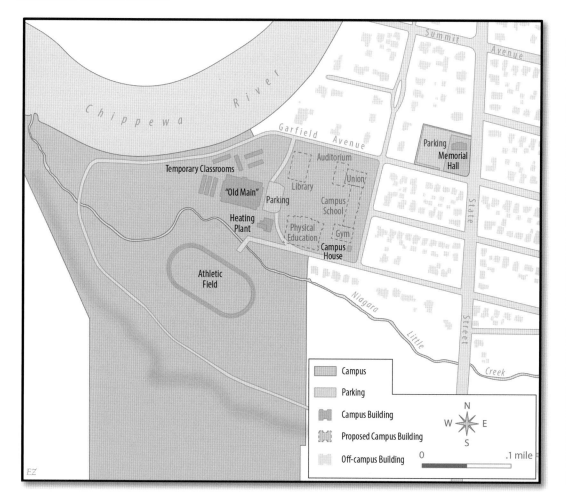

Map 4.1

Efforts to secure accreditation from the North Central Association (chapter three) were also disappointing. Walter Morgan, president emeritus of Western Illinois State Teachers College, made a preliminary visit to Eau Claire in the fall of 1946 on behalf of the NCA. His evaluation of the college was tepid. He was favorably impressed by tenure protection for the faculty and their "complete freedom" in teaching, as well as the advising and orientation programs Davies had worked hard to develop. He was not impressed by the academic qualifications of the faculty and their lack of scholarly publications and was bothered by the fact the least qualified teachers in these respects had the highest salaries. Despite the increased responsibility Davies had given to faculty committees—or perhaps because of it—Morgan found confusion on campus about the role of faculty governance. He further reported, "Some members of the staff [feel] that the standards of scholarship are not set high enough for students." Morgan also noted the absence of a student government and the paucity of financial aid and felt the regent secretary and the local regent were too involved in day-to-day management of the college. His conclusion was Eau Claire State was a "border-line case" for accreditation, and consequently Davies chose to "defer" a formal request to the NCA for accreditation.

In addition to dealing with the NCA, Davies faced another problem in the postwar years with which Harvey Schofield had repeatedly struggled—legislative efforts to terminate Eau Claire State as a separate institution. The underlying problem was the continued rivalry between the teachers colleges and the University of Wisconsin. By expanding into each other's domain, the institutions came into heightened competition after World War II when the teachers colleges began to offer extension programs and the UW widened its system of two-year campuses around the state in an effort to relieve overcrowding on the Madison campus. The UW at this time also initiated an elementary education program, which had previously been exclusively a domain of the teachers colleges. As relations deteriorated, an alarming report in 1948 by a special UW Functions and Policy Committee (the "Ingraham Committee") envisioned a statewide UW incorporating the teachers colleges. Later that year the special Commission on Education, appointed by the governor and included Eau Claire businessman Earl Hale, endorsed this idea of a merged system of higher education on grounds of efficiency and economy, and Governor Oscar Rennebohm (who had taken office on Goodland's death) proposed it to the legislature in January 1949.

Strong support came from Superior and Milwaukee, where there was a desire to have four-year liberal arts and professional programs with the prestigious University of Wisconsin brand, but backing also came from Eau Claire. A petition with three hundred signatures asked the legislature to make Eau Claire State a branch of the university. The Eau Claire Chamber of Commerce also gave its support to the proposal, citing benefits from the recent incorporation of the teachers college at Duluth into the University of Minnesota. For their part, spokesmen for the teachers colleges denounced the proposal, alleging it would lead to centralized control and the neglect of teacher education. Davies described it as "a grandiose scheme that may not be practical and sound." He proposed "voluntary cooperation should be tried for two years longer." In a letter to the chamber of commerce jointly written with Haas and physics teacher Parker Clark, Davies perhaps relied on the fact the Morgan report was not public knowledge and directly "challenge[d] [Hale] to substantiate his inference [*sic*] that the instruction at the college is not equal to that now offered on the campuses at Wisconsin or Minnesota." The Area Committee supported Davies by voting against the idea of a single governing board for public higher education (but only by a 14–9 margin). For the time being, the UW regents also favored the status quo, and the assembly ultimately rejected the merger proposal on a 49–38 vote even after it had been slimmed down to make only Milwaukee State and Superior State part of the university. The most widely read newspaper columnist on state politics ascribed the defeat to the "selfish interests" of "the men who run the colleges [who] had no appetite for downgrading in position, prestige and authority."

Davies had succeeded in keeping Eau Claire State a separate institution. As he explained to an Area Committee member, "We feared that this was merely the opening wedge to make our teachers colleges junior college feeders for the university." The *contremps*, however, showed the college had lost the support of a significant component of the Eau Claire community. This problem was exacerbated by an unseemly row between Davies and the chamber of commerce when the pro-merger chamber declined to pay the expenses of an out-of-town speaker who opposed the integration proposal at the chamber's public forum on May 10. To keep community support, it seemed more urgent than ever for the college to expand beyond teacher education and obtain new facilities. In the summer of 1949 Davies renewed his pitch to McPhee and the governor, explaining, "To implement the liberal arts status of the college would not be difficult nor costly."

The Transformation of Eau Claire State, 1946–51

The Morgan Report provided the impetus for changes in the college, some of which Davies had already been advocating. James Wallin headed a faculty Committee on Accrediting Agencies (the "North Central Study Committee"), which worked during the late 1940s to oversee efforts to prepare the college for a successful accreditation review.

To address the most glaring deficiency noted in the NCA report, the administration encouraged existing faculty members to use summer sessions when they were not teaching to pursue their own education and complete doctoral degrees. In addition, for new faculty appointments they sought individuals who were at least close to receiving a doctorate. "[W]e are attempting rather abruptly to build up the academic standards of the local faculty," Davies explained, "which stood next to the lowest in this respect" among the teachers colleges.

The administration also further strengthened the emergent system of faculty governance. Davies defined the responsibilities and regularized the meeting schedules of faculty committees. In 1948 Haas also put together a formal faculty handbook specifying college policies. The handbook stressed faculty members must "become an integral part of the community," and it also outlined the regents' elaborate salary scale, which ranged from $2,000 to $5,600 (about $20,000 to $56,000 in 2016). By increasing the responsibilities and authority of the faculty, Davies was going against the tradition of authoritarian management in Wisconsin teachers colleges, and his policies met with disfavor in Madison. In a last warning-before-dismissal letter, McPhee, writing on behalf of the regents, reproached Davies because "you seemed to give more weight to the decisions of some of your faculty members" than to the board.

The faculty remained too small to set up academic departments (except in English), which the Morgan Report seemed to want, but Davies created four "divisions" with elected chairs: Education and Psychology, Humanities, Natural Sciences and Physical Education, and Social Sciences. This differentiation among the faculty lessened their overall cohesiveness, but it strengthened academic standards, as the administration wanted. The NCA Study Committee recognized, "Teachers who are assigned courses outside their field dare not be exacting in their demands," and Haas regretted " a time . . . when this was common practice and when standards were reduced accordingly."

The Student Personnel Committee, headed by physicist Parker Clark, addressed another of the issues raised by the Morgan Report. In 1949 it drafted a new form of student government for approval by the student body, including an elected executive, legislature, and judiciary, to replace Schofield's 1940 Student Life Committee. The *Spectator* subsequently introduced an "According to Justice" column, which detailed the judgments of the student judiciary, mostly "convictions" for gambling in the student union. Students publically complained, however, about lax enforcement of gambling regulations by student legislators and judiciary officials, who themselves were accused of gambling. In the fall of 1950 an almost annual series of confrontations between the *Spectator* and the elected student executive began; the student executive replied to the charge he had plagiarized some of his public remarks by arguing he was a "Robin Hood" who had "stole from the mentally rich for the purpose of enlightening us, the mentally poor." For its part, the student legislature impeached this executive, although it failed to remove him from office. It was obvious it was going to take some time for a responsible student government to develop.

In the meantime, scholarship aid, privately funded by individuals and organizations, strengthened the college. "There were just no scholarships," Haas later pointed out, before "the decade of the 40s." By 1949, the *Catalog* identified fourteen scholarships available to students and supported by an "endowment" of pooled gifts organized in 1945. Including direct awards from organizations, twenty-six scholarships were awarded in the spring of 1949. Davies himself generously gifted a scholarship in memory of his daughter, Kathryn, an Eau Claire State graduate, who died of diabetes in 1948. The president memorialized her by pointing out her mother had died, her boyfriend had drowned, and she had gone blind, but she had "learned to do impossible things." In addition to this private aid, about fifty students in the early 1950s received Legislative Scholarships (chapter three). This aid was needed. At the end of the 1940s, half of Eau Claire State students relied on at least some paid work.

The transformation of the college was not completely from the top down. Students pushed for higher academic standards, echoing the recommendations of the NCA report. They publically criticized the scheduling of Thanksgiving break in the middle of exam period, the lack of alignment between different sections of the same course, the practice of giving the same exam to multiple sections at different times, and the refusal of faculty members to tell "disgusted" students who had actually graded their exams (apparently a criticism of peer grading). Perhaps in response to such critiques, and in line with a recommendation of the Morgan Report, Dean Haas began to make regular visits to the classes of untenured faculty. He also promoted higher academic standards by simultaneously publicizing the 20 percent or so of students named to the Dean's Honor Roll and "dropping" about 5 percent for low academic performance.

The Faculty in the Late 1940s

As he had done for music and speech during the war years, in making faculty appointments in the postwar period President Davies sought individuals with academic qualifications that would impress the NCA and who would be able to provide leadership in building the departmental organization he envisioned for the college. Among the faculty members who fit this profile, and who would serve the college for at least fifteen years, were Lawrence Wahlstrom in mathematics, who would also encourage the organization of a Scandinavian area studies program; William Cochrane in history, who mediated a long-standing temperamental clash between Sutherland and her colleague Vine Miller; and Lee Hench, who developed a minor in journalism which was added to the curriculum in 1953, while advising the *Periscope* and, in particular, the *Spectator* to become more professional publications.

Just as the student body became male dominated in the aftermath of World War II, so did the faculty. Long-time women faculty members retired, including Lyla Flager in 1952 and Hilda Oxby in 1953, adding to the void in women on the instructional staff. (Oxby remained feisty to the end, retiring when she was displeased with a room assignment given to her by Haas.) There were a few exceptions to this pattern. For example, Lois Almon, with a PhD from the University of Wisconsin, extensive experience at the state hygiene lab, and a commitment to environment preservation, came to Eau Claire in 1947. She added a specialist in plant science to the faculty. Almon, however, left in 1953 for a position at North Dakota State. Her replacement was a man, Mark Fay, who provided strong leadership for the biology program for the next thirty years.

As the faculty changed during the postwar years, it struggled to find its collective voice. Traditional groups continued to play an important role. The Association of Wisconsin State Teachers College Faculties brought together all teachers in the system for a biennial meeting (which was in Eau Claire in 1944) with presentations by administrators, adoption of recommendations to the regents, and conferences among subject-matter specialists. John Schneider was a leader in this organization at the state level before World War II, Kjer and Fay were active on the campus level after the war, and Cochrane provided leadership for the state organization during the 1950s. Davies also urged his faculty to join the Wisconsin Education Association and participate in the annual meeting of the Northwest Education Association, which always met in Eau Claire; beginning in 1953, Wahlstrom was a member of the association's executive board.

In addition, as labor union membership swelled in postwar America (reaching about 35 percent of the labor force by the mid-1950s), the American Federation of Teachers (AFT) organized a chapter at Eau Claire State in 1946, which by its affiliation with the American Federation of Labor connected the campus to a different component of the community than did Davies's efforts with the Rotary and chamber of commerce. Although an early member recalled, "I don't think that it was looked upon with as much favor by President Davies . . . as was AWSCF," about one-third of the faculty belonged to it by the mid-1950s. When Davies spoke to the union group in September 1949, he carefully focused his remarks on advocating for more research on working-class youth attending college and did not discuss issues of teachers' rights, wages, and working conditions or their role in college governance. The presence of the union, he feared, made the college seem like a high school, exactly the impression he did not want the NCA to get.

Finally, largely through the efforts of Hilda Oxby, a chapter of the American Association of University Professors was established at Eau Claire State in 1946. Smaller in membership (thirty-five individuals in 1952) than the AFT chapter, this group focused on protecting the academic freedom of the faculty and connected the campus to the professoriate at major colleges and universities around the country.

Davies believed in academic freedom for his faculty. For instance, in 1948 he did not interfere when several faculty members, including Schneider, Wallin, and Kolka, organized campus support for the controversial presidential campaign of Henry Wallace, who was endorsed by the Communist Party. Furthermore, in response to a demand in 1949 from the American Legion to ban a speaker from an upcoming campus conference, Davies asserted that membership in a group "which eventually came under Communistic influence" should not be a disqualification and the president pointedly denounced political "witch hunting."

While respecting his faculty members' right to form their own political views, Davies did not allow them to act in ways that seemed openly critical Eau Claire State or its leadership. Enforcing this position led Davies into conflict with English teacher Robert Brigham, which resulted in the most serious compromise of academic freedom in the history of the college. Brigham had a PhD from the University of Missouri and came to Eau Claire State in 1948 from the Illinois State University, where he earned a favorable recommendation from Bjarne Ullsvik, a former mathematics teacher at Eau Claire. Davies envisioned him as head of the English Department and was not disappointed by his performance of teaching and service duties and his publication of poetry.

Brigham, however, was also an ardent unionist, and in the fall of 1949 he was elected vice president of the Wisconsin Federation of Teachers. In a guest column in the *Spectator*, he denounced teachers who "in their desire to be 'respected' or 'professional' often disguise themselves as Elks, Chamber of Commercities, or real estate salesmen" who "shun action, mental or otherwise." He asserted the "company unions which they form to keep telling each other they are professional fail to make them teachers." (That the *Spectator* would publish such a piece showed the greater freedom it exercised after Hench became its faculty advisor.) Davies was further bothered by Brigham's remarks at public meetings, including one on labor-management relations that was attended by Regent McIntyre.

Davies terminated Brigham's employment at Eau Claire State at the end of the fall 1950 semester, as was his legal right. He told Brigham this was due to his "lack of mature judgment," not his politics. Privately, the president explained his decision to the regents on the grounds of Brigham's *Spectator* column, his criticism in class of the Reserve Officers Training Corps, and a fear he would not "keep still" if allowed to gain the protection of tenure. Haas later admitted that, in addition, "the more conservative elements in the community wondered about this radical." Several of his colleagues, including Schneider and Wallin, came to Brigham's defense; students and community members supported him; and Brigham himself groveled to Davies by admitting "bad judgment" and difficulty in communicating his ideas clearly. Davies, sensing a better attitude in Brigham and fearful of censure by the American Association of Colleges for Teacher Education for a lack of sufficient notice of the termination, reconsidered his decision. McPhee, however (showing where authority now ultimately resided), firmly insisted the course of Brigham's elimination continue. The regents formally denied Brigham's appeal in January 1951, without making public any justifications. Although a "citizens committee" which supported Brigham made public Davies's temporary "change of mind" regarding the termination, in the end the president steadfastly stood by his decision to dismiss. Haas "was not that concerned" about the incident but admitted, "It may have shaken a few faculty members."

Campus Improvements

While waiting to receive the go-ahead for the construction of a new building, Davies accomplished a few important improvements to the campus physical plant. With the assistance of bridge financing provided by three Eau Claire businessmen, the president was able to use some of the 1945 state building appropriation to purchase the Dulany property at the corner of State Street and Garfield Avenue, which Schofield had eyed before the war (chapter two). The college remodeled this elegant Queen Anne-style home (1909) into a dormitory for sixty-two women, which opened in January 1947. The total cost to the state was around $150,000 (over $1.5 million in 2016). The building's basement and first-floor rooms, which retained features from its period as a private residence, provided both a lounge for residents and space in which college and community organizations could meet. For Laura Sutherland, Memorial Hall "was a dream come true for the college."

The college also acquired property for future expansion. Early in 1947 Ralph Owen, son of lumberman John S. Owen who had offered an alternative site for Eau Claire Normal in 1910 (chapter one), sold the college twenty-one acres at the top of the bluff south of campus extending to US Highway 12. The price was a reasonable $5,000. Putnam Park, which Henry C. Putnam donated to the City of Eau Claire in 1909 as a nature preserve, separated this property from the original campus, but Putnam's heirs (who conveniently included Director McPhee's wife) agreed to an informal easement which allowed the

Memorial Hall

Originally the residence of lumber baron Daniel Dulany, this home was at the northwest corner of State Street and Garfield Avenue. After its purchase in 1946 as the college's first residence hall, the third story was added.

college access across the park to the top of the bluff. Davies envisioned a residence hall, field house, and athletic fields on the new parcel, and a two-page sketch in the 1947 *Periscope* showed how they would look (the sketch also included a large "new college building" between Old Main and Park Avenue). The Owen purchase in effect committed the college to expanding on top of the bluff; unlike other colleges with campuses in increasingly congested urban areas—such as the Minnesota teachers colleges at Duluth and Mankato—Eau Claire State was not going to relocate to a suburban location.

The field house proposal came close to fruition. Pledges of financial support came from Eau Claire County and a local booster group, which envisioned it as the venue for high school athletic matches and other community events. In January 1948 the regents authorized the creation of a non-profit corporation to operate the field house and use revenues to repay construction costs borrowed from the state retirement board. Envisioning it as the basis of the new arena, Zorn oversaw the acquisition of a surplus World War II aircraft hanger and had it disassembled and shipped to Eau Claire. The final go-ahead for the project waited in the governor's office when money for new campus construction finally became available in 1949.

A Satisfying End to the Decade

After a decade of struggle, between 1950 and 1952 the college achieved three major goals—it constructed a second building, redefined itself as a liberal arts college, and secured regional accreditation.

Against strong opposition from the Wisconsin Chamber of Commerce, the legislature approved Governor Ronnebohm's entire $25 million building program for the 1949–51 biennium along with a 25 percent income tax surcharge to balance the budget. By far the largest project in the teachers college system was a $1.3 million "college building" for Eau Claire State. Lester Emans headed the committee which considered different proposals on how to spend this money and finally resolved on an interconnected set of buildings which faced Park and Garfield east of Old Main. The prominent Milwaukee architectural firm of Eschweiler and Eschweiler, which had just completed the Milwaukee Arena, prepared the plans. The complex included a 2,750-seat College Gym for physical education classes with a "king-sized" fifty by ninety-foot court for Zorn's basketball team; a classroom and office building for Emans's teacher education program; a four hundred-seat Little Theater for Kjer's Campus Players; and a Campus School with a state-of-the art observation deck for watching kindergarten through eighth grade classes through one-way mirrors. The front entrances to these buildings faced the street, not Old Main, and invited school children, theatergoers, and athletic spectators from the community onto the campus.

Ronnebohm broke ground for the complex in October 1950, the cornerstone was laid in September 1951, and the new buildings were fully ready for use in the fall of 1952. At the dedication ceremony on October 8, student body executive Charles Jenks accepted the building on behalf of the students and observed there had been "remarkable advancements" at Eau Claire State during his three years on campus.

One of these advancements was the formal initiation of liberal arts degree programs. At the end of its 1949 session, having failed to enact the consolidation of higher education proposed by Ronnebohm, the legislature authorized the teachers colleges to offer four-year liberal arts courses. The governor hesitated to sign this bill, which had been introduced by Senator Arthur Padrutt from Eau Claire. McPhee and Regent President William Anderson persuaded him to approve it provided the legislation would not take effect until 1951 and require no funding during 1949–51. Subsequently, on July 1, 1951, the Eau Claire State Teachers College became Eau Claire State College and James R. Mors, a French major, received the college's first bachelor of arts degree in January 1952.

By that time, the college had also accomplished its goal of receiving NCA recognition. In the fall of 1949 the college reapplied for accreditation and submitted detailed reports on a half-dozen topics prepared by faculty members—Davies recognized the application was a collective effort, telling students

Campus View, early 1950s

The Campus School (renamed Park School in 1973) and the Little Theater (renamed Kjer Theater in 1965) faced Park Avenue. The Education Building (renamed Brewer Hall in 1960) and the Physical Education Building (renamed several times, finally Zorn Arena in 1988) faced Garfield Avenue.

Observation Deck, Campus School

Pupils in the Campus School quickly adapted to the see-through mirrors above them and generally behaved un-self-consciously when observed by aspiring elementary education students from the college.

and faculty that "[w]e sink or swim together." When NCA examiners made their site visitation, they were not impressed by the administration's repeated efforts to blame every problem on Harvey Schofield, who had been dead and buried for almost a decade. They acknowledged, however, the college had corrected many of the deficiencies noted by Morgan in 1946 and they issued a report in January 1950 recommending accreditation of Eau Claire State.

The report noted favorably the college's efficient administration; the widespread membership by the faculty in professional organizations; good faculty salaries and, especially, retirement benefits (local remonstrances to the contrary); a strong curriculum in the elementary education program; "pleasant and well-maintained" student housing; an "excellent" student government (the student executive had yet to be impeached); and a "spirit of friendliness" on campus. There remained areas that needed improvement: the academic qualifications of the faculty were low (which meant limited depth in the advanced undergraduate program); the faculty teaching load was too great; the secondary education program needed more careful planning; and the student health service, financial aid, and the athletic staff were still inadequate. After receiving its evaluators' report, the NCA still hesitated to approve Eau Claire State because of the crowded facilities in Old Main, but by showing blueprints for the recently approved building complex Haas convinced the accreditors in March 1950 to vote favorably.

Everyone on campus greeted the news about accreditation with satisfaction. The administration cancelled classes for one hour and students enjoyed an "all-school snack" courtesy of Regent McIntyre. Davies and Haas had demonstrated to critics that amalgamation with the University of Wisconsin was not necessary for Eau Claire State to provide a high-quality, nationally recognized education for its students.

In January 1951 Davies summed up his ten years as president by singling out the NCA accreditation as the "greatest significant educational advancement of the decade." He also identified as important the college's contribution to the war effort; the addition of a dormitory; the development of "closer contact" with the community through the Area Committee; the introduction of organized student government; the expansion of the speech and music programs; the initiation of scholarship aid for students; the presence of foreign students on campus; the work towards developing a cooperative nursing program with Luther Hospital; the legislature's approval of liberal arts programs for all Wisconsin teachers colleges; the establishment of chapters of national honorary societies; and the construction of a second building.

Looking to the future, the president asserted, "The goal is a college of education that will rank as one of the best in the Middle West, with a wide enough offering to truly serve the needs of the college youth of Northwestern Wisconsin." The college's "Long Range Development Plan and Program 1952" foresaw an institution in 1962 with 1,500 students. Where Davies had overestimated post-World War II growth, he now dramatically underestimated the transformation the college would see between 1952 and 1964.

1952-64
The College Leonard Haas Built

Between 1952 and 1964 as dean of instruction and later as president, Leonard Haas shaped the transformation of the Wisconsin State College-Eau Claire.

He self-consciously made it a "liberal arts college" rather than a "teachers college." New programs began; academic standards became stronger; facilities expanded; enrollments swelled; students became more engaged with the college; a better-educated faculty took on new responsibilities; student self-government matured; the administration became more elaborate; and the campus community proudly shared a sense of self-accomplishment, although not without expressing some self-doubts. Haas navigated the college during these years through a national context of burgeoning prosperity tempered by a Cold War fear of communism; a state context of competitive scrabbling among institutions to overcome deferred needs in higher education; and a local context in which community members welcomed the benefits and prestige provided by the transformed college, but worried about what its impact might be on them. Ironically, in the mid-1960s, just as Haas could see the blossoming of his liberal arts college, the institution would have to transform itself into something different—a multi-purpose regional university.

Growth in Enrollment and Expansion of Program

The 1952 long-range plan (chapter four) underestimated the 1962 enrollment at Eau Claire State by almost 70 percent: it was actually 2,500 instead of the predicted 1,500. Already in 1963, *before* the baby boomers came to campus, 2,900 students enrolled—3.6 times more than in 1952. This pattern reflected the fact the annual number of high school graduates increased in Wisconsin during this period from 29,791 to 48,416. A growing proportion of these graduates (35 percent by 1962), buoyed by postwar optimism and a widely shared economic growth, continued on to college. Throughout the entire state college system, enrollment swelled even more than at Eau Claire—it was 3.8 times larger in 1963 than it had been in 1952, an increase which far exceeded the national rate of growth in college enrollment. "Numbers *are* necessary," Haas emphasized to the faculty, concerned about a possible dilution of the quality of the student body because "they enable us to do some of the things which we all want to do."

What was the profile of these students? Although the most local-centric of the state colleges, the geographical origins of Eau Claire State students gradually broadened during this period. In the fall of 1963, about 62 percent came from Eau Claire and adjacent counties, whereas about 80 percent had in 1950. Out-of-state enrollment had grown to about 3 percent of the total. Students' socio-economic backgrounds also broadened: by 1961, more than 80 percent worked to pay for at least part of their education, up from about 60 percent before World War II. The cost for them to attend Eau Claire State in 1964—fees and room and board—was about $770 (about $6,000 in 2016), an increase of around 10 percent in real terms since 1952. In the early 1960s, about 20 percent of students received scholarship aid, mostly Legislative Scholarships (chapter three), and 25 percent took out loans.

Most students continued to enroll in teacher education curricula, but the liberal arts programs formally introduced in 1951 were increasingly popular—about one-third of graduates in the early 1960s had liberal arts majors. Indeed, by 1960 Eau Claire State had the highest number and the largest proportion of liberal arts graduates of any of the state colleges. Among graduates with teacher education majors, about 40 percent were in secondary education, the second-highest proportion among the state colleges. Secondary education and liberal arts graduates were overwhelmingly male, so overall enrollment in the college continued to tilt masculine, more so than any at other state college. In the spring of 1963, over 55 percent of students were men.

With this gender ratio in mind the local newspaper pointed out, "Dating odds at Wisconsin State College continue to favor women." During the postwar decades, the personal quest for security in a world overhung by the threat of nuclear war and the memory of the economic privations of the Great Depression encouraged dating customs to shift from "playing the field" to finding a "steady." As divorce rates fell, marriage seemed to be an even steadier form of security—the median age at first marriage dropped dramatically in the United States during the 1950s to less than twenty for women. Correspondingly, the percentage of college students nationwide who were wed increased. At Eau Claire State it was 12 percent by 1960, and 40 percent of the graduating class of 1959 were already married.

By 1964 students had a greater choice of academic programs than they had in 1952. The 1964 *Catalog* identified twenty liberal arts majors. In 1959 the college also added a minor in philosophy and, with pre-theology students in mind, became the first state college to offer Greek. In 1962, Haas reported that in the previous four years there had been a half-dozen graduates whose education had "served them well" for study in Lutheran seminaries.

Teacher education programs also expanded. "Outside of agriculture, home economics and industrial arts," Haas told the *Milwaukee Journal*, "we believe all the colleges should be training teachers for all other fields." He later admitted, "[U]nder the umbrella of economics we taught commercial subjects." Economics professor Albert Sweester got national recognition for Eau Claire State in 1957 by self-publishing a six-hundred-page textbook on commercial banking, *Financing Goods*. Marshalling support from the Area Committee (chapter four), President Davies overcame objections from the established program at Whitewater State and in 1958 got the regents to approve a major in business education. Additionally in 1959, instruction in special education began with the approval of a program for teachers of the "mentally handicapped," the first in the state. Effective in 1959, art also became both a liberal arts and a teaching major. In 1962, instruction started in "speech correction" and the regents authorized a major in February 1963, which was first outlined in the 1964 *Catalog*.

The college also initiated majors in fields other than liberal arts and teacher education. Beginning in 1955 it offered a four-year BS degree program in medical technology, which included a one-year hospital internship. By the spring of 1963, almost one hundred students enrolled in this popular program. Building on the business education program, the college introduced a major in business administration in 1961. Eau Claire State also provided one year of academic instruction for students at Luther Hospital School of Nursing, and President Davies wanted to make this cooperative effort into a degree-granting program.

General Education and the 1959 Curriculum

Leonard Haas believed the intellectual foundation of all of these academic programs was the liberal arts. "[L]iberal Education should be at the base of the whole educational program," Haas emphasized in his initial address as president to the faculty in 1960. As part of his responsibilities as a member of the Board of College Education of the American Lutheran Church during the 1950s, he visited church-related liberal arts colleges around the country. He was deeply impressed by personalized instruction aimed at developing knowledgeable and articulate graduates who would become civic leaders, which he observed at institutions such as St. Olaf College in Minnesota (which eventually awarded him an honorary doctorate). As much as could be possible in a public institution, Haas wanted Eau Claire State to resemble these colleges.

Eau Claire State's efforts to define what should be foundational learning for its students also took place within a national discussion during the 1950s about "general education" or "liberal education." Even before World War II several high-profile general education programs had reacted against the "elective system" of broad student choice in course selection which dominated major universities and liberal arts colleges in the first third of the twentieth century. At the University of Chicago, for instance, President Robert Hutchins espoused a "core curriculum" for all students based on "great books" designed to "cultivate the intellect" of individuals. Also influential was the 1947 report by President Harry S. Truman's Commission on Higher Education, *Higher Education for American Democracy*, which differed from the Chicago model by emphasizing the *social* utility of general education. In New Deal-like fashion it championed expanded higher education as a force for international peace, responsible citizenship and family life, and healthy "social adjustment" by individuals. Regarding general education, it denounced a focus on "eternal truths" and argued that colleges should transmit a "common cultural heritage" not by a uniform curriculum but by a "consistency of aim," i.e., the "service of democracy."

General Education in a Free Society—the title of a 1945 proposal, which proved to be more influential than that of the presidential commission—suggested a somewhat different focus. The Harvard faculty members who wrote what came to be known as the *Redbook* wanted colleges to produce "responsible" citizens who could bear the burdens of the international struggle between democracy and totalitarianism. In order to meet this goal, college curricula needed to provide a "common ground" for all students. The report proposed students take six yearlong courses especially designed for "general education," including a common course in humanities and a common course in social science. As general education was implemented at Harvard, however, students were allowed to choose from among increasingly numerous course alternatives to meet categorical requirements in humanities, social science, and math/science.

As Haas and the faculty put together the curriculum at Eau Claire State during the 1950s, they incorporated parts of these national trends and also included unique local features. A new statement of purpose appearing in the 1958 *Catalog* in some ways would have pleased the Truman commission. It promised to provide students an "appreciation of democracy" and a "well-rounded personality," in addition to "academic preparation" in a subject area. However, it also promised students a "liberal education." To achieve this goal, during the 1950s Eau Claire State students could meet part of their general education requirement by taking Humanities 50: Art, Literature, and Music, an interdisciplinary course in the spirit of the Harvard *Redbook* taught by foreign language professor Eldon McMullen.

Haas blamed the eventual demise of Humanities 50 on an inability to recruit other broadly educated faculty to teach it, but his own thinking encouraged electives rather than core courses as the way to meet general education requirements. "There should be no stereotyped straitjacket into which all are poured," he told a statewide teacher education conference in 1961, "but a program provided which is tailored to the needs of the individual," rather than the general needs of society.

Haas's thinking underlaid the curriculum adopted by the faculty in 1959, which codified practices developed during the previous decade and basically remained in place until 1972. For "general education," students had a wide choice to pick courses to meet the requirements of three broad categories—science and mathematics, humanities, and social science. These requirements were essentially the same for liberal arts, teaching, and medical technology students. More credits were required in science/math for the BS than for the BA; fewer were required in humanities. Both required fifteen credits in social science, including six in history. There were also freshman composition and physical education requirements for all students. A final requirement was distinctive to Eau Claire State—three credits in philosophy (or in the history and philosophy of education for teaching majors). The 1959 curriculum omitted any foreign language requirement, which had previously existed for BA students.

The 1959 curriculum continued the requirement of 128 credits for graduation. It also set standard majors at thirty-six credits, comprehensive majors at sixty credits, and minors at twenty-four credits.

With sixty credits required in general education and physical education, it was feasible for liberal arts students to graduate in four years, but it was more difficult for education majors. The college told secondary education majors (there were now fifteen programs from which to choose), who had to take twenty-five credits of professional course work, that they "will need to realistically face the fact that summer session attendance or even an additional semester may be required" for graduation. Similarly, music professor Leo Christy's annotation in his copy of the 1960 *Catalog* (now in the university archives) shows that in practice elementary education majors needed to take 135 credits.

Faculty Growth in Mid-century

Presidents Davies and Haas worked strenuously to hire additional faculty to teach the growing number of students and provide expertise for the expanding programs at Eau Claire State. The faculty grew in size from about sixty-five in 1951 to about 170 in 1963, 55 percent of whom had come to Eau Claire in the previous four years. Overall their academic qualifications were stronger—37 percent had doctorates by 1963—which enabled them to teach the advanced courses needed in the college's new majors and specialized programs. Over 80 percent of the faculty in 1963 were men (while 75 percent of emeriti faculty were women). Nationally, women with PhDs were becoming less common—ten times more men than women received doctorates in 1955, compared to only about six times as many in 1940. During a search in 1954, Davies learned that getting a PhD "is quite an undertaking for a woman who at any time has a possibility of becoming married and leaving the profession to be a homemaker." Perhaps aware of the growing gender imbalance within his faculty, for some positions Davies specifically required women.

Hiring new faculty continued to be the president's responsibility. After reviewing all applications for a position, Davies would usually consult with the faculty member with whom he was working to "build up" a discipline. He would then invite to campus the most promising candidate—ideally, someone with a PhD or close to receiving it. On campus, the candidate received close scrutiny from the administration. "We would meet trains that came in here at two o'clock in the morning to meet the applicants," Hass recalled, "take them to our homes, put them to bed, have breakfast ready for them in the morning."

By the early 1960s some department heads began to take on the responsibility for recruiting and interviewing. For instance, after his appointment as chair of the English Department in late 1961, Thomas Barnhart, who "was well known nationally" according to a colleague, recruited extensively at the Modern Language Association meeting during the last week of December. On his recommendation, Haas—now president—began making job offers at the beginning of January. Several persons declined before Haas and Barnhart were able to staff the English Department. "[W]e really had to scramble with the faculty" because of the strong job market for academics in the early 1960s, a department member recalled. That only three of the seven new appointees to the English faculty in 1963 had high school teaching experience was an indication the background of the Eau Clare State faculty was becoming more academic.

Administrators also worked hard to *retain* the faculty they recruited. They lobbied incessantly with the public and with legislators for better salaries. "We are finding it increasingly difficult to secure able members of the faculty at the present salary base," Haas told Director McPhee in 1962 in support of his request for 10 percent salary increases in each year of the 1963–65 biennium. Even the fiscally conservative local newspaper endorsed better pay for teaching staff. Among the faculty, history chair William Cochrane, in particular, joined in these efforts as a leader of the statewide Association of Wisconsin State College Faculties (AWSCF). Comparative data from the American Association of Colleges of Teacher Education (AACTE) actually showed salaries at Eau Claire State were competitive compared to those at teachers colleges, but there were other institutions that paid better and successfully lured away professors. Sixteen of the thirty-eight faculty members who left Eau Claire State between 1955 and 1960 were called to better-paying positions. A significant back-door salary improvement did come to all faculty in the state college system in 1956 when summer session teaching—which was sought by almost everyone—began to earn additional pay rather than be part of the regular assignment. Furthermore, in addition to participating in the state retirement system, beginning in 1958 faculty members earned Social Security benefits and in 1959 joined the newly organized State Health Plan, paying half the premium.

Another problem, repeatedly emphasized by the AACTE and the North Central Association in their accreditation reports, was the faculty assignment of a five-course teaching load. As Cochrane pointed out to legislators in 1961 in a vain effort to secure a reduction, this policy hindered faculty recruitment and resulted in "factory-method teaching." As past president, Cochrane attended the 1964 meeting in Eau Claire of the delegate assembly of the AWSCF that formally asked the regents to "consider" a maximum teaching load of eleven to thirteen credits per semester.

Davies and Haas also mandated some departures: eight faculty members were "released" during the 1955–60 time period. If the faculty member did not have, or was not making progress toward obtaining a PhD and was at best only an average teacher, the administration did not want him or her to remain more than four years and earn tenure. In the early 1960s, the president and one or two administrations made these decisions at a series of meetings during the Christmas recess without input from the faculty.

As at the other state colleges, in 1954 the Eau Claire State faculty was ranked into four categories from "instructor" to full "professor." The cohesiveness that came from everyone being a "teacher" was now lost, and some faculty members resented the inferior ranks into which they were placed. Eau Claire State now resembled more closely other collegiate institutions. For Davies and Haas, though, recruiting new faculty direct from graduate programs now became more complicated because of the regents' requirement that four years of teaching experience was needed for the assistant professor rank.

While retaining ultimate authority, Davies continued the practice he began in the 1940s (chapter four) of involving the faculty in decision making. Regarding athletics the 1953 Statement of Policies by the Wisconsin Intercollegiate Athletic Conference said the faculty had the same power regarding athletics that it had "in other areas of the institution's educational policies" and all coaches should be "full-time faculty" with "regular teaching duties." In practice, faculty athletic representatives scrimmaged with athletic directors and the college presidents about issues of scheduling, athletic scholarships, and academic eligibility for athletes. Davies took the position that as the state colleges expanded, the presidents should recognize they could no longer directly supervise activities such as athletics and should instead defer to the faculty representatives—such as chemist Floyd Krause from Eau Claire—to set policies.

Despite its growing size and increasing responsibilities, the faculty remained "close-knit" into the early 1960s, according to Arnold Bakken, who taught zoology beginning in 1953. In addition to the regular monthly meetings of the entire faculty, the campus chapters of the American Association of University Professors and the American Federation of Teachers brought colleagues together from different disciplines. These monthly meetings not only discussed occupational-related issues, but also heard presentations on topics of general interest. At the February 1956 meeting of the AAUP, for example, English professor Alan Lehman spoke about textual and semantic issues in translations of the New Testament. The wives of faculty members also met regularly through the Faculty Dames association. "It was very rare that any wife would miss one of those meetings," Haas later emphasized. His wife, Dorellen, played a prominent role in this organization and was its chair for the 1952–53 year.

The Haases also encouraged sociability among the faculty by regularly entertaining all of them in their home. "[I]t helps people understand each other," Dorellen Haas explained, "if they get away from an impersonal setting into a home setting and sit down together and enjoy some fellowship." Neighborliness aided this social cohesion. In 1955 two-thirds of the faculty lived in the Third Ward neighborhood adjacent to the college campus. In the late 1950s, Davies, Haas, Lester Emans, and Earl Kjer built homes next to one another on the south side of the 100 block of Roosevelt Avenue, across the street from the college, with rear lawns sweeping back across Little Niagara Creek to Putnam Park. With faculty and administrations living so close by, "everything happened around our dining room table," Delpha Davies explained.

Aerial View of Campus, c. 1955-56

At the lower left are the four homes built on Roosevelt Avenue in the early 1950s by President Davies and other faculty members. By the mid-50s, increasing automobile use necessitated the construction of a large parking lot where Schneider Hall stands in 2016. "Temporary" World War II-era buildings are still evident in front of Old Main. This photograph also shows the campus lawn and the Council Oak to the south of the new Women's Dormitory. Putnam Park appears as a dense barrier between the college and the open land—at the top of the bluff in the upper left of the photograph—that it did not yet own.

Leonard Haas provided a model for faculty involvement in community affairs by serving on the Eau Claire City Council. In these roles, faculty members often provided counterweights to socially conservative attitudes in the community. For instance, at a heavily attended public meeting in 1953 Davies and several faculty members spoke against a proposed board of review which could ban publications from sale at newsstands in Eau Claire. "Let them go to Chippewa" Falls for graphic comic books, shouted a supporter of the proposal from the audience, apparently referring to the Gomorrah of the Chippewa Valley. The leading advocate for the board of review was the chair of a student Committee for Better Entertainment, who was also a member of the college's debate team. But the administration also had to shield students from attacks by community members. Letters of protest bombarded Haas about the 1962 issue of the *Tatler* [sic], the student literary publication. The president admitted he was "revolted" by its contents but emphasized, "The exercise of undue restraint and censorship often defeat the purpose of their use."

Their heavy teaching load limited the time faculty members could commit to other professional activities. Their eagerness to take on overload and extension teaching responsibilities, towards which the accrediting agencies repeatedly cast a critical eye, cut further into time available for public service or scholarship. The administration also kept the focus of the faculty on teaching: an applicant who seemingly expressed excessive interest in working on his own scholarship, even though he offered to accept a reduced salary, had his on-campus interview cancelled. In response to a question from the National Academy of Sciences in 1960, Haas explained, "The place of research has not been recognized in the load of the faculty members."

Eau Claire State College and the City Council

This photograph probably dates to 1963, when Charles Hornback was initially elected to the council and when Richard Hibbard, who was first elected in 1957, took over from David Donnellan, a prominent real estate broker, as council president. During this period, other council members from the college included Leonard Haas (1949-57), William D. McIntyre (1949-52), and history professor Edward Blackorby (1966-68). Shown left to right are Hibbard, Donnellan, and Hornback.

Slowly, however, the faculty worked to make an impact beyond their classrooms. In 1953 three faculty members—Frank Yuhas, the principal of the Campus School; Mary Rowe, one of his teachers; and Louis Slock, his predecessor who had become head of placement and extension programs—wrote a formal survey and made recommendations that were implemented regarding the elementary education program in the Stanley public schools. The introduction of new programs also provided opportunities for faculty to work with the community. As the business administration program developed, in 1964 economics professor Fred Armstrong proposed Eau Claire State develop a partially self-supporting "contract research center" to do economic development planning, specifically for a shopping mall in Eau Claire.

In addition to their other responsibilities, some newly appointed faculty members, in particular, began to pursue active research programs. An example was Donald Warner, who came to Eau Claire State in 1956 after a decade of teaching at Macalester College. Warner won the Frederick Jackson Turner Award in 1959 from the Mississippi Valley Historical Association, the principal scholarly organization of historians of American history, for his book *The Idea of Continental Union*. There was a burst of publications from the history department in the early 1960s, including books by Edward Blackorby and William Kaldis. Two historians, Jack Thomas and William Rodemann, were among the seven Eau Claire faculty members who received grants from McPhee's office to support their research in 1963. These awards were part of a new program to encourage scholarship among state college faculty. (Only one other college in the system received more such grants than did Eau Claire.) By the early 1960s, the history department, along with the biology department, was completely staffed by faculty with PhDs.

The results of faculty research sometimes strained relations with the business community. For instance, in the summer of 1960 John Gerberich, head of the medical technology program, directed a faculty-student research project in conjunction with Eau Claire's City-County Health Board. The research group's finding of E-coli contamination in commercially marketed cottage cheese received statewide publicity. After the local health board consequently moved to regulate sales of cottage cheese, and the Wisconsin Board of Health became interested in adopting regulations, the Intra-State Milk Commission angrily attacked the report as misleading and damaging to the dairy industry. Haas retreated in response, apologizing for the "unauthorized" release of the report and promising that further reports will only "be released through responsible channels" (i.e., with his approval). As the character of Eau Claire State changed, the principle of the faculty's right to uncensored publication of their research findings still had to be defined.

Creating a More Elaborate Administration

As dedicated as he was to developing Eau Claire State into a strong liberal arts college, there was a limit to Haas's energies. "I can't imagine today," he said in 1985, "how I did it to tell you the truth. It goes beyond me." As the college rapidly grew, President Davies gradually added other administrators to his staff. Just as the faculty became more specialized, Eau Claire State administrators began to take on specific responsibilities.

In the late 1950s, Richard Hibbard, a political science faculty member, took over from Haas the responsibility for admissions and, later, the registrar's duties. Hibbard was an Eau Claire State graduate who earned a PhD from Northwestern University and taught in Greece and at Muhlenberg College before World War II. During the war he worked for the Office of Strategic Services (OSS), the wartime espionage and intelligence agency, and later as head of the Bureau of Representation in the State Department. He was eager to return to Eau Claire after the war to be with his wife's family, and Davies found a position for him in the veterans' counselling office. Hibbard later returned to the clandestine service for a two-year assignment as a Middle East analyst with the Central Intelligence Agency, the successor to the OSS, but he found academic work preferable. Davies and Haas were pleased to have him return to Eau Claire in 1955 and become their key person in building the political science department. Highly efficient as an administrator, deeply dedicated to the college, an advocate of higher academic standards, and "excellent with students" according to Davies's wife, Hibbard was Haas's choice to succeed him as dean of instruction when Haas become president in the fall of 1959.

Not wishing to seem to slight teacher education, Haas also began his administration by adding the title of dean of administration to Lester Emans's position as director of teacher education and placement. As a result Emans took on the responsibility for alumni relations and, because of his successful work on the Campus School complex (chapter four), the planning and management of campus construction. At the same time, Haas lightened Hibbard's duties by hiring James Dean, from Berea College in Kentucky, as registrar. In the spring of 1960, Haas also made personnel changes in student affairs. As part of a career change, Stella Pedersen stepped down as dean of students. Haas filled Pedersen's dean of women duties with an outsider to Eau Claire, Margaret Nolte, who had been assistant dean at Ohio Wesleyan. He left the dean of students part of Pedersen's position in hiatus for a year. Then in the spring of 1961, not satisfied with the performance of newcomer Nolte, Haas turned inside and appointed psychology professor James Benning, an Eau Claire State graduate who had headed testing services since 1959, as dean of students. Benning had the overall responsibility for student welfare and discipline, as well as orientation programs, financial aid, class attendance, student organizations, and counseling and testing services.

Haas completed his new administrative structure for the college during 1963–64. Hibbard became vice president for academic affairs and headed three newly organized schools: Arts and Sciences, Education, and Graduate Studies. Emans remained as dean of the latter two schools, while most of his other administrative duties went to Lester Hunt, who came to Eau Claire in the fall of 1963 as vice president for business affairs and who worked closely with Haas on budget and physical plant matters. Ormsby Harry, from Shepherd College, West Virginia, succeeded Benning and became vice president for student affairs. Reporting to him was John Kearney, newly appointed as director of admissions. Slock continued as director of extension and took on the duties of secretary of the alumni association; Willis Zorn remained as director of athletics; and Haas by now had a special assistant, William Peters, who handled public relations (in an innovative arrangement, 25 percent of Peters's salary was paid by the newly organized Eau Claire State College Foundation). In all, where Harvey Schofield and three part-time faculty members had provided the administration for a college of 735 students in 1939, a quarter century later there were fourteen administrators (and more than fifty classified staff) for a college of 3,573 students.

The administrative reorganization of the college included an increasingly important role for department chairs. Paralleling the demise of the interdisciplinary Humanities 50 course, in the spring of 1957 Davies eliminated the divisions with elected heads—five by 1957—into which departments had been grouped for the previous decade. In their place he gave front-line responsibility for supervising the faculty to appointed department chairs. Lawrence Wahlstrom in his capacity as president of AFT local 917 strenuously protested the change, but Haas and Davies felt conditions in some departments were "chaotic" and firmer leadership was necessary. Haas argued publically the change would eliminate "electing a poorly qualified faculty member as chairman" and would help to attract new faculty by offering them the possibility of a "permanent chairmanship." He told Davies, "I don't believe we should hesitate to pay top salaries for a few positions of leadership in the academic areas where needed." When he became president, Haas continued the practice begun by Davies in the mid-1940s of building academic programs around ambitious individuals with strong administrative skills.

Women's Dormitory, 1955

The first residence hall built by the college was renamed Katherine Thomas Hall in 1960. Thomas, a member of the original faculty, taught in the Campus School for thirty years, the last two of which she was principal.

Building a Bigger Campus

The completion of the Campus School complex in 1952 began two decades of frenzied building construction on the Eau Claire campus. Davies, and later Haas, spent much of their time in the 1950s and 1960s bent over architectural drawings and building plans. In 1954 Davies outlined to McPhee what buildings would be needed for the next twenty years: more residence halls, a student union, a library, a fine arts building, another classroom building, and renovations to the existing buildings (including adding a pool to the arena).

Their first priority was residence halls. Haas's vision of a liberal arts college was that of a residential community, where closely supervised extracurricular life could flourish. The administration also felt the limited housing available on campus in the early 1950s discouraged students from enrolling at Eau Claire State. The board of regents addressed these needs in 1953 by using a newly authorized financing mechanism to approve construction of a dormitory to the west of Old Main for 138 women. It set up the Wisconsin State College Building Corporation, of which the regents were the directors, to borrow money for the construction of non-academic buildings and to pay off the loans from revenues the structures generated. The still-unfinished Women's Dormitory opened in the fall of 1955; the $580,000 project (over $5 million in 2016) was completed in December. Its ground floor contained a spacious lounge facing south with a fine view of the "campus lawn," Little Niagara, the Council Oak, and the bluffs above them, which provided a more attractive space for campus and community social events than had been available previously in Old Main and Memorial Hall. Meanwhile, Memorial Hall became a male residence until a new building for 235 men, west of the Women's Dormitory at the edge of Putnam Park, opened in 1958.

Using the mechanism of the building corporation in the late 1950s all of the state colleges built student unions. At Eau Claire, the new $750,000 building authorized by the regents in 1956 replaced the makeshift arrangements that had existed since 1940 in Old Main and in the barracks on the campus

Students Picnicking on the Campus Lawn, early 1960s

The space between the newly constructed dorms and Little Niagara Creek, highlighted by the Council Oak, was a popular gathering place from the mid-50s to the mid-60s.

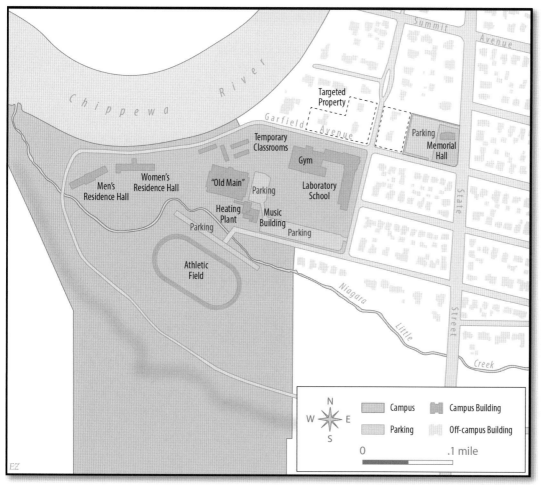

Map 5.1

THE COLLEGE LEONARD HAAS BUILT

lawn. Reflecting Haas's goal of having Eau Claire State resemble other colleges, the eighteen-person student-faculty Planning Committee ignored charges by the *Spectator* of extravagant travel expenses and visited other campuses to get ideas. The location they selected for the new building was south of Old Main, which required a relocation of Little Niagara, and an underground tunnel connected the new union to the original building. Groundbreaking was in November 1957 and the College Center was completed in time for Davies to host a graduation reception on June 4, 1959. It included a cafeteria (which could be converted to a ballroom), snack bar, lounge, meeting rooms, and "a real honest to goodness college book store," according to Haas. At the insistence of Regent President McIntyre, the new center could not compete with off-campus businesses. Consequently, "sweatshirts and things like that" were "completely out" as items for sale in the bookstore.

College Center, c. 1959

The view is from the south before later additions altered the center's appearance.

By the time the College Center opened, construction had begun on the library, a $1,140,000 project built with state-appropriated funds. The library's collection of 63,000 books had long since outgrown the capacity of its room at the west end of the second floor of Old Main, which had even been cramped for study space when the enrollment in the college had been half what it was in 1959. The new building, connected to Old Main by a glass-walled walkway, doubled shelf space for books; provided

Terrace Lounge, College Center, 1959

The new College Center was furnished in what can be loosely labeled as a mid-century modern style. The furniture was smooth, bare, and rectangular. Lamps were mounted on floor-to-ceiling poles or ceiling tracks. The open staircase's railings and its clean, sweeping lines added to the room's geometric appearance. Natural light for the lounge came from large exterior windows as seen in the top photo.

separate reserve and main reading rooms; added a room for the curriculum library which had been in the Campus School, as well as additional classrooms; and provided more cutting-edge technology such as microfilm readers. Director McPhee returned to Eau Claire to give the principal address at its dedication on October 28, 1960, and pledged there would be no enrollment restrictions adopted in the state colleges that would "halt capable students in their race toward college graduation."

The successive moves during the 1950s by the Campus School, gymnasium, cafeteria, and library to new buildings freed up space in Old Main. In 1952 Davies moved his office and the college's business office from the second floor of Old Main into what had been kindergarten and first-grade classrooms on the east corridor of the first floor. Haas and Pedersen moved into adjacent offices around the corner from Davies on the north corridor in what had been the music classroom. To the west of them was Emans's office. Dean of Men Zorn was right across the hall, next to the admissions office when it became a separate unit. "We were much more convenient to the general public" than before, Haas explained, "If we're going to keep the kind of philosophy that we have, [we] should be very accessible," especially to students. When the college obtained its first computer, however, it had to be placed on the ground floor underneath the administrative suite—the weight of a mainframe machine in 1962 was too much for the floor beams of even a massively constructed building such as Old Main.

As more space became available in Old Main, academic departments also relocated. For example, the Biology Department, which had been located in two rooms at the northeast corner of the second floor, moved to the cafeteria's former space at the east end of the ground floor. Here the previous kitchen's tile floor, water piping, steam supply, and drainage were ideal for labs. Down the hall on the north side of building was the former boys' shower room, no longer needed when the College Gym replaced Old Main's gymnasium. This space was ideal for the turtles used in anatomy classes by professor Karl Shilts. "[T]hey lived very happily in the bottom of that shower," recalled department chair Mark Fay.

The college still needed more buildings, however. The biology faculty argued that relocation to makeshift facilities could only be temporary. Davies agreed, and a new science building headed his list of campus needs. Second on the list was Haas's great goal: a fine arts center. During the 1950s the music program had to make due in noisy quarters on the second floor above the small heating plant building which was attached to the northeast corner of Old Main by an underground tunnel. No doubt influenced by his observations of St. Olaf College's strong music program, Haas saw music as central to liberal arts education, and he envisioned a fine arts center for Eau Claire State with an auditorium seating two thousand or more concertgoers from the community as well as the campus. Planning also had to take into account that the new library and student center had been designed for a campus of 2,500 students and needed additions within a few years of opening.

Chemistry Lab, mid-1950s

The need for new laboratory equipment and space is evident from this photograph.

The decade concluded with the expanded array of buildings on campus getting new names. With the approval of the regents, in the spring of 1960 Old Main became Schofield Hall, the Education Building became C. J. Brewer Hall, the College Center became the W. R. Davies College Center, the Women's Dormitory became Katherine Thomas Hall, and the Men's Dormitory became Emmet Horan Hall (it would later be redesignated Katherine Putnam Hall). The buildings may have been new or remodeled, but they kept alive the spirit of the faculty members, regents, and administrators who had led the college through its first forty-five years.

A Larger Campus Footprint

Before there could be additional construction, more land was needed. In the late 1950s and early 1960s Eau Claire State added significant acreage on both the original ("lower") campus and on the "upper" campus, where it had begun to acquire land in the late 1940s (chapter four). The acquisition of additional space, however, inflamed relations with the community and as enrollments spiraled ahead of projections still left the campus severely confined.

Davies jumped at an opportunity in 1957 to acquire Putnam Park, a two hundred-acre tract given to the City of Eau Claire as a nature preserve in 1909 by lumberman Henry C. Putnam, whose heirs had become dissatisfied with the city's failure to maintain it. The college had gained access across the park in 1948 for a road and stairway to link the upper and lower campuses, and in 1954 it had picked up two acres from the park at the base of the bluff where the Men's Dormitory was eventually built. With possession of the entire park, the college could block up its landholdings and, Haas envisioned, develop an arboretum similar to the University of Wisconsin's in Madison. Furthermore, the press reported when the regents approved the transfer from the city to the college that "the board hopes to use the land for its building program."

In response to the building proposal, the Citizens Committee for Keeping Our Parks mounted opposition to the transfer. A deep suspicion of the college's motives emerged in heated public debate during the first months of 1957. Opponents expressed numerous, although sometimes contradictory, arguments: the college did not need the land, the public would lose the access to untrammeled nature that Putnam had envisioned, the portion of the park that extended to US Highway 12 (West Clairemont Avenue) should be sold to private developers and put on the tax roll, building a road to the top of the bluff would waste the college's money, and the transfer amounted to an illegal "giveaway" of city property of which "every human soul" owns a share.

The college mobilized a strenuous response to its critics. It somewhat uneasily asserted it had an "acute need for more space" but "there are no plans to build on the park area," only to gain access to the upper campus. The college's plans mentioned two new dormitories on the upper campus, but it left vague whether they would be built in the park or on the land the college already owned. Actually, as Haas later admitted, "We had gone so far as to have all of the architectural work completed" for the new dorms "when we still did not own the land." With strong editorial support from the local newspaper, the college prevailed at a dramatic public hearing before the city council on February 12 (in which Council President Haas did not participate). Certainly reassuring to the influential property owners on the south side of Roosevelt Avenue, who had been among the critics of the transfer of the park, was the pledge at the meeting by McIntyre that there would be no construction "east of the present boundary of the college" (i.e., into their backyards). The college also promised to maintain public access to the park through Putnam Drive. Biology chair Fay soon developed printed guides and led nature walks in the park for community members.

Before the year was out, the college further expanded its presence at the top of the bluff. McIntyre reached a private agreement with local attorney Francis Wilcox, representing Sacred Heart Hospital, which was eager to relocate from its cramped location on Dewey Street overlooking downtown Eau Claire. The understanding was the regents would purchase—without a competing bid by Sacred Heart—about thirty-five acres extending southward from the bluff. The college would retain twenty-seven acres (the "Wilson Purchase") and resell the rest to Sacred Heart at the original purchase price. (The two already planned dormitories—what in 2016 are Horan and Governors Halls—which were quickly built at the edge of the bluff above the river on land that straddled the boundary of Putnam Park and the Wilson Purchase.) Although his arrangement with Wilcox was not made public, rumors circulated on campus about some sort of agreement by which McIntyre had sold out the interests of the college. Eau Claire State appeared to become hemmed in further when the Eau Claire Technical Institute and the State of Wisconsin, looking for a site for an office building, each purchased half of the forty-acre tract between the Wilson Purchase and West Clairemont Avenue.

Haas later concluded that the college Planning Committee, which he chaired, "probably yielded too easily" to McIntyre's willingness to concede space on the top of the bluff. To be fair, the future enrollment growth of the college was not evident to most people in 1957. McPhee said triumphantly after the Wilson Purchase that the college "had enough land to last for a hundred years." Furthermore, encouraging Sacred Heart to locate next to the campus enhanced the possibility of initiating a nursing program at the college. Hoped-for benefits from proximity to the technical school and the state office building did not immediately develop, but the college eventually obtained use of the northern part of the state building site, and Sacred Heart informally allowed the college to build a parking lot and outdoor recreation facilities on the northern edge of its plot.

Despite the benefits they gave to the college, Haas and his successors as chancellors had good reason to look wistfully at the hospital, school, and office building that secured prominent frontage on what became the principal east-west traffic artery in Eau Claire. The technical school also had the opportunity to expand onto adjoining property south of West Clairemont, which was still open land in 1959. (The college had to settle in 1967 for a non-contiguous thirty-eight-acre plot south of MacArthur Avenue which Haas envisioned as a site for a "coliseum" and married student housing, which in the twenty-first century is Bollinger Fields, used for intercollegiate and intramural athletics.)

Partly because of the limited amount of land it was able to acquire on upper campus, the college pressed to expand eastward from the lower campus. In the fall of 1962, by now anticipating an enrollment of 7,500 in a decade, the college's Long-range Planning Committee decided the "area north of Garfield Avenue and West of Memorial Hall [at the northwest corner of State and Garfield] should be declared an expansion area for the college." It recommended the regents buy properties in the area as they became available. Less than a week later the owner of 110 Garfield Avenue offered to sell his home—at 50 percent greater than its appraised value! (The Ecumenical Religious Center, rather than the college, eventually secured this property.)

The following year an opportunity emerged for the college to acquire (for over $600,000 in 2016 money) the two homes on the east side of Park behind Memorial Hall. When newspaper reports said the college planned a high-rise dormitory or a large academic building for the site, the neighbor across the street on Park immediately protested to Haas. She joined with other residents of the Third Ward, for whom Episcopalian Bishop William Norstick became the spokesperson, to object to the college's incipient expansion as wasteful of the taxpayers' money and threatening to the integrity of the neighborhood. Eventually, five hundred "taxpayers" signed a protest and sent it to the regents and 150 residents confronted Haas on March 12 at a meeting in the Little Theater. They suggested the college sell Memorial Hall and use the proceeds to buy land still available south of West Clairemont Avenue for future expansion. Haas calmed the waters by explaining, "The college has no plans in the foreseeable future for any further acquisition of property in the city of Eau Claire."

This town–gown clash ended in a standoff. The college never constructed any sort of building between State and Park, but quietly acquired the four properties at the southwest corner of Park and Garfield which eventually became the site for a classroom building. The wrecker's ball eliminated Memorial Hall, and a parking lot ultimately extended from State to Park, but stained-glass windows and wood trim from Memorial Hall were saved and helped to decorate a dining room in an expanded Davies Center. When the state architect suggested the college expand by acquisition of the properties on the south side of the 200 block of Roosevelt Avenue, Haas—appreciating the concerns that had been expressed in 1963 by neighbors in the Third Ward and aware of the high cost of buying these properties—disagreed, even as it meant further delays for his long-sought fine arts center.

Student Life in an Emergent Liberal Arts College

As Eau Claire State grew in the 1950s and early 1960s students chose to experience it in different ways. Some of their experiences helped to build the liberal arts college environment Leonard Haas wanted to see develop, others did not.

What Audiences Saw in the Little Theater

The 1965 *Periscope* said Earl Kjer's "immortality" existed in the memories audiences had of the sixty-six main stage shows by the Campus Players he directed between 1943 and 1964. As many as four thousand students and community members saw each production by the end of the Kjer era. These audiences attended shows that were examples of the well-crafted, entertaining, and usually uplifting works that made live theater-going a frequent and community-building experience for middle-class white Americans during the first half of the twentieth century.

All but three or four of the shows performed by the Campus Players during the Kjer era (including a few with directors other than Kjer) had been produced successfully on Broadway within the previous twenty years or so, and over 80 percent had become Hollywood films. Kjer kept the Campus Players closely in touch with this contemporary commercial theater by organizing annual theater-going trips to Chicago and, subsequently, New York. A few of the shows the Campus Players put on with this inspiration are largely forgotten—the comedy *Two Blind Mice* performed in 1951, for example, seems to have received little interest following its 150 performances in New York, starring Melwyn Douglas, and a national tour in 1949–50. A few others, such as the once-popular *Teahouse of the August Moon*, part of the Campus Players' schedule in 1957, became inappropriate to perform because of ethnic or gender sensitivities. Most of them, however, would be familiar to twenty-first-century theatergoers, at least through their film versions.

Audiences saw serious dramas such as *Joan of Lorraine*, *The Little Foxes*, *The Diary of Anne Frank*, *Inherit the Wind*, and *The Miracle Worker*, as well as lighter fare such as *I Remember Mama* and *Life With Father*. Kjer's roster also regularly included comedies such as *You Can't Take It With You*, *Tall Story*, and *Mrs. McThing* and thrillers such as *Night Must Fall* and *Witness for the Prosecution*. Beginning in 1959 with *The Boy Friend*, one of the Campus Players' three-to-five yearly productions was a musical. Theater classics also had a significant place on the schedule. The Campus Players put on works by Moliere (twice), Sheridan, Wilde, Shaw (three times), Ibsen, and Shakespeare (comedies *Twelfth Night*, *Comedy of Errors*, and *Merry Wives of Windsor*). The French avant-garde theater of the 1930s and 1940s was also well represented by stagings of multiple works by Jean Giraudoux and Jean Anouih.

Eau Claire audiences, however, did not see some dimensions of contemporary theater. Kjer steered clear of the postwar Theater of the Absurd, associated with playwrights such as Samuel Beckett and Eugene Ionesco. Casting considerations no doubt prevented staging plays that tackled the issue of race, such as Lorraine Hansberry's 1959 *Raisin in the Sun* (which the Campus Players saw in New York). Kjer's playbill also largely avoided the work of the most important postwar American playwrights—Arthur Miller, Tennessee Williams, and William Inge (President Davies's political views may have explained the exception, the 1955 production of Miller's *The Crucible*, an unsubtle and critical allegory of McCarthyism). Nor were there any examples of plays from the 1930s by Robert Sherwood, Maxwell Anderson, or Clifford Odets which had engaged Depression-era social and political issues. Perhaps most strikingly from the perspective of the twenty-first century, the Campus Players did not perform anything by Eugene O'Neill, either from among his 1920–35 work, which had already won him the Nobel Prize for Literature, or from his posthumously produced postwar work, such as *Long Day's Journey Into Night*, which only further enhanced his reputation.

Even during the Kjer era in Eau Claire, the American theater was changing. Its mass-entertainment function gave way to television. By the end of the 1950s, the American theater also was becoming less Broadway-centric and was experimenting with forms other than the well-constructed three-act play and the book musical with hummable songs. By the 1970s and 1980s the theater program at Eau Claire would reflect these changes. During the first two decades after World War II, however, Earl Kjer's selection of shows for the Campus Players reached a wide audience of students and community members by hewing to a format playing to an America that was confidant, eager to be entertained, and usually willing to overlook its problems.

Campus Player's Production of *The Madwoman of Chaillot*, 1963

Opportunities increased for students to participate in campus organizations—the 1964 *Periscope* identified about forty-five campus groups. "There were so many organizations . . . you could belong to," recalled Mary Friederich, a student from the 1950s. The largest was the Concert Choir with seventy voices directed by Caldwell Johnson, which took a ten-day tour of the eastern United States in 1964. Friederich, who met her husband in the choir, recalled an earlier tour to the west in which she participated, "It was supposed to be one railroad car for women and one for men, but it didn't end up that way." There were also seven intercollegiate sports teams for men in 1964. Wrestling had become a varsity sport in 1960 and the newly hired coach also directed an "all-school intramural wrestling tournament (females excepted)." Coach Jim Rice's football team had won the conference championship in the fall of 1963.

Nancy Blomlie, who graduated in the early 1960s, felt students in specific activities formed "cliques," such as the "artsie" group associated with the National Collegiate Players. Mary Jean Hazelton was part of that group and later recalled thoroughly enjoying its annual theater-going trip to New York. Similarly, athletes bonded with their teammates; football player Jerry Bersoth's strongest memory of his campus years was his team's victory over River Falls State in 1957. Students did not necessarily know much about what was happening on campus outside of their group. Bersoth admitted, "I knew who Dr. Haas was, but that was about it."

Greek life evolved from its foundations in the 1940s with the cautious blessing of President Davies, who had been a fraternity man as an undergraduate at Ripon College. By 1964 there were four social fraternities and four sororities on campus, with over three hundred members. The *Spectator* gave their activities prominent coverage and editorialized they were a counterweight on a campus becoming increasingly impersonal as it grew larger. "I cannot remember that we did a lot of good work," Friederich—a sister of Sigma Phi Kappa—recalled, "but we had fun . . . The social life at the [college] was great."

The major organized social events on campus during the 1950s were Homecoming, Winter Carnival, and Prom (for which the student government took over responsibility from the junior class). Students chose a queen for each event, and the social highlight was a dance. Homecoming and Winter Carnival also included parades, bonfires, and skits and games. Homecoming, in particular, was an occasion for pranks by students from the colleges involved, which sometimes got out of hand. Most spectacularly, in 1960 five Eau Claire football players were seriously injured when ten gallons of gasoline in milk cans, intended to be thrown from a pickup truck onto the Stout State College Homecoming bonfire, exploded prematurely. Sarah Hibbard, Dean Hibbard's daughter and one of the organizers of the 1961 Homecoming parade, later recalled it was difficult to get high school bands to participate because the college students had become so "naughty" at the event.

Snow Sculpture for Winter Carnival in Front of Schofield Hall, 1963

Homecoming Parade, 1962

The Homecoming parade continued to go through downtown Eau Claire throughout the 1970s.

For some students, informal social activities became the focus of their college years. Responding to complaints there was nothing to do on campus, especially on weekends when most students went home, Haas initiated a foreign film series; scheduled well-known guest speakers, especially in the Forum Series; arranged for the YMCA pool to be open to students on Sunday afternoons; booked classical music groups to perform; and arranged for free Saturday night movies. Many students, though, preferred informal alternatives of socializing and card playing in the Blugold Room on the ground floor of Old Main and later in the College Center. Popular in the evenings were the Hoot (designated by the *Spectator* as the "north campus") in the town of Hallie and other clubs outside the city of Eau Claire which served beer to eighteen to twenty year olds. Students also partied, away from the gaze of Dean Zorn, at Bull Frog Slough in the town of Seymour, in Carson Park, in Rod and Gun Park, and in Putnam Park at the junction of Little Niagara and the river. Mary Jean Hazelton recalled, "Little Niagara was well-strewn with [beer] bottles." Like other collegians around the country in the late 1950s, male and female residents of the new dorms at Eau Claire State engaged in water balloon fights, dunkings into Little Niagara, and panty raids. Zorn summoned the police to a break in and theft of "several pairs of panties" at Putnam Hall in the spring of 1964, but the *Daily Telegram* archly reported, "There is some question whether or not there was someone inside the dormitory aiding and abetting the raiders."

Bonfire at Homecoming, 1963

A similar event at Stout State College in 1960 was a near tragedy for the Eau Claire students who tried to throw gasoline on the bonfire. The cartons of Walter's beer bottles, a local Eau Claire product shown in this photograph, were responsible for problematic behavior at Homecoming.

In Between Classes at the Blugold Room

As Eau Claire State grew rapidly in the 1960s, the most popular part of the Davies Center was the Blugold Room, often shortened to "The Blugold," a site students claimed as their home on campus. The 1963 *Periscope* even coined a participle for hanging out at the Blugold: "Blugolding."

Sharon Tripp ('73) recalls the Blugold as "a big hangout for commuters." Kirk Ausman ('72), who lived at home while attending the university, remembers the Blugold as subdivided into different affinity groups that sat at different tables around the room: "There were Townie tables, there were tables for the Vets Club, there were fraternity tables . . . because we [Townies] didn't have a dorm to go to between classes, we would go to the Blugold."

The three groups Ausman identified were important at Eau Claire State in the 1960s. The self-described "Townies" were the students who enrolled at the university but chose to live at home. They were not the same as students who chose to live off campus after having experienced residence hall life. Townies made up about 35 percent of the student body in 1965–66, even as more residence hall rooms and off-campus housing became available (chapter six). However, during the mid-to-late 1960s, the Townies were noteworthy for their daily presence at the Blugold. The Vets Club was started in 1967 and had a mix of mostly men who had served in the armed forces, often in Vietnam, before coming to the university. At its peak, the Vets Club had more than two hundred members. One alumna recalled them as well integrated into campus and another said they were generally on the anti-war side of campus events. The fraternity (and sorority) tables at the Blugold functioned in some ways like those of the Townies, in that the Greek chapters did not have their own houses to retire to between classes.

With these and other groups looking for a place to hang out, it's no wonder the 1966 *Periscope* titled a section on student life, "Chairs were scarce at the Blugold," and then captioned a photo of the crowded room: "Time: 12 noon any day. Place: The Blugold. Wanted: one chair."

Students Eating in the Davies Center, early 1960s

Many other students experienced college life differently, especially those who were older than twenty-five, married, veterans, working, or living with their parents. To them college was a place to earn a career-enhancing degree, and they were less engaged with activities outside of the classroom. Don Gilbertson, a 1959 graduate, admitted he was "not one who got involved in campus activities."

Gay students had to stay in the closet at Eau Claire State during the 1950s and 1960s. Reflecting the dominant homophobic attitudes of the time, administrators did not want to be responsible for recommending gay graduates as teachers for the public schools. When they detected homosexual behavior they encouraged students to seek a medical cure. In order to learn the names of other gays on campus, they also tried to make them become informers. Same-sex behavior attracting notoriety resulted in expulsion.

A growing number of students with disabilities—nineteen in 1952 and sixty by 1960—enrolled at Eau Claire State, assisted by scholarships from the rehabilitation division of the Wisconsin Department of Vocational and Adult Education. Frank Huettner, who had been left a quadriplegic by a school bus accident, received widespread media attention when he attended the college for two years in the mid-1940s by using "teachaphone" technology before earning bachelor and law degrees at the University of Wisconsin. Sophomore Robert Southard became a quadriplegic as a result of a diving accident in 1954 at Big Falls, a popular spot for students on the Eau Claire River. After two years of rehabilitation, he returned to college using a wheelchair, became active in campus activities, and was elected student government executive for 1957–58. The day-to-day difficulties of these students became a bit easier when special education professor Ellyn Lauber, who joined the faculty in 1962, became their advocate.

The organized activities and informal social life of the college did not distract some students from primarily focusing on academics. For a portion of them, this was because their courses seemed demanding. "I have never felt so lost in my life," a freshman wrote to her parents a few weeks into the fall 1959 semester. Despite non-stop studying, she felt, "I just don't seem to learn anything." Similarly, pre-veterinary student George Gannon found himself underprepared for the freshman science courses on his schedule. Mathematics professor John Menard "saved me," he later acknowledged. He "understood what you were doing," Gannon explained, an opinion of Menard shared by many students in the 1950s. (But not by Davies: the president eventually told Menard, who wore manure-spattered boots in his classroom, he had to choose whether he wanted to be a teacher or a farmer, and Menard reluctantly chose the latter.)

Some students blossomed academically in the more rigorous liberal arts college atmosphere Haas encouraged. "College was an amazing freedom to me," recalled John Geske (who paid for his education by working nights at the US Rubber plant in Eau Claire). "You either did the work or you flunked out," he emphasized. Geske particularly liked his philosophy courses. By 1964 academically oriented students could belong to six national honorary societies. Haas believed these chapters "brought prestige to the institution . . . [p]articularly for those who are going to go to graduate school." Annually at Honors Day he proudly publicized graduates who earned fellowships and assistantships for postgraduate study—in 1959 Ronald Christenson received a prestigious Woodrow Wilson Fellowship to prepare for a college teaching career, and altogether in 1964 there were seventeen graduates who received graduate fellowship and assistantship awards.

In Loco Parentis at Eau Claire State

Even as Eau Claire State grew in size, Davies and Haas tried to continue the paternalistic oversight of student behavior Harvey Schofield had maintained before World War II. The professionalization of student personnel activities by use of modern psychology supported this goal. Dean of Students Benning—a psychologist—believed the students accepted this oversight. With the support of the student government, in the fall of 1963 the administration turned aside requests to relax the weekday curfew of 10:30 pm for women living in the dorms. Dean Zorn also pronounced, "[S]tudents should not be wasting their time playing cards," which usually involved gambling. Freshmen grumbled but continued to wear beanies (veterans were exempted). When they went to dinner at the College Center, with the men wearing coats and ties on Sundays, students reluctantly ate what they were told was food for "cultured" people, such as beef stroganoff and veal parmesan, rather than the hamburgers and hot dogs they preferred.

The administration listened to students, however, and accommodated them in some ways. By 1964 a daily list of students formally excused from classes continued to circulate, but the judgment of each professor, rather than the automatic trigger of three unexcused absences, now determined which absentees were sent to the dean of men or women. Daily assemblies gave way to weekly convocations, with mandatory attendance only by freshmen after 1955, and by 1964 all students only had to attend four events of their choice during the year.

The deans of men and women handled serious behavior infractions. For instance, in the fall of 1962 Zorn accompanied the police on a post-midnight raid of an off-campus party. A sensationalist article in a local newspaper reported the officers found liquor bottles in every corner and "female underclothes . . . hanging on a door knob" in "one of the most miserable garrets" in the city. The college suspended the party's hostess, placed five partygoers on probation, and terminated a drunken English instructor who was in attendance. Like all offenders, they were allowed to appeal their punishment to the president but had no formal due process rights.

Most of the problems Zorn dealt with were minor—shortchanging the college as ticket collectors, entertaining women in off-campus apartments, stealing traffic signs, creating a disturbance outside a women's residence hall at 2 am, using false parking permits. He often handled them informally, sometimes in conjunction with penalties imposed by the student judiciary. In the 1963–64 academic year, among over 1,500 men he placed only sixteen on probation, suspended three, and ordered one to pay child support.

Zorn commanded the respect of students, parents, and community members. A half century after the event, Don Gilbertson recalled how impressed he was with Zorn's fairness and judgment when he believed Gilbertson's account of how he was injured in a bar fight. Parents also trusted him: in an incident that probably led to a youthful marriage, a parent wrote to Zorn asking him to have a student "get in touch with me at once, he has some very serious business to discuss with my daughter and I immediately." In some situations, rather than prefer charges, the police remanded miscreants to Zorn's discretion for punishment. Similarly, without informing the police Zorn himself sometimes punished students for what could have been misdemeanors or even felonies. Judge Merrell Farr trusted Zorn so much he assigned him in 1962 to supervise the yearlong probation to which he sentenced two students convicted of burglary (they were among a half-dozen students who committed such petty crimes during the early 1960s).

The Beloit Incident

For Davies and Zorn the most serious issue regarding student behavior during the 1950s was the Beloit Incident in March 1955. Zorn took his 20–1 conference-champion basketball team to Beloit College to play for a birth in the National Association of Intercollegiate Athletes tournament in Kansas City. At least twenty male students were part of a group of fans who traveled to the game in a party bus bedecked with Blugold banners. The team lost the game, but the by-now highly intoxicated fans were consoled by cheerleaders who joined them for the return trip. The bus stopped multiple times for passengers to urinate at the side of the road.

Reports quickly reached Eau Claire about the Beloit Incident—a Lutheran pastor from Tomah told Davies the fans' behavior showed the college and its athletes "do not justify their existence." Punishment was swift, although Davies (who blamed the incident on Wisconsin's lax drinking laws) relented on expulsions and in the end about six students wound up on "strict probation." More significantly, by decree on March 21 Davies proscribed alcohol on campus, in off-campus student housing, and "in public places or performances in any way connected with college activities." He further required in the future all "traveling groups" from the college have "faculty chaperons." Davies enforced the new rules in the spring of 1957 when he learned students were drinking vodka on a field trip for a physical geography course. (Interestingly, the penalty for the male involved was suspension, while that for his "disgraceful" female accomplice was only a failure grade for the course.)

Although the student government unhesitantly backed Davies's handling of the Beloit Incident, the consequence of his new policies would be squabbling for the next several years between the president and the student leadership. What groups needed chaperons? Who was going to pay for them? When could the administration move unilaterally and by-pass the student judiciary on disciplinary issues, as they did in the Beloit Incident? What exactly was the "behavior unbecoming a student" that could result in suspension?

God and Man at Eau Claire State

Organized religion waxed in the United States during the 1950s; a survey in Eau Claire in 1955, for instance, found 98 percent of its residents identified with a denomination. Davies and Haas, fittingly, were deeply Christian men. Haas regularly filled in as a supply minister in Eau Claire-area pulpits (as did several of his faculty colleagues) and publically advocated for increased release time for public school children to receive religious instruction. Davies planned for the College Center to include a chapel, and he drafted a dedicatory sermon until McPhee ruled it out. Instead denominations sponsored their own student centers located close to campus. At the Lutheran center, the "counselor" reported that because of its worship, social, and service programs, Lutheran students "need not suffer a great deal from attending this college rather than a church-related one." In 1964 the Campus Lutheran Congregation was at the southeast corner of McKinley and Park Avenues, across from the Campus School, while Catholics and Methodists occupied large properties on the west side of State Street, between Memorial Hall and Summit Avenue.

The college cooperated closely with the five officially recognized student religious organizations. Until the late 1950s, it avoided scheduling activities on Monday nights so as not to conflict with their programming. One evening during the four-day freshman orientation period in early September was also set aside for them. In addition, the deans of men and women referred students to religious organizations for counselling. The college also organized a Religious Emphasis Week and presented special convocations for Easter, Thanksgiving, and Christmas. At these programs Davies felt there should be "an avoidance of ritual, but [that] readings and silent prayer are quite in order." As part of graduation ceremonies, the college scheduled a baccalaureate service in the Old Main auditorium on the Friday evening preceding commencement on Sunday. Students wanted such opportunities to express their faith: in 1961 they (unsuccessfully) petitioned Hass to cancel classes on Good Friday to enable them to attend services.

Davies carefully cultivated good relations with Catholics, who were about one-quarter of students during the 1950s. At the 1958 dedication of the Newman Center near campus, in the presence of the bishop of La Crosse, the president explained the "college is not interested in disrupting the foundations established by . . . the church." Davies passionately emphasized he was "everlastingly concerned that the young people of this college have an abiding faith in the Almighty" and he encouraged Catholic students to attend daily Mass.

Nationwide at mid-century, however, many Catholics remained wary of becoming absorbed by Protestant America. In Eau Claire, Davies had to field a complaint from a local priest that Vine Miller was "intolerant" in insisting the correct answer to her examination question "Who Was the First Pope?" was Saint Gregory the Great, who was elected in the sixth century, rather than the Apostle Peter, who by Catholic tradition had been chosen by Jesus Christ. Catholics also knew Davies's pastor gained national attention in 1960 for his sermons repeatedly denouncing Catholics as unfit to become president of the United States.

On campus, the issue of Catholic sensitivities boiled over in February 1962. The Newman Club chaplain, Father James Lovejoy, sent a memo to Catholic students mandating attendance at the organization's meetings. If students did not attend, Lovejoy told them ominously, the bishop will "take steps through the parents and pastor to have [them] removed." Specifically, the memo said, Lovejoy and the bishop would recommend the college administration not give recommendations "for job placements at the time of graduation" to negligent students. Lovejoy emphasized his memo was secret, but of course it quickly spread across campus. History professor Howard Lutz, a prominent Quaker who as a conscientious objector during World War II had participated in the Minnesota Starvation Experiment, immediately drafted a response calling for the administration not in any way to "lend its support to coercion regarding religious affairs of the student" and asking religious organizations with "coercive practices" be disqualified from using college facilities.

The College and Public Affairs During the 1950s

The highest-profile public figure in Wisconsin in the years following World War II was US Senator Joseph R. McCarthy, who served from 1947 to 1957. Fortunately, McCarthy's efforts at uncovering Communist sympathizers in Washington kept him from spending much time looking for subversives at Wisconsin colleges. McCarthy's politics, however, did not endear him to Davies, although they were both Republicans. The president took bold action in 1952, which attracted statewide attention, when he joined 150 other Eau Claire-area residents in signing a newspaper advertisement which attacked McCarthy and endorsed Henry S. Reuss, a former Republican, in the Democratic primary to select a candidate to oppose McCarthy for reelection. In the end, former Progressive Thomas Fairchild edged Reuss in the primary and ran a strong race against McCarthy in the general election, but he could not overcome the strength of Dwight D. Eisenhower at the top of the Republican ticket.

By taking a public position and signing the advertisement, Davies and several other faculty members—including conservatives like Laura Sutherland and liberals like John Schneider—probably influenced student political attitudes. Like most collegians in the United States, Eau Claire State students preferred Eisenhower for president in 1952—65 percent supported him in a straw poll, exceeding his support nationwide, in Wisconsin, and in Eau Claire County. In the race for senator, however, students supported Fairchild over McCarthy, as did their colleagues at the University of Wisconsin. (That the local newspaper endorsed Fairchild, and that the Eau Claire County Republican party was unfriendly towards McCarthy, no doubt also contributed to the students' preference.)

Davies continued to oppose what he saw as ill-conceived proposals from the political Right. In particular he objected to the positions of the American Legion, of which he was a long-time member, that criticized higher education and the United Nations and supported a theologically fundamentalist "back-to-God" program. Moderate Republicanism also continued to appeal to students. When a critic of McCarthy, political science instructor Arthur Peterson, campaigned unsuccessfully for Congress as a Republican in 1956, three-quarters of them supported him, which exceeded even their enthusiasm that year for Eisenhower's reelection. At the same election, only half of them supported fellow student Roger House, a Democrat, in his campaign for state assembly.

An Uneasy Campus in the Late 1950s

Despite, or perhaps because of, the widely shared prosperity that characterized the United States in the postwar years, an uneasiness about themselves, their nation, and its institutions began to afflict Americans in the last years of the 1950s. Administrators, faculty, and students at Eau Claire State, for their part, began to think more critically about their institution.

The launching of the space satellite *Sputnik* by the Soviet Union on October 4, 1957, provoked widespread fear that the United States was "losing" the "space race" to the Russians, in part because American education had become flabby. Congress responded by passing the National Defense Education Act of 1958. Federal research funding had already transformed major American universities, including the University of Wisconsin, in the postwar period. Now, through the NDEA, national government programs affected public colleges such as Eau Claire State. Title II of the NDEA provided for student loans, 116 of which were awarded to Eau Claire State students for the 1962–63 academic year. By then a total of 368 Eau Claire students had borrowed over $200,000 under the program. To qualify for these loans, students had to take a loyalty oath, a legacy of McCarthyism; the campus AFT and AAUP chapters joined the *Spectator* in protesting this requirement.

Critics during the 1950s blamed poorly trained teachers for the shortcomings of high school graduates, especially in mathematics, science, and foreign languages. Consequently, one of the goals of the NDEA and other programs was improving the content knowledge of these teachers. Eau Claire State responded by offering special summer institutes for in-service teachers. In the summer of 1961, the National Science Foundation funded an eight-week Science Institute for thirty middle school teachers and a Mathematics Institute for secondary teachers. Also that summer the Ford Foundation and the American Historical Association awarded the college grants for a one-week History Institute for thirty high school teachers. Focused on Latin America and Canada, it was designed to equip teachers to refute anti-American propaganda from newly Communist Cuba. Overall, these federal- and foundation-supported initiatives built on Davies's long-standing internationalist interests, clearly expressed through the Forum Series. They made an awareness of global issues part of the democratic citizenship colleges throughout the United States sought to develop in their students during the 1950s.

The *Sputnik* launch had a deeper effect on the Eau Claire campus, however, than just initiating programmatic responses. By the fall of 1958 Davies had become uneasy about the "morale and work" of the college. He especially expressed concern about the criticism by elementary and high school teachers of "our concept of teaching," particularly in the English Department. The president prompted a discussion of this issue at the general faculty meeting on October 6, and five days later he solicited from the faculty written suggestions for "improvements" in the college.

This unusual offer by a college president resulted in a thick folder of responses. Some faculty members took the opportunity to tout their own accomplishments, call for salary raises or more convenient parking, or simply emphasize the need for better "public relations." Others made thoughtful suggestions. Political scientist Karl Andresen eloquently defended the proposition that the college should not just serve, but also critique society. It was apparent from other responses, however, that this sort of criticism was exactly what was not wanted. Several members of the Department of Education asked Davies to proscribe criticism of the public schools and the Wisconsin Education Association. English professor John Morris, on the other hand, called for the "college [to] continue to strengthen its academic program" and for content departments to have more involvement in teacher education. English instructor William Lemons felt, "Criticism of the grade schools and high schools is justifiable . . . [and] badly needed." It appears by the end of 1950s, the transformation of Eau Claire State into a liberal arts college had opened schisms within the faculty.

Academics in the College Leonard Haas Built

Between 1952 and 1964 the quality of students at Eau Claire State continued to be good—most came from the upper quartile of their high school classes (as had been the case before World War II and continued thereafter through the university's centennial). Indeed, of the 1,064 new freshmen in the fall of 1963, sixty-four had been awarded "A" Legislative Scholarships (chapter four) for being at least among the top four in their high school class.

The college's graduation rate, however, lagged that of all the other state colleges—only one-quarter of freshmen who entered in 1954 returned to begin their senior year in 1957. In part the issue was balancing the college's historical role of providing access to college education with its increasing emphasis on academic quality. Specifically, Haas blamed the retention problem on weaker students admitted on probation from the lowest quartile of their high school classes. He reported only six of forty-two such students admitted in 1957 were in good standing a year later, and twenty-nine were not enrolled at all. For several years in the mid-1950s the college required less well-prepared students to take non-credit remedial courses—unfortunately designated as Math 0 and English 0—but this initiative was abandoned as unsuccessful. At the same time a University of Wisconsin report documented almost half of the state's high school graduates of "top ability" did not go on to college. Consequently Davies told the faculty in 1957 the issue was "the problem of the good students who don't come and the poor students who do."

Even many students from above the lowest quartile of their high school classes did not continue to graduation. For example, of the 910 freshmen who enrolled in the fall of 1960, only 737 registered for the spring semester. During that semester, just 438 of them earned a grade point average above 2.00, 172 of the others were given probation, and 123 were placed on suspension. With transfers, the sophomore class in the fall of 1961 did grow to 608, but in turn a third of them earned GPAs below 2.00 that semester. Dean Hibbard explained that fall, "If the college continues to maintain high standards of instruction, [then the] rate of dropout will be higher than in other institutions [with similar standards] with higher admission policies" than Eau Claire State. Overall, in the early 1960s the median semester GPA for freshmen was barely above 2.00 and was only about 2.30 for all students.

Freshmen English was the biggest academic hurdle for most students. In 1954, in order to receive full transfer credit to the University of Wisconsin, the college revised its previous "communication" course for freshmen, which included oral presentations and analysis of mass media, into a "composition" course with ten student "themes" required each semester based on analyses of pieces of fiction and non-fiction. The course was rigorous. In the fall of 1959, the average grade in freshman English was a D+. The department tried to explain its standards to high school teachers, who were upset by the failure of so many students they had recently taught. "We no longer have any problem with spelling," Professor Roland Lee wrote. "The students have one, but we don't." Work with misspellings was just not accepted, he explained.

There was a further reason, in addition to the weak aptitude of some students and strict faculty grading, for the seemingly poor academic performance (at least by twenty-first-century standards) of Eau Claire State students in the 1950s and early 1960s: students did not feel pressured to earn high GPAs. "Grades weren't as important as they are now," Nancy Blomlie, a 1962 business education graduate, recalled in 2013. "We were in college so we were already part of the elite." "Jobs were easy" to get, explained Albert Guiz, a 1960 graduate with a mathematics major. "It's not like now." Since public schools were scrambling to find staff to teach swelling numbers of baby boomers, if "you spoke English and you knew the alphabet there wasn't [a] place you couldn't get a job," 1951 graduate Carol Endl admitted.

The college's own surveys showed almost all graduates quickly moved into employment. In 1961, only one of eighty-six secondary education graduates and one of 141 elementary education graduates did not immediately find jobs. The picture was almost as good for liberal arts graduates.

Given the contentious discussions at the end of the 1950s about the state of the college, Davies and Haas also wanted evidence about the academic outcomes for Eau Claire State graduates. Beginning in 1959, seniors had to take the Graduate Record Examination in their major or the National Teacher Examination if they were in elementary education or certain other teaching majors. Haas's annotation shows he paid attention to the scores he received from the Educational Testing Service for students in each major who took the exam. He saw in 1959 that history graduates—from a department with accomplishments in faculty scholarship—collectively earned the highest median score among the majors, and the following year he saw English graduates—from a department under attack for its rigorous grading—collectively earned the highest median score among the majors. Haas's encouragement of the liberal arts appeared to be paying off.

Vexed Female and Student Debate on Gender Roles

Another dimension of the self-criticism that occupied the campus during the 1958–59 academic year was a discussion among students about gender. No other topic in its thirty-five-year history had attracted so many letters to the *Spectator* than an extended exchange in the pages of the newspaper in the spring of 1959 about male and female roles.

The episode began with a letter to the *Spectator* published on February 26. Trying to be "cool," the anonymous author adopted a *Playboy*-like pose and explained he liked to "watch the skirts and sweaters go by." (He had probably enjoyed ogling the women presented in the "Miss Photogenic" spread in the 1958 *Periscope*.) The letter writer was frustrated, however, when he wanted "to talk to a chick in class" and instead wound up sitting next to a "grandma" who was "a curve pusher (but not in the right places)" and who gabbled about the Civil War (it was true that 12 percent of 1959 graduates had started college before 1950). In succeeding issues, several "grandmas" heatedly responded to the ageist dimension of this letter. The most interesting responses, however, addressed the letter writer's ideas about women.

On March 19, Vexed Female wrote to the *Spectator* claiming the anonymous letter writer was among the "undesirable" half of men on campus who were "so inebriated that they can't tell a girl from a lamp post." This letter produced a deluge of ungentlemanly responses. They alleged in order to make her claims, Vexed Female herself had to be spending too much time in the bars; to attract a man, she should not "be fussy" or "look like a lamppost;" men drink because of the lack of "effecton" [sic] they got from Eau Claire State women; and "the minority of females on this campus that are kind, considerate, understanding, etc., are either married, engaged or spoken for." Over the next two years articles, letters, and editorials in the *Spectator* complained about the campus sexual atmosphere and returned to issues raised by Vexed Female. A survey of students in 1961 reported women thought men were "cheap" and too interested in fishing, sports, and drinking, while men thought they needed to be half-drunk so they could "see better" when they asked women for dates—in other words, that was the only way they could see female students as attractive.

The Vexed Female episode hinted at dissatisfaction that lurked at the end of the 1950s, at Eau Claire State and around the country, which during the next decade would explode into challenges to gender and family roles—men rejecting the idea their primary obligation was to be economic providers and women desiring partners who would treat them as more than housekeepers and sexual objects.

Leadership Changes at the End of the 1950s

The decade of the 1950s ended with changes in leadership in Washington, DC, and at Eau Claire State. Sensing the national uneasiness, Massachusetts Senator John F. Kennedy launched a campaign which represented him as a presidential candidate who could reinvigorate the nation. In preparation for what was anticipated to be a crucial primary contest against Minnesota Senator Hubert H. Humphrey, Kennedy campaigned across western Wisconsin in mid-November 1959. Former student government president Edmund A. Nix, who was now the Eau Claire County district attorney and secretary of the statewide Kennedy-for-President organization, arranged for Kennedy to speak on November 12 to an overflow crowd in the Little Theater. As part of his campaign strategy to present himself as a knowledgeable and serious candidate, despite his relative youth, Kennedy delivered a long and detailed speech on Latin American policy. Anticipating what would become his Alliance for Progress program, Kennedy called for the United States to promote economic development in Latin America to meet the Cold War threat in the region from the Soviet Union. In March, Senator Kennedy returned to the city, and his brother Robert spoke on campus. Although Humphrey narrowly beat him in western Wisconsin, the more conservative Kennedy was successful statewide in the April primary. In the general election in November, Kennedy edged Vice President Richard M. Nixon in a straw poll among students (although the *Spectator* dismissed the results because of ballot stuffing by both sides), while losing statewide and in Eau Claire and most adjacent counties. If the poll had any validity, it suggested Eau Claire State students were trending Democratic: in addition to their presidential preference, they supported the reelection of Democratic Congressman Lester Johnson by a significantly greater margin than he received in the general electorate and in Eau Claire County.

Leonard Haas Greeting John F. Kennedy, College Center, November 12, 1959

The Spectator *barely noticed Kennedy's visit, but did editorially praise an appearance by his brother Robert a few weeks later because it roused the campus from "lethargy" and encouraged students to "think big."*

At Eau Claire State, illness increasingly kept President Davies away from campus during the late 1950s, just as President Schofield had become incapacitated twenty years previously. In late August 1959, Davies announced he intended to retire in January 1960 and took leave for the fall semester; Haas became acting president.

The regents quickly chose Haas to succeed Davies. A strong endorsement from Davies, his widespread community involvement in religious and political affairs, respect from the faculty, and admiration from the students (Janice Kneer was amazed, but found it in character, when Haas remembered her by name when he encountered her on the street years after she graduated) made sure Haas would become the third president of Eau Claire State. Haas had eyed the presidency. In 1958 he declined Director McPhee's invitation to apply to be president of Platteville State, emphasizing, "I cherish the hope that I may be given consideration should a vacancy occur in another State College presidency." His reputation was such that only a dozen persons, just one from Wisconsin, applied for the Eau Claire position. Just to be sure, at a September 11 meeting Lester Emans and others friendly to Haas arranged for the faculty to endorse his candidacy and provided "the opportunity" for individuals to sign a petition to the regents registering their feelings. While no one had any objection to Haas, many of the untenured faculty, at least, saw this tactic as a not-very-subtle form of coercion. In any event, McPhee later emphasized the regents did not give the petition special weight. However, they did waive their usual preference for external candidates, and after interviewing five applicants, the regents formally chose Haas at their meeting on November 16.

A special convocation in the Fieldhouse the following morning celebrated his appointment and marked Davies's final public appearance on campus. Increasingly frail, Davies died on December 10. Haas eulogized his friend and mentor (as he had Schofield eighteen years previously) the following day at a memorial service in a packed Old Main auditorium. Haas praised Davies's faith in God and love for the college and emphasized that by his cooperative leadership style "a way was formed in the wilderness to bring about a new kind of a college community."

The First Years of the Haas Administration

In the fall of 1960 Haas told the *Spectator*, "I hope that I will be here long enough to witness dispersal of [my] authority over the entire faculty and the entire student body." He was intrigued by the idea of developing a student-faculty senate that would set policies for the college (subject to his veto, of course). While the faculty hesitated to share with students any of their newly gained power, Haas did establish a "commonwealth system" with authority over non-academic areas which replaced the previous student government and the board that managed the College Center. A College Senate, with seventeen students and eight faculty and administrators, administered this new system. The editors of the *Spectator* advocated at least two of the student positions be reserved for women, but in the spirit of the respondents to Vexed Female they were denounced as "crackpots, traitors, or just plain gutless." When the commonwealth system began in 1961, however, a woman served as student government president for the first time.

Although it took a few years, Haas also accomplished the better integration of Catholic students into campus life. The spirit of the Second Vatican Council, which opened in 1962, encouraged interdenominational cooperation rather than Catholic separatism. The chancellor of the diocese of La Crosse, Monsignor James P. Finucan, attended the council and was characterized in the press as a "liberal" and a "controversial" exponent of its principles. In 1962 Finucan wrote a friendly letter to Haas in which he apologized for "our chaplain's embarrassing you last spring." Haas reassured him, "It appears to me all proper lines are reestablished in relations with foundation chaplains." Haas then invited the subject of the controversy, Father Lovejoy, to give the invocation at the 1963 commencement. Catholic students began to participate in joint activities with other campus faith groups. They also took to heart the council's call for a larger lay role in Church affairs. Beyond the campus, as president of the National Newman Club Federation, Julius Gilbertson, a 1963 Eau Claire State graduate, called for a "pro-student" movement which would operate "outside the ecclesiastical framework of the Church but within the spirit of it" and prevent clerics from "submerging . . . the laity."

Haas also continued to strengthen Eau Claire State's academic program. To help address the high freshman failure rate, in the fall of 1960 faculty started to submit mid-semester grades for first-year students. Also in 1960 a summer orientation program began in which first-year students and their parents came to campus for a day of testing, advising, and registration. The fall orientation program added a freshman-faculty "cultural discussion" session; in 1962 it was "Is Man an Animal?" In addition, together with the other state colleges, in 1962 Eau Claire State began to require freshmen to take the American College Test (ACT). Its intention was to enable the college to better evaluate applicants from the lowest quartile of high school classes, the group said to be responsible for the college's low retention rate, but the local newspaper endorsed the ACT as an elimination of "fun-loving young men." In 1962 the college also dropped its two-year program for rural teachers. Henceforth, it would give them no diplomas and no pictures of graduates would appear in the *Periscope*. Davies had long criticized the program and students had called for its abolition, but McPhee had resisted. Now Haas was proud the faculty had "the strength to say: We stand only for that which is quality." He was also proud that in 1959 Eau Claire was the first Wisconsin state college approved for a chapter of the American Association of University Women.

The civil rights movement of the late 1950s and early 1960s slowly came to Eau Claire State. In the fall of 1960 newly appointed political science professor Paul Carlsten openly called for recruiting more African American students as part of an attack on the "provincialism" he found at Eau Claire. Little racial diversity developed in the early 1960s, but Al Green did become the first African American student athlete when he played for Zorn's 1961–62 basketball team. Three students and the Wesley Foundation minister joined the famous August 1963 March on Washington for Jobs and Freedom. Reflecting these emerging public concerns, in the fall of that year the college adopted an employment policy which officially proscribed "discrimination based on age, race, color, creed, sex, national origins, or ancestry."

The most dramatic event at Eau Claire State during the early part of the civil rights movement was the presentation by the Reverend Martin Luther King Jr. in the Forum Series on March 29, 1962. He told a jammed Fieldhouse that the racial problem in the United States "must be uprooted not because of diplomatic expediency but because it is morally compelling." John Schneider, the long-time and sometimes lonely voice from the Left on campus, heard King's message and was "so overcome," in the words of Sarah Hibbard who was present, he collapsed and died. "It just seemed to be the fulfillment of his life that [King] had come there," explained Haas, who was sitting in the gym with Schneider.

Students showed their emergent support for the civil rights movement by their political choices in 1964. In a mock election in which most students participated, two-thirds preferred incumbent Democratic President Lyndon B. Johnson to Republican US Senator Barry Goldwater, an outspoken opponent of the just-adopted Civil Rights Act of 1964. Johnson's margin among students significantly exceeded his statewide margin. Students also preferred the reelection of Democratic US Senator William Proxmire and supported the unsuccessful congressional candidacy of Edmund Nix, the Eau Claire State alumnus and Kennedy supporter in 1960, against incumbent Republican Alvin O'Konski.

Reshaping Higher Education in Wisconsin

As the size and role of Eau Claire and its sister state colleges changed between 1952 and 1964, relations among the components of higher education in Wisconsin became more complex and more contentious as partisan divisions also widened in the state.

In 1953 Governor Walter Kohler proposed an end to duplication and rivalry by "integrating" the state colleges and the University of Wisconsin into one institution with a single governing board. The focus at the colleges would be on undergraduate instruction and at Madison would be on graduate study and research. Davies supported the idea, as did the local newspaper and a majority of the state college regents. Other state college faculty and administrators, however, fearing diminished direct access to the legislature, opposed the governor's plan. The university faculty also mounted a strenuous objection, fearing integration would lower the prestige of the UW and give the president of the Madison campus the authoritarian powers exercised by the state college presidents. The state assembly ultimately rejected the proposal.

Governor Kohler was also a fiscal conservative. In presenting the executive budget in January 1953 he told the legislature, "The people want less government, fewer regulations, smaller budgets and lower taxes." Director McPhee and Regent President McIntyre needed all their skill to get a 4 percent increase in the state college system budget for the 1953–55 biennium, when the overall state budget was 2.5 percent lower. Their success stood out in contrast to the cut in appropriations the University of Wisconsin received from legislators, who were inflamed by the discovery it was carrying over surplus tuition revenue from previous years and by the audacity of its faculty to oppose the football team's participation in the Rose Bowl. Given the budgetary outcome, resentment towards the state colleges increased at the university.

Kohler tried again for integration in 1955. The positions of the university and the state colleges were even more sharply delineated than they were two years previously, with McIntyre strongly supporting the governor. The final compromise outcome was more acceptable to the UW than it was to the state colleges: a new Coordinating Committee for Higher Education, comprised of regents from both boards and citizen members, would get to approve each system's budget proposal to the legislature but have no direct management authority. Davies saw it as a "sell out to the U." In related developments, the state college system lost Milwaukee State, which became part of the University of Wisconsin, but added the Stout Institute and the Wisconsin Institute of Technology, which eventually merged with Platteville State.

Although he had been a skeptic, Davies believed the initial work of the Coordinating Committee—statistical reports, surveys of needs, recommendations for more efficient utilization of existing institutions—encouraged a healthier relationship between the state colleges and the university. Viewed retrospectively, however, the work of the committee mainly served to deflect energies into meetings and reports rather than resolving the conflicting ambitions of the two systems of higher education. For instance, in what would have made a wonderful episode of *Yes, Minister*, the 1980s BBC television spoof of Whitehall bureaucracy, a "working group" of the "subcommittee on duplication" of the "committee on elementary education" of the Coordinating Committee worked for months before learning a "duplication study" was also underway by the Coordinating Committee's own research staff.

Suspicion continued to exist between the UW and the state colleges. Davies scorned the university for using its growing system of two-year extension centers around the state, which were emerging as competitors to the state colleges, primarily as training sites for its PhD candidates. The UW, for its part, bluntly told Haas in 1956 that as a result of the performance of transfer students at Madison it felt, "[Y]our courses in Engineering Drawing are not as rigorous as those given at the University."

Engineering Drawing Lab, 1950s

The University of Wisconsin did not believe instruction in this subject at Eau Claire State was up to Madison's standards.

That all state college administrators did not respect faculty the same way Davies and Haas did was also troublesome. Most significant was the 1957 dismissal by Jim Dan Hill, president of Superior State, of tenured professor George Ball and the subsequent financial punishment of colleagues who came to his support. McIntyre and McPhee brushed off the intervention of the AAUP and strongly supported Hill, but Ball prevailed in litigation ultimately decided by the Wisconsin Supreme Court. Subsequently, in early 1964 the governor was "shocked" and UW faculty were appalled when the regents suddenly moved Hill from his presidency to be co-director of the staff of the Coordinating Committee. The shift damaged the Coordinating Committee's credibility, while the AWSCF, meeting in Eau Claire in April, criticized the regents for not following their own guidelines when they omitted faculty participation from the search for Hill's replacement at Superior.

The political landscape for Republicans McPhee and McIntyre changed with the breakthrough election of Democrat Gaylord Nelson as governor in 1958. (Democrat John Reynolds, elected with Nelson as attorney general, declined to defend the regents in their litigation with Ball.) Democrats soon dominated the board of regents. McPhee and McIntyre, however, continued to work effectively to promote the interests of the state colleges by rallying bipartisan legislative support, especially outside of Madison and Milwaukee, for the state colleges as the "conservative" alternative in higher education to the cosmopolitan and radical-tinged University of Wisconsin.

Nelson advocated, largely in vain, for more efficiencies and greater cooperation between the university and the state colleges. At a joint meeting of the UW and state college regents in April 1962 he insisted on the need for more planning by the Coordinating Committee to meet the anticipated doubling in undergraduate enrollment in the state during the next decade. He also advanced twenty-six specific points. Some were eventually adopted—more college credit for high school work, more part-time faculty, limits on the number of out-of-state students at the UW, a new college in southeastern Wisconsin, and greater financial aid. Most of his suggestions, however interesting, got nowhere: a centralized admissions system, a longer academic year, balancing the admission of new freshmen between September and January, class schedules assigned by the institution rather than selected by the students, and appointment of University of Wisconsin teaching assistants to positions in the state colleges.

With the branches of state government divided along partisan lines, the 1961 and 1963 legislative sessions were long and combative. At the heart of the problem was Republican insistence on the introduction of a sales tax to fund increasing state expenditures and to reduce reliance on the income tax, with which Republicans had been unhappy since 1911 (chapter one). Eau Claire State Area Committee member Corwin Guell, a Thorp lawyer and former Republican assemblyman, wanted students and parents to "assume a larger portion of the costs of higher education" because "we cannot stand any further increase in corporate and individual income taxes." If students "can afford beer they can afford larger fees," a letter writer to an Eau Claire newspaper asserted.

For Haas, retaining and recruiting faculty for the fall were difficult when the legislature could not decide the number of faculty positions or their salaries. In July 1963 he publically reported that three faculty members had left for other jobs because of the stalemated budget situation in Madison. Playing hardball, in the absence of a budget the Republican co-chair of the Joint Finance Committee told the state colleges to prepare to operate at 85 percent of 1962–63 levels. The regents (including Republican McIntyre) unanimously refused to adopt any such plans and condemned the proposal as the "liquidation of higher education in Wisconsin." The state Republican chair in turn denounced the regents: "[W]hen faced with the possibility of a reduced standard of living they utterly reject the idea of planning for it." A compromise finally ensued. Reynolds, now governor, persuaded enough Democrats in the legislature to accept a 3 percent general sales tax which, with a small increase in the income tax and other revenues, allowed for spending in 1963–65 at levels close to what he wanted; state college faculty received a 6 percent salary increase in the fall of 1963. The Eau Claire AFT local gave McIntyre kudos for his efforts on the college's behalf. In their electoral choices in 1964, however, Eau Claire students joined a statewide reaction against Reynolds for advocating higher taxes and preferred moderate-Republican challenger Warren Knowles in their mock election for governor.

All in all, regardless of the partisan orientation of officials in Madison, the post-World War II years were good for the Wisconsin state colleges. In 1964 dollars, per-student appropriations by the state (which accounted for about two-thirds of the colleges' operating budgets) increased from $339 to $579 between 1947 and 1948 and 1964 and 1965. The expansion and strengthening of the state colleges contributed to the relative gain in human capital the state achieved during these decades. In 1940, the proportion of Wisconsinites over age twenty-five with a bachelor's degree was 15 percent below the national level and trailed all four neighboring states. By 1970 Wisconsin had moved ahead of Iowa and Michigan and was only 5 percent below the national level. Correspondingly, per-capita income in the state rose from 92 percent of the national level to 99 percent between 1940 and 1960. As Haas pointed out in his inaugural address in 1960, "We must recognize that all of us are beneficiaries of higher education."

At his 1960 inauguration, Leonard Haas emphasized the need for "a striving for excellence in every human activity." By 1964 he saw Eau Claire State had moved a long way in that direction since 1952. Achieving excellence, however, would be a more complex challenge for Haas and the institution in the decade following 1964. The college became Wisconsin State University–Eau Claire on July 1, 1964, when the regents retitled the Wisconsin state colleges as Wisconsin state universities. In a sense, Haas's goal for the institution to become a liberal arts college had been overtaken by its own success. He would have to deal with his next set of challenges in an academic and social context much different than that of the two decades following World War II.

1964-71
The New University: Excellence and Growth

The audience expectantly assembled in Schofield Auditorium in January 1960 for Leonard Haas's first faculty meeting as president of Wisconsin State College-Eau Claire.

President Leonard Haas at Commencement Exercises, c. 1967

Haas began his remarks by stating the faculty were the heart of the college and his job as president was to recruit, retain, and help develop an excellent faculty who combined teaching, research, and service, in that order. Haas then turned to the students and told them he wanted to build the college as a place that would attract the best applicants for admission and to make it an outstanding residential college. Next, the president stated the college would continue President William R. Davies's outreach to the community, particularly in public policy debates, in the arts, and by housing an outstanding library open to the public. Eau Claire and Chippewa Falls, the communities most closely tied to the college, could expect an institution that would serve them in many ways. Haas then turned to a new theme, or at least one not previously emphasized by presidents Harvey Schofield or Davies: the college must develop a "culture of excellence" in all that it does.

Looking back twenty-five years later on that convocation, Haas admitted the word "excellence . . . was a strange word in 1960. It was like a new word in the vocabulary insofar as being attached where the university was concerned." That may have been so in regard to Eau Claire State, but the concept of "excellence" was to receive widespread use in John F. Kennedy's 1960 presidential campaign, particularly Kennedy's often-quoted saying that "the ancient Greek definition of happiness was the full use of your powers along lines of excellence." The future president had visited Eau Claire State in November 1959, two months before Haas's address (chapter five). Thereafter, President Haas nourished a special feeling for the Harvard-educated Kennedy, more so than for his successor in the White House, the Southwest Texas State Teachers College-educated Lyndon B. Johnson.

President Haas certainly felt his twenty-one-year term as president and later chancellor at Eau Claire lived up to the promise of that January 1960 address, especially the building and maintaining of a culture of excellence. The irony of Eau Claire's adopting the "excellence" slogan, of trying to build a "culture of excellence," of fostering "excellence in everything we do at Eau Claire," is the institution Haas envisioned at the beginning of 1960 was a small, residential, liberal arts, and teacher-preparation college modeled on St. Olaf College and the other Lutheran colleges Haas had visited during the 1950s (chapter five) and not the university it soon became.

President Haas was also interested in the so-called "commonwealth" model of college governance at Antioch College in Ohio. Antioch featured a single representative assembly consisting of the president, faculty, and students. That body made decisions about curriculum and extracurricular matters. At his January 1960 speech to the faculty, Haas concluded by suggesting Eau Claire State consider adopting the Antioch "commonwealth" system of campus governance. Rather than take up the challenge of the commonwealth idea, however, the college's faculty decided it wanted more emphasis placed on the Faculty Council established in 1959 to advise the president on curricular and extracurricular matters. In 1960, the faculty was cool to the concept of student participation in such a council, especially regarding curriculum.

From the "Little Commonwealth College" to the University as "Gothic Cathedral"

Almost seven years after delivering his "cult of excellence" speech, President Haas once more crafted an address setting out his vision of the university. He did so in a different venue than a regularly scheduled faculty meeting. Instead, in December 1966 he inaugurated an "Arena of Ideas" series in which, separately from the University Forum, one or more speakers could discuss an idea in depth. Jo Dahle, the newly hired director of university activities, took on the task of coordinating the Arena of Ideas and he asked Haas himself to begin the series by speaking on the topic of the modern university.

Haas began his address with a description of the old Eau Claire State, which was a "single-purpose" institution with the sole task of granting bachelor's degrees. The new Wisconsin State University–Eau Claire, in contradistinction, was a university granting undergraduate and graduate degrees. The job of a college was to transmit old knowledge to students; the task of a university was to discover new knowledge and convey that, as well as to teach established knowledge to students. Moreover, Haas argued a state institution had a responsibility to serve the public in its quest for new knowledge and in the dissemination of knowledge. A college had a simple form of governance: the president, aided by the faculty, or perhaps even the Antioch "commonwealth" system. A university, consisting of different schools or colleges and furthermore consisting of different types of students and faculty, required a more complex form of governance. Haas explained Eau Claire State needed separate faculty and student senates, with rights and responsibilities set out in written charters or constitutions. It was at his "Arena of Ideas" address Haas proposed the concept that the modern university could be understood as the twentieth-century equivalent of the Gothic cathedral: a complex edifice of interlocking supports aspiring toward grace, beauty, and excellence.

This was quite a different mission that Haas set for Eau Claire State in its new role as WSU–EC. The type of excellent college he sought to build was modeled on the St. Olaf or Antioch residential example of a committed faculty and fine student body who were motivated by a broad sense of spirit. Instead, the challenge of excellence at Eau Claire turned out to be how to build a large Gothic cathedral of a public regional comprehensive multiversity, without losing sight of the cult of excellence. For the half-century since President Haas's Arena of Ideas address of December 1966, that has remained the challenge of excellence for WSU–EC and the University of Wisconsin–Eau Claire. The balance of this chapter takes up the history of how the university understood, built, and sought to enhance excellence during the 1960s.

Excellence by Democratization: Growth in Numbers of Students, Faculty, and Staff

In just a few decades, the modest-sized Eau Claire State Teachers College changed, first into a liberal arts institution and then into a regional comprehensive university. Enrollment exploded in the 1960s as the college annually grew at double-digit percentage rates. It topped two thousand in 1961 and doubled to more than 4,500 five years later. Enrollment nearly doubled yet again to more than 8,600 by 1971–72, when WSU–EC became University of Wisconsin–Eau Claire.

What caused the unprecedented enrollment growth at Eau Claire? Cynics believed American colleges and universities grew in the 1960s as a refuge from the military draft. Even President Haas, looking back in the 1980s after his retirement, thought this was part of the reason for Eau Claire's growth. The problem with this explanation is the number of women students at Eau Claire State grew even faster in numbers than men, and under the laws Congress set for the US Selective Service System, women were ineligible for the draft. Moreover, if men sought college at Eau Claire as a haven from the draft, the university proved rather inhospitable as between a quarter and two-fifths of the freshman class each year dropped out or were asked to leave for academic reasons. The Selective Service System gave deferments from military call-up to male college students attending full time with good academic standing, so those Eau Claire men who dropped out (or were suspended) were eligible to be drafted.

Another explanation for the rapid growth of college attendance in the 1960s was the delayed effect of the baby boom. This explanation stresses the large number of children born to US parents between 1946 and 1964, with an eighteen-year wait from birth until college readiness. In Eau Claire's case, however, the growth in student enrollment began before the expected effects of the baby boom; that is, enrollment began its upward surge in the 1950s and early 1960s, before the first baby boom high school graduating class of 1964.

At the time Eau Claire State Teachers College changed into the liberal arts Wisconsin State College–Eau Claire in 1951, educational analysts in the state forecast only a modest growth in college attendance by the state's baby boom generation over the next two decades (chapter five). The nine state colleges that year enrolled 8,500 students, with a prediction that in 1971 enrollment would top 13,000. The University of Wisconsin campus had 18,000 in students in 1951 and was expected to grow to 21,000 by 1971. Instead, by 1971 the nine WSU campuses enrolled 65,000 students and the four campuses of the University of Wisconsin enrolled another 40,000 students. Actual college attendance was three times greater than forecast in 1951, even though planners were aware then that the baby boom had begun.

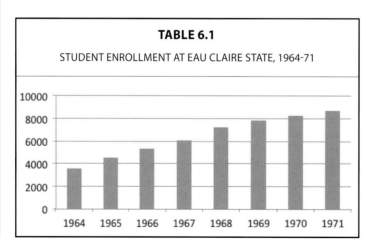

TABLE 6.1
STUDENT ENROLLMENT AT EAU CLAIRE STATE, 1964-71

Director McPhee knew better than to invoke a simple demographic explanation for the growth of the institutions in his system. The cagey administrator explained in an oral history that enrollment growth at Eau Claire and the other state universities "didn't come about as a result of bulges in the population as much as it came about in the higher percentage of students going to college." McPhee noted that in 1946, even with college enrollment increased by returning veterans, only 25 percent of Wisconsin high school graduates attended college; a generation later by 1970, fully 40 percent of the state's high school graduates attended college, higher than the nationwide average of 33 percent. Moreover, Wisconsin students in the 1960s became more likely to complete high school than had earlier generations, thereby increasing the pool of potential college applicants. The state's high school graduates overwhelmingly chose to enroll at the campuses of the WSU and the UW. The contrast between the students at WSU–EC in 1970 and their parents is striking: more than 85 percent of Wisconsin school children twenty-one and under in 1970 (baby boomers) had completed high school. By contrast, the high school completion rate for those born in the 1920s or 1930s was barely half of those born in the 1950s.

Throughout the 1960s, a series of Wisconsin governors and legislatures embraced the idea that college should be available to all Wisconsin high school graduates. Eau Claire State's admission standards were somewhat above "open enrollment," but not much. In 1964, prospective Blugolds with a high school diploma and whose class rank placed them in the top three-quarters of their high school graduating class could gain automatic admittance. They also had to take a standardized test, the American College Test, for purposes of "counseling." Applicants additionally had to submit a letter of recommendation from their high school principal or counselor. The university also accepted some students from the lowest quartile of their high school graduating class, a decision that depended in part on their ACT score, but placed them on academic probation. The prevailing attitude, expressed by McPhee, was every person with a high school diploma deserved a chance at college, "and if he can't make it, ok."

If state officials underestimated the demand for access to college in 1951, they over-estimated the future demand in the late 1960s. The Coordinating Committee on Higher Education (CCHE), a body created by the legislature in 1955 consisting of representatives from the University of Wisconsin, the Wisconsin state colleges, and the public, forecast in 1968 only more growth in college admissions. That fall, WSU–EC enrolled 7,248 students, but the CCHE told the university to prepare for a student body of 12,500. This study predicted enrollment at new University of Wisconsin campuses would increase 366 percent at Green Bay and 600 percent at Parkside, in each case reaching 11,000 students. The CCHE proved guilty of groupthink, the tendency to talk and write among the same insiders, saying the same things. It became a cliché to write the baccalaureate would be the "minimum" qualification for most future employment, and advanced graduate degrees for many jobs would become the norm.

The administration at Eau Claire State had little time to engage in long-range planning or strategic thinking about a campus that might reach 12,500 in enrollment. They were too busy trying to keep up with each year's influx of new students, especially first-year students. The growth in student enrollment was not evenly balanced across the four years of undergraduate status. The ratio of first-year students in the student body never fell below one-third and sometimes reached as high as 40 percent. Sophomores typically numbered about one-quarter of the student body in the 1960s, but juniors and seniors made up a much smaller percentage. In 1966, for example, seniors comprised just 12 percent of the student body.

Some of this imbalance was due to the simple arithmetic of growth by adding ever more first-year students. However, some was due to a high dropout (and washout) rate at the university. In the 1963–64 academic year, the chair the Committee on Student Admissions and Retention, professor Helen Sampson of the English Department, reported 11 percent of the student body was on probation and an additional 7 percent had been suspended for poor academic performance. The problem of poor academic performance was particularly acute, or at least public, in student government as over the course of the decade many officers had to resign their positions because they did not meet the minimum grade point average (GPA) for good standing—a 2.00 on a 4.00 scale.

In an oral history, alumnus Robert Sinz ('69) remembered his first Freshman Assembly in the fall of 1965 when President Haas said to the 1,500 first-year students, "Look to the left and look to the right. Two out of three of you won't be here in four years." A few years later, Director of Admissions John Kearney estimated 40 percent of students entering the university would never complete a degree, with one-half of that figure dropping out the first year. Not all those who left the university did so for reasons of poor academic performance. Some transferred to other institutions, and some students, both men and women, dropped out to wed and start a family. They considered themselves "College Men" or "College Women" even if they did not complete the Eau Claire baccalaureate.

In 1964–65, Sampson reported one-quarter of first-year students did not return for their sophomore year, and further, 30 percent of sophomores did not come back for their junior year, a retention rate essentially unchanged since the 1930s. WSU–EC in the 1960s was not able to address the dropout rate for first-year students, despite Sampson's call for action. Not until the following decade did the university begin to add more services to help students succeed, and even then retention of first-year students into their second year remained a problem well into the twenty-first century. What did begin to change over time was an increased retention rate for students who completed their sophomore year and returned for a junior year.

Why did students choose Eau Claire State in the 1960s? Oral histories provide varied answers. Certainly one reason was the growing reputation Eau Claire had as a good, even excellent, institution for teacher training. Sue Miller came to Eau Claire from Oshkosh with the intention of becoming an English teacher (she changed her mind and became a social worker), but she had heard even across the state of Eau Claire's excellence in preparing English teachers. Patricia (Ehlers) Poppele ('68) remembered the education faculty were serious professionals, very much concerned with training future Wisconsin leaders in the classroom. She recalled a steady regimen of hard work: "I think it was mostly all of it was listening to the lecturer, the instructor, the teacher, the professor, and then being tested . . . maybe all the time there was a paper to do, some sort of research paper . . . as I moved into the methods classes we were judged on our teaching abilities . . . we were also judged on whether or not we could put together good ways to teach material."

Eau Claire State remained very much an institution that attracted students preparing for a career in teaching. During the 1960s the number of students who enrolled in teacher education programs increased each year. In 1966, for example, 2,528 of the total enrollment of 5,326 students identified themselves with one of five programs within the School of Education: elementary education, secondary education, special education, business education, and for first-year students, pre-professional education. That number was 1,100 higher than it had been in 1960–61, Leonard Haas's first full year as president. The number of students in the School of Education, or who declared an intention to get an education degree, was higher than the number of majors in all the departments in Arts and Sciences (1,844), in the new School of Business (596), or in the new School of Nursing (284). Indeed, it was almost higher than the number in those three schools combined. Two years later, in the fall of 1968, WSU–EC students preparing for a teaching career numbered 2,753, again more than the other three schools, even if the relative proportions had started to swing towards Arts and Sciences, Business, and Nursing. Students chose the profession of teaching because long-term changes in the economics of the labor market caused by the baby boom provided more opportunities, especially for women, in elementary education.

Some students chose Eau Claire State because it was conveniently close to home and therefore more affordable. In the fall of 1964 56 percent of the student body came from Eau Claire or a contiguous county, such as Chippewa or Trempealeau (see Map 6.1). Susan Oberstar ('71) chose Eau Claire State in 1967 because she was from the area, and as she recalled, "[A]ll my friends went there." Mary Rambo ('68), who chose Eau Claire in 1964 for its elementary education program and later had a successful career as a third-grade teacher, lived at home to save money, and she remembered she never even considered going to a university farther away from home because of the greater cost. Rambo was hardly alone in choosing to live at home: some two-fifths of the first-year class of 1968 made the same choice.

That pattern changed in the 1970s as living on campus, at least for one year, became the norm of the Eau Claire experience in a large part because of the increasing geographical scope of student recruiting and enrollment.

Long-time Director of Admissions Roger Groenewold recalled the admissions office consisted of just two persons when he began as a counselor in 1970. There was no plan for how many students to accept, little recruiting, and no attempt to shape the entering class. Admissions simply let the market send eligible students Eau Claire's way. According to Groenewold, the admissions office did not even have a target for the first-year class: "If 1,900 students matriculated, that was fine, and if the number was 2,100, that was fine, too."

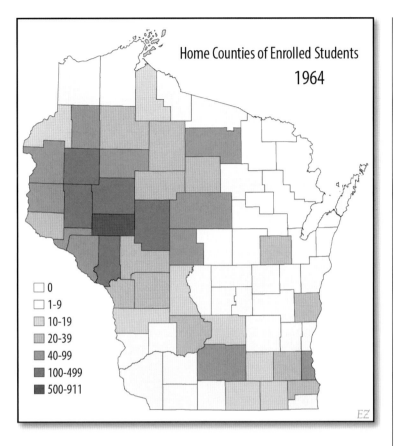

Map 6.1

When Eau Claire State became a university in 1964, it recruited a student body primarily from west-central Wisconsin.

Women made up a steadily growing percentage of the students who enrolled at WSU–EC between 1964 and 1971. Academic year 1966–67 was the last in which men constituted a majority of the students. The changing trend had become apparent during the previous years as more women than men entered the first-year class each fall. By 1966, women students accounted for 52.5 percent of the entering class, and just three years later that figure had risen to 57 percent. For the second fifty years of Eau Claire's history, the university would be an institution where women made up a majority of the student body, never falling below 54 percent and sometimes rising to as high as 61 percent. It was only a matter of time before the implications of that change were debated, contested, eventually understood, and became the basis for institutional change.

Yet another reason student enrollment rose so rapidly at Eau Claire State in the 1960s was costs were still low. The state colleges had a policy of not charging tuition to students from Wisconsin, believing the state received back far more from the corps of teachers they prepared than the state paid to them in support. The no-tuition policy continued after 1964 when the college became a university. The WSU institutions, however, did levy fees on students for books and extracurricular student activities and tuition on residents of other states. In 1968, the cost of attending Eau Claire State for a full academic year by a Wisconsin resident was $1,300: $600 for room and board in a residence hall, $300 in fees over the two semesters, and $400 in "incidental expenses." In real terms, tuition and fees more than quadrupled between 1966 and 2016 and the cost of room and board increased by more than 50 percent.

To a remarkable extent, Wisconsin taxpayers paid for the cost of education at Eau Claire State. Those state appropriations included monies for the capital costs of construction of academic buildings, for the buildings and grounds maintenance, and for instructional support. Students paid all the costs of their rooms in the residence halls and for their food from the cafeterias (in Davies Center and after 1968 in

Hilltop Center on upper campus). As seen in chapter five, federal student aid to college students started in 1958 with the National Defense Education Act, and this policy expanded in 1965 with the Higher Education Act. Both acts committed the United States to funding individual college students on the basis of student need and the needs of the national interest—for example, to produce more scientists and engineers. WSU–EC benefited somewhat in the second half of the 1960s from these new federal monies, but for every federal dollar that came to the university in 1968, the State of Wisconsin sent ten dollars.

At the same time student enrollment rose at such a rapid rate, the university struggled to hire and retain faculty to teach the new students. The faculty numbered about one hundred in 1959–60, the year the regents appointed Leonard Haas to lead Eau Claire State. By 1964–65, this number exceeded two hundred. In its review of the college in 1963, the North Central Association of Colleges and Secondary Schools (NCA) called for Eau Claire State to hire more faculty members with terminal degrees, especially the PhD. This proved difficult for the rest of the decade as newly produced PhD-holders enjoyed a seller's market for their services. Wisconsin kept an eye on distant California, mindful of the 1966 statement from the University of California president that the UC System's need for new faculty was such that California could absorb every single PhD produced in the country for five years.

The regents took note of the NCA's directives for a satisfactory student-faculty ratio of 18-1 for the nine-campus university system and later lowered it to 16-1. They authorized 272 faculty positions for WSU–EC to start academic year 1965–66, and the board added another forty-five faculty lines for the next year. By the end of the decade, the faculty at WSU–EC numbered more than five hundred and climbed to 567 for the 1972–73 academic year before reversing itself. Even so, each year the university struggled to find enough instructors to staff classrooms filled with ever more students. In the fall of 1967, students petitioned the dean of the School of Arts and Sciences, John Morris, for relief from overcrowded classes in the Department of English. They—not the faculty—asked that specialized literature courses be limited to thirty-five students and the freshman composition course required of all students be limited to twenty-five students per class.

At the same time, increased numbers made faculty decision making more cumbersome. "The faculty meetings had become long and arduous," Haas realized. As a result of recommendations from a committee headed by long-time psychology professor Inez Sparks, beginning in January 1965 a Faculty Senate of elected representatives took over the "real work" of governance, and meetings of the full faculty became usually pro-forma.

The curriculum the faculty designed rested on a wide base of general education courses in the liberal arts for students majoring in all subjects. The 1959 curriculum (chapter five) affirmed that general education "emphasizes the cultural heritage that is the possession of a free and responsible citizenry." The elementary education major, for example, required at least 128 credits of work, with the standard class counting for three credits. Elementary education majors had to take fifty-five credits of general education; twenty-seven credits of professional education courses; and another thirty-one credits of liberal arts courses such as speech, leaving just fifteen credits for electives. In 1964, secondary education majors preparing for careers at the senior high school level had to complete as many as 142 credits for the degree: fifty-five credits of general education, twenty-seven credits of professional education classes, a thirty-six-credit major, and a twenty-four-credit minor. This program left almost no room for electives. The secondary education major was, in effect, a five-year program. Students majoring in nursing also faced a long road to the degree: 136 credits, starting with fifty-five credits of general education. The faculty in the new School of Nursing, beginning in 1964, designed a degree program for the BSN that took eight semesters plus a summer session. The faculty in the new School of Business, starting in 1966, sought to build an accounting major "in the direction of a liberal education, rather than in the direction of a purely vocational orientation." The faculty further stated: "It is part of our mission to imbue others with the understanding that the pursuit of profits through the achievement of efficiency and effective performance makes a significant and necessary contribution not only to the affluent society but . . . to all of us for the good life. This becomes evident by a comparison with those societies which are economically under-developed and which have a correspondingly low development of the accounting discipline."

The prominence of general education in the Eau Claire State curriculum meant the faculty hired was tilted heavily toward the liberal arts. In 1967, the total faculty across the four schools of Business, Education, Nursing, and Arts and Sciences numbered 344. Of them, three-quarters (257) were in the School of Arts and Sciences. The combination of a faculty heavily weighted toward the liberal arts, and a student body weighted toward first-year students, meant the typical college course offered at Eau Claire State was an introductory-level lecture: Biology 1, Chemistry 1, History 1, Sociology 1, and so forth.

Eau Claire State prided itself on offering smaller class sizes than the University of Wisconsin, so instead of having just one or two big sections of an introductory course in a large lecture hall, the university offered many sections of the same course in smaller classrooms. Eau Claire's pride in this fact was to some extent a result of lack of facilities. Except for Schofield Auditorium, the campus lacked a large lecture theater until L. E. Phillips Science Hall opened in 1965, and that building only had one such room. The design for the new Social Science Building that opened in 1968, soon named Schneider Hall, also included only one room that could seat more than sixty students. Only the opening of the Humanities Building in 1974 gave the university four large lecture theaters in which to offer introductory courses.

Chemistry Class, c. 1970

Small classes were characteristic of WSU-EC.

Geography Lecture, Phillips Hall, late 1960s

Until the mid-1970s, large classes were held only in Schofield Auditorium and the first-floor lecture halls in Phillips and Schneider Halls.

One of the most important planning decisions Haas and Hibbard made in 1966–67 was to assign each academic department a target for generating student credits per faculty position. A department had to show it produced student credits at, or above, the product of the total number of students enrolled multiplied by the total number of credits per each class, divided by the total number of faculty in the department. At the high end, the departments in the social sciences such as Economics, Political Sciences, Psychology, and Sociology, as well as History, had to average four hundred student credits per faculty member, or since most classes were three credits, 133 students per faculty member. At the low end, the departments that offered individualized studio instruction, for example Art, Music, and Speech, had a target half the level of the social sciences, just two hundred student credits per faculty member. To meet these targets, faculty members were expected to teach four and sometimes five courses per semester, and the bulk of that for Arts and Sciences instructors came in introductory courses.

The idea of the student credit target for each academic department proved a durable management tool for presidents, chancellors, vice presidents, and deans, as it remained in use the entire second half of the university's history. It was devised at a time of rising enrollments as a way to allocate additional faculty positions; in the decade of the 1970s, however, when enrollments stalled and the legislature reduced appropriations, it would be used to eliminate faculty positions (chapter seven). It also remained in place when, in the late 1980s, academic departments began to take advantage of the auditoriums in Hibbard and Schneider Halls and shift towards a three-course teaching load for faculty, which meant larger class sizes.

The total number of faculty positions authorized masked a much larger number of instructors coming to and going from the university. In the 1966–67 academic year alone, WSU–EC made more than one hundred new faculty hires to reach its target size of 317. To encourage candidates to accept his job offers, President Haas maintained a policy of not reimbursing travel expenses for applicants who visited campus but declined an Eau Claire appointment. The rapid growth of the faculty at the entry level led to an imbalance in the ranks. The university had relatively few full professors at the start of the decade or even associate professors holding tenure. The vast increase in new faculty came at the bottom of the ranking system: instructors without the PhD or as untenured assistant professors with the terminal degree. This misshapen distribution of faculty-by-rank had consequences for the university for the next several decades: in the establishment of rules and procedures to govern faculty promotion and tenure decisions for so many untenured persons and then later over continued faculty development of those hired in the 1960s and the eventual replacement of a generational cohort of faculty.

Much as the student body had a large percentage of first-year students leaving the university, so, too, did many new faculty hires spend only a year or two at Eau Claire and then move on. Thirty-four faculty members left the university after the 1964–65 school year, and that number increased in the following years. In April 1968 the *Spectator* took note of the phenomenon of churning among the faculty ranks when it reported more than fifty instructors and professors would not be returning to campus for the 1968–69 academic year. "Why Did They Leave?" the newspaper asked in a lengthy feature, interviewing as many of the departing faculty members as possible. The reasons varied, from salary concerns to geographical preferences, to expressions of political disapproval of the university administration (too stuffy), to condemnations of life in a small Wisconsin manufacturing city.

Faculty grading policies continued to be rigorous throughout the 1960s. Kirk Ausman ('72) recalled when he began at the university in the fall of 1968, a faculty advisor in his major told him, "'You should start with a full load of credits' and so I started out right away with seventeen credits." Many alumni interviewed in 2013 recalled their favorite instructor's class as "hard," "demanding," or "difficult." A "C" grade standing for "satisfactory" really was the average, and few "A"s were awarded. In 1964–65, the median GPA of first-year students in all courses was a 2.19 on a 4.00 scale, just above a "C." Sophomores and juniors had a median GPA of 2.30 and 2.36, respectively, about a "C+." Even seniors earned a median GPA of just 2.54, a "B-."

The 1960s also saw a large increase in the staff on campus not directly offering instruction. This included persons working in the Davies Center, housing office, registrar's office, business services, and other offices. Eighty professional positions, in additional to classified staff, were devoted to these activities in 1970–71. Schofield Hall increasingly became a building devoted to offices and administrators, rather than the "Old Main" classroom building it had been up through the mid-1960s.

In 1963 President Haas chose Orsmby Harry as dean of students to supervise the growing number of student services. Dean of Men Willis Zorn reported to Harry. Dean Harry temporarily replaced the position of dean of women with a "Council of Head Residents," highlighting that a main task of his office was overseeing residential life. In an oral history he gave after his retirement in 1983, Harry recalled with pride how he recruited residence hall directors with graduate training or advanced degrees. They not only managed the residence halls, but for some years in the 1960s they served as the main academic advisers for students residing in them.

In 1970, James Bollinger, a basketball star for Zorn in the 1950s (chapter five), returned to campus as vice president for administrative services, overseeing personnel, buildings and grounds, and other activities. The following year, Charles Bauer, who had come to UW–EC in 1965 as director of business services, became executive vice president with responsibility for alumni relations, development, public relations, and institutional research.

Physical Growth—The Emergence of "Wisconsin's Most Beautiful Campus"

The university's logo in the 1960s might well have been a blueprint and the campus mascot a construction crane, what with all the building that took place in the decade. Students and their families coming to campus in the fall, and faculty on the way to work, all had to plan their walks around cyclone fencing and construction pathways. Each new building promised a much-needed solution to the space crunch for classrooms, laboratories, offices, and residence halls. Eau Claire State was hardly alone in experiencing dramatic growth in its physical campus. President Haas estimated that over the course of the decade the Wisconsin State University system constructed more than sixty buildings across its nine campuses. Behind this sometimes mad scramble for space and facilities lay the idea, sketched by Haas at his 1960 talk to the faculty, that the university could promote excellence by having a beautiful setting for teaching and learning. It was in the early 1960s that the college began printing on its letterhead the phrase, "Wisconsin's Most Beautiful Campus."

Until the end of the decade, the growth in student and faculty numbers always seemed to outpace the architect, the construction foreman, and the electrician. The most dramatic expansion in the first half of the decade took place on lower campus southeast of the new Davies Center: the new Science Hall. The legislature authorized $2.5 million for its construction at a time when the Biology, Chemistry, Geography, Geology, and Physics Departments had a total of about a dozen faculty members. Nonetheless, the small science faculty, along with faculty in the Department of Mathematics, secured grant funding from the National Science Foundation starting in 1961 for science teacher education and continued for several years to sponsor summer workshops for elementary, junior high, and high school teachers on campus and at the WSC cooperative facility at Pigeon Lake. The sciences had run out of room in Old Main and badly needed their own building with laboratory space. Moreover, the science faculty members Haas hired expected to have private office space for telephoning, writing, and meeting with students and colleagues.

The plans for the new Science Building, led by Chemistry Department chair Floyd Krause, included lecture halls, laboratories, faculty offices, and the Newman Bird Collection, all set astride Little Niagara Creek. Unlike in President Davies's time when Little Niagara was relocated for the building of the College Center, the construction of Science Hall took place without disturbing the creek. The new building welcomed visitors to cross the creek, to examine the specimens in the Newman Bird Collection, and to see the biggest and newest lecture hall on campus. The planners situated labs on the east and west sides of the building and placed faculty offices along the south side facing Putnam Park.

Aerial View of Campus, 1969

The construction of the upper campus residence halls, student center, and physical education center had been completed. This photograph shows how the university's buildings were separated from West Clairemont Avenue by the technical school, the state office building, and Sacred Heart Hospital (partially off-photo at lower right).

Groundbreaking took place in 1963 and the construction managers expected completion in time for the fall 1964 semester. Alas, inflation in building material and construction costs ate away at the final plans for Science Hall. Construction ran behind schedule and the state's allocation of $2.5 million proved inadequate to complete the planetarium and all the laboratories Krause's Science Hall Building Committee had sought. In the fall of 1963, Haas learned the budget was some $250,000 short of what was needed to complete the building as planned. He took the unusual step of asking a private donor, Eau Claire industrialist Louis E. Phillips, to contribute the funds needed to equip the laboratories in Science Hall. Haas walked away from a meeting with a pledge from Phillips for a quarter million dollars, at that time the largest single gift made to any Wisconsin State College. The appropriately named L. E. Phillips Science Hall opened in the fall of 1965, with Governor Warren Knowles taking part in ceremonies including a keynote speech by Nobel Prize-winning astrophysicist James Van Allen. Barely two years into occupancy of Phillips Science Hall, the university started planning an expansion of the building to accommodate more labs and equipment for the growing physical science and life science programs.

The lead news story in the September 15, 1966, *Spectator* greeting new and returning students to campus had the headline, "Current Program Initiates $30 Million Building Plans." It noted plans to open a new heating plant on the upper campus and a "footbridge" across the Chippewa River. After the completion of Phillips Science Hall, building focused on the upper campus with Bridgman and Sutherland residence halls opening in 1965. The latter was named for history professor and Dean of

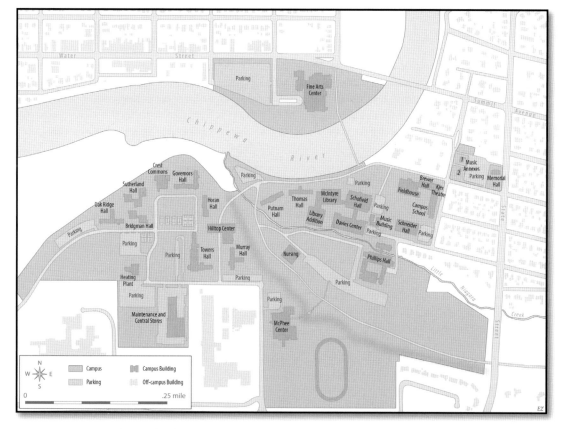

Map 6.2

The campus by 1970 had expanded dramatically into upper and lower parts and also on both sides of the Chippewa River.

Women Laura E. Sutherland, who died in 1964. Murray Hall, named for an English teacher on the original faculty, opened the next year. By far the biggest construction project on the upper campus started in April 1965 when the regents approved Towers North and South, a pair of residence halls which opened in 1967. The two new buildings provided more than six hundred double-occupancy rooms, enough to house more than half the first-year class for the 1967–68 academic year. For the next half-century, the first-year experience for many Eau Claire students included a year in Towers. The design for Towers came from WSU–Oshkosh, an example of the WSU System economizing on architects' fees by simply copying plans from one campus to another.

The dramatic expansion of residence halls on the upper campus was completed by the opening of Oak Ridge Hall, with beds for about 350 women, in 1969. Residence hall construction was accompanied by the construction of support buildings. The Eugene McPhee Physical Education Building and a second student union, Hilltop Center, opened in 1969. Consequently, the upper campus emerged as the location where students spent much of their time, especially the first-year students and sophomores who were living in the new halls.

Construction of McPhee Physical Education Center, December 1967

Similar disruptions occurred across most of both upper and lower campuses between 1965 and 1975.

THE NEW UNIVERSITY: EXCELLENCE AND GROWTH

It was on the north bank of the Chippewa River that President Haas met a significant defeat in "town–gown" relations. The issue was the university's plans for a concert hall fronting on the Chippewa River with ample parking on the north side of Water Street. Again, recalling his 1960 speech to the faculty, Haas had long wanted a concert hall as a showcase for the finest music where faculty, students, and visiting artists could perform. The Kjer Theater was no longer suitable and neither was Schofield Auditorium or the fieldhouse, although the Minneapolis Symphony (forerunner to the Minnesota Orchestra) and the Milwaukee Symphony made annual visits to the fieldhouse throughout the 1960s. Haas thought the north bank of the river, between the water's edge and Water Street, would be a fine site for a 2,500-seat theater.

The difficulty was the state had no taste for spending that much money on a concert hall that would primarily benefit the Eau Claire community. Consequently, the regents capped their bonding request to the legislature at $1 million. In 1966, therefore, Haas proposed a joint venture with Eau Claire County: a building that would combine classrooms, recital rooms, and faculty offices with a large concert hall. The state would put up $1 million, and the county would issue bonds for another $1.5 million. The president organized a "Friends for the Community-University Concert Hall" to encourage citizens to contact the county board with their support for a bond issue.

To Haas, the matter was straightforward: the county (and the larger Chippewa Valley) could have an excellent $2.5 million concert hall at a cost of just $1.5 million. To faculty and music supporters, the idea held out the promise that Eau Claire could become a leading regional center for music performances. To some county board supervisors, however, the idea seemed more like the university getting a $2.5 million concert hall for just $1 million with local property-owners picking up most of the tab through higher taxes. Some supervisors objected to the location, on the Chippewa River flood plain, but the bigger objection was to raising property taxes for bonding and debt service on a project that seemed to benefit mainly one party, the university. The county board chair told Haas that $1.5 million would never get a majority of the board's support. Haas cut his request to just $800,000, but even that proved too much. The board rejected the proposal by a 7–28 vote. In the end, the state approved money for the new Fine Arts Building at WSU–EC but with a concert hall nowhere near as large or as splendid as the one originally contemplated by Haas. The lesson was the little college on the Chippewa was no longer so little, and its town and county neighbors did not always think what was good for the university was good for the rest of Eau Claire.

Art Class, 1970-71

The Fine Arts Building provided modern studio art facilities, replacing makeshift spaces in Brewer Hall and elsewhere around campus.

Schneider Social Science Hall, 1967-68

John Schneider taught history and sociology from 1930 to 1961. In the community, he was a director of the Consumers Cooperative Association, member of the Eau Claire County Democratic Party Executive Committee, an active Mason, and a member of the First Congregational Church.

Between 1968 and 1974 the university filled in parts of the lower campus with additional academic facilities. The regents directed WSU–EC to use the design for a building at WSU–Stevens Point as the basis for a structure which would house social science departments and where the university's new School of Business would also have its home. That building, named after sociology and history professor John Schneider, opened in 1968. The School of Nursing also needed its own building and in 1969 got one on a parcel of lower campus which jutted into Putnam Park behind Putnam and Katherine Thomas Halls. The university also began planning in 1970 for the academic high-rise building President Haas had held out for in the 1964 dispute with Third Ward residents (chapter five). Plans for this new Humanities Building proposed it as the largest of any academic building on campus: five large lecture theaters, fifteen smaller lecture/classrooms, eleven seminar rooms, and of great importance to the faculty—175 offices. Until the Humanities Building opened in 1974, faculty in departments such as English or Foreign Languages, if they even had an office, held their office hours in the trailers that remained on the lower campus.

The final building of the Haas presidency, the Ecumenical Religious Center, fondly known as the ERC, opened on non-state property in 1975. This building's plan echoed Haas's 1960 speech to the faculty calling for a residential college that encouraged the spiritual growth of its students, faculty, and staff. The Catholic Diocese of La Crosse in 1963 bought the property at 110 Roosevelt, west of where the Humanities Building would be constructed, for a campus Newman Club. Reflecting the changing orientation of the Catholic Church following the Second Vatican Council, the Newman Center, along with the Lutheran Student House, became an intellectual center on campus in the mid-1960s. In the spring 1964 semester, Father James Lovejoy, the Newman chaplain, hosted a forum on "Vatican II—Its Contents and Impact." During the 1966–67 academic year, the Newman Club held monthly forums on current topics ranging from abortion to the Vietnam War, to premarital sex to suicide, to the more beseeching "Has Modern Society Dismissed Religion as a Moral Force in the 20th Century?"

Ecumenical Religious Center, 1974

Reverend Robert McKillip, shown here with plans for the ERC expansion, was chaplain of the Newman Club. He opened the May 6, 1970, Cambodian protest rally by asking for four minutes of silence in memory of the students shot to death at Kent State University.

Later in the 1960s, an interdenominational Cooperative Campus Ministry, formally independent of the university, emerged in an effort by denominational and campus leaders to make available to students, faculty, and staff worship services, pastoral counseling, and seminars, forums, debates, and lectures on topics about religion in American life. In 1970, Haas reaffirmed to the Catholic bishop of La Crosse, "It has been the deliberate policy at WSU-EC to give every encouragement possible in a non-sectarian state supported institution to efforts of those who are concerned with the spiritual life of students." Building on these efforts, in 1970 the ERC was incorporated. Catholics and Lutherans—both of whom organized congregations which included students, faculty, and community members—participated in the ERC at 110 Roosevelt with the United Campus Ministries, itself a cooperative arrangement of four mainstream Protestant denominations. The ERC deflected the efforts of Haas to obtain the property for university uses, and in 1975 it completed construction of an addition to the building—a 285-seat chapel.

In retrospect, this campus interest in the inner life led directly to two permanent changes at the university. The first was the decades-long cooperation by mainstream Protestant denominations, eventually joined by Catholics, which led to the establishment in a prime site adjoining the campus of the ERC and came to serve as the university chapel President Davies had desired (chapter five). The second was the faculty saw the importance of the academic study of religion by starting a minor in the discipline, which eventually became a major offered by the Department of Philosophy and Religious Studies. Appropriately, Willis Gertner, who had been the campus Lutheran minister, became the department's first religious studies professor.

TABLE 6.2 BUILDING PROJECTS, 1961-75		
Year	Academic Buildings	Residence Halls
1961		Horan Hall
1962		Governors Hall
1963	McIntyre Library	
1964	L.E. Phillips Science Hall	
1965		Bridgman / Sutherland
1966		Murray
1967	Schneider Social Science Hall	Towers
1968	L.E. Phillips Hall expansion	Hilltop
1969	McPhee Phy Ed Center	Oak Ridge Hall
1969	School of Nursing Building	
1970	Fine Arts Building (HFA)	
1971	McIntyre Library Addition	
1974	Hibbard Humanities Hall	
1975	Ecumenical Religious Center	
Other Facilities		
1966—Heating Plant		
1967--Carillon		
1970—Footbridge		

Academic Program Growth: The Creation of a Regional Comprehensive University

Contemporary and subsequent explanations about post-secondary enrollment in the 1960s tend to focus on one side of the story—the student demand for access to college. They overlook the other side—the supply of admission spaces in colleges. Certainly no one at Eau Claire State in 1960 even remotely expected a decade later the college would accommodate more than eight thousand students. However, the leadership on the board of regents and in Schofield Hall began to prepare for growth.

The preparations began with a modest increase in the mission of Eau Claire State: the offering of graduate work by college faculty in cooperation with the University of Wisconsin's College of Education. Starting in 1960, Eau Claire State faculty taught summer classes for students working on master's degrees in education, almost all of them in-service teachers in the Chippewa Valley. The cooperative agreement intensified the existing friction between Eau Claire State and the UW, while the students who enrolled soon demanded they be able to complete their degrees entirely at Eau Claire. The faculty quickly decided to request permission from the regents and the Coordinating Committee for Eau Claire State itself to offer graduate degrees, a pattern also followed by the other WSC campuses. Beginning in 1964 Eau Claire began to award the MST degree, a combination of pedagogy, liberal arts, and subject matter courses for teachers. This program was an important stage in the development of the college into a university.

In another important aspect of becoming a university, Eau Claire State reorganized its academic administration in 1964 under Vice President Hibbard into a series of "schools," later somewhat confusingly called "colleges." The first school was Arts and Sciences and consisted mainly of liberal arts departments that offered both general education introductory courses and their own majors. The School of Arts and Sciences also housed some departments outside of the liberal arts, including the university's medical technology program. Haas and Hibbard appointed a political scientist, Robert Gibbon, as first dean of Arts and Sciences. Two years later, John Morris, chair of the Department of English, succeeded Gibbon.

At the same time the School of Arts and Sciences was established, the teacher education departments—Elementary Education, Secondary Education, a new Junior High School program, and Special Education—were gathered under Dean Lester Emans in a School of Education. In 1965, education students began an experiment that dramatically changed teacher training, as well as the staff doing the training. That year a large number of senior education majors received paid internships that lasted a full semester and gave education majors a real-life experience in leading a classroom. After Rodney Johnson became dean of the School of Education upon Emans's retirement in 1969, he worked to increase the number of paid student-teaching internships to 120 per year. The state budget crisis in the early 1970s, however, largely put an end to this Wisconsin Improvement Program. Other initiatives continued in the School of Education. Beginning in 1970, Lloyd Joyal, Max Poole, and Juanitta Sorenson, supported by a grant from the Wisconsin Research and Development Center, directed the Individually Guided Education program, which became an emphasis within the MST degree.

The next school to be created was Nursing. Throughout the 1950s, with the permission of the regents, Eau Claire State planned for a baccalaureate degree program in nursing. The two hospitals in Eau Claire—Luther and Sacred Heart—had run diploma nursing education programs as part of their mission, although Sacred Heart abandoned its program during the Great Depression. As seen in chapter five, Eau Claire State had cooperated with Luther by providing classroom instruction for first-year students in its diploma program. In the early 1960s, when Sacred Heart constructed its new building adjacent to the upper campus, it also wanted to establish a nurse-training relationship with WSU–EC. For its part, Luther Hospital did not want to abandon nursing education, as the growing hospital wanted a guaranteed supply of highly trained nurses, but they were not able to compete with the new WSU–EC/Sacred Heart alignment. The university agreed to accept students from Luther's diploma program when that hospital suddenly terminated its program in October 1965.

Eau Claire State agreed to take on the task of nursing education at a time when none of the nine universities in the WSU System offered a BSN degree. In western Wisconsin, only Viterbo College in La Crosse offered such a degree. There was a significant difference between the diploma nursing program, such as Luther Hospital's, and the baccalaureate program Eau Claire State contemplated. Students graduating from a diploma program received a certificate qualifying them to seek a license as a practical or registered nurse; students with a BN degree became registered nurses who could assume additional duties and administer a floor unit in a hospital or medical center. The first nursing class at WSU–EC began in the fall of 1965.

The administration in the new School of Nursing had no idea of how great the demand would be for admission in the 1966–67 school year. The first faculty, led by Dean Marguerite Coffman, set a minimum entry GPA of 2.30; the dean was stunned when more than two hundred students sought admission to the one hundred places set aside in the first class. The average GPA of those admitted was 3.60. From the very start, the School of Nursing taught some of the most high-achieving students in the university.

An external accrediting agency—the Wisconsin State Board of Nursing—granted temporary approval in 1965 for WSU–EC's nursing program. Full-fledged accreditation depended on the university's ability to show it could educate nurses at a high standard of excellence, a task that began with recruiting a faculty with the mix of earned doctorates and clinical leadership experience. Dean Coffman began 1965–66 with three faculty members. By January 1967, the School of Nursing faculty had grown to nine. For the start of the 1967–68 academic year, it had increased to twenty-two faculty members. Each year, Coffman made the case to Hibbard and to Haas they needed more and better-trained faculty to earn long-term accreditation. By 1969–70, when the School of Nursing expected to reach its full complement of four hundred students, she asked the administration for twenty-eight full-time faculty positions. The important point is the decision to expand the university into nursing education had significant consequences for the allocation of budget support.

Eau Claire State's School of Business also started in the mid-1960s and experienced a similarly rapid growth. Unlike the School of Nursing, the School of Business had its origins in teacher training, specifically the preparation of high school teachers in business and office education. Building on a business education program initiated in 1959 (chapter five), in 1960 the college added a new degree in business administration, administered by the faculty in the Department of Economics, and four years later began offering classes toward a major in accounting. In academic year 1965–66, the university decided to create the new School of Business with departments of Business Administration, Business Education, and Economics. The School of Education, led by Dean Emans, protested the loss of Business Education, and the School of Arts and Sciences, led by Dean Morris, objected to the loss of Economics. In the end, Business Education moved to the new school, but Economics remained in Arts and Sciences. Enrollment in the new School of Business surged dramatically in the late 1960s, especially by students pursuing the bachelor of business administration degree. Just five years after its creation, its enrollment topped two thousand.

The graduate school also expanded rapidly after its formal organization in 1963. A record 714 graduate students enrolled in the summer of 1971 and 480 that fall. R. Dale Dick, a psychologist, succeeded Emans as dean in 1966. His selection was part of a sometimes contentious shift of WSU–EC's orientation in graduation instruction from kindergarten through high school education programs towards the liberal arts. In the late 1960s MA and MS programs, not limited to teachers, began to be offered in biology, chemistry, communication disorders, English, history, and medical technology. Correspondingly, the number of MST graduates fell by 23 percent between 1969 and 1971 and, much to the chagrin of the faculty of the School of Education, there was discussion among the liberal arts faculty of eliminating, or at least deemphasizing, that program. Meanwhile, in 1968 the regents designated WSU–EC as one of the two sites in their system for development of doctoral programs to prepare the next generation of teachers at state universities. Strenuous objections to this ambition, supported by the Coordinating Committee, came from the University of Wisconsin, which further increased bad feeling between the UW and WSU Systems.

Confirming Excellence by External Evaluations

The postwar decision by President Davies to seek external accreditation from the North Central Association (chapter five) meant every ten years Eau Claire State faced self-studies, campus visits, external reports, and responses to lists of matters for attention in order to keep the seal of NCA accreditation. In similar fashion, Eau Claire State had joined the American Association of Colleges of Teacher Education (AATCE) in 1928 (chapter three). The college continued to be accredited by the

National Council for Accreditation of Teacher Education (NCATE) when that organization morphed out of the AATCE in 1954; NCATE reaccredited Eau Claire State in 1963. The college was also a founding member in 1960 of the American Association of State Colleges and Universities (AASCU). This organization began as a way to make sure the voices of the old normal schools and state teachers colleges—like Eau Claire—were not drowned out by the power of bigger schools and colleges of education within the flagship state universities. AASCU did not offer accreditation or certification, but it did provide a network for administrators to meet and learn from one another. Leonard and Dorellen Haas were annual attendees at the AASCU summer workshops.

The impact of external accrediting agencies turned out to be something of a double-edged sword. One edge brought plaudits and external recognition of the excellence Eau Claire State sought to build in its undergraduate programs. The external reviews also put pressure on the board of regents, and through them the legislature and governor, to provide the necessary funding to maintain excellent programs. However, the external reviews also made Eau Claire State vulnerable to negative evaluations by authorities beyond the control of the campus or the state. That became a major problem in the 1980s.

More broadly, NCA and NCATE reviews compelled Eau Claire to measure itself against changes and trends in US public higher education. The biggest such challenge was the impossibility of reconciling President Haas's vision of the small residential liberal arts college with the realities of a rapidly growing regional state university. An accrediting team from NCA led by Samuel Gates, dean of education at Colorado State University (and later president of WSU–La Crosse), came to Eau Claire State in February 1963. Its resulting report recommended reaccreditation of the liberal arts baccalaureate programs, the teacher education program, and the graduate program in education. The report, however, pointed up some areas of concern for Eau Claire State. Gates called for the college to become more of a regional comprehensive university and less of the residential commonwealth that Haas had envisioned in 1960. The NCA called for more support for faculty scholarship, including the provision of regular sabbatical leaves for faculty renewal and development. It also called for an immediate focus on recruiting more PhDs to the faculty, a lower student-faculty ratio, and a decreased teaching load in order to support more faculty scholarship. The NCA also recommended scrapping the commonwealth type of campus government in favor of a multiversity-style system of different colleges led by semi-autonomous deans, especially the dean of education.

The NCA and NCATE reports of 1963 came at the cusp of Eau Claire State's boom in campus growth. In the next few years, WSU–EC made decisions to expand its curriculum in a way that the switch in governance to the multiversity model was inevitable.

Celebrating Excellence: The Golden Jubilee, 1965–66

Soon after taking office as the third president of the college, Leonard Haas began talking to his faculty about the importance of the year 1966—the centennial anniversary of normal school education in Wisconsin and the golden anniversary of the establishment of Eau Claire Normal. Haas appointed a planning committee in 1960, which got to serious work in 1964. Academic year 1965–66 was devoted to reflecting upon the beginnings and accomplishments of Eau Claire and the other eight campuses in the Wisconsin State University System. The October 1965 dedication of the new Phillips Science Hall, with Governor Knowles in attendance, proved a stirring kickoff to the Golden Jubilee year.

Alas, all did not go well with the combined Eau Claire Golden Jubilee and WSU Centennial. The expected highlights of the celebration included a volume recounting the history of Eau Claire State to be authored by retired faculty member Laura Sutherland. She died before she could revise her book manuscript and the fragment she did leave was not included in a centennial-themed volume of essays on each state university that did get published. Instead, Hilda Carter of the University News Bureau undertook the research and writing of a chapter on Eau Claire. The WSU history volume began with an unusual, if enthusiastic, simile presented by WSU–River Falls President Walker D. Wyman which compared the state colleges and universities to a "deep well thrust down through the middle and lower economic layers of society," with the gratifying result that the sons and daughters of Wisconsin were "drawn upward to new levels of service and status." Carter's characterization of Eau Claire State's fifty-year history was more modest, but still positive. More than ten thousand persons received a degree or a diploma from the institution, she emphasized, surely improving their own lives and that of the state of Wisconsin.

Professor Wilmur Pautz of the School of Education undertook a jubilee year project by devising a questionnaire for Eau Claire alumni. The alumni office had addresses for almost six thousand living alumni, and 3,550 completed and returned this survey. Among the data Pautz gathered, one comparison stood out: the extent of the social mobility on the part of Eau Claire Normal/Eau Claire State graduates, as measured by years of education compared to their parents. Not even 30 percent of men who had graduated from the college could say their fathers had completed high school, and about the same percentage (28 percent) reported their fathers had not even completed the eighth grade. The women alumni had slightly better educated mothers: 40 percent were high school graduates and only 19 percent told Pautz their mothers had not completed the eighth grade. The takeaway from the Pautz survey was Eau Claire alumni came to college from households with low educational backgrounds, and yet these same alumni used their college degrees to pull themselves up into the professional part of the middle class as teachers and principals (chapter three).

The highlight of the jubilee celebration year was a June 4, 1966, banquet in the Davies Center. President Haas invited US Vice President Hubert H. Humphrey to give a keynote address, but he could not secure the Minnesotan's participation. Haas himself gave the address to an audience of six hundred diners, including five faculty and fourteen students from the opening class of 1916. The university advertised the jubilee widely, paying for celebratory supplements in the *Eau Claire Leader*, the *Spectator*, and the *Periscope*. In addition, Haas asked each academic department to name students and faculty worthy of receiving an "Excellence" medallion, awarding 150 of them at the banquet. Department of Art faculty member Kenneth Campbell designed the image on the medallion and it remains on the university's seal in 2016. Campbell placed the Council Oak (chapter three) at the center of the seal and surrounded it with the name "Wisconsin State University-Eau Claire" and emblazoned the word "Excellence" at the bottom. Haas stated in 1985 that he never tried to define the word "excellence" for the campus, but he thought the "average faculty member" likely understood it to be "doing the best you can with the talent you have and with the resources you have available." For students, excellence meant "challenging themselves academically and as future leaders; for faculty, the most important element of excellence was teaching, excellence in and out of the classroom working with students."

To underscore the importance of excellence in teaching, in 1966 the university started an annual award under that name. The award came with a cash prize, a medallion, and the recipient's name featured on a plaque outside the president's office in Schofield Hall. Recent alumni selected these Excellence in Teaching recipients. Graduates from between two and four years before the time of the selection received ballots. The faculty member who came in first in the balloting won the award. In subsequent years, the university added Excellence awards to faculty and academic staff for Scholarship, Academic Advising, and Service and Excellence in Performance awards to Administrative and Professional Staff and to Classified Staff.

University Seal, 1966

Kenneth Campbell designed the seal and taught art and art history from 1964 to 1988. Off campus, Campbell designed the initial exhibits in the Chippewa Valley Museum, a history museum located in Eau Claire's Carson Park.

Who was a Blugold? Recruiting Minorities and the "Disadvantaged"

Just two years after his "Gothic Cathedral" address on the change from college to the university, President Haas once again addressed the faculty on the need for change. His topic at a November 26, 1968, faculty meeting, as reported in a *Spectator* headline, was "Haas talks on 'U' Direction, Issues." The president offered suggestions about changes in student life, including proposals to improve the academic experience, residence hall living, and student government. However, from the perspective of nearly a half-century later, perhaps the most important part of Haas's remarks was his call to recruit more minority and "disadvantaged" students to attend the university and for the institution to devote more resources to topics related to minorities and the "disadvantaged." In the language of 1968, Haas sometimes used the phrase "culturally distinct" to refer to minority students, sometimes in the same phrase as the term "culturally disadvantaged," by which he meant to include poor white students.

Haas's call for change at WSU–EC came at the end of perhaps the most tumultuous week in the history of the Wisconsin State University System. At WSU–Oshkosh, on November 21 African American students occupied the office of President Roger Guiles and tried to compel him to discuss with them a set of demands they had presented the previous month. When Guiles refused to discuss the students' demands, some in the gathering destroyed property in his office. Guiles called the city police and ninety-four students were arrested, booked at the Winnebago County Courthouse, and then jailed at various facilities around the Fox Valley. Guiles closed WSU–Oshkosh for five days, and while the Winnebago County District Attorney contemplated prosecutions, the president suspended *en masse* the "Oshkosh 94." After an appeals hearing in December, the regents expelled ninety of the protesters. At UW–Stevens Point, the decision by its president, Lee Sherman Dreyfuss, to deny a campus charter to Students for a Democratic Society (SDS) led to a confrontation between students and faculty, on the one hand, and the board of regents on the other, as SDS–Stevens Point continued to meet on campus despite the regents' ban.

At six of the nine WSU campuses during the week before Thanksgiving in 1968, telephoned bomb threats shut down academic buildings until emergency service personnel could check for safety. WSU–Eau Claire was one of the six affected campuses, with the main switchboard receiving a call stating a bomb would go off in Phillips Hall. That fall, the university also had ongoing controversies over a successor group to SDS, the Campus Involvement Association (CIA), over the expulsion of a popular African American student and Dean Zorn's questioning of two African American students for hosting an off-campus interracial party. Student leaders staged a teach-in on November 26, 1968, at which more than one thousand protesters came to discuss the Vietnam War, race relations in America, and the future of WSU–EC. The teach-in lasted all night, and for once women students from the residence halls were allowed to stay out later than curfew without punishment. One alumna later recalled the 1968 teach-in as "where we were up all night trying to educate one another."

Haas told the faculty on November 26 that the university needed to recruit more minority students. Haas had already shown interest in American Indian students from Wisconsin reservation communities and in African Americans. In 1962–63, for example, the Harvard-Radcliffe Indian Project contacted Veda Stone, a Wisconsin social worker, about placing its students to work with American Indian children from Wisconsin reservations. Stone needed a Wisconsin partner to host such a project and turned to Haas. In turn, the president made campus facilities available during the summer of 1963 for the first Midwest Indian Youth Leadership Program (MIYLP). Haas turned to professor John Hunnicut in the Sociology Department to coordinate the event. Hunnicut and Stone, working with Harvard and Radcliffe faculty, invited twenty-five high school-age native youth to Eau Claire State for two weeks from the Red Cliff, Bad River, St. Croix Ojibwe bands, and Winnebago (now Ho-Chunk) tribal communities at Neilsville and Black River Falls.

Hunnicut and Stone repeated the MIYLP the next year and subsequent summers. Some of the established and emerging American Indian leaders came to campus to work with the MIYLP, including Robert Bennett (Oneida), President Kennedy's commissioner of Indian Affairs; Vine DeLoria Jr. (Standing Rock Lakota), the executive director of the National Congress of American Indians; Ada Deer

Ann Devroy's Work as a Spectator *Journalist*

Ann Devroy ('70) pursued a career in journalism, holding positions at the Eau Claire *Leader-Telegram*, the Bridgewater (New Jersey) *Courier-News*, the Associated Press, and the *Washington Post*. At the *Post*, she became White House Bureau chief, where she earned a reputation as a fine reporter and editor. As a measure of respect for Devroy's determined journalism, there was a story repeated that in the 1990s, the five most feared words in Washington offices were "Ann Devroy, on line one."

Her career was cut short by cancer, and after her death at age forty-nine in 1997, her husband, Mark Matthews of the *Baltimore Sun*, established the Ann Devroy Fellowship at UWEC in 1998, awarded annually to a *Spectator* staffer. It carried with it an internship at both a local newspaper and at the *Post*. Each April, the university hosted a Devroy memorial event featuring a prominent journalist who addressed both current events and Ann Devroy's legacy as a Washington journalist.

Ann Devroy learned her journalism in classes at the university and in covering the campus and city beats for the *Spectator*. Her first bylined story appeared in September 1967 when she reported on the campus visit of US Representative Allard Lowenstein. In a fine pyramid style of writing, she reported the who, what, when, where, and why in the first paragraph: "The elimination of Lyndon Baines Johnson as a candidate in the 1968 presidential election is the main objective of Allard K. Lowenstein, a Democrat from New York, who spoke to Wisconsin State University-Eau Claire students last Tuesday afternoon."

As a reporter, she maintained an interest in covering national politics, including the March 1968 Wisconsin Democratic primary. She interviewed Paul Newman, who spoke to a crowd in Owen Park that Devroy estimated at three hundred, where the film star led a campaign rally for Senator Eugene McCarthy (D-Minnesota). Devroy wrote in her story that Newman asserted he came to speak to Eau Claire students, "Not as a movie star, but because I've got six kids . . . and we can't put up with four more years like the ones we've had."

Devroy published other bylined stories in the *Spectator* about the anti-war movement, including one on the founding of a group called Campus Involvement Action that preferred to be called by its initials. At a CIA meeting in September 1968, students mixed calls for reform on campus with calls for radical change in the United States. Devroy reported that CIA also demanded an end to "ridiculous" restrictions on visiting hours in women's residence halls. CIA, according to Devroy's reporting, also hoped students would see there were "two Americas, the America of President Johnson and the America of President Haas," on the one hand and on the other a future "our America. The two are in direct opposition to each other."

Contemporaries remembered Devroy's journalism in varied ways. Alumna Sandra Lindow ('74, but who started at Eau Claire State a year behind Devroy's class) remembers Devroy's journalism as "subtly" radical in outlook and tone. One-time *Spectator* faculty adviser Elwood Kirwand did not recall anything subtle about Devroy: "There was a lot of unhappiness with the (Vietnam) war. Ann definitely spoke her mind, and it didn't really seemingly matter to Ann the fact that they happened to be a professor or an editor. If she had something to say, she said it." Whether subtle or blunt in her journalism, the student-journalist did not suffer fools gladly, even if she might have sympathized with their politics. For example, she wrote about four Eau Claire students who traveled to Washington in October 1967 to march at the Pentagon in response to the call by the National Mobilization Committee to End the War in Vietnam. She learned in her interviews with the quartet that they left Eau Claire for the weekend not to take part in the levitation of the Pentagon, but because, as they said, "They simply got bored . . . and [wanted] to see the action . . . to do their anti-war thing."

In addition to working as a student-reporter, Devroy joined the *Spectator* editorial board in the fall of 1967 as organizations editor. In that capacity, she directed coverage of student groups on campus, often taking her notebook to report directly on events. She covered Student Senate meetings and journeyed to Stevens Point to cover the 1968 meeting of the inter-campus United Council of Student Governments, a group that included delegates from all nine WSU campuses (chapter ten). She showed a particular interest in covering issues related to residence hall life and off-campus student housing. She also covered student government elections and even wrote a letter to the editor decrying the influence of the Tau Kappa Epsilon fraternity in running candidates for office.

During her junior year at Eau Claire State, 1968–69, she held two editorial positions at the *Spectator*: copy editor and news editor. Her reporting that year included a number of articles and "news analysis" commentaries about the ongoing issue of student and faculty rights versus the prerogatives of the administration and regents. Her news stories covered these issues in a straightforward manner, but her opinion pieces made clear her support for student and faculty rights to due process. She had little regard for the WSU Board of Regents and its belief it could run the state universities as it saw fit. In 1967–68, Devroy covered the conflict on campus over the non-renewal of the faculty contracts of English Department faculty members Neal and Elizabeth Resnikoff, including a boycott of classes and a teach-in at the Davies Center. During the summer of 1968, she observed the WSU Board of Regents as it discussed issuing a faculty and a student conduct rulebook. In a series of opinion columns, Devroy questioned the board's actions in limiting free speech and the right of assembly and carving out exceptions to rules about due process. She ended one "Soapbox" column in the *Spectator* with this hard-hitting finale: "The Regents can now breathe a sigh of relief. Their all-important face has been saved. The only losers in this political game will be the unfortunate people who happen to carry the sad name of students."

Whether it was the WSU Board of Regents in the 1960s or the Clinton White House in the 1990s, Ann Devroy lived up to the best traditions of journalism: she comforted the afflicted and afflicted the comfortable. The "Ann Devroy on line one" of White House journalism may be clearly seen in the work of Ann Devroy, student-journalist, in the pages of the *Spectator*.

Ann Devroy

After learning journalism on the Spectator *and in class at Eau Clare, Devroy went on to a career with the* Washington Post, *including a stint as White House Bureau chief.*

About the Author

Ann Devroy, Green Bay sophomore, is a journalism major and Organizations Editor of the Spectator.

"I don't claim to be any expert on the legality of the Code, but I think the Regents are going too far when they try to control every aspect of our lives, including things we do while we're off campus."

Midwest Indian Youth Leadership Seminar, c. 1965

Veda Stone, a social worker who helped organize this program, later returned to UW-EC to teach in American Indian studies. In 1973 she earned an award from the National Indian Education Association for "outstanding and dedicated service" and in 1975 received the UW-EC Alumni Distinguished Service Award.

(Menominee), later President Bill Clinton's assistant secretary of the interior for Indian Affairs; and Nancy Lurie of the Department of Anthropology at the University of Wisconsin and later head curator of anthropology at the Milwaukee Public Museum. One of the students who attended the MIYLP was an Ojibwe from the Lac Courte Oreilles Reservation, Richard St. Germaine, who chose to attend the university. After obtaining his doctorate, he joined the faculty. By 1968, the MIYLP expanded to an April on-campus weekend seminar in addition to the two-week June program. More than one hundred American Indian young people came to Eau Claire for a taste of college.

Haas and other faculty members used the success of the MIYLP to begin to recruit African American high school students to an expanded summer program at Eau Claire. A sociologist colleague of Hunnicut's, John Stoelting, led the WSU–EC program for "high-risk and disadvantaged youth." He planned a 1969 summer program that would draw 160 high school students to campus, who this time would not be limited to American Indians but would also include African Americans.

After the November 26, 1968, faculty meeting, Haas appointed Stoelting to head a campus task force on the topic of recruiting more minority students by offering them more in the way of curriculum and extracurricular activities. The proposed curriculum would include courses in black history, black literature, and possibly even a black studies program. Stoelting's task force worked with the Afro-American Association, a student group, to begin a Black Culture Week in early February, including extending an invitation to the folk singer Odetta to perform on campus. The *Spectator* began running a "Black Essence" column that it opened to the officers of the Afro-American Association. AAA President Michael Simmons wrote a piece entitled "Call Me Black," telling the campus, "I am no longer a Negro, but I am proud to be Black." Other students wrote opinion pieces in the "Black Essence" op-ed slot about "The Feeling of Soul" and about "Black Hair." The following year AAA Vice President Debi Johnson wrote an essay about the death of Chicago Black Panther leader Fred Hampton.

WSU–EC's abrupt, sometimes awkward, attempt in 1968–69 to address issues of race had some successes and some setbacks. It was one thing to bring American Indian or African American high school students to campus for part of a summer session but more of a challenge to ask the students, faculty, and staff to change the university to make it more welcoming to minority students, especially African Americans. Black Culture Week in February 1969 was a success, as seven hundred students, mainly white, attended a dance sponsored by the AAA at which a Milwaukee group, the Commodores, played soul music. A popular African American student, Bill Bolden, was elected Winter Carnival King. That same month, the University Senate approved new course proposals and planned new books and curriculum materials on black studies for McIntyre Library. Nonetheless, the pace of change felt too slow for a group called the Black Students Coalition (BSC). In April, they staged "black-white" confrontations in twenty classes, to the surprise of unknowing students. A follow-up teach-in revealed the instructors in the classes gave permission to the confronters to enter their classrooms.

What the Kids were listening to in the 1960s: From the Four Preps to Jefferson Airplane

The students at WSU–Eau Claire were part of the rock 'n' roll generation. The Beatles and the British Invasion began the year the college became a university. Eau Claire State student choices in music kept up with changes in the decade. A look at the types of musical groups that came to campus shows those changes, as well as some of the tug of war between what the students wanted and what others thought they should hear.

In addition to live concerts, students also listened to jukebox music and drank beer at under-twenty-one taverns such as "The Hoot" in Hallie, Corky's in Fall Creek, and the "Beer Bar" in the town of Washington. As a non-alcoholic alternative, a coffeehouse opened in the Davies Center in February 1968, soon to be known as "The Cabin," a venue where many musicians, poets, and writers performed their work. The university also programmed musical events as part of the Artist Series, and until 1967 first-year students were required to attend Forum and Artist Series events to receive "convocation credit." Such events ranged from symphony orchestras to Louis Armstrong and included an annual visit by the Tamburzitans (a Duquesne University ensemble which sang and danced Eastern European music).

However, what students remember were the groups that appeared in the Davies Center for Homecoming and Winter Carnival dances and also so-called "big-name" groups that appeared in the fieldhouse for special concerts. In 1964–65, the Four Preps ("26 Miles to Santa Catalina Island," also known as Rickie Nelson's backup band on the *Ozzie and Harriet Show*) came to play the Homecoming dance. For Winter Carnival, the Lettermen played at the Davies Center. In 1966 the Kingsmen, a group previously denounced by the governor of Indiana and investigated by the FBI for allegedly obscene lyrics in its cover of "Louie, Louie," made an appearance at Eau Claire State. The student crowd was enthusiastic, so much so that fights broke out and campus police had to halt the show. That experience taught university officials to go cautiously in booking bands the students wanted to hear.

The dean of students office, which oversaw Homecoming and Winter Carnival, always seemed a step or two behind students in picking music. The 1967 Winter Carnival had the folk group Brothers Four singing "Greenfield" in snowy and subdued Eau Claire. Tamer offerings came in 1967–68, including variety artist John Davidson for Homecoming and the piano duo of Ferrante & Teicher for Winter Carnival. For Homecoming 1968, WSU–EC played it safe and invited the Lettermen back once again. In January 1969, the campus successfully hosted different African American music groups as part of "Black Culture Week." Students wanted more such music, but when the Winter Carnival planners booked the all-black vocal group Fifth Dimension ("Age of Aquarius") for Homecoming the next fall, at a cost of $6,500, the Afro-American Association called for boycotting the show on the grounds the Fifth Dimension played white music.

Student activity fees and admission charges paid for the music performed at the Artist Series and at the Homecoming and Winter Carnival dances. Promoters of other musical events on campus could book the Davies Center or the fieldhouse but could not draw on student activity fees. Only ticket sales could fund such events. In 1965, the singer Johnny Mathis ("Chances Are") gave a concert at the fieldhouse, a quickly scheduled event when a Duluth appearance was suddenly cancelled. Mathis's talent agency took care of the promotion and any possible shortfall in receipts.

Other efforts at promotion on campus were not so successful. In 1967, the Interfraternity Council (IFC) thought it had booked the duo Chad and Jeremy ("Yesterday's Gone") for a pre-Christmas concert. The Englishmen cancelled and IFC scrambled for a replacement, finally securing Sergio Mendes and Brasil '66 ("Mas que nada" and "Fool on the Hill") to play the fieldhouse. Mendes demanded more than $5,000 and when ticket sales barely topped $3,000, the IFC had to dun its member fraternities and sororities on campus for the shortfall. The IFC did not give up on promoting live music, booking (and losing money) on the Righteous Brothers ("You've Lost that Lovin' Feeling") and Kenny Rogers ("I just dropped in to see what condition my condition was in") in 1969 and in 1970 on the Association ("Along Comes Mary").

The IFC and other campus groups that wanted to host a big-name group needed permission from Dean of Students Ormsby Harry. That official had his own ideas about appropriate music. When a group of students asked to transform the fieldhouse into the "Fillmore North" to hear the "San Francisco Sound" of the acid-rock group Jefferson Airplane, Dean Harry's immediate reaction was to say no.

Off campus, Eau Claire students shopped for music at record stores on Water Street. In 1969–70, the pages of the *Spectator* featured music reviews by student critic Mike Puccini of new albums and of on-campus performances. He panned the Association and also Neil Diamond's performances at the fieldhouse, but then again, he was a difficult critic to satisfy. When the Beatles released the album "Abbey Road" in September 1969, Puccini quickly got himself a copy. "'Sgt Pepper,' in my opinion," Puccini wrote, "is the greatest rock album ever recorded. 'Abbey Road,' while not bad, is nothing special."

The 1969–70 academic year saw a greater focus on academic and extracurricular programming on black studies. Reverend Jesse Jackson was the speaker at a special University Forum on black economic empowerment. The "Arena of Ideas" featured several faculty members speaking on black power, urban life, and other topics related to race relations. The year was not without tensions, however, as the BSC's "Black Culture Week" had one day of panel discussions and presentations where black speakers demanded white attendees be evicted from the room. The resulting bad feeling caused BSC President Emmet R. Griffin Jr. to apologize and cast blame on non-WSU–EC persons for the actions. The episode, however, showed the BSC was tugged in the same way as black intellectuals across the country, between an integrationist direction on the one hand and a nationalist one on the other. Vice President Hibbard rejected a request by the BSC and some faculty supporters that the university begin a black studies program on the grounds he could not justify spending scarce resources on a program that would appeal to so few students. A parallel request from the BSC for its own building received a polite rejection from President Haas, who said he did not have the funds for such a project.

The state did not help WSU–EC recruit more African American students, at least ones from Illinois: in 1969 the legislature insisted the regents raise out-of-state tuition, quite publicly as a way to reduce the number of black students from Chicagoland attending WSU schools. The board of regents raised out-of-state tuition from $750 to $1,250 per year, a move the *Spectator* reported was intended to "to keep militants out of state universities." Although WSU–Oshkosh and WSU–Whitewater may have been uppermost in the thinking behind this action, WSU–EC was hurt, too. Students from Illinois—not Minnesota—made up by far the biggest number of out-of-state matriculants in 1968–69. Haas and the regents worked at cross-purposes when it came to increasing black student enrollment.

The president did not give up. With Stoelting and other faculty leaders, he decided to approach the group of historically black colleges and universities with the idea of an exchange. After contacting several other institutions, Haas visited Grambling College in 1967, and Eau Claire State agreed with Grambling to exchange up to a dozen students per year, one set coming to one campus one semester and then reversing the next. Those students involved in the exchange served as both ambassador-representatives and as ambassador-hosts. Despite initial opposition from the successor organization to the AAA, the Eau Claire Black Coalition, on the grounds that Grambling students should not be subjected to racism in Eau Claire, the exchange proved initially successful and lasted until 1975. Looking back on the Grambling–Eau Claire exchange after his retirement, Haas said the interest eventually waned on both sides. Eau Claire students did not care for the restrictive campus life at Grambling (or the cafeteria food), and the parents of Grambling students did not care for the lack of supervision given their sons and daughters at WSU–EC.

Grambling State College Exchange Program, 1970-71

President Haas welcomes Grambling State students to Eau Claire State, Fall 1971.

The Downfall of *In Loco Parentis*: Student Housing, Student Assembly, Student Speech

For much of the 1960s, the board of regents, headed by Eau Claire's William McIntyre and served by Executive Director Eugene McPhee, was distant, if not invisible, to most students and faculty at Eau Claire State. However, when the board chose to exercise its power over the university, it usually did so in a ham-handed and sometimes illegal manner and often provoked a student backlash. The basic tension at Eau Claire State was students wanted to be treated as adults, capable of making their own life decisions, and the regents and often the university administration sought to act in ways that did not regard students as fully adult. In short, much of the student unrest on campus was a conflict between student insistence that they enjoyed rights and the board's—and by delegation, the university administration's—belief it acted *in loco parentis*, that is, it took the actions a parent would take in protecting a minor child. Eau Claire State and the WSU System were hardly alone in experiencing this generational conflict: nearly every institution of higher education in the United States also experienced it.

The conflicts at Eau Claire State over *in loco parentis* flared up in 1964 over rules governing students over twenty-one and continued to the end of the decade regarding rules regulating the lives of first-year students under twenty-one. *In loco parentis* gave way in the early 1970s, as students' rights as individuals were recognized in 1971 by the Twenty-sixth Amendment to the US Constitution, granting eighteen year olds the right to vote in federal elections, and soon thereafter, by a 1974 amendment to the Higher Education Act guaranteeing student records privacy (chapter seven). Along the way, the board of regents, encouraged by Director McPhee, fought stubbornly to maintain its prerogatives and the image of the Wisconsin State Universities as conservative bastions in an era of social upheaval.

The beginnings of the "Sixties" at Eau Claire State can be dated to May 1964, not to matters of free speech or freedom of assembly, but to the college's insistence on controlling the lives of students living off campus. That spring, Dean of Students Ormsby Harry reminded full-time students that if they did not live on campus or at home, they could only live off campus in private housing the college approved. A landlord had to submit an application to get on the "approved list;" among other requirements, the landlord had to live in the building where students rented and could only rent to Eau Claire State students. Rachel Montik ('66) recalls having rented a room on Chippewa Street "from an elderly lady, a seamstress." Resident landlords had to share the names of their tenants with the dean of students office and also had to show the rent charged was less than what the university charged for a room in the residence halls. For the safety of the students, landlords had to submit a certificate of inspection from the Eau Claire City Fire Department. Also for the safety of women students, the landlord had to maintain a daily sign-in/sign-out sheet and also enforce the same curfew as in the residence halls.

The furnished room in a one-family rooming house, not the unfurnished student apartment in a multi-unit building, is what Dean Harry had in mind for a landlord to get on the approved list. Even during the spring of 1964, there were not enough such rooms on the approved list. Students gathered in the Blugold one day to protest Harry's decision. Their specific grievance was the dean's edict applied to all students, including those over the age of twenty-one. Some students constructed and then hanged an effigy of Harry in front of Katherine Thomas Hall as one hundred students watched and cheered.

Recently designated Vice President Harry and his subordinates, Dean of Men Willis Zorn and Dean of Women Patricia Watt, continued the policy in the 1964–65 school year. Watt took the policy to an extreme in the case of Sally Dickinson. The senior medical technology student lived in an unapproved apartment at 430½ Water Street. In a January 20, 1965, letter Watt ordered her to move or face the consequences. Dickinson, who was a part-time student and over twenty-one, did not think the policy applied to her. Watt insisted, and when Dickinson was still living at the Water Street apartment on March 1, Watt suspended her from the university. Dickinson's appeal eventually reached President Haas, and he ordered Watt to reverse her decision and apologize to Dickinson and her family, not because the housing policy was flawed but because Watt had not recognized Dickinson's exemption from it as a part-time student.

The problem was exacerbated each school year as the number of rooms available on the approved list increasingly fell short of demand. During the fall 1965 semester, 1,100 students sought off-campus rooms with only 183 rooming houses on the approved list. The first student protest group on campus, "Student Leadership Action Movement," organized protests in the Davies Center in May 1966 against the off-campus approved list policy.

The completion of Towers Hall in 1967, with space for 1,272 students, promised to alleviate the shortage of rooms for WSU–EC students and ease student complaints about the administration's housing policy. Instead, the regents inflamed the bad feelings over housing with a policy directive in March 1967 requiring all students but seniors to live on campus for academic year 1967–68. The board worried students might not choose to live in the many high-rise residence halls it had built across the nine campuses. The reaction was vocal student protest at WSU–EC. At the start of a spring semester when only a small handful of students gathered on or off campus to protest the Vietnam War, far more were energized to protest the board's new on-campus housing policy. Many showed up for an open forum on university housing policy on March 20. Robert Witte, the head resident of newly opened Murray Hall, told the audience, "The state universities have gotten into the housing business. Now they are finding themselves in an embarrassing financial position if they cannot fill their dormitories." Professor Karl Andresen of the Political Science Department blamed the university's "babysitter" approach to the off-campus housing approved list and urged its abolition. At its April meeting, the Student Senate voted condemnation of the regents' new housing policy. Showing some appreciation of the controversy, nine members of the state assembly came to campus to listen to students on the housing issue; the legislators wanted to educate themselves on past and future requests from the WSU System for money to build more campus housing.

The uproar over the administration's off-campus housing policy and the regents' on-campus housing policy merged that April with protests over free speech and freedom of assembly on campus, with protests about the Vietnam War and new interest in the Black Power movement in the North. The administration retreated slightly on its policies, saying seniors under the age of twenty-one could live off campus, but still only in approved housing. Eau Claire City Police Chief Arvin Ziehladorff also fostered campus–community harmony by encouraging his officers to gain experience as students by enrolling in courses at the university. WSU–EC ended the spring term quietly.

At WSU–Platteville, however, student anger at the regents' housing policy exploded into a full-fledged riot that required a large police presence to suppress. A few students attacked an electrical transformer, causing a power blackout, and then two thousand went on a rampage through the city. President Bjarne Ullsvik, a close friend of Haas's, called an all-student assembly at which 3,500 students, out of an enrollment of 3,875, discussed their grievances over housing, cafeteria food, and other issues. After Platteville, the regents met in Eau Claire and retreated even further on their housing policy. Now, only first-year students had to live on campus in residence halls, while presidents were given the option of also requiring sophomores to live in residence halls. The board's new policy, adopted on May 19, 1967, was that juniors and seniors, even if under twenty-one, could live off campus.

One upshot of the statewide student protests about housing in 1967 was the legislature decided not to authorize any additional new residence halls. WSU–EC's plans to build married student housing for graduate students on Stein Boulevard (chapter five) were rejected. Instead, private capital built a great swath of rental housing on the streets south of upper campus. By 1970, as enrollment ceased to grow, the on-campus housing crunch eased. The university also liberalized its strict off-campus and on-campus housing rules. As of 1971, off-campus housing simply had to meet city building and fire safety codes; gone were the requirements about landlords living on site, keeping check-in and check-out records, and the other bothersome rules Karl Andresen had called "babysitting."

Other stalwart supports of *in loco parentis* rules fell one by one between 1968 and 1972. One significant change was the cession of enforcement power from the dean of women to a student judiciary board in the matter of student violations of residence hall life rules. Valena Burke, appointed dean of women in 1967, convinced women students in 1968 to hold a referendum on the idea of a "J-Board." The referendum passed and students took on the task of hearing complaints and enforcing punishments for violations. The following year the men took the same step, creating their own J-Board for men's residence halls. The next year, in response to public cries by women that "we're sick and tired of these hours," another irritant about residence hall life fell when the dean of students assigned to students the responsibility for setting their own hours when women residents could entertain male visitors in their rooms. Finally, in 1972–73, much to the chagrin of Director McPhee, the first Eau Claire residence hall went co-ed.

While Eau Claire State administrators grudgingly gave way on *in loco parentis* in housing, they were much more accommodating to student and faculty freedom of speech and freedom of assembly. The university in the 1960s continued to benefit from the tradition begun by President Davies of bringing compelling and important speakers to campus as part of the University Forum. In addition, President Haas's encouragement of faculty discussion of issues in the "Arena of Ideas" series began in 1966. Eau Claire State never had a "Free Speech Movement," as did the University of California, Berkeley, because Eau Claire did not seek to restrict student and faculty speech in the name of a supposed impartiality or neutrality. That had been the issue at Sproul Plaza in 1964—the ban by the UC on so-called political advocacy because of the appearance that the UC endorsed a particular point of view or a particular party or candidate. Eau Claire State, by contrast, made its facilities open to many points of view in the 1960s. The irony of conflict over freedom of speech at Eau Claire—with one significant exception—was not that students could not hear or voice different opinions, but rather that students were forced to listen to so much speech.

Students at WSU–EC had to complete a "University Convocation Credit" requirement. That meant students had to attend at least four events involving extracurricular speakers, whether at the University Forum, the Arena of Ideas, or some other speaker series, such as those of the Newman Club or the Cooperative Campus Ministry. Students had to obtain a signature from a faculty marshal showing they had attended enough forums to qualify for the convocation credit. The system broke down in 1966–67, in part because of the hostile heckling and booing Eau Claire students gave to Harvard professor Henry Kissinger when he lectured them in a January 1967 University Forum about the necessity of winning the war in Vietnam; the students made clear they did not want to be forced to listen to someone they had no say in selecting. About the same time, the newly appointed director of student activities and university programs, Jo Dahle, also stated there was an increasing difficulty in booking enough events for the convocation credit to satisfy the growing number of students on campus. Dahle asked the faculty to make University Forum attendance voluntary, starting in 1967–68, as a one-year experiment, a move the University Senate and President Haas endorsed. The experiment was deemed a success and the University Convocation Credit disappeared from the list of graduation requirements.

First-year students, however, still had to attend weekly Freshman Forums. The size of the entering class meant Freshman Forums could no longer be held in Schofield Auditorium. By the end of the decade, the weekly event was too large to be held at one time even in the fieldhouse; it had to be subdivided into 10:00 am and 11:00 am sessions. The topics at the Freshman Forum were seen by students, and increasingly by faculty members, as wasted time. Furthermore, the two-hour block on Friday devoted to Freshman Forum meant the same 10-to-noon slot on Monday and Wednesday was largely unusable for lower division classes, thus resulting in Saturday morning classes.

Freshman Forum was only part of the Eau Claire State first-year experience. The sophomore class took charge of the socialization of the first-years to campus; from 1963 onward, sophomores sold beanies (skullcaps) to all first-year students and demanded they wear their beanies in public. If caught without the headgear, they were subjected to "kangaroo courts" that levied fines and sometimes humiliating punishments. The hazing period ended with a bonfire built by the first-year students when they could toss their beanies into the blaze and become full-fledged student-body members. By 1966, the annual rites of initiation were so marred by fistfights between the classes that student leader Robert Shaw

Freshmen Assembly, Schofield Auditorium, c. 1966

First-year students were still wearing their despised freshmen beanies.

called for an end to beanies and sophomore tyranny over the first-year students. Dean Zorn sought to keep beanies and asked for "cooperation in this tradition, which is good, and cut out the horseplay and violations on both sides."

The freshman beanie lived on two more years before student activists made it an object of farce. The Campus Involvement Association (CIA) staged a pair of "guerilla theater" episodes during Freshman Forums in 1968, the first of which had an imagined first-year student being arrested by pretend police for failing to wear his beanie and for being late to the Forum. The second CIA invasion of Freshman Forum featured clowns throwing candies and welcoming first-year students to the "circus." Zorn was enraged by the interruption as he was trying to deliver a speech to the assembly. He demanded a student conduct board convene to try one of the CIA disrupters, and under the newly promulgated regents' rules on student behavior, President Haas granted him his hearing. Zorn presented his case and called for the expulsion of the student, Winston Baker, who was defended by two young faculty members, historian Carl Haywood and political scientist Morton Sipress. The faculty board Haas appointed to hear the case listened to four hours of testimony before voting to suspend Baker for his violation of the regents' conduct standards.

Dean Zorn, not President Haas, had taken the lead in pushing for a disciplinary hearing in the Baker/CIA disruption case, and consequently Zorn received criticism for trying to hold onto a relic of *in loco parentis*, the infantilization of first-years through beanies and hazing. What Zorn called a good tradition finally died out in 1969–70, as did Freshman Forum.

There were times, however, when Haas was front and center in responding to issues of student freedom of speech and freedom of assembly. In February 1967, American Nazi Party leader George Lincoln Rockwell was touring Wisconsin college campuses, speaking to student groups about his party's call for white supremacy. Rockwell angled for an invitation from a WSU campus and quickly accepted one from Eau Claire—not from the University Forum or the Arena of Ideas, but from the College Republicans and the College Democrats, who saw a fundraising opportunity. Those two organizations announced the event before securing a meeting place, thereby putting the university on the spot. Haas stepped in and decided the invitation to Rockwell must be honored in the name of free speech, but only university students, faculty, and staff would be admitted. This would not be a University Forum event where non-university residents of the Chippewa Valley were welcome.

Rockwell came to campus, found a packed fieldhouse with 3,500 students, and had to sit and listen to a withering introduction by political science professor Karl Andresen, who said WSU–EC opened its doors to Nazis precisely so students could know the would-be brown-shirts for what and who they were. In the aftermath of the Rockwell speech, congratulations poured into Haas and the university for not fearing extreme political speech and not fearing that a rabble-rouser would unduly sway students. David Duax, one of the student organizers, concluded that the invitation to Rockwell had been a mistake, but Haas had handled the students' mistake splendidly. Haas's actions stood in contrast, for example, to those of Acting President Kingman Brewster of Yale University, who blocked Alabama Governor George Wallace from his campus in 1963. To many people on and off campus, the Rockwell event was an outstanding example of Eau Claire's excellence.

During the same month Rockwell spoke to thousands of students, President Haas was weighing a decision on what to do about what he regarded as another proponent of extreme speech, the Students for a Democratic Society (SDS). Founded in 1962, the group claimed a dedication to "participatory democracy" and from its Chicago headquarters built campus chapters across the country, more than three hundred by the beginning of 1967. The main attraction of SDS to students was its unswerving opposition to the war in Vietnam. By 1967, it had chapters at the both the Madison and Milwaukee UW campuses, as well as at WSU–Whitewater and WSU–Stevens Point. The Madison chapter became well known for its use of civil disobedience to disrupt the speech or meetings of those it deemed part of the war machine—notably recruiters for the Dow Chemical Company. When SDSers at WSU–La Crosse applied for a charter to become a recognized student organization with access to campus facilities, the new president, Samuel Gates, refused to give his assent. SDS had followed proper procedures in making its application—it had an organizational constitution and bylaws and it had a faculty sponsor—but Gates nonetheless denied the charter on the grounds that the student group was violent and had no place on his campus. The Wisconsin Civil Liberties Union promptly filed suit against Gates and the board of regents. The state attorney general cautioned Gates and the board that it could grant or deny organizations campus charters based on their furtherance of the educational mission of WSU–La Crosse, but it had to do so on an equitable basis and also not violate the free speech rights of students and faculty.

It was WSU–EC's turn, specifically President Haas's turn, to face an application for a campus charter for SDS. As at La Crosse, the SDS proposal came properly prepared. The group had its constitution, bylaws, and many faculty sponsors. It wanted to have a regular meeting place on campus where its members and the public could assemble to hear ideas. SDS-Eau Claire submitted its application to the Student Senate, which approved it, despite opposition from the dean of students office, which recommended rejection. The group got a "provisional" or temporary charter, good until April 14, 1967, and subject to presidential approval for permanent status.

SDS made the most of its provisional status by holding numerous meetings. At one, faculty sponsor Morris Dickson from the History Department spoke about racism in Eau Claire; at another, SDS National Secretary Greg Calvert tried to fit WSU–EC into the national critique of higher education as part of the war machine. According to Calvert, "The university I saw today at Eau Claire reminded me of a factory where students, receptacles or garbage cans for data, are passed along the assembly line." SDS-

Eau Claire then appealed to President Haas to support the Student Senate and the numerous petitions in favor of granting SDS a charter. The board of regents privately communicated to Haas its wish that he follow Gates's lead at La Crosse. Haas also received the same reading materials as had Gates, speeches by Federal Bureau of Investigation Director J. Edgar Hoover about the dangers of SDS and by US Senate Internal Security Committee chair James O. Eastland (D-Mississippi) on the international Communist conspiracy behind SDS. Haas deliberated for weeks and only issued his decision during spring break week when the campus was empty: SDS was denied a charter because, Haas said, it would not recognize campus rules and procedures and because elsewhere SDS chapters had engaged in breaking the law.

Haas, like Gates at La Crosse, believed granting a student organization a charter represented an endorsement of the organization itself, and neither president could do that for SDS. Haas also took seriously the argument of some of his aides that students needed to be protected from joining SDS on the grounds that a youthful involvement with the radical group could come back to hurt those students after their college days, perhaps much later in their careers and their lives. A genuine fear of some future Joseph McCarthy punishing those who at some point joined SDS prompted this objection to granting a charter.

That spring of 1967 was a study in contrasts as to how the university viewed freedom of speech and assembly: on the one hand, in the confidence with which the university listened to an American Nazi; on the other, the fearfulness with which it considered granting a charter to SDS. In his oral history given almost twenty years later, Haas defended his decision in the SDS matter, pointing out that President Gates had reached the same conclusion and made the same decision. Besides, Haas argued, SDS could still meet, just not as a recognized student organization. Indeed, figures from the national SDS office did visit Eau Claire and gathered on campus; the national secretary for 1969, Mark Rudd, was even scheduled to visit for a presentation at the Arena of Ideas, an invitation he did not fulfill because he was otherwise engaged with his "Weatherman" faction in attempting to start a violent revolution in Chicago in October 1969.

Opposition at WSU–EC to the War in Southeast Asia

In the late 1960s, disappointment, even anger, with the continuation of the Vietnam War by the administration of President Richard M. Nixon drove many students to participate in teach-ins on campus and in marches off campus in Eau Claire. WSU–EC students and faculty were enthusiastic participants in the fall 1969 "Mobilization Against the War" protests. Twenty-five hundred Eau Claire students and faculty participated in the October 15 "Moratorium" on business-as-usual. Turnout was also high for marches in November. In the new year of 1970, however, student and faculty activity on campus against the war slowed as the national Moratorium movement waned, in part because of some acceptance of President Nixon's "Vietnamization" policies. In April, a new issue engaged students on campus: concern about the natural environment and the desire to do something to stop air and water pollution. According to the *Spectator*, more students took part in an April 23 teach-in on the first "Earth Day" than did in earlier anti-war events.

Feelings about the Vietnam War were still strong on the campus in the spring, even if students were no longer marching. A continuing issue was the willingness of the campus to host a Reserve Officer Training Corps (ROTC) unit. In 1967, the university sought to attract an air force ROTC unit to campus, but the air force already planned units at other WSU campuses. The real need for an ROTC came from the army. The regents instructed WSU–EC, and other WSU universities without ROTC, to prepare invitations. Eau Claire did this in 1969 to the army, an action that prompted the Student Senate in December to ask the university to reconsider and retract the invitation. The Faculty Senate debated the ROTC at numerous meetings during the spring semester, and on April 20 they voted by more than a 2–1 margin to affirm the invitation.

Just ten days later, President Nixon ordered US troops to invade Cambodia in what many students and faculty throughout the country saw as a shocking escalation of the war. Protests began and then

Cambodian Invasion Protest Rally, May 6, 1970

President Leonard Haas admitted he was nervous about facing an angry crowd at an unprecedented event, but his calming remarks successfully balanced individual and institutional rights in a tense situation.

accelerated in intensity after the shooting deaths by National Guardsmen of four young people at Kent State University on May 4 who were protesting the Cambodian invasion. WSU–EC students and faculty members called for a student strike to protest the war and the Kent State deaths. The students organized a mass meeting for midday on Wednesday, May 6. Contemporary estimates placed the crowd at 3,500. Student leaders who spoke urged the university to participate in what was becoming a national student strike against the war, noting that almost all WSU and UW campus student bodies had declared strikes. After hearing a lucid explication of the principles of non-violent resistance in the face of oppression from history professor Howard Lutz, the students turned the microphone over to the university president.

Haas began by addressing the crowd as "Fellow Students." He proceeded to say that WSU–EC "cannot have an official position . . . but morally every member of the University community can register a personal position." He acknowledged the strike call and said Davies Center meeting rooms would be available for teach-ins. He also told students they had "the choice to boycott your classes," even as the university remained open and expected all faculty to meet their classes "for those who wish to be there."

Haas reminded instructors in attendance that the Faculty Senate had recently decided class attendance results would no longer be an official university record reported to the registrar. In other words, students faced no disciplinary action for skipping class. Nevertheless, he cautioned students who took part in the strike to use the time to keep up with their schoolwork, even as they read, discussed, and debated the issues of the Cambodian invasion and the Kent State shootings. Haas closed with a defense of the role of ideas in a university: "Use the art of persuasion to justify your position to other students . . . but respect learning and others. Freedom cannot exist in an atmosphere of fear or violence." The students then voted for a strike which concluded peacefully on May 8 with a solemn ceremonial planting of four trees between Putnam Park and the Davies Center in memory of the four slain Kent State students.

The testing of President Haas was not at an end, however, with the winding down of national passions over Cambodia and Kent State. Although the Faculty Senate had voted to welcome the army ROTC, the events of April 30 and May 4 caused a shift in attitudes. A meeting of the entire faculty, called by petition, resulted in a clear repudiation of the vote, as well as the position of the board of regents: by 185–105 the faculty voted to reject ROTC. Haas faced a dilemma: use the power granted him by the board of regents and overrule the faculty or back his faculty and defy the regents. He chose the latter course, saying in his oral history, "Although I didn't like the conclusion they [the faculty] had reached, I determined that I would not be in the way."

The other issue that tested President Haas in the days after the end of the May 1970 strike was a *Spectator* cartoon some regarded as an obscene comment on the Cambodian invasion. Haas was inundated with angry letters from parents, alumni, legislators, and friends of the university, most of them demanding he censor the student newspaper. Although he expressed his unhappiness with the cartoon to the *Spectator* editors, he also answered the angry readers with a strong defense of student journalists and their right to freedom of expression.

The 1960s and Leonard Haas as an Extraordinary Leader

Alumni, emeriti faculty, retired staff, and subsequent student-historians have commonly believed that Eau Clare State was fortunate in the 1960s and 1970s to have had Leonard Haas as president. The sentiment is usually expressed that he "kept the lid on" the campus, or words to that effect. The National Guard never had to be called out to patrol the campus; not even the Eau Claire City Police Department or the Eau Claire County Sheriff's Office intervened on campus, a policy which students applauded. There was almost no vandalism or destruction of university property. A complementary explanation, offered by history professor Richard Marcus, was WSU–EC students were solid midwesterners and moreover were paying for their own education—they had neither the inclination nor interest in destroying what they valued so much.

Contrast is often made to the University of Wisconsin campus in Madison, or even to Columbia University or the University of California, Berkeley, but also sometimes to other WSU campuses such as Whitewater, Oshkosh, or Platteville. One significant difference between how Eau Claire students viewed their university, and by contrast how Columbia students viewed their university, was much protest at the latter school was directed at the institution's participation in military research. Columbia's membership in the Institute for Defense Analysis (IDA) was a flash point in 1967–68 for students who did not want their school engaged in research that aided the Pentagon's war effort in Southeast Asia. SDS at Columbia engaged in building occupations, including the president's office, as a protest against the IDA on campus. WSU–EC was not a member of the IDA. Nobody accused WSU–EC of being part of the military-industrial complex.

Along similar lines, SDS students at the University of Wisconsin in February, and again in October 1967, protested that school's invitation to Dow Chemical Company, manufacturer of napalm and other war-related chemicals, to recruit on campus. Subsequent protests at the UW targeted General Electric as a recruiter trying to hire students to join the corporate war machine. Events during the month of February 1968 revealed a contrast between the student body at Eau Claire State and at the UW. On February 5, the Central Intelligence Agency sent a recruiter to Eau Claire State, without student protest. Ten days later, Dow Chemical scheduled a visit to WSU–EC, and despite some apprehension by the Eau Claire Police Department, its appearance on campus drew no protest. Only when the U.S. Marine Corps attempted to recruit did Eau Claire students protest and only then in the fall of 1969 when members of the Campus Involvement Association handed a mock coffin to a lone, surprised U.S. Marine Corps recruiter.

WSU–EC students did not believe their university was part of the war machine, and as a result, did not lash out at buildings on campus or institutional leaders. Neither did Eau Claire students believe their university was complicit in promoting white supremacy and the white "power structure." Never did any significant part of the student body formulate a critique of American capitalism as the source of imperialism, war, and racism. When, between 1967 and 1970, students marched against the war, they did so in front of off-campus symbols of power, such as the federal building at Lake and Barstow Streets and the Army Reserve Center on Keith Street. WSU–EC students felt, to be sure, they had much to complain about and were not shy about doing so. Their complaints, however, were mostly about campus conditions: freshmen beanies, restricted choices for housing, restricted hours for women in the dormitories, and, of course, food service.

Eau Claire students did not complain about academics, except when radical teachers such as the English Department couple Neal and Betty Resnikoff had their employment terminated by Haas, Hibbard, and the Arts and Sciences dean, John Morris. In the spring of 1968 the Resnikoffs, neither of whom held tenure, were told their contracts would not be renewed. Students sought access to administrative offices in Schofield Hall to protest the non-renewal and also picketed in front of Haas's house on Roosevelt Avenue; Dorellen Haas came out to greet the students with cups of hot cocoa on a cold day, helping to defuse the tension. Haas, Hibbard, and Morris stuck to their position that personnel decisions were entirely in their purview and students did not have a say.

Most of the characteristics of students at Eau Claire State may also be said to have applied at WSU–Oshkosh, WSU–Whitewater, or WSU–Platteville, and yet those campuses had student bodies that were radicalized at critical points in the 1960s. In the spring of 1967, as thousands of WSU–Platteville students rioted and caused vandalism on and off campus over the regents' housing rules and city alcohol rules, Eau Claire students had meetings and signed petitions but otherwise kept peaceful. Also, in the spring semester of 1967, President Gates of WSU–La Crosse denied SDS a campus organization charter, setting off a semester's worth of protests and eventually landing himself and the board of regents in a lawsuit charging violations of constitutional rights. When President Haas did the same thing at WSU–Eau

Resnikoff Protest, 1968

Students unhappy with the university's decision not to renew the teaching contract of English instructor Neal Resnikoff demonstrated outside the home of Leonard and Dorellen Haas at 117 Roosevelt Avenue.

Claire, by contrast, there were reprimands from the Student Senate and from some faculty members, but nothing like the reaction at La Crosse. In the fall of 1968, as WSU–Oshkosh shut down for five days in the aftermath of a mass suspension of African American students, Eau Claire students watched quietly as a prominent African American student was suspended for disrupting Freshman Assembly. That same year, there was also no protest on the Eau Claire campus against the state's decision to raise out-of-state tuition and consequently to limit the number of black students coming to WSU campuses from Illinois.

President Haas showed a deft touch in dealing with student protests that other university presidents, including some in the WSU System, seemed to lack. He delayed his 1967 decision to deny SDS a charter until spring break, allowing passions—and students—to disperse. He, and the board of regents, bent on some housing rules at the end of the spring semester that year, again diffusing some of the anger students felt against *in loco parentis*. Dorellen Haas's generous touch in March 1968 in greeting chilled student protesters marching in front of her house with cups of hot cocoa showed a basic humanity and concern for students that many college presidents did not display. Haas's November 1968 address to the faculty certainly marked a turning point in his self-awareness of the need for institutional change, expanding shared governance with the faculty and broadening the student body to include the "disadvantaged." Haas showed a respect for shared governance when he accepted that the faculty had spoken definitively in May 1970 against inviting ROTC to campus, despite a direct order from the board of regents to prepare such an invitation.

Most of all, Haas's basic belief in free speech and more of it, despite his actions in the denial of the SDS charter, served him and the university well in 1969–70. Students and faculty participated peacefully in the October Moratorium protest and in the May strike against the Cambodian invasion and the Kent State deaths. The president's May 6, 1970, speech to thousands of students brought calm to a tense campus, and unlike other Wisconsin universities, WSU–EC remained open, both to those who wanted to attend classes and those who wanted to use university facilities to promote their strike. A few campus radicals might have seen President Haas as the problem, but far more students, faculty, and staff saw him as someone trying to work toward peaceful solutions.

1971-80
Pursuing Excellence Within a New State System

In 1968, the board of regents redefined its domain as the "Wisconsin State University System," an indication of its changing thinking about the relationship among the state universities it oversaw.

At the board meeting which considered it, Leonard Haas and the other eight presidents opposed the name change, making clear the idea that their institutions made up nine autonomous universities which were under a single board, to be sure, but were not part of a "system." The board heard the presidents' concern and amended its resolution with the statement that "the resolution in no way is intended to diminish the individual importance of each university."

Despite that reservation, for the next three years the WSU acted more like a system by planning different missions for its different campuses. The board challenged WSU–EC and the other state universities in 1968 to think about their future, and the Eau Claire faculty responded with proposals for new majors, new professional schools, and even for granting earned doctorates in selected fields. WSU–EC expected to grow to 12,500 students by the end of the 1970s. The university's response to the board's challenge is a good example of what higher education scholar John Thelin has called the "Golden Age" of Higher Education in the United States (1945–70). Growth and access to the university for all, yet with expectations of excellence of all, were the hallmarks of Eau Claire as the Golden Age came to a close.

Planning its mission within the WSU System was only a foretaste of what Eau Claire would experience after the system merged with the University of Wisconsin in 1971. WSU–EC had largely achieved excellence through growth and ever-increasing spending by the state on campus facilities and instruction (chapter six). Its proposals during the 1960s for new academic degree programs had largely sailed through the board and were approved by Wisconsin's Coordinating Committee on Higher Education (CCHE) (chapter five). In the 1970s, the challenge of maintaining excellence as part of a system, first the WSU and then the UW System, would prove more daunting, especially as the economic recessions of 1969–70 and 1973–75 squeezed state resources. WSU–EC, along with most other public regional universities belonging to the American Association of State Colleges and Universities (chapter six), had now entered the post-Golden Age, a period Thelin has called the Troubled Age characterized by public disdain for campus radicalism, retrenchment due to economic troubles, and more scrutiny by elected and appointed state officials.

The Merger of Wisconsin's Higher Education Systems

A merger between WSU and the UW had been discussed on and off in the 1950s and 1960s (chapters four and five). Finally, a gubernatorial candidate put the issue front and center before the public in the summer of 1970. Running for the Democratic nomination, former lieutenant governor Patrick J. Lucey put the WSU regents on notice in June that, if elected, he intended to ask the legislature to merge the two university systems. The specific trigger for Lucey's statement was the board's decision to create a new assistant executive director position to assist Eugene McPhee and to fill it with WSU–La Crosse President Samuel Gates. Lucey asked the board not to proceed with the Gates hire, as he expected there would soon be no WSU to administer. The board ignored the candidate's request and hired Gates, who looked to be in line to succeed McPhee.

Frustration among elected officials at the seemingly endless squabbling between the two higher education systems in Wisconsin, which the CCHE seemed unable to resolve, now boiled over. Lucey won the election in a November landslide, and shortly after assuming office he restated his intentions about the merger. Lucey chose not to accept the recommendation of a panel appointed by his predecessor, Republican Warren P. Knowles, to place both systems under a new higher education board. Instead, his February 1971 budget message asked the legislature to merge the two university systems into one, with the UW president in charge and a plurality of former UW regents on a new board. Supporters among the newly dominant Democratic majority in the assembly introduced the governor's budget bill with Lucey's preferred merger language: one system president; one board with a plurality of former UW regents; chancellors for each campus; and local advisory boards to assist the campus chancellors, such as the Area Committee at WSU–EC (chapter four).

The governor's bill in many ways favored WSU over the UW. It called for major cuts in graduate education, especially at the doctoral level, which disproportionately affected the Madison and Milwaukee campuses of the UW. The governor further called for comparable pay for comparable workloads for faculty coming from the two systems, and in a nod to the existing inequity between WSU and UW faculty, Lucey asked the legislature to fund higher salaries for WSU faculty.

Lucey's insistence that a merger be part of the budget bill enhanced his power to push his proposal: if there were no merger provision passed by the legislature, he threatened a veto of the budget. Even as the UW regents, administration, faculty, and alumni issued statements of opposition to merger, initially the WSU regents and Executive Director McPhee cautiously welcomed it. The WSU board voted on March 5 to ask the governor to appoint an ad hoc Joint Regents Study Committee consisting of members from both boards to "iron out" the "wrinkles" in the merger proposal. At the same meeting, McPhee expressed his support of Lucey's proposal, provided the new system honor faculty tenure granted by WSU.

That spring, legislators introduced amendments to the governor's budget. The WSU Board opposed some of them, such as a mandatory minimum faculty teaching load of fourteen student credit hours per week (McPhee and the board wanted the existing standard of faculty teaching twelve credit hours each week). The board also opposed a Senate bill that would, in effect, have created a super-state education board. In June 1971 the WSU Board voted against a merger "at this time." Regent John Lavine of Chippewa Falls, however, favored a modification of the Lucey budget bill proposed by Republican Senator Raymond Heinzen that took the merger proposal out of the budget and placed it into a separate bill. In a similar vein, the Republican floor leader in the Senate, Raymond Johnson, an Eau Claire State alumnus, worked during the summer and fall to overcome UW opposition to a merger.

Opinion within the WSU Council of Presidents was even less certain about the benefits of a merger than was opinion among the board members. President Haas recalled eight out of nine presidents opposed the idea in the spring of 1971, with only Lee Sherman Dreyfus of WSU–Stevens Point in favor. The presidents wanted to preserve as much of their campus autonomy as possible. They distrusted the central administration model that had emerged at the University of Wisconsin under President Fred Harvey Harrington in the 1960s, which had subordinate campus chancellors at Milwaukee, Green Bay, and Parkside; the two-year centers reported to Harrington's office, not to the UW Board of Regents. The WSU presidents instead preferred an executive director of the unified system with a small research staff and wanted direct access to the new board, unfiltered by any central administration. They also desired a geographically dispersed board with representatives appointed from each congressional district,

Wisconsin State University System Presidents, 1970

President Haas and his all-male colleagues projected a certain insouciance on the eve of their institutions' incorporation into the new University of Wisconsin System.

continuing the practice since the inception of state normal schools in the nineteenth century of having a local regent for each campus. Haas recalls he was indifferent to the proposed name change to "University of Wisconsin-Eau Claire," but other presidents insisted the new system be called the "State University of Wisconsin System" with each campus adding its geographical name, for example, Eau Claire State University.

Faculty members at WSU–EC voiced differing opinions on the governor's merger proposal. An ad hoc committee of the Faculty Senate reported it could support the merger provided there was no central administration to the new system, no diminution of tenure to WSU–EC faculty, no change in the role of the Faculty Senate in its powers, and, significantly, a raise in pay for faculty. Most faculty members did not see any more prestige in the name "University of Wisconsin-Eau Claire" than in the existing "Wisconsin State University-Eau Claire." Rather, they supported the merger on the basis of Governor Lucey and Senator Johnson's promise of "parity," also expressed by some faculty members in 1971 as "equal pay for equal work." That phrase, usually associated with movements for racial and gender equity, meant something different to WSU–EC instructors: they would receive the same pay for teaching the same classes as UW faculty. "That was one of the things that we were looking for," Haas explained.

Among the faculty, the discussion of a merger became intertwined with that of unionization. Faculty members at the nine WSU campuses had organized themselves into a professional association known after 1964 as the Association of WSU Faculty (AWSUF), which at Eau Claire superseded American Federation of Teachers (AFT) local 917 and the campus chapter of the American Association of University Professors as the voice of the faculty (chapters four and five). AWSUF became increasingly vocal about the issue of lagging salaries in the biennial state budgets of 1967 and 1969. There was severe disappointment with Governor Knowles's proposal for raises of only 7 percent for each year of the 1967–69 biennium, an adjustment AWSUF found so meager as to term it "disastrous." In 1969, AWSUF's Eau Claire State chapter voted 248–51 to pursue collective bargaining as part of a statewide faculty labor union. A measure of AWSUF militancy is the Eau Claire chapter further voted 203–79 to proceed with forming a labor union, even if the board declined to enter a collective bargaining agreement. At its January 1970 meeting, the board declined that request, saying only the legislature could grant collective bargaining rights to AWSUF; in May 1970, the board on the same grounds refused to recognize the International Brotherhood of Teamsters as the faculty representative at WSU–Whitewater. The fact that faculty at a WSU campus could turn to Jimmy Hoffa's union was a measure that militance on campus could include the professors, not just the students. A merger with the University of Wisconsin appeared to Eau Claire State faculty in 1971 as the best way to get the pay raise they thought they deserved.

WSU–EC students did not express a strong opinion one way or the other about Governor Lucey's merger proposal. Oral histories show Blugolds in 1971 did not pay much attention to the matter. Susan Oberstar ('72) said a merger "didn't impact me very much." Marie Stadler ('72), when asked what she recalled about the merger issue, replied, "Okay, could've fooled me. I didn't even know it happened." The Student Senate voted in favor of the merger in May 1971, as did the inter-WSU United Council of Students, headed by former WSU–EC Student Body President Robert Jauch. Some students argued there was prestige in graduating with a degree from the "University of Wisconsin" as opposed to WSU. Others supported a merger on the basis of the governor's promise to improve undergraduate education statewide and distribute state support more equitably.

The merger bill easily passed the assembly but stalled over the summer in the Senate, despite the leadership of Heinzen and Johnson. In light of the delay, WSU regents at their July meeting made plans for a national search to replace McPhee as executive director. They seemed to have no sense of urgency as McPhee indicated he would continue to serve for another full year until July 1, 1972, when he reached the mandatory retirement age of seventy. At its September 17 meeting, the board appointed a search committee for the executive director position, still uncertain if the merger would take place. However, the hold-up in the Senate ended on September 21 with approval of a bill containing most of the features sought by Governor Lucey and Senators Heinzen and Johnson: abolition of the CCHE, a new board of regents comprised equally of former UW and WSU regents, a two-year trial period before the merger became complete, a new name—the "University of Wisconsin System" with hyphenated campus names following, and campus autonomy based on prior mission statements.

As approval neared in the assembly, and Lucey indicated he would sign a stand-alone merger bill, the *Milwaukee Journal* reported that despite the months of amendments, substitutes, and parliamentary maneuverings, "The average citizen is not overly concerned about the question." A conference committee between the two chambers resolved the differences and the governor signed the bill into law on October 8, 1971, with the new University of Wisconsin System set to begin operations three days later.

The WSU Board met for the last time on Thursday, October 7, and knowing the merger bill was about to become law, made one last maneuver. It accepted McPhee's immediate resignation as executive director, and since Gates preferred to return to Colorado to accept a comparable position, it turned to Leonard Haas to oversee the nine-campus system. The board appointed Haas as executive director of WSU—for four whole days—and gave him a leave of absence from WSU–EC until June 30, 1973, the end point of the trial period for the two systems under one board of regents. WSU–EC Vice President for Academic Affairs Richard Hibbard became interim president at Eau Claire during Haas's leave of absence, and Arts and Sciences Dean John Morris stepped into Hibbard's position.

The board's last action indicated its intention to have a representative of the old WSU System play a prominent part in the new system administration. The governor had indicated only that he wanted UW President John Weaver to head the

John W. Morris, 1979

Morris was vice chancellor for academic affairs from 1971 to 1982. In the community he was on the board of the L.E. Phillips Memorial Public Library from 1966 to 1977, was president of the local Rotary Club in 1981-82, and—continuing the tradition of service of Leonard Haas and Richard Hibbard—sat on the Eau Claire City Council from 1994 to 1997.

new system. Weaver might well have wanted to bring in the existing UW administration as the new UW System administration; Haas's appointment showed the WSU wanted at least one of its leaders at the top in the new system. Haas and Weaver began planning for this possibility the prior spring. Haas invited Weaver to give the 1971 spring commencement address at WSU–EC, and while he was on campus the two men discussed the possibility of a merger. Haas had a further connection to Weaver, having known Weaver's father through debate activities when Haas had been a student in Madison in the late 1930s. The two men were convinced should a merger happen, they could work together to oversee the new system and its component parts during the two-year trial period: Weaver or perhaps some designate of his would look after the old UW campuses, and Haas would oversee the old WSU institutions.

This arrangement was implemented when the UW System regents appointed Haas as executive vice president. He was able to bring two former WSU administrators to the system office, Robert Winter and Robert Polk, to help him oversee budget affairs and academic affairs, respectively, for the nine former WSU schools. Haas concentrated on working with Weaver on getting acquainted with all twenty-seven two- and four-year campuses across the state and on drafting the language of the formal statute governing the new UW System.

Implementing the Merger

An important part of the merger legislation provided a Merger Implementation Study Committee (MISC) set to work during 1971–73 to recommend to the legislature adjustments to the merger law. The expectation was the legislature would revisit the merger in its 1973 spring session and make any changes by the June 30 deadline at which the merger would be complete. AWSUF president and UWEC mathematics faculty member Marshall Wick joined the MISC in November 1971 and worked to shape the report about the operating procedures of the newly merged system.

Wick helped defeat a proposal from the Lucey administration making faculty tenure subject to periodic review and revocation. Instead of this proposal, he embraced the language of Chapter 36 of the state statute that had applied to the UW about the faculty's "primary responsibility" for curriculum and for faculty personnel decisions; Wick argued the sections of Chapter 36 about faculty rights and responsibilities should now apply to all UW System institutions, replacing the Chapter 37 provisions that had applied to the WSU institutions.

Wick argued Chapter 37 had been deficient in spelling out faculty rights and responsibilities. WSU faculty could earn tenure by merely teaching for four complete years, but they had little or no say in the reappointment and tenure decisions made by their campus president. Indeed, for non-renewal of untenured faculty, the WSU Board of Regents had successfully gone all the way to the US Supreme Court to defend the position that untenured faculty deserved no due process whatsoever in cases of non-renewal. Several incidents during the 1960s abridging academic freedom, most notably involving George Ball at Superior (chapter five), had led the American Association of University Professors to censure the WSU System.

After the merger everyone agreed the language giving faculty "primary responsibility" in the areas of curriculum and faculty personnel decisions was much preferable to such arbitrary decision making by administrators. UWEC administrators soon learned there were other advantages to making use of the old UW personnel rules for local governance. The tenure granted a faculty member at Eau Claire State applied to the entire WSU System; a tenured faculty member dismissed at one campus stood first in line to reclaim a job at any other WSU school. By contrast, tenure at the UW was granted by the board of regents, not by statute, and was specific to one campus; a tenured faculty member dismissed from UW–Green Bay could not claim the next spot open at the UW–Milwaukee. In the end, the 1974 legislation implementing the merger followed input from the MISC and adopted the old UW tenure rules for the entire UW System, spelling them out now in statutes.

The adoption in 1975 of the Wisconsin Open Meeting law also affected faculty personnel decisions. A product of the Watergate-era drive toward government accountability to the public, the Wisconsin Open

Meeting statute required the public announcement of meetings in advance of their start and the meetings be open to the public unless the subject matter involved personnel decisions. The law applied to UWEC, as a state institution. In practice, this meant the publication of a weekly "Notice of Meetings" (known as the "pink sheet" for the color of the paper handout). The University's Rank, Tenure, Salary Committee, a four-person group consisting of the chancellor, vice chancellor for academic affairs, and relevant school dean and department chair, faced the prospect of posting five hundred separate public notices per year, one for each of the five hundred personnel cases about tenure, promotion, and reappointment it met to discuss in an academic year. Vice Chancellor John Morris decided instead to devolve the meetings to department personnel committees, consisting of the department's tenured faculty, and let them call the meetings in accordance with the Wisconsin Open Meeting law. From the time the legislation passed in 1975, the deans, vice chancellors, and chancellors did their review work in their own offices and not actually meeting under the terms of the law.

Nonetheless, the new law about faculty rights and responsibilities carried with it a fundamental ambiguity: just exactly who was the "faculty?" The previous UW practice had been the faculty was understood primarily as the academic department's tenured faculty. This group originated all personnel actions such as recommendations for hiring, retention, tenure, and promotion. An alternate interpretation was the faculty was the entire university faculty, without regard to academic department. UWEC soon had occasion to learn, painfully, that the two definitions of faculty could be at loggerheads.

In 1976, Chancellor Haas appointed a new chair for the Department of Sociology, J. Kenneth Davidson. His appointment, however, was at the rank of assistant professor without tenure. When Davidson applied for tenure and promotion the next year, the Sociology Department Personnel Committee (DPC) voted no. Its objections to Davidson were not based on his teaching or scholarship but on his administration of the department. Haas asked the committee to reconsider, only to have that body reaffirm its negative decision. Not wanting to seem to overrule his faculty, Haas directed a faculty committee to review Davidson's request for promotion and tenure, got a favorable report from that ad hoc group, and then made his own recommendation in favor of Davidson to the board of regents. When the board granted Davidson promotion and tenure, the Sociology DPC filed a lawsuit in state court, with the backing of AWSUF's successor group, the Association of UW Faculty (TAUWF). In this litigation, the DPC unsuccessfully maintained it was the "faculty" defined by the statute, and only it could recommend tenure and promotion. For thirty years, Haas had worked to increase the decision-making role of the faculty; in the Davidson incident, he skillfully used faculty decision making, broadly defined, to thwart the attempt of a departmental majority to use the new statute establishing UW System procedures to act against the wishes of the administration and in what appeared to be an unfair manner towards Davidson.

The new personnel rules (Wisconsin Statutes, Chapter 36) also carried over another old UW practice, the titling of professionals not on the faculty as "academic staff." In addition to jobs in areas such as student services and the registrar's office, this category included instructional academic staff teaching courses in UWEC classrooms but without even the protection the untenured faculty now had to due process. UWEC eagerly embraced this new job category, and in the years after 1974 more and more Blugolds received their classroom instruction from a floating academic proletariat of instructional academic staff. By 1981 more than a quarter of the 543 teaching positions in the university were instructional academic staff.

The merger legislation allowed the newly designated UW–Eau Claire keep to the mission statement it had drafted in 1964. That statement had expressed the ideals of "excellence" in a liberal arts college: "The University aims at excellence in intellectual development, conducted in a democratic atmosphere, through a curriculum designed to meet the needs and interests of a changing society. It is devoted to augmenting, organizing, and presenting knowledge. The University is concerned with students as individuals and seeks to bring them into close contact with a faculty who, by its scholarly attainments, devotion to studies, and concern for teaching, is able to instill a love of learning."

This statement continued to stand as UWEC's mission when President Weaver and Executive Vice President Haas halted all new proposals from across the system for additional academic programs until 1973. Their reasoning was the new system administration needed time to study the problem of overlap and duplication among campuses. At Eau Claire, the faculty and administration busied themselves with plans to design some of the new programs McPhee's office had previously encouraged them to propose. When the program expansion pause ended in 1973, UWEC consequently pushed to become the "cooperative" graduate center campus for West Central Wisconsin, where post-baccalaureate students from UW–La Crosse, UW–Stout, UW–Superior, and UW–River Falls would come to study. Even more ambitiously, UWEC proposed to host a new graduate school of social work, a new school of veterinary science, and a second UW law school.

Before the university could get approval for these new degree programs, it needed approval of a new mission statement by the board of regents. UWEC, as well as the other former WSU campuses, ran up against skepticism from UW–Madison about the expansion of their graduate and post-baccalaureate professional offerings—UW–Madison regarded that task as part of its mission. The regents held hearings around the state in the fall of 1973, including one at UWEC, to listen to opinions about the mission statement. The faculty and administration insisted that graduate education at UWEC was high quality and bristled at any attempt to write it out of the university's mission statement. It took more than two years of discussion and debate, but the mission statement the regents approved for UWEC in 1976 did include graduate education, based on existing undergraduate strengths in teacher education, the liberal arts, business management, and the health professions. However, instead of the university becoming the graduate center for western and northern Wisconsin, the regents directed that it cooperate with the campuses at River Falls, Stout, and La Crosse, an initiative that soon became the West Central Wisconsin Consortium.

Tellingly, this new mission statement omitted all mention of excellence. In the post-Golden Age of American higher education, furthermore, none of the ambitious proposals from the end of the WSU years advanced very far when they were considered by UW System administration. The state managed to do without a second UW law school, and in 1979 the regents eventually placed a school of veterinary medicine on the Madison rather than the Eau Claire campus, despite the latter's centrality in the federal dairy price support program.

There were programmatic changes during the 1970s, to be sure, especially the new master of nursing degree and the new master of business administration degree, which was at first in cooperation with UW–La Crosse but later became a stand-alone program. New departments of Computer Science and Communication Disorders were organized and began offering majors, and a comprehensive major in criminal justice was introduced by the Department of Sociology. However, the array of UWEC's academic programs in 1981 was essentially the same as it had been in 1971, in marked contrast to the expansion during the previous two decades. Here was an example of Eau Claire's fate in the new state system: the faculty's ideas about what majors to teach and what degree programs to offer was now subject to a new bureaucracy in Madison, even before reaching the board of regents for consideration.

Campus Expansion and Environmental Awareness

In the 1950s and 1960s, Presidents Davies and Haas had built Wisconsin's most beautiful campus. In the 1970s, UWEC spent much of its energy defending that beauty from a host of despoilers, some from upstream, some from downstream, and some from on campus itself.

One threat to campus beauty came from the Wisconsin Bureau of Capital Development, which had definite ideas about where to place the new humanities tower. Haas wanted to locate the building, proposed to be as many as ten stories of offices atop four floors of classrooms, at the corner of Garfield and Park Avenues. In 1970, the state bureau heard complaints from residents in the campus neighborhood who opposed the university's expansion toward State Street and decided to place the humanities tower on the lawn in front of Schofield Hall, blocking the view of the Chippewa River from the campus's original building. Apprised of the decision, Haas vowed "to fight it in every way."

Throughout 1970–71, Haas and the Bureau of Capital Development were locked in a standoff. Finally, in the summer of 1971, the state agency gave in to Haas's wishes and agreed to sign off on the architect's plans to build at the Park and Garfield corner. Construction started in 1972 and the building opened in September 1974, eight stories tall and named for the late Richard E. Hibbard. The last academic building of the Davies-Haas era had a grand opening with lectures, poetry readings, and seminars by leading academic humanists from all the academic disciplines housed in the tower. It left homeowners on Park and Garfield Avenues, however, "really furious" at the university, and at Haas personally, according to a long-time neighborhood resident.

Activities associated with the first Earth Day in April 1970 expressed more broadly the growing national concern about environmental issues. One week later a campus group formed called Eau Claire Area Ecology Action (ECAEA). That group promised to combine research and advocacy to defend the Chippewa River Valley ecosystem. One hundred miles upstream from campus, the Lac Courte Oreilles Band of Lake Superior Chippewa (LCO) sought to deny the Northern States Power Company (NSP) a renewal of the license on the company's dam at Winter, Wisconsin. LCO wanted to assert control over the dam that, against the band's wishes, had been authorized in 1921 by the Federal Power Commission and which flooded six thousand acres of the band's reservation. When the commission took up the company's renewal request in late 1971, LCO leader Eddie Benton-Benai came to speak at a University Forum and rally opposition. ECAEA and the UWEC Student Senate went on record in support of the tribe as the best steward of the upper reaches of the Chippewa River, upon whose proper management rested the safety of the campus from flooding. (NSP's license for the dam was eventually renewed, but under terms more favorable to the tribe than had been the 1921 license.)

Twenty-five miles downstream from campus and two years later, Northern States Power proposed a nuclear power plant on the Chippewa River that struck students and faculty members in ECAEA as a threat to the water quality of the river, a danger to the Chippewa Valley, and an uneconomical boondoggle. Worst of all, argued chemistry professor Melvin Gleiter, NSP had not addressed "the hazards associated with segments of the nuclear fuel cycle such as mining, refining, enrichment, fuel reprocessing, and the disposal and storage of radioactive waste." Instead of a new nuclear power plant at Durand that would mainly send electricity to the Twin Cities, ECAEA urged conservation and less power usage. The research and testimony in public forums by ECAEA helped stall NSP from receiving permitting approval, to the point where its costs became prohibitive, even before the 1979 accident at Pennsylvania's Three Mile Island plant put an end to any new construction of nuclear power generating stations.

ECAEA mobilized the campus in defense of one more watershed, Little Niagara Creek and Putnam Park. Again, Earth Day 1970 inspired faculty and students in defense of this treasure. On May 13, ECAEA led a volunteer cleanup group to remove debris from the pathway through the park. ECAEA pointed to other threats to the park, including motorized vehicles and dumping of waste by contractors. The bigger threat, however, came from the newly created Wisconsin Department of Transportation (WDOT), previously known as the Wisconsin Highway Commission. The WDOT wanted to build another exit from Interstate 94 and run a four-lane highway northward directly to downtown Eau Claire following a route that bisected Putnam Park and disrupted Little Niagara Creek. In an ECAEA campus poll, 92 percent of respondents agreed with the statement, "It is important to keep Putnam Park in its wilderness state." Chancellor

Students in Putnam Park, August 1977

The trail along the side of the bluff west of the lower campus was restored and river overlooks were constructed in 1974.

Haas joined biology professor Mark Fay and others in the fight with the WDOT, which lasted almost as long as that with NSP over the nuclear power plant, and the highway boosters eventually gave up and Putnam Park was saved.

In sum, during the 1970s, maintaining excellence from within UWEC overlapped considerably with the preservation of Wisconsin's most beautiful campus against forces from without.

Anxiety in a Troubled Age

At the beginning of the trial period of the merger into the new UW System in 1971–72, UWEC seemed to have gotten most of what it wanted out of the new system. It had its president-on-leave, Leonard Haas, as the number two executive in the system with many of the job duties McPhee had held in his position as the WSU executive director. It also had a prominent seat at the table for every meeting of the regents: W. Roy Copp, the former chair of the WSU Regents, became chair of the new UW System Board. It also had its former AWSUF president, Marshall Wick, on the MISC to write the procedural rules that would spell out shared governance among faculty, campus administrators, system administration, and the board of regents. In the decade that followed, however, UWEC learned it had less control than it thought over its fate, due to a quartet of externalities: a declining population of college-age people, a downturn in state revenues due to national economic recessions, a governor and legislature with new and competing priorities for state budgeting, and finally, a university system where it was just one of fourteen campuses.

Even if the main cause of Eau Claire State's growth in the 1960s had been expanded demand for higher education (chapter five), the growing number of young Wisconsinites in the eighteen- to twenty-two age cohort played a part on the supply side. That supply continued in the 1970s, but its growth slowed. Even before merger, WSU–Whitewater had seen a troubling decline in its enrollment, attributed by the president of that school to aggressive recruiting among Whitewater's usual pool of applicants by UW–Madison. Whatever the cause, the result was a reversal of the 1960s pattern of continuous growth. No one in the UW System had direct experience since the early 1950s with shrinking enrollments and corresponding shrinking in state support.

In the fall 1972 semester, there was a modest drop in enrollments system-wide, but the distribution was uneven as the Madison, Milwaukee, Green Bay, and Parkside campuses grew, and the Platteville, Oshkosh, and Stevens Point campuses showed sharp declines. UWEC grew, but barely, with just fifteen more students enrolled in 1972 than in 1971. Furthermore, in the 1973–75 budget, Governor Lucey and the legislature demanded 7.5 percent more in productivity from state workers. The governor estimated UW campuses could make this improvement in efficiency, in part, by teaching more students. In the case of UWEC, this meant that whereas 540 faculty taught 8,686 students in 1972–73, just 515 would be needed in 1973–74 and only 496 in 1974–75. As Interim Vice President Morris caustically observed, when Lucey accomplished the merger, "[H]e claimed to save money; and then he immediately proved that it did by cutting our budget and creating all kinds of turmoil and problems."

By the spring of 1973, System President Weaver had looked at enrollment and productivity numbers and decided firing more than four hundred faculty members was the way to balance the system's budget. At the former UW campuses, this was accomplished through the non-renewal of untenured faculty, not because of their performance, but rather as a matter of finances. At the former WSU campuses, however, especially ones with severe enrollment drops, there were not enough untenured faculty members to dismiss to meet Weaver's target. On April 4, 1973, the president told the campus chancellors (the title the former campus presidents received in January 1972) they should inform the faculty that some tenured faculty members would have to be terminated. "I guess it was legal really, but it certainly wasn't proper procedurally," Morris later acknowledged. Weaver's number came to eighty-six tenured faculty layoffs across the system, with Oshkosh losing twenty-two, Platteville and Stevens Point fifteen each. Even Eau Claire, which had not suffered an enrollment loss, stood to lose eight tenured faculty members. The system-ordered layoffs proved deeply damaging to faculty morale at every campus that experienced them. At UW–Oshkosh, one faction among the faculty used the crisis as an opportunity to get rid of their political rivals on campus.

The chancellor who had to send the intent-to-layoff letter to the UWEC faculty was Leonard Haas. His interim replacement, Richard Hibbard, had died suddenly of a heart attack at the Homecoming dance in the Davies Center on October 17, 1972. After Hibbard's death, and knowing difficult personnel decisions faced UWEC, Haas decided to resign his position in Madison and resume campus leadership at Eau Claire. "I missed the campus so much," he explained. "I missed the faculty, I missed the students." To resolve the issue of faculty reductions, Haas and Morris decided to employ the student credit-hour targets for departments Hibbard had established in 1967. They particularly looked at academic departments with at least three full-time-equivalent faculty below their targets. In early May 1973, Haas and Morris decided seven of the tenured faculty to be dismissed would come from four of what they deemed over-tenured departments: History (three positions), Art (two positions), Foreign Languages, and Political Science (an eighth position came from a non-instructional academic staff member whose tenure under the old Chapter 37 law carried over after merger).

Haas's May 29, 1973, letter to the group, soon known as the Eau Claire Eight, sought to explain the rationale for who was to be fired and why, but it met with strong opposition from campus faculty leaders, including members of TAUWF. "There were a few mornings that summer," Haas later admitted, "when I really wished I didn't have to go to the campus and face the faculty." TAUWF engaged a Madison law firm to fight the layoffs at every campus. Hearings at Eau Claire in October publicly established the arbitrary nature of the Haas and Morris layoff plan. They had not used seniority to determine who would be fired, but rather the credit-hour targets, which had never been adjusted when the curriculum changed and students took more credits from some departments and fewer from others. Haas, however, believed it was advantageous for UWEC to have credit-hour targets, as it provided a measure of objectivity to the administration's decision making.

The October hearings and subsequent lawsuit did not result in any stay of dismissal for the Eau Claire Eight. Governor Lucey and the legislature proved unsympathetic to the arguments by TAUWF that faculty tenure was a property right and could not be revoked by a mere budget reallocation. The governor stated in an Eau Claire appearance, "It appeared logical that when we had an over-run of students we hired additional faculty members; when we have an under-run we released faculty members to keep the ratios in balance." He explained the universities had benefited from increased state expenditures when enrollment surged, and now they would have to learn to live with fewer state dollars when enrollments fell short after Lucey's productivity increases were introduced. Fortuitously, the university had decided to close the Campus School in June 1973 and lease the building to the Eau Claire Area School District for continued use as a public school. By doing so UWEC lost an important connection it had since 1916 with the community, but its financial bottom line got a much-needed boost. Finally, an unexpected late surge in registration of almost two hundred students, along with a few regrettable deaths and timely resignations that happened over the course of 1973–74, gave Haas and Morris the flexibility to rescind the layoffs of the Eau Claire Eight.

Still, damage was done to the tight bond that had formed between Haas and Morris and the faculty up through 1973. "It left a scar," Morris acknowledged. What followed in the 1970s was a sharpening of the divide between UWEC faculty and administration. For the post-Golden Age, Haas and Morris, whom Haas promoted to the permanent position of vice chancellor for academic affairs, implemented a department-by-department position control plan, setting forth a tenure management system based on dampened enrollment projections through the end of the twentieth century. Departments deemed over-tenured might not expect to hire a new faculty member for decades under this plan.

The system-wide pattern of uneven enrollments by campus continued after 1973–74. After a pause in enrollment in 1972 and 1973, total student enrollment at UWEC surged by more than a thousand to almost ten thousand by 1975. Other campuses, however, continued to lose enrollment. These disparities caused system administration to investigate how much the UW spent per student at each campus, resulting in a statistic known as the Composite Support Index (CSI). UWEC ranked at the very bottom of state instructional support, just as it usually had according to less-sophisticated metrics during the eras of Presidents Schofield and Davies. System administration also learned on-campus and off-campus housing for students at Eau Claire was "saturated." To address these issues, the board of regents decided at its March 1975 meeting to impose admissions caps on some campuses in the system, including Eau Claire, while instructing other campuses to be prepared to accept up to six thousand additional students, supposedly because they did not need any increase in faculty or instructional support.

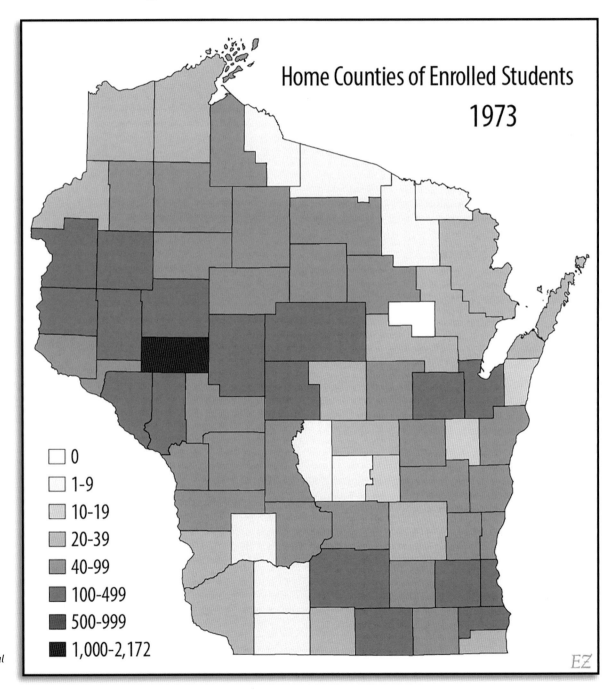

Map 7.1

UWEC students by 1973 increasingly came from state ppulation centers outside west-central Wisconsin.

UWEC, therefore, as part of a statewide system, entered a new phase in its history: admissions control. The 1960s era of seeking excellence through expansion and ever-more growth had decisively ended. An immediate effect of the new policy was UWEC informed high school guidance counselors that prospective, qualified students had best apply before May 1 if they wanted admission to the fall class. A longer-term effect was enrollment targeting became an important part of campus management. The position of admissions director became more important as funding through the CSI formula was closely tied to the number of students enrolled. Director Roger Groenewald recalled, "There was no concept of enrollment management when we started. We just enrolled." After 1975, "every campus had a target . . . and funding was based on that target." Groenewald's office began by setting the target for the first-year class at two thousand and then accepting transfers on a space-available basis. "Competition got greater for the better students," he recounted. "Only UWEC and UW-Madison had special scholarships for National Merit scholars" at this time.

Another era ended for UWEC with admissions control: the time when Eau Claire had a regional service area over which it exercised a territorial suzerainty. In the new era of the UW System, high school seniors from across the entire state were fair game for admissions recruiters, and other UW campuses could recruit those from the Chippewa Valley. Whereas a decade earlier, almost 60 percent came from Eau Claire or contiguous counties, now barely 40 percent did. Milwaukee County sent almost as many students to Eau Claire as did next-door Chippewa County; Dane and Waukesha Counties both sent more students than Marathon or Barron Counties. Haas pointed out in an era when "students wanted to get away from home," because the new Interstate 94 had been built through Eau Claire, "It was possible for a student to live in Milwaukee or Milwaukee suburbs without having a traffic signal between their home and the campus in Eau Claire." The UWEC student body was changing in the 1970s, and in so doing, changed the university.

Faculty, and to some extent administration, opinion about the merger had soured considerably by the mid-1970s. TAUWF took a formal stand against the 1974 bill that proposed to make the merger permanent. The legislation nonetheless passed, and after Governor Lucey signed the bill into law, TAUWF (led by UWEC faculty) returned to the task of securing recognition as a labor union to bargain collectively for faculty. System administration opposed TAUWF on this move, and the union found little support among former UW faculty, so the stage was set for more than three decades of conflict.

While allowing that "some things we have gained on have been balanced by some things that have been losses" as a consequence of the merger, Haas acknowledged the "disappointment" of those "people who had great expectations one way or the other." Specifically, faculty salaries did not move towards equality with those at UW–Madison, but rather, as inflation ravaged the United States during the 1970s, they declined in real terms: UWEC professors earned about 15 percent less in 1981 than they had in 1971 and associate and assistant professors about 20 percent less.

The UWEC faculty expressed their disappointment with the legislature for not providing the expected salary increases, but perhaps a larger grievance lay against the UW System administration, if not the board of regents, for failing to advocate for equity in faculty salaries across the system. This became clear to UWEC faculty and staff in 1976 and 1977 when the legislature asked the UW System to report on the matter of salary equity. The reply from the system administration was that inequity was proper between campuses given "mission difference." UW–Madison and UW–Milwaukee, as research universities granting doctorates, had to pay higher salaries to attract and keep top faculty; UW–Eau Claire and the other cluster campuses had a different mission and did not have to compete for top talent.

This view from system administration angered UWEC faculty who continued to advocate for their own notion of "equal pay for equal work," that is, equal pay to everyone who taught at any UW campus. Edward Muzik, a UWEC faculty member and the executive director of TAUWP, spoke for many when he said the system administration's reply to the legislature ". . . has seriously undermined the confidence of many faculty members in the ability of Central Administration to treaty all faculty fairly."

What is clear in retrospect is events in Wisconsin were part of a national trend in the early 1970s of consolidating public higher education under one directorate, with close supervision by governors and legislatures. Some states followed the Wisconsin example of having a single governing board; others had a powerful higher education board overseeing separate state colleges and universities. In 1960, only eleven out of fifty states had a single group of persons with power comparable to those of the merged UW System and its regents; by 1980, forty-six out of fifty states had gone that route. Legislatures and governors felt they were spending so much on higher education they wanted more and closer control. The yearning by some faculty members at UWEC for the good old days overlooked the fact that the growth and spending of the 1960s was not sustainable. Elected officials across the country, the ones responsible for paying the bills for higher education, all sought to put the brakes on that spending in the 1970s, a trend which extended to the federal level in subsequent decades.

The budget crises of the 1970s resulted in the end to the historic rule of no tuition for Wisconsin residents at UWEC. Wisconsin made the turn in 1973 and began formally charging tuition to state residents. Tuition came on top of the existing segregated fees for extracurricular activities, health services, and textbook rental, which already had been steadily increasing for decades. UWEC students paid $280 in tuition and fees per semester in 1973 (about $1,500 in 2016). Under the new policy, UW System officials and state lawmakers sought to limit student tuition to no more than a quarter of instructional costs, but that percentage proved to be elastic over time. Consequently, almost without a break, tuition and fees increased every academic year; in real terms, they tripled between 1973 and 2016. Payment for room and board at campus facilities remained a separate matter; the fee for 1973–74 was $461.50 (about $2,500 in 2016 dollars, about a third lower than what it actually was that year).

The switch toward an explicit student contribution to the cost of UWEC's instruction in the form of tuition coincided with an increase of federal support for higher education, based on the Higher Education Act of 1965 (chapter six). In 1972, legislation expanded the range of federal support for students, although not for UWEC directly. This amended HEA included a new provision for a federal guarantee of student loans at a low interest rate; the law also included the first federal grant to college students not tied to national defense. That grant, formally known as the Basic Educational Opportunity Grant but referred to in the popular press as the "Pell Grant" after its Senate sponsor, Claiborne Pell (D-Rhode Island), sent federal dollars to UWEC for students in need. The implementation of student tuition at UWEC, therefore, was somewhat softened by federal support for students through increased access to loans, grants, and work-study funds.

In addition to increasing access to loans and grants for students and their families, Congress in 1974 adopted the Family Educational Rights and Privacy Act (FERPA), which required higher education institutions that accepted federal student aid to respect student rights about access to their academic and non-academic records. The UWEC Student Senate had called in 1972 for an end to the university's practice of sending student grade reports each semester to parents or guardians. FERPA ended that practice and others, such as keeping letters of recommendation confidential unless a student waived the privilege of seeing them. FERPA came about with the dismantling of *in loco parentis* (chapter six). Student complaints in the 1960s about too much university control over their lives had centered on residence hall living and off-campus entertainment; with FERPA, the university and its staff also had to respect students as adults in regards to academic matters.

In sum, the merger for UWEC brought fairness and equity of a sort, but not of the immediate type the faculty and administration had hoped for in the way of additional state monies for the university, especially higher faculty salaries in line with what the UW–Madison faculty earned. Rather, fairness and equity lay in the more stringent protections of due process for faculty and students adopted by the new UW System. The UW System and its regents appeared less interested in promoting Eau Claire's particular vision of excellence than had been the case in the more-loosely federated WSU System. If UWEC wished to continue exalting its "cult of excellence" it would have to do so from within and not from without.

Continuing Excellence in the 1970s

One suggestion for promoting excellence came from Assistant Chancellor Ormsby "Bud" Harry. In the aftermath of merger, he observed the university mainly recognized student excellence in academic performance at the end of a student's career at Eau Claire, commencement day. Why not, Harry asked, acknowledge and celebrate academic excellence with an "Honors Week" in the spring term? Involving the academic honor societies tied to specific disciplines, which Haas had worked hard to initiate during the 1950s and 1960s (chapter five), was the way Harry organized Honors Week. He worked closely with foreign languages professor Roma Hoff, advisor to Sigma Delta Phi, the Spanish honor society. For the first such event, in 1973, five academic honor societies were led by Phi Kappa Phi (which honored high achievement in general by juniors and seniors), presenting a week's worth of events capped with a Saturday evening banquet and an address by Circuit Court Judge Thomas Barland. The next year, eight academic societies joined in the event, and by 1977 seventeen honor societies took part. That year also marked a change as a student-initiated competition produced the keynote speaker who addressed the banquet audience of more than one thousand. During the following decades, UWEC Honors Week denoted a celebration of academic excellence from within. During the week, each academic honor society had its events, its awards, and its addresses and activities. The Saturday night banquet program listed these achievements, as well as the overall "Outstanding Senior" award.

The high degree of student involvement with academic honor societies marked UWEC as different in yet another way: although social fraternities and sororities had existed off campus since the 1940s, their membership and campus reach had been limited. This was partly due to the lingering power of *in loco parentis* in the form of the university's reluctance to authorize off-campus fraternity and sorority houses and partly due to the cost of pledging and annual dues. By contrast, student honor societies flourished at Eau Claire because they offered some of the same avenues for fellowship and camaraderie as did Greek organizations, but with affinity ties based in academic studies side by side with faculty members.

One event started in the 1970s symbolized the commitment to excellence and to financing student success in the midst of economic uncertainty: the Viennese Ball. The idea was to celebrate elegance in music, dance, and pastries, with the net proceeds going to fund scholarships for students in the Department of Music. Largely through the efforts of Ada Bors of the University Centers staff, the event was an almost immediate success, involving faculty, staff, students, and community residents. By 1978, attendance was over one thousand. In 1980, two thousand tickets were sold for two nights of the ball, with Governor Lee Dreyfus in attendance to dance the first waltz. Over the next four decades, the Viennese Ball was consistently the social highlight of the spring semester, drawing thousands and raising hundreds of thousands in scholarship money. Excellence could be fun, especially in formal evening wear.

Viennese Ball

Governor Lee S. Dreyfus and his wife, Joyce, opened the dancing at the 1980 Viennese Ball. In the background are Leonard and Dorellen Haas and Adam and Ada Bors.

One signifier of excellence was the accomplishments of alumni. Beginning in 1961, the alumni association annually had given Distinguished Service Awards to alumni for service that "brings credit upon the recipient and the university." In its first decade, four recipients were Haas, Hibbard, McPhee, and Ade Olson—deserving selectees, but reflective of a somewhat inward view of what represented distinguished service. By the early 1980s, the selection turned outward, defining service more as a successful career after graduating from the university. Some of the award recipients made their marks as leaders in public education in the state, reflecting the university's historical role in teacher education; increasingly, however, distinguished alumni had careers in academia, business management, science research, and other areas.

Rethinking the Curriculum in the 1970s

Not every internal effort to promote excellence in the 1970s could be counted as a success. For example, the faculty labored for years to devise a replacement for the general education requirements adopted in 1959 (chapter four) which had stressed the importance of a wide grounding for students in the liberal arts, particularly in the "cultural heritage that is the possession of a free and responsible citizenry." General education was also supposed to be the foundation for "advanced courses in the liberal arts, professional and pre-professional programs." The faculty's certainty about general education wavered in the late 1960s, as it did at most other American colleges and universities, in the context of the general challenge to authority that characterized American society in those years. The question posed by general education programs—what should a college student know?—became problematic.

In 1968, the Faculty Senate convened a special committee to revise general education. That committee worked two years and came up with a proposal for a new general studies program, which provided students with a much-less prescribed grounding in the liberal arts. Students could take as few as thirty credits from a wide variety of liberal arts courses spread over four categories with such lofty names as "Man and His Cultural Achievements" (a category which encompassed the arts and humanities). After an additional two years of debate, the Faculty Senate voted to begin general studies for first-year students entering in the fall of 1972. "[T]he faculty was really becoming a part of a nationwide . . . fad," a less-than-enthusiastic Haas explained.

The Class to Take: Robert Fossland's Biology 130, Human Sexual Biology

The faculty's implementation of general studies in 1972 encouraged many departments to create new courses to help students satisfy the new requirements. In the context of greater social openness in the early 1970s about sexuality, the most popular such offering came from the Department of Biology: Biology 130, Human Sexual Biology taught by Robert Fossland. The 1972–73 *Catalog* promised the course would address "structure, function and coordination of the human reproductive organ system. Formation and function of sex cells. Problems of lactation, fertility, sterility, sexuality, birth control. Human population challenges."

That first year, 237 students (217 of them first-year students) enrolled in Biology 130. Fossland lectured twice weekly to the entire class and then met separately with eight discussion sections. Fossland had a reputation among students as demanding with high expectations, but also as fair and caring about student learning. He made certain every lecture and every assignment asked students to learn and apply science concepts, not just to the material in Biology 130, but also to other areas of study. On the first exam, Fossland asked students this multiple-choice question:

The term *inter alia* means…(*)
  a. Buried without children
  b. Between drinks such as ale
  c. Among other things
  d. Within
  e. I don't know

Students also fondly remembered Fossland for his sense of humor. For the final exam, he asked an "optional" question: "Males—will you state how much time in terms of hours, days or weeks (or never) since you last had a seminal emission prior to [this] final exam and how this happened: nocturnal emission, masturbation, coitus, fellatio, spontaneous ejaculation on seeing the exam, or whatever."

(*) correct answer is "c"

General studies had little direction, at least that students could see. Almost all the old distribution courses that made up general education credits could still count for general studies. Given little guidance about the importance of the liberal arts as a foundation for specialized study or professional study, students took as few general studies courses as possible. Since the other requirements for baccalaureate degrees remained the same—a sixty-credit major-and-minor combination and 128 total credit hours—students now had more electives, but little in the way of advice about how to use their freedom.

The switch from general education to general studies was an example of UWEC stumbling in trying to find its way, and not just within the new UW System. Recalling the discussions of the 1940s (chapter five), a general reaction against what critics decried as the excessive number of choices in a "cafeteria-menu" type of general education soon developed within American higher education. Just the year after UWEC switched from GE to GS, Harvard College sought to answer the question about what every undergraduate should know with a revised "core curriculum," a task that took that college's faculty six years to draft and implement. The Harvard Core Curriculum did make prescribed statements about what every student should know and master.

For their part, UWEC faculty and students soon tired of general studies and in 1978 the Faculty Senate adopted a new general education component of the curriculum with more specificity than GS had. The new schema required students to take thirty-nine credits of general education, in addition to freshmen composition, in ten disciplines from four conventionally titled categories—communications, natural sciences, humanities, and social sciences. Eau Claire students could now continue to pursue degrees in professional and pre-professional fields, but they would do so based on a broader understanding of the liberal arts.

During the 1970s students got to make known their opinions about general studies courses and the faculty that taught them, as well as all instructors on campus. In 1967, the Student Senate had proposed a pilot project to involve willing faculty in a program of course evaluation by students, but the request met with no reception. The Student Senate revived the idea during 1969–70, but the Faculty Senate tabled the issue. The Student Senate did not give up, and when a survey it sponsored showed more than half of the five hundred faculty members indicated willingness to participate, the Faculty Senate voted in the spring of 1971 to allow the Student Senate to conduct evaluations in classes where faculty members gave their approval. However, only about sixty instructors actually carried through on their promise to allow evaluations.

After the spring 1971 introduction, the Student Senate continued to underwrite the taking and collation of student evaluations, but with only modest participation by volunteer faculty members. The Student Senate expressed its view about the importance of "student participation in retention, rank, salary and tenure at departmental level," an extension of student power far beyond what the faculty were willing to cede. Then suddenly, by order of the regents in September 1974, student evaluations of courses and instructors became mandatory at every UW campus. The regents' policy stated, "Student evaluation of teaching is an important source of information on classroom performance."

The regents took care to say their directive did not conflict with the statutory requirement in the new Chapter 36 that gave UW faculty the primary responsibility for faculty personnel and curriculum decisions. Rather, they affirmed respect for the faculty's lead role by proclaiming that student evaluations should be used for "the improvement of teaching quality." They went further and insisted student evaluations be used as part of faculty personnel policies regarding reappointment, tenure, promotion, and other reviews.

Mandating student evaluations of faculty did not mean students got to vote on who would teach them. Students did not get to review faculty scholarship or public service, which were important parts of personnel decisions. Nonetheless, students gained a powerful voice on who was reappointed, tenured, and promoted. Vice Chancellor Morris heard from faculty members that "too much weight is put on student evaluations, and it runs the risk of affecting adversely a faculty member's rewards . . ."

The university now had to devise a campus-wide policy for how student evaluations would be conducted and how the resulting data would be used. The Faculty Senate appointed an ad hoc task force to propose a standard evaluation instrument with general questions about the instructor and the course. Academic departments reserved the right to edit the questionnaire and add items related to specific disciplines. Questions remained, however, about who was entitled to see the evaluations. If student evaluations, in accordance with the regents' directive, formed part of personnel decisions, did that mean other faculty, department chairs, deans, and other administrators could see them? Did that mean students could see the results? Other questions also persisted: what was the standard for acceptable, not to mention excellent, student evaluations? And who made that decision?

What the Kids were listening to in the '70s

The Student Senate's Social Commission oversaw the two big annual campus events, Homecoming and Winter Carnival. In 1968–69, the Social Commission promised the student body it would work to attract "big-name entertainment" to campus, which meant rock 'n' roll groups. The Social Commission, however, had to balance its promise of bringing big names to Eau Claire against the economics of hosting rock concerts in the fieldhouse. That facility was limited to three thousand seats, and the Social Commission tried to make sure it at least covered its costs, as it could not charge expenses to the funds generated by student segregated fees, instead drawing on a separate state special account that had to be balanced annually.

In 1969–70, the Social Commission lost money on concerts by Neil Diamond, the Righteous Brothers, and the Association. For Homecoming 1970, the Social Commission contracted with Melanie ("Look What They've Done to My Song, Ma"), but she cancelled. Some hurried phone calls revealed Jefferson Airplane was available to play Eau Claire, but their agent demanded a steep fee. The Social Commission signed the contract and got to work selling tickets. They nearly sold out the Arena, as it was now named, in a matter of days. *Spectator* music columnist Mike Puccini wrote, "I've seen the 'Airplane' twice and they're the best American rock & roll band. Thank you very much Social Commission for a job well done. The Jefferson Airplane in Eau Claire—beautiful!"

Still, the event lost money for the Social Commission, an outcome which once again highlighted the problem of bringing big-name entertainment to a small venue. The Social Commission took a poll of the student body in 1971–72 to find big names it could afford and yet would draw student ticket-buyers. The top choices, such as Santana, Chicago, and Creedence Clearwater Revival, all charged more than the Social Commission could pay, given its estimate that students would not pay more than $6.50 for a ticket. Topping the list of those groups that polled well with the student body, yet were affordable, was the Carpenters.

One group that played the Arena twice in the 1970s was the Grass Roots ("Midnight Confession"). A disgusted Mike Puccini wrote of their March 1971 appearance: "The Arena jammed with 15-year-olds. The Grass Roots in concert . . . Look! In The Arena. It's the Byrds. It's the Jefferson Airplane. No, it's the Grass Roots. Strange visitors from another state, who came to Eau Claire with powers and abilities far below those of normal men. The Grass Roots! Who can change the course of bubblegum music, bend ears with a single off-key note." At least the Grass Roots did not lose money for the Social Commission at their 1971 date. This was one reason they came back in September 1973, although they did not draw as well the second time around.

There was no accounting for students' taste in music, the Social Commission found throughout the 1970s. Nearly every group booked wound up losing money. Some lost more than others, notably Frank Zappa and the Mothers of Invention in 1974 (with the audience improbably warmed up by Dion and the Belmonts), but so did Kris Kristofferson and Rita Coolidge (twice in 1974) and the Nitty Gritty Dirt Band and Kansas in 1976. Fleetwood Mac and Styx did better, but still could not sell out; John Denver played to a half-empty arena. Only Johnny Cash in 1975 had enough cachet to fill the Arena with paying students.

Lettermen Singing in the Student Crowd in the Arena, March 1973

Expanding Opportunity: Who was a Blugold in the 1970s?

In the Golden Era of growth in enrollment and programs up through 1971, UWEC made clear its expectations of high academic achievement among students, but for the most part it connected with students as individuals. It provided almost open access for all who could benefit, and if students did not succeed, that was their problem. The university did its part, it reasoned, by hiring a good faculty, providing good facilities, and encouraging an atmosphere conducive to learning. Administrators and faculty in American higher education in the 1970s, however, began to pay more attention to the social characteristics and past experiences students brought with them to campus. UWEC was part of this change in thinking.

The answers to the question of "who was a Blugold" began to change in the 1970s. As seen from the discussion of the expansion of student services, a Blugold now was no longer just an atomized individual who swam or sank on his or her own, but rather a social human being who came with a past and an identity and who was a person the university realized might need extra attention or help to realize academic and personal success. This was especially true for minority students, students of non-traditional age, and—although by now a majority on campus—women students.

The enrollment crisis of the early 1970s made campuses across the UW System more aware of the need to work to keep their students enrolled, both as a matter of fairness and as a matter of institutional self-preservation. In 1974, the university administration appointed Mark Olson to head a new office of academic and career advising. Olson's office reported to Vice Chancellor Morris in academic affairs, rather than to Assistant Chancellor Harry in student affairs. Academic and career advising also took on the task of overseeing new student orientation, the two-day summer program for first-year students and their families to introduce them to the university and enable them to select their fall course schedules (chapter five). At the same time, the career counselling and placement office, under Director Wayne Puttmann, moved from student affairs to the jurisdiction of academic affairs. The university had come to see the need to help students succeed in the classroom and afterwards as a long process, beginning with summer orientation and continuing post-graduation with assistance in seeking a job.

Even as the WSU merged with the UW in 1971, the former was under investigation from the US Civil Rights Commission for allegations of racial discrimination. Congress had established the commission as part of the 1957 Civil Rights Act. The commission's midwest office took up the complaint of African American students at WSU campuses. The commission paid the most attention to complaints of students at Whitewater and Oshkosh, but Eau Claire also came in for criticism. The commission's 1971 report, *The Black Student in the Wisconsin State University System*, found WSU–EC in 1970–71 enrolled ninety-seven of what the authors of the report called "American Minority" students, defined as black, American Indian, "Oriental," or Spanish surnamed. Fifty-two of those students (six-tenths of 1 percent of the student body) were African Americans, and the commission urged Eau Claire and the other campuses to aim for an enrollment of at least 2 percent African American with a focus on recruiting students from Milwaukee. The commission commended the efforts of WSU–EC's admissions office to recruit more black students and to provide resources to ensure academic success. Yet when the commission recommended the campus triple the number of black students enrolled, administrators doubted they could do much differently. Their response was Eau Claire "was first and foremost a regional institution," that is, far from Milwaukee, and furthermore, "the desires of black students and the cost of education suggest it will be difficult to reach that figure [of 2 percent]."

African American students and faculty members, with the help of the University Center staff, offered their own programs to expand racial diversity on campus. For a few years, a group called "Ebony Ladies, Inc" (ELI) put on programs, including fashion shows. The Black Students Organization sponsored Black Liberation Month in 1974 and Black Aesthetics Week in 1977. However, African American students and their supporters in the faculty were not able to convince the university administration to begin a black studies program.

American Indian students and faculty were energized, even radicalized, by the events inside and outside of Indian Country in the 1970s. Native students on campus worked with the Student Senate in 1971 to take a stand against renewing the license to the Winter Dam to the Northern States Power. The campus group "Native American Student Nationalists" (NASN) also expressed its support for the Menominee Warrior Society as that group battled for a restoration of federal recognition of that terminated Wisconsin tribe. Speakers on campus included Ada Deer, head of the DRUMS group of Menominee members. In addition to student activism, NASN began in 1973 to host an annual powwow and native banquet. The banquet kicked off "Native American Awareness Week" each April and the powwow closed the week. Noted speakers included Vine De Loria Jr., a prominent author and activist for Indian rights who was then a faculty member at Western Washington University.

In March 1973, native students and faculty at UWEC protested the Federal Bureau of Investigation's actions against American Indian Movement (AIM) activists at the Pine Ridge Indian Reservation in South Dakota. The NASN led a march from campus to the federal building on Lake Street, the same locale anti-war protesters targeted between 1967 and 1970. The UWEC protesters carried a banner exclaiming, "Their Stand Should Be Our Stand" and demanded FBI and US marshals pull back from the Wounded Knee Compound and end the armed standoff. After the seventy-one-day siege ended, and the United States put the AIM leaders on trial for conspiracy and assault of federal officers, NASN invited the lead defendants, Russell Means, Dennis Banks, and Clyde Bellecourt, along with their attorneys, William Kunstler, Mark Lane, and Larry Leventhal, to campus in April 1974 for a rally and fundraiser for the Wounded Knee Legal Defense/Offense Committee.

Wounded Knee Demonstration, March 1973

About 130 protesters marched from campus to the federal building in downtown Eau Claire. In the background of this photograph are the Ecumenical Religious Center property before the construction of its chapel (chapter five) and the Humanities Hall under construction.

Anthropology Class, 1970s

Professor Helaine Minkus, who taught anthropology from 1972 to 2008 and encouraged expanded international education, is shown teaching in Schneider Hall 303 using Native American objects from the Adin T. Newman Collection of Historical Artifacts and Memorabilia. In the community, Minkus was president of Temple Sholom for thirteen years.

In addition to student activism, NASN forcefully pressed for native student interests. NASN students and their faculty supporters in 1972 decided to ask UWEC's administration to begin an American Indian studies program, starting with courses offered by the English Department in American Indian literature and the American Indian in film. By 1974, the faculty supporting native studies put together a proposal for a twenty-four-credit academic minor.

It was NASN and its faculty supporters who insisted the administration could do more to include American Indian students and the rigorous academic study of American Indians into UWEC. In 1976, when a subcommittee of the regents visited UWEC to inquire about how the university supported the education of minority and "disadvantaged" students, NASN leaders confronted Chancellor Haas about the lack of support for American Indian students. Haas responded by hiring Veda Stone, the American Indian education leader at UW–River Falls. Stone soon began an Indian Adult Education project at UWEC designed to start students of non-traditional age in a weekend college. That initiative, along with the expansion of the curriculum to support a new academic minor in American Indian studies, jump-started UWEC's efforts to expand the idea of "Who is a Blugold" to include Wisconsin's native people. Haas also responded to the 1976 campus hearing by starting an American ethnic coordinating office, tasked with recruiting and retaining minority students to UWEC.

Campus and system leaders expanded their thinking about who was a Blugold, in part because of federal pressure and in part because they thought they had a duty to help educate the next generation of leaders of American minority groups. There was little discussion in the early 1970s about how the majority-white student body would benefit from what would later be called diversity. In effect, it was up to the minority groups themselves, by events such as Native American Awareness Week or Black Aesthetics Week, to teach the majority student body about themselves.

The sense that diversity was not a two-way street in the 1970s was certainly not true of another group largely new to the university: international students. The Department of Foreign Languages had a few study-abroad programs for their majors, and beginning in 1974 Roma Hoff annually led three-week travel seminars to Spain and nearby countries for students and community members. For the most part, however, the term "international education" meant welcoming foreign students to study at UWEC. Campus leaders worked hard to attract foreign students, more than tripling the number of such students between 1964 and 1973 and then doubling the number again by 1980. In the tradition of President Davies, campus leaders such as Haas thought Eau Claire students would benefit from learning next to foreign students.

The university had begun an "international festival" in the mid-1960s, but not until 1971 did the campus link the festival to United Nations Day in October and to a new event called the "International Folk Festival." Much like the Viennese Ball, the International Folk Festival quickly became popular in the Eau Claire community. By 1974, the event took over almost the entire Davies Center for a Sunday afternoon, with students from different nations displaying their folk traditions of music, dance, and food to the public. By 1980, an estimated four thousand persons attended the folk festival; Haas told festival organizer professor Barbara Rolland it was "an event that has found its place in the life of the University."

International Folk Festival, c. 1980

Professor Irene Lazda (center) taught German in the Foreign Languages Department from 1969 to 2012. She and her husband, historian Paulis Lazda, were deeply involved with international education programs between the UWEC and Eastern Europe and Baltic nations.

Second-wave Feminism at UW–Eau Claire

The social upheavals in the United States during the 1960s included a movement by women for gender equality, including enhanced legal rights, greater job opportunities, alterations in family patterns, and recognition of female sexualities. American colleges and universities were among the institutions challenged by this new feminism.

In July 1972, at the urging of the regents and system leaders Weaver and Haas, each UW campus hired an assistant to the chancellor for affirmative action. UWEC assigned a faculty member in the Department of English, Sarah Harder, to provide guidance and leadership to the campus regarding women's issues. Following congressional passage of Title IX of the Education Act of 1972, system and UWEC administrators had to pay attention for the first time to how UWEC complied with the federal law mandating equality of opportunity by sex in higher education. The 1972 legislation gave institutions receiving federal support, such as student financial aid, one year to collect and present data to the US Department of Health, Education and Welfare about their compliance with Title IX. In the spring 1973 semester, the Faculty Senate created a Commission on the Status of Women (CSW), with a mandate to explore issues relating to women in areas of university life aside from employment (the responsibility of the affirmative action office). Newly returned Chancellor Haas appointed faculty members Lorraine Missling and Helen Sampson, along with Dean of Women Valena Burke, to the CSW. There was plenty of work for both affirmative action and for the CSW. Four issues took up much of the time and attention of the commission in the 1970s: childcare for adult students, especially single mothers; reproductive healthcare for women students; the initiation of a woman's studies program; and women's participation in varsity athletics.

In its first year of work, the CSW identified the lack of childcare for students with youngsters as a significant barrier to their academic success. There had been some awareness on campus of non-traditional students as early as the 1940s (chapter four), but equal access to opportunity had not been recognized as a barrier for them. As the issue of childcare finally emerged, the university's first Children's Center opened in 1973 under Marie Evans's directorship on the west side of Eau Claire at a house at 109 Chippewa Street, supported by the parents' cooperative effort and donated labor and by modest fees. In an interview with the *Spectator*, Evans said, "Our purpose is to promote our children's growth socially, emotionally, physically, as well as intellectually."

To make excellent childcare available for parents required a more permanent facility and better financial support. The CSW took such a request to the Student Senate in 1974, but at first that body voted against supporting the Children's Center with student fees. The Senate eventually reversed itself, and additional funding came to the Children's Center in 1978 through a federal grant. Then in 1981, the Children's Center found a new home on campus in the old Campus School, now known as Park School, in a space it occupied for the next three decades.

After obtaining the provision of childcare to adult students, CSW determined the next most important issue related to women's success at the university was access to reproductive health services. This was part of the larger issue of University Health Services (UHS), a small entity when Eau Claire State was a college and one that struggled to keep pace with the university as it grew. In 1964, the Student Health Service consisted of a part-time nurse, supplemented by a physician who visited once a week. The health service had a small clinic in the fieldhouse, but the location was so obscure that in 1967 the Health Committee recommended placing a "sign over the door 'Health Service' so students can readily see it." There was no pregnancy testing and no contraception prescribed. *In loco parentis* governed women's access to reproductive health services: one alumna recalled her sophomore-year roommate went to the Midelfort Clinic, a large multi-specialty off-campus clinic, for a pregnancy test and was chagrined to learn it sent the results to her parents. In the decade after the widespread introduction of the birth control pill in early 1960s, Eau Claire State refused to prescribe it to unmarried women students. The director of the Student Health Service wrote the Tri-County Medical Society in 1972 that "prescribing contraceptives to unmarried individuals and minors is against state law . . . and I do not see how we can condone it." The next year, in response to an inquiry from a student reporter from the UW–Oshkosh *Titan*, the director stated, "We do not give BC pill to students unless they are married." Not until 1976 was Wisconsin's statutory ban on prescribing birth control to unmarried persons reversed.

In 1975, the CWS undertook a survey of men and women on campus about their experiences with University Health Services. The results received from 1,100 questionnaires showed a sharp split: men who used the service reported a good outcome; women did not. Two-thirds of women students said they would not use UHS for "sex-related problems such as suspected venereal disease or pregnancy," and just 31 percent of women students said they would recommend UHS to a friend. Many of the women respondents reported a lack of privacy and confidentiality at their clinic visits. Worse, women students felt bothered by physicians who asked them questions about sexually transmitted diseases and about their sexual partners, even on visits when the women sought help for the flu or upset stomach. Increasingly, UWEC women sought help for pregnancy testing and contraception from a free women's clinic in Eau Claire, Karma House. One 1975 report said on any given evening, twenty-five to thirty university women visited Karma House.

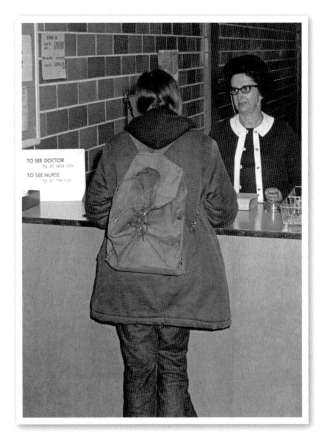

Student Health Services, 1960s

Health services were located in cramped facilities with little patient privacy in the University Fieldhouse, what in 2016 is Zorn Arena.

The CSW used the results of the survey to push for two changes in health services: the employment of a female physician to see women student patients on reproductive health and the establishment of a contraceptive clinic. The university saw to both between 1976 and 1978, first by hiring a female staff physician, Dr. Theresa Rice, and second by setting up a contraceptive clinic with assured patient confidentiality. The health service also hired a physician's assistant to head a Family Planning Clinic, open to all students without regard to marital status. In 1983 health services finally moved to larger facilities in the Crest Commons.

UWEC's CSW also appointed a representative to the system-wide Task Force on Women's Studies. Following the task force's meetings, English professor Nadine St. Louis returned to campus with the challenge of building an inter-disciplinary women's studies program that would "become neither isolated nor identified as a segregated area for women only; instead, courses about women must be an integral part of the entire University curriculum." Here was an early benefit of membership in the UW System: collaboration with colleagues across the campuses, and the push from system administration and the regents supporting new programs it valued.

UWEC, like every American college or university accepting federal funds, had to comply with the equal access provision of Title IX of the 1972 Higher Education Act. Lack of access to varsity sports for women students quickly emerged as an issue on campus. The CSW investigated the status of women athletes at UWEC and found wide disparities in access to varsity sports, access to facilities, and salaries paid to coaches. Equality of access, in practice, meant equal access to funding from student fees, since every varsity sport cost more in expenses than it reaped in ticket revenue. Title IX required institutions receiving federal funds to prepare a response within twelve months about how they provided equal access to women students. The UW System missed that deadline, as did UWEC.

In 1975, the Commission on the Status of Women investigated equality of access for women athletes at UWEC. The results made plain to the campus that there was a widespread disparity in access and resources for women varsity athletes. Even accounting for men's football—a sizable squad and an expensive sport to equip and coach—UWEC was clearly not adhering to federal law.

The CSW investigation of Blugold athletics revealed additional disparities by gender in salaries paid to coaches. All the coaches at UWEC held faculty appointments in the Department of Physical Education (in 2016 the Department of Kinesiology). Their faculty status as teachers covered most of their salaries, yet the men's basketball coach earned at least 50 percent more than the women's basketball coach, although their academic credentials were comparable. Some of the salary gap was due to different faculty ranks held by men and women in the department—all the full professors and associate professors were male and all but one of the women were instructors. However, the salary gap persisted even between men and women at the assistant professor rank.

Table 7.1
Commission on the Status of Women's 1975 Findings on Varsity Athletics at UWEC

Category	Men	Women
# of sports	9	6
Eligible athletes	351	211
Coaches	13	5
PE Staff (FTE)	6.9	4.8
Athletic staff (FTE)	4.0	1.5
Total budget	$108,125	$13,000

The CSW held a public hearing to listen to the experience of UWEC women athletes and coaches. The testimony was shocking about the shoestring budgeting for women's sports. Women's basketball had only eleven uniforms for fourteen players, and even those at hand were borrowed from the University Recreation Department. Women's swimming did not even provide racing suits for its athletes—the women had to provide their own. The same held true for women's gymnastics—the athletes had to buy their own leotards. More significant for the health of women's athletes was the absence of athletic training personnel to assist varsity teams. Those who suffered a sports injury did not have access to the trainers who worked with men's varsity teams.

The solution to these problems was obvious: more money. Women faculty leaders, especially physical education instructor Judith Kruckman, repeatedly made the point they wanted to expand access for women, not take away opportunities for men. The way to do that was to spend more on women's athletics, which meant increasing student fees or reallocating the distribution of fees from competing requests from non-sports student organizations. The Student Senate agreed and voted to increase support for women's athletics. Expanding excellence in athletics for all students could not be done on the cheap, a lesson UWEC learned in 1975.

Old Enough to Fight, Old Enough to Drink?

There was another way UWEC students in the 1970s differed from those who came before them. They could—and did—consume alcohol legally, even on campus. The doctrine of *in loco parentis* was in full retreat at Eau Claire in the 1970s, and perhaps in no area was this clearer than in student drinking. The changes also had a profound effect on the social geography of the city of Eau Claire, particularly Water Street on the lower west side, as it developed into a full-fledged student strip, anchored by many taverns.

Ever since the end of Prohibition in 1933, America's states, counties, and municipalities had a patchwork of different laws and ordinances about the sale and consumption of alcohol. Wisconsin chose in 1933 to prohibit the sales of liquor to minors (someone under age twenty-one). At the same time Wisconsin ended the Prohibition Era by allowing eighteen- to twenty-one-year-olds to consume beer with an alcohol content of no higher than 3.2 percent. The legislature further amended its drinking laws in 1955 to give municipalities the option to ban all drinking by persons under twenty-one. Many of the towns and cities that housed WSC campuses chose to enact such a local ban, including the City of Eau Claire. At this time, President Davies also helped to fend off a proposal in the legislature that would have allowed all colleges in Wisconsin to sell alcohol on campus, a policy already in place at the University of Wisconsin (chapter five). The legislature acted in 1963 to further restrict beer consumption among eighteen- to twenty-one-year-olds by confining it to licensed establishments and by prohibiting carryout sales.

With its central European heritage, however, there was a strong tradition of alcohol consumption and a drinking culture in Wisconsin which worked against these restrictions. Smaller municipalities surrounding Eau Claire, including the towns of Hallie and Washington as well as the village of Fall Creek, ignored the option given them by the 1955 legislation and continued to issue licenses for beer bars open to the eighteen to twenty crowd. Much to the chagrin of Davies and Haas, establishments such as Corky's in Fall Creek, the Hoot in Hallie, and the Barr in the town of Washington all catered to Eau Claire State students as places to drink 3.2 beer and listen to live music (chapter five). The bars ran buses to and from campus on weekend nights. Alcohol consumption and student purchase of alcohol from liquor stores became increasing problems. In the fall of 1971, intoxicated students at a football game in Carson Park who were openly drinking in the bleachers engaged in a melee with Eau Claire City Police, resulting in injuries to four officers from hurled wine, beer, and liquor bottles.

In 1971, the Twenty-sixth Amendment to the US Constitution ensured the right to vote for persons eighteen and older. The next year Wisconsin went further and changed the age of adulthood from twenty-one to eighteen. This had the effect of repealing the 1933 ban on the sale of intoxicating liquors to those under twenty-one. As of March 1972 the right to purchase and consume alcohol, and not just 3.2 beer, now belonged to all of the student body except a few seventeen-year-old first-year students. The Hoot and its counterparts soon went out of business, and in their place fourteen taverns operated on Water Street between Third and Fifth Avenues.

Several factors came together at about the same time to make Water Street the center of student drinking: the footbridge connecting lower campus to the new Fine Arts Building and Water Street opened in 1970 (chapter six); the suspension of new dormitory construction by the state after 1968 meant almost all juniors and seniors, and quite a few sophomores, left the dorms, looking for rental housing on the lower west side near to campus; and cheap retail spaces became available in Water Street storefronts and a Water Street Merchants Association started promoting the district. Above all, the university was in full retreat from its *in loco parentis* policy, especially for student behavior off campus.

Water Street was merely one of many student strips to emerge in college towns after the 1972 change in law. At almost every campus with a sizable residential population, students used and abused their right to drink and get drunk. The resulting problems became apparent when Water Street turned violent in 1976 at the tenth anniversary party of an event dubbed as "Tornado Watch," sponsored by the Tau Kappa Epsilon fraternity.

In its early years, the Tekes held their party outside the city limits in the town of Brunswick, with modest attendance by the fraternity brothers and their friends. After the change in the drinking age, Tornado Watch became more popular, not just among Eau Claire students but by drawing students from other campuses. The Tekes stretched the event into a three-day party in early May, and the crowds grew in number. By 1976, according to one estimate, 7,500 students gathered on Friday, May 7 for the party, consuming over five hundred half-barrels of beer on the first day alone. However, when the music stopped at the festival grounds on Friday evening, the partygoers did not wish to end their revelry. Instead, as many as three thousand students converged on Water Street and continued to drink in and out of taverns, including the Oar House, Shenannigans, and the Old Home. When police told them to disperse, students reacted angrily with bottles, cans, and other missiles and vandalized businesses and automobiles. Seven officers suffered injuries in what police called a riot; they did not clear the street until 4:00 am.

Tornado Watch

Thousands of young people from around the state gathered for the TKE party off campus and outside the city limits.

TKE cancelled the last two days of Tornado Watch. City officials submitted a bill for property damage and police overtime to UWEC, which promptly forwarded it to Tau Kappa Epsilon for payment. The Tekes refused to pay, claiming they were not responsible for the Water Street riot. Assistant Chancellor Harry suspended their charter as a campus group and the Student Senate moved to make student organizations responsible for, in effect, collateral damage resulting from sponsored events. When TKE attempted to revive Tornado Watch in 1979, the dean of students office warned them off.

The Tornado Watch riot stamped Water Street in the community's mind as a place where students ran wild. The Water Street Business Association responded with an attempt to upgrade the district. Of more importance was the legislature's action to increase the drinking age to nineteen in 1981 and to twenty-one in 1986; both changes were due to public pressure to reduce alcohol-related traffic accidents among young people. After 1986, Water Street remained a student strip filled with taverns, but one most UWEC students could not legally frequent until later in their college careers.

End of the Haas Era and the Selection of a New Chancellor

During his fortieth year on the UWEC faculty, Leonard Haas announced he would step down as chancellor at the end of the fall 1980 semester. He would continue, though, at the university for three more years as an academic advisor and as a member of the History Department, where he taught Wisconsin history. Finding a new leader for the campus who would be as respected and as effective as Haas would have been difficult for any institution, and it proved to be particularly so for UWEC. Serious problems also developed at the end of the Haas era which the new chancellor would have to face immediately.

Haas's last year as chancellor at UWEC was filled with tributes for the work he and Dorellen Haas had done in building the university. Impressive events were hosted in the visual and performing arts to celebrate that legacy. For example, in the winter of 1980, the Foster Gallery in the Fine Arts Building hosted a collection of the works of pop-artist Roy Lichtenstein, and the artist himself came to campus to open the exhibit and to speak at a University Forum. In September, Haas gave his last academic-year opening speech to the faculty and reflected upon his twenty-year run as campus leader. He returned to the theme of excellence and pronounced the faculty, through their hard work and dedication, had made the UWEC a university noted for excellence in curriculum, instruction, and learning. The university had set and achieved high goals, Haas concluded.

Students Partying at 1980 Homecoming Parade

The Haases also had fun in 1980; they were grand marshals of the Homecoming parade, and at the Homecoming dance Leonard proclaimed Dorellen his "homecoming queen." The fall 1980 semester was filled with tributes and awards, which left Leonard Haas a little embarrassed at the effusiveness of the kudos. One proposal was to spend $5,000 to commission a statue of the chancellor, an idea he sensibly nixed. System President Robert O'Neil deferred another suggestion, to name the Fine Arts Building after Leonard and Dorellen Haas, saying system rules prohibited naming buildings for currently employed faculty and staff (the building was finally dedicated to the Haases in 1986). After leaving the chancellorship in January 1981, Leonard Haas began his new university duties nine thousand miles from campus, as an exchange professor with UWEC's new partner in Japan, Kansaid Gadai University.

Leonard and Dorellen Haas, 1978

The Fine Arts Center (left center) was named in honor of the Haases in 1986.

The process of selecting Haas's successor as chancellor taught the UWEC the power of UW System administration and the board of regents. The consensus choice among the faculty was Vice Chancellor John Morris. However, for the first time, the chancellor search had to proceed under UW System rules; the new chancellor could not glide into the position almost by acclamation, with the overt endorsement of the faculty, as Haas had done in 1959 (chapter five). Consequently, the shock on campus was palpable when the regents announced in June 1980 that Morris was not even one of four finalists. One faculty member said he went from being "stunned" at the omission of Morris to "appalled" at the quality of the four finalists. President Robert O'Neil rejected a hastily assembled faculty petition asking the regents to reconsider and add Morris to the short list. Then in July of 1980, after interviewing the finalists, the regents selected M. Emily Hannah, vice president for academic affairs in the Minnesota State College and University System (MNSCU), as the next UWEC chancellor.

Emily Hannah favorably impressed the regents on the Search and Screen Committee when they interviewed her at an airport hotel in Bloomington, Minnesota, in late June. She especially impressed President O'Neil. He noted Hannah had experience with faculty governance as an administrator at St. Cloud State which included experience negotiating with unionized faculty, a looming prospect in Wisconsin, O'Neil thought. He was also impressed she had done her homework about how to make the best use of Leonard Haas's talents: "Haas could continue to represent Univ. in community. Build on strength," O'Neil jotted as he talked with Hannah. Hannah told O'Neil and the regents that her priorities would be to build up the women's studies program at Eau Claire, improve the funding and status of the Children's Center to help non-traditional student-parents, and to recruit, enroll, and retain more "minority and disadvantaged students." Clearly, Hannah had absorbed the meaning of the changes of the 1970s about the broadened identities of who was a college student and, specifically, who was a Blugold.

The UWEC faculty's future was also on O'Neil's mind that June. He had just read the reaccreditation report of the North Central Association, which noted the lack of faculty scholarship at UWEC.

That report said, in part: "[The] low level of scholarly activity and the minor importance attached to scholarship are not surprising in an institution with UW-EC's history. The System's declaration that UW-Eau Claire is not and is not to become a research university is taken very earnestly here. [However,] The quality of teaching to which it otherwise attends so determinedly will soon suffer if it does not."

O'Neil acknowledged to Haas that the NCA report was "a bit pejorative [with] the phrase 'minor importance attached to scholarship.'" Nonetheless, he asked all the finalists at the Bloomington interviews what they would do to raise the importance of research, scholarship, and publication among the UWEC faculty. Hannah went further than any other finalist saying, according to O'Neil's contemporary notes, she saw from afar a "good faculty 'stale' at UWEC." She proposed to motivate the faculty with additional rewards for research and publication and by beginning new graduate programs in liberal studies, nursing, and library and information science. Most significantly, she said she would demand more in tenure and promotion reviews and would begin post-tenure review of faculty to determine who was performing at an expected high level and who was deficient.

Although most of the faculty did not welcome Hannah's selection, other voices around the region and the state were pleased. Regent Lavine, publisher of the Chippewa Falls *Herald-Telegram*, wrote Hannah applauding her appointment as an upgrade of the quality of administrators around the UW System and the first of what he hoped would be many new women and minority academic leaders. Two faculty members from UW–Superior wrote Hannah saying, "We no longer need to be embarrassed by the absence of women in the campus chief executive position." In his letter of appointment, President O'Neil wrote, "Your appointment has brought much excitement and enthusiasm not only to Eau Claire but throughout the state . . . I know you will bring to one of our finest institutions a rare and humane quality of leadership."

Emily Hannah came to Eau Claire at age forty-four after a rapid career rise, including short stints as a high school teacher; as a faculty member, department chair, and assistant dean at St. Cloud State University in Minnesota; and in the president's office at MNSCU. A graduate of Grinnell College in Iowa, with master and doctorate degrees earned at the University of Iowa in speech and communications, Hannah was the first woman chancellor of any UW System campus. Upon her selection, Hannah visited Eau Claire to meet faculty and students and sit for an interview with the *Spectator*. She stated her intention "to back faculty governance at Eau Claire. I believe it avoids the tendency that collective bargaining has to polarize the faculty and administration," a red flag to the sizable majority of the faculty who belonged to TAUWF and were pushing the legislature to award it the right to engage in collective bargaining.

Hannah announced she would begin her chancellor's duties on January 1, 1981. During the fall semester she asked O'Neil for authority to hire her MNSCU assistant, Sara Chapman, as an assistant to the chancellor at the UWEC, a post that did not exist under Haas. John Morris duly organized a search for an assistant to the chancellor position, and in November he announced Chapman had been selected for the job.

Before Hannah would arrive on campus, during the fall 1980 semester, the most serious scandal to beset the university during the Haas era occurred. On October 20, the dean of the School of Arts and Sciences, Frederick Haug Jr., pled no contest to two counts of sexual assault. The special prosecutor handling the case revealed in his charging statement the defendant had committed the offenses prior to 1980, but when they came to the knowledge of Haas and Morris, he had merely promised to change his behavior and had retained his position. The special prosecutor stated Haas and Morris had "failed miserably" in their oversight of Haug. On November 4 the dean was sentenced to two years probation with required counselling. "[U]nless we have a loud and clear message," the special prosecutor emphasized, "the university can look upon itself . . . as above the law." A defiant Morris countered that the police "were unnecessarily aggressive" and the special prosecutor had "overreacted." "Personally," Morris told the *Spectator* about the investigation and decision to charge Haug, "I resent all the tax dollars spent on it."

The criminal behavior by Haug revealed an insularity into which UWEC had drifted in the 1970s. Campus leadership, starting with Haas and Morris, protected their associates and ignored the seriousness of sexual harassment. They showed themselves insensitive to matters of the power differential between a dean and a subordinate. Despite speaking about equality of access for all, they showed themselves indifferent to matters important to women on campus.

To fill the void created by Haug's resignation, Assistant Dean Robert Fraser took over as interim dean of Arts and Sciences, even as he continued as interim chair of the faction-riven Department of Sociology as it struggled with the tenure dispute regarding Kenneth Davidson. Almost the first task Emily Hannah had to face was a search for a new Arts and Sciences dean; instead of looking inside to her faculty, she went outside to hire a department chair from Moorhead State University in Minnesota, Lee Grugel, whom she had known from her MNSCU service.

In addition to dealing with the crisis in leadership in Arts and Sciences, Hannah took office just as Lee Dreyfus, the former UW–Stevens Point chancellor who had been elected governor as a Republican in 1978, imposed a pay freeze on all state employees in response to a budget shortfall. Hannah voiced the frustration felt on campus when she told the faculty: "[T]he overwhelming response of a typically dedicated professor is HURT—a sense that his or her effort and talent is unappreciated . . . Faculty are recruited nationwide. They belong in their minds and in mine to a national community of scholars more than to a local group called state employees. UWEC will keep its established faculty, but lose its junior faculty and not attract the new, best faculty."

The tone was happier when President O'Neil and other state dignitaries came to Eau Claire for Honors Week in April 1981, as the signature event was planned to coincide with Hannah's inauguration as chancellor. The chancellor, very much aware of Eau Claire's motto, dwelled on the theme of excellence in her prepared remarks: "Excellence: the word of ancient origins emblazoned on the university seal as our goal . . . It is a word which reminds us that leadership of a university is not a function of a chancellor only, but of all members of the university community."

Lecture Theater, Hibbard Humanities Hall, 1970s

Journalism professor Gerald Connor is teaching his Mass Media Law course. The lecture hall facilities in the new Humanities Building were state of the art.

President Haas's second run as campus chief executive, from 1973 to 1980, was less successful than his first had been from 1960 to 1971. Above all, the challenge of Haas's second term was maintaining excellence rather than expanding it. Regarding the physical shape of the campus, the great building boom of the Golden Age came to an end with the completion of Hibbard Humanities Hall. Protecting Wisconsin's Most Beautiful Campus against external, unwanted development, such as highways bisecting Putnam Park, took on a greater priority. Maintaining excellence in the new UW System proved a challenge as well, particularly when the regents and the system administration seemed to favor the doctoral campuses at Madison and Milwaukee over UWEC. Keeping UWEC excellent in the face of budget cuts also challenged Haas and his administrative team. The 1970s was the decade in which the state began to shift the financing of public higher education from taxpayers to students and their families. At the same time, federal and state authorities made new demands upon UWEC to ensure equality of opportunity.

Haas faced the challenges of the 1970s with most of his administrative team (minus the late Richard Hibbard) from his first presidency at Eau Claire, and most of the faculty having arrived before 1971 as well. By 1980, Haas's team and faculty were well set in their ways and confident in the excellence of those ways. The university Leonard Haas built was a mature institution, expecting to continue his call to pursue excellence.

1980-90
Conflicting Paths to Excellence

Students on the "Hill" from Lower to Upper Campus, c. 1980

By the 1970s, "hill" had replaced the more geographically correct "bluff" in common usage.

UW–Eau Claire developed excellence in new ways during the 1980s. These achievements occurred in the national context of the most intensive debates about American education in a quarter of a century.

External financial constraints and—as feared at the time of the merger in 1971—a growing number of mandates from the University of Wisconsin System also increasingly shaped the campus during the decade. Finding paths to excellence was difficult in this atmosphere, but at the beginning of the decade UWEC's controversial new chancellor identified some promising new directions, which were blazed later in the decade behind leadership with which most of the campus was more comfortable.

UWEC in the "Education Decade"

President Jimmy Carter selected Ernest Boyer as his first commissioner of education, a post he served in until 1979 when he moved to the Carnegie Foundation for the Advancement of Teaching. At Carnegie, he began a study of the American high school, which found it to be an area of concern for the country and urged partnerships between secondary education and higher education. Boyer called his study "Excellence in Education: A Prospectus for a Study of the American High School."

The newly named chancellor at UWEC, Emily Hannah, met with Boyer twice before she began her duties on January 1, 1981. She wanted Carnegie to fund UWEC as the go-to expert on how to change the education of twelve million American high school students. Hannah arranged a December 1980 meeting in Madison for what she thought would be a deal-clinching, face-to-face sit-down with Boyer and his Carnegie associates on one side of the table and herself and UW President Robert O'Neil on the other. Boyer told her Carnegie was not yet ready to accept Eau Claire's proposal, but neither did he discourage her from pursuing a future partnership. Hannah had to postpone the announcement with which she had hoped to open her chancellorship the following month: a Carnegie/UW–Eau Claire partnership that would serve not just the region or even the state of Wisconsin, but the entire nation, and in doing so, drive UWEC to new heights of excellence in teaching, scholarship, and service.

Hannah was not discouraged. Soon after arriving on campus in the winter of 1981, she convened a northwest Wisconsin working group of high school principals and UWEC School of Education leaders to prepare a grant proposal to send to Boyer at Carnegie. Assistant Dean of Education Charles O. Larson led the team that worked during the spring and summer of 1981 and submitted to Carnegie a "Study of High Schools in Northwestern Wisconsin: Prospectus for a Proposal." The Larson group proposed a close working relationship among UWEC and the dozen participating high schools, including Eau Claire's two public high schools, Memorial and North, as well as Chippewa Falls High School. The draft proposal featured articulation agreements between the university and its partner high schools so the graduates of the high schools would be ready for admission to UWEC.

Chancellor Emily Hannah

Hannah was the first woman chancellor in the UW system and led UWEC from 1981 to 1984.

At the same time the Larson group was at work on its proposal, Hannah reached out to the Corporation for Public Broadcasting for support of a proposal which included UWEC producing educational television programming for high school students. Hannah, Education Dean Rodney Johnson, O'Neil, and UW Regent (and state superintendent of public instruction) Herbert J. "Bert" Grover met with Boyer in Madison in November 1981 to go over the Eau Claire proposal. To Hannah's dismay, Boyer told her at that meeting Carnegie was so far behind schedule on funding grant proposals for its American high school project she should just forget the foundation as a funding source and look elsewhere for support.

The same month she received the disappointing news from Boyer, Hannah and the School of Education faculty made an important decision: UWEC would not pursue re-accreditation from the venerable National Council on the Accreditation of Teacher Education (NCATE). The chancellor had asked the faculty to research the pluses and minuses of NCATE certification. The resulting report was a model of policy recommendations based on survey research. The faculty reported to Hannah that students seeking a career in teaching did not pick a program on the basis of NCATE certification and, just as important, school districts in Wisconsin did not hire teachers on the basis of their holding a degree from an NCATE-certified school. UWEC, as did some other UW schools, left NCATE because research showed certification by an external accrediting agency was not cost effective.

By the time Ernest Boyer and the Carnegie Foundation finally finished their American high school study in 1983, the nation had moved on to a new report commissioned by President Ronald Reagan's new secretary of education, Terrel Bell's *A Nation at Risk*, which had a sharper, more alarming critique of elementary and secondary public education. That report famously began with the statement, "The educational foundations of our society are presently being eroded by a rising tide of mediocrity that threatens our very future as a Nation and a people."

Mediocrity in education clashed with UWEC's proclaimed mission of "excellence," yet the university did not escape the scrutiny of *A Nation at Risk* and its aftermath. The authors very publicly compared US students to their peers in other nations, notably Japan, and found American pupils lacking. Above all, the authors stated the US education system, including colleges and universities, was not doing its part in "workforce preparation." The Bell report laid bare the tension between a growing number of Americans who saw college almost entirely in vocational terms as workforce preparation for immediate post-baccalaureate employment and those who held the older view that regarded college as preparation for life.

UWEC struggled to address this tension through on-campus curriculum debates and off-campus exchanges with external audiences, including governors, legislators, and the public. In the mid-1980s, the board of regents created a study commission, led by then-UW System Vice President for Academic Affairs Katherine Lyall, on the future of the University of Wisconsin. That group, too, leaned toward workforce preparation as the main reason for mass access to UW higher education. The Lyall group asked for a reconsideration of the place of the university and the "Wisconsin Idea" from the early twentieth century: whereas the UW once served the state by serving farmers in their barns and fields with new knowledge, in the 1980s it would serve the state by generating new economic development. The "Wisconsin Idea" was refurbished, but the inspiration was from the higher education–business connections of California's Silicon Valley and Massachusetts's 128 Corridor.

Another Boyer–Carnegie initiative at the end of the decade proved significant in changing UWEC. Carnegie funded a study of the American college and university professoriat entitled *Scholarship Reconsidered*. Boyer, as the lead author, reported American faculty members at almost all institutions saw themselves as teachers first. He called for a wider view of scholarship beyond peer-reviewed publication of research. Boyer combined his findings and his call for a different type of American researcher into a new "Scholarship of Teaching and Learning."

UWEC, in its own fashion and after some twists and turns, embraced Boyer's *Scholarship Reconsidered* and found it a guide to a renewed purpose of excellence. As will be seen later in this chapter, at the end of the 1980s, the regents proclaimed UWEC a "Center of Excellence" in faculty–student collaborative research. This variant on Boyer's new definition of scholarship proved to be a productive and innovative outlet for engaging the university's best faculty and best students, as will be detailed in chapter ten.

New Leadership at UWEC, 1981–90

Emily Hannah's positive start at UWEC was soon offset by her decision to circumvent the campus governance embodied in the constitution of the Faculty Senate. She appointed three ad hoc task forces to report to her on the future of graduate education, on the future of international education, and on the organization of student support services. Hannah chose to rely on task forces to give the university a new direction, rather than asking the Faculty Senate to take up the issues. She revealed her thinking about how to make change at UWEC in a talk she gave at a North Central Association (NCA) meeting in Chicago in March of 1981; the speaking notes she wrote to herself read: "New initiatives. DON'T give to Faculty Senate or to Existing VPs or Deans; DO create task forces charge with specific objectives and staffed with secretarial help."

The first task force Hannah convened concerned the state of graduate education at the university. The 1980 NCA reaccreditation report of UW–Eau Claire had concluded the "role of the Graduate School is ambiguous and that of the Graduate Dean is weak." The criticism was not specific to the then-graduate dean—instead, the NCA report complained the graduate program in nursing and also the graduate program in business were both separate from the graduate school. The NCA report called this "an awkward separation" and "an unfortunate situation." Hannah recognized this problem, but wanted more from the graduate education task force than mere recommendations about how to organize the graduate office; she wanted the task force to call for more faculty scholarship in the form of research and publication if UWEC was to continue offering master's-level graduate education. What she had in mind was an enhanced graduate office that also promoted faculty research and creative activity.

Hannah asked a second task force to look at international education and to chair this group she turned to Leonard Haas. This task force, therefore, had to wait to complete its work until Haas returned from his exchange semester in Japan. Its proposals shocked the campus at their audacity, particularly in the area of curriculum changes. The task force called upon every student to take twelve credits of "International Studies," including at least three credit hours in "non-western" studies. In addition, the task force proposed a requirement that every UWEC graduate should show subject competence in a foreign language at the two-semester level. The task force reported to the Faculty Senate that the university should create three new full-time staff positions in international education, including a director and coordinators for foreign students on campus and for UWEC students studying abroad.

The curriculum committees of all four schools, as well as the Faculty Senate's Academic Policies Committee, rejected the recommendation for requiring twelve international studies credits. Only the School of Arts and Sciences voted to require its students to show competence in foreign languages, and then only for those pursuing the bachelor of arts degree, not the bachelor of science. However, the administration did hire a full-time director of international education. The successful candidate came to campus and announced in his view, UWEC students along with other college students had a "dismal preparation in American politics, foreign policy and world affairs" and this shortcoming "must be addressed." The critique echoed President Davies's evaluation of Eau Claire State when he became president in 1940 (chapter three)—finding fault with students because of their provincialism, their homogeneity, and their ignorance—but the remedy in 1981 was corrective action through compulsory registration in a new course.

The third task force was charged with making sense of the proliferation of staff positions serving different student groups on campus, but outside the supervision of the dean of students office. Hannah stated this review was necessary because, as she put it, faculty members were asking the question, "Why so many resources are devoted to special students, and not enough to regular ones?" The Task Force on Student Services, chaired by Philip A. Chute from the Department of Physics, received a charge to examine possible duplication of services to students and also to look at the ways in which students were referred to different offices.

The Chute task force learned that in 1962 Eau Claire State had just three student service offices outside of the dean of students: one for counseling, one for new students, and one for placement. By 1982, eleven independent student services existed. Most of the new offices had been created in the 1970s in response to one or another initiative: the American ethnic coordinating office served minority students; the adult students office served non-traditional aged students; the special services office served students with inadequate academic preparation for college; the educational opportunity office served low-income students; and the academic skills center served students in need of tutoring in reading, writing, and mathematics to perform at the college level. These offices did a mix of academic, personal, and career counseling.

After much study, the Task Force on Student Services' report emphasized that academic advising was the responsibility of academic affairs, a decision made in 1974 when the office of academic and career advising had been established (chapter seven), but which was not clear in everyone's mind by the early 1980s. Specifically, the Chute group reiterated the policy that every student with a declared major have an academic advisor in the relevant department, and students undeclared as to major have an assigned advisor in academic and career advising. Centralizing and streamlining, with the hope of cost reduction, was the task force's message.

The task force reports contributed to a growing sense of turmoil on campus in the fall of 1981. Graduate Dean Dale Dick resigned in September 1981, pointedly saying he did not want to be an obstacle to any change the faculty might want to make in graduate studies. New Arts and Sciences Dean Grugel called for all faculty members to engage in research and publication, not just those who wanted to earn tenure and promotion. The campus was further rocked by the resignation of Vice Chancellor Morris, who publicly said he wished to return to full-time teaching in the Department of English, but also said he had been isolated and unable to perform his job by the combination of Hannah and her assistant, Sara Chapman. Dean of Nursing Suzanne Van Ort resigned in October 1981, also saying she could not work under Hannah and Chapman. The departure of Van Ort, the highest-ranking woman leader on campus before Hannah's arrival, suggested it was not just males with whom Hannah could not work. Former Faculty Senate chair Nadine St. Louis, who a year earlier had been very excited for UWEC to have the first woman chancellor in the UW System, was by the fall of 1981 thoroughly disenchanted with Hannah and Chapman.

The "Roaring Inferno:" Blugold Basketball in the Era of Ken Anderson

The success of the men's basketball program during the 1970s increased UW–Eau Claire's profile, connected it more closely to the community, and became one of the major focuses of student life. The person most responsible for this success was Coach Ken Anderson.

As a Blugold, Anderson played basketball and baseball and graduated in 1955. He successfully coached at four Wisconsin high schools and succeeded Bill Zorn as basketball coach at the university in the spring of 1968. Taking over a program that had one winning season among the previous eight, he was immediately successful. His 1968–69 team was 14–8, and they won the title in what became the Wisconsin Intercollegiate Athletic Conference (WIAC) in eleven of the thirteen seasons between 1970 and 1982.

Student and community interest in Anderson's teams was so great three thousand or more "basketball mad fans," as they were characterized by the local newspaper, often crowded into the Arena for their games. Recalling campus life in the early 1970s, Sally Gordon explained, "Our greatest thing to do was to go to the Blugold basketball games." Students queued up for hours in the cold to get into what local sportswriter Ron Buckli described as "a roaring inferno called the University Arena." By tradition, the crowd stood and yelled until the Blugolds scored their first basket. With this fan support, the Blugolds won 90 percent of their home games during the Anderson era.

Unfortunate fans who were shut out of the Arena listened to the games on WBIZ radio or saw them on WEAU-TV several times a season. In an era before cable television every night brought a half-dozen games from around the nation into homes in the Chippewa Valley, in which the UW–Madison basketball program floundered and got little attention, and when statewide newspapers still had sports desks large enough to staff key WIAC games. Blugold basketball developed a strong following across the northern part of the state.

The success of the basketball team brought national attention to UWEC. A flattering article in 1971 in *Sports Illustrated* emphasized, "The members of Eau Claire's varsity are bright, articulate, well-informed and congenial and they fit in neatly with a student body that cares far more for pep rallies than protest meetings." The article's author was clearly impressed by Wisconsin's Most Beautiful Campus and reported, with a bit of exaggeration, "When a new building is planned, the first considerations are mainly esthetic. How many trees will have to be cut down?"

Infected with "Blugold Fever," thousands of fans followed the Blugolds to Kansas City for the National Association of Intercollegiate Athletics national tournament, in which UWEC participated fifteen times while Anderson was coach and was twice runner-up. Commenting on their enthusiasm, a tournament official explained in 1980, "I wish we had more fans like Eau Claire's."

In 1982 Anderson declined the opportunity to become the coach at UW–Madison and remained at Eau Claire until his retirement in 1995. (Interestingly, a Badger assistant coach in 1982 was Bo Ryan, who later coached the UW–Platteville teams, replacing UWEC as the dominant power in the WIAC in the late 1980s and 1990s, and who in 2001 successfully took over the UW–Madison program.) In 2016 Anderson's 631 wins remained the most in WIAC history (Zorn was third on the list). He was a three-time NAIA Coach of the Year.

In 2012 the site of the Roaring Inferno officially became Ken Anderson Court at Zorn Arena. To make this so, former players and other alumni raised $100,000, the same amount as was needed to dedicate a classroom. At the dedication ceremony, Anderson jokingly responded to a video which included congratulations from Ryan by pointing out the Blugolds had defeated his UW–Platteville teams ten out of eleven times on that floor. The naming of the floor also highlighted the significance of the Zorn-Anderson connection: just as Laura Sutherland's many contributions to the university included boosting the appointment of Leonard Haas to the faculty in 1941 (chapter two), Zorn's list of contributions included the identification of Anderson as his successor. Both selections profoundly affected the history of UWEC.

Ken Anderson Coaching Six-hundredth Win, 1993-94 season

Problems mounted as the semester progressed. In November, Elwood C. Karwand, chair of the Journalism Department since 1964 and advisor to the *Spectator*, was charged with embezzlement of funds from the student newspaper. Karwand had stolen over $20,000 from *Spectator* accounts over at least a four-year period. Then, in December, Wallace R. O'Neill, the chief of University Police, was arrested because of his warrantless search at the off-campus apartment of a suspect in a residence hall theft. The chief entered the apartment and found the stolen goods, but nonetheless was charged by the district attorney and convicted of burglary (a judgment eventually set aside on appeal). In still another incident, Frederick Haug, who had returned to campus to teach while on probation for sexual assault (chapter seven), was arrested and later pled no contest to sexually harassing a colleague.

Relations between the chancellor and her faculty worsened after Morris's resignation. The faculty, working under Governor Dreyfus's pay freeze, reacted with outrage when they learned Chapman, the chancellor's assistant, had received a job reclassification and a substantial pay raise. When the *Spectator* reported Hannah and Chapman shared not just a house, but also a joint bank account, some faculty members accused Hannah of benefiting personally from Chapman's appointment. The unsubtle whispering campaign was the new chancellor was engaged in a lesbian relationship as well as nepotism.

Chapman spared the campus further turmoil by resigning her position in December and accepting a fellowship at the National Humanities Center. Her resignation and departure from Eau Claire, however, deprived her partner of needed workplace and private support. Hannah told the *Milwaukee Journal* in an interview that UWEC had enough trouble adjusting to one strong woman leader, "two was two too many."

At a tumultuous faculty meeting on December 17, Hannah faced her critics, spoke of her hopes for Eau Claire, and listened to faculty complaints. However, many faculty members came away furious with their chancellor when she told them she regarded them as the heart of the university, but one that was "atrophied, blocked [and] flaccid." No one could accuse Hannah of sugar coating her opinion of UWEC faculty.

Even before her atrophied-heart comment, University Senate chair Ronald Schlattman had prepared a letter that amounted to a resolution of no confidence in Hannah. He listed four specific complaints: 1) Hannah had bypassed the Senate in favor of unelected task forces; 2) by emphasizing faculty research and publication as criteria for tenure and promotion, Hannah had unilaterally changed the faculty personnel rules; 3) she had proposed a differential pay plan for faculty with raises pegged to individual evaluations of merit; and 4) she had changed the motto on university stationary from "Excellence" to "Accepting the Challenge."

After the December faculty meeting, Schlattman sent his letter to O'Neil and asked the system president to come to Eau Claire. Schlattman told O'Neil, "We have reached a critical period on this campus . . . the most important juncture in the history of our campus." At the same time, a faculty senator demanded O'Neil perform a personnel evaluation of Hannah, presumably as preparation to remove her from office. O'Neil journeyed north to Eau Claire and listened to faculty and also met with Hannah. His handwritten notes of that January visit show he struggled to understand its complicated dynamics: "Causes? A) change—Haas Era difficult; b) External Conditions; c) Faculty Passivity; d) Style; e) Personal Chemistry. How Serious? Depends on next couple of weeks."

O'Neil did conduct a personnel review, of sorts, of Emily Hannah, but rather than acting to remove her from the UWEC chancellorship, he awarded her the largest possible raise for a new chancellor. Around the state, too, voices spoke up in favor of Hannah's leadership, including the state's leading newspaper, the *Milwaukee Journal*. One citizen wrote to O'Neil cautioning him, "The turbulence at the University of Wisconsin-Eau Claire threatens to become an academic lynching bee. Please keep a close watch on a campaign that now endangers the career of the UW System's first woman chancellor." O'Neil toyed with the idea of asking a senior woman academic leader, Donna Shalala, then president of Hunter College, to mentor Hannah on being a woman university president, but Hannah stated she was not the one who needed mentoring.

On campus, the Student Senate took Hannah's side. Three female students and faculty members also castigated the *Spectator* for reporting on Hannah and Chapman's financial arrangements, alleging it was cheap payback for the chancellor's decision not to give the newspaper the money Karwand paid in restitution for his embezzlement.

The ill will between Hannah and the faculty flared up again during the spring 1982 semester over the search for a replacement for John Morris as vice chancellor. The Search Committee, following existing campus rules, refused to share the names of applicants in the pool, instead telling Hannah she could only see the names of the four persons they recommended as finalists. She found this unacceptable and when the Search Committee would not budge, she rejected the four names they provided her as not qualified. Before authorizing another search, she demanded changes in the personnel rules that would give her greater power in any future search. In the meantime, Larry Schnack continued for another year as interim vice chancellor for academic affairs.

Hannah was so angry with the faculty and its governance rules that in May 1982, she single-handedly resolved to bring Sara Chapman back to Eau Claire and install her as vice chancellor for academic affairs. "I am tired of being bullied," Hannah wrote O'Neil, telling him of her decision. In turn, the president cautioned her against this move, warning with understatement it "would cause possible public relations problems," and before she did anything, he would like to "run it past the Regents." Hannah let the proposal drop, and Chapman instead became dean of Newcomb College at Tulane University.

Emily Hannah's Vision for UW–Eau Claire

June is usually the time when students and faculty are away from campus, enjoying summer break. For administrators in almost any organization, however, July 1 is the due date for the annual report and June is devoted to compiling material for that document. Chancellor Hannah wrote hers in the form of a private letter to O'Neil, almost as if she was an external consultant, reporting on the state of somebody else's college. She began with a backhanded reproach of O'Neil and of the board that selected her: "Perhaps no one could possibly have estimated fully enough what the coming of a change in chancellorship would mean at Eau Claire; had they done so, surely none of the principals would have made the decisions of July 1980—certainly not without simultaneously vacating the vice chancellorship."

Hannah lumped the faculty into the same category as the students, saying they suffered from "homogeneity" and were full of "insecurities." She did not doubt herself or the actions she had taken and instead told O'Neil, "The challenge ahead is to engage other faculty in leadership of their enterprise, much as was done in this year's task forces." In a private letter later that summer to a friend at the American Council of Education's Office of Women in Higher Education, Hannah gave her opinion that O'Neil and the others in the UW System Administration had "absolutely no understanding of what is involved in making a minority or a woman succeed."

Chancellor Hannah was still far from done trying to change UWEC. She created additional task forces, one of which was charged with starting an honors program. Hannah also decided the way to make change on campus was replace the existing academic and student affairs leadership, one by one. To that same friend at the American Council of Education, she wrote UWEC "is a bit of a piranha tank of power players" and in her search for a replacement for John Morris, she insisted "the chief academic officer must be unerringly patient and persevering." To replace the graduate dean, she asked for names of women as the dean's job was "a good one for a bright young woman who wants to try university-wide administration."

A year later, Hannah wrote her annual report from the perspective of the year 1993, looking back a decade at UWEC. This time traveler, she wrote, would see in the UWEC of 1993 four differences from the university of the earlier "growth era." First, the faculty had developed "an emerging self-identity as a community of scholars, rather than an [sic] homogeneous family of teachers." Hannah helped lead this transformation, she claimed, by insisting all tenure and promotion decisions address the matter of faculty scholarship. Second, the university stopped looking to the legislature for an increase in funding and instead looked to higher tuition and private fundraising. During the 1982–83 year, Hannah had called upon O'Neil to ask the regents to grant UWEC the right to levy a tuition surcharge, and once again he had told her the time was not right. Her crystal ball gazing indicated she thought such a surcharge was inevitable, and not far into the future. Third, in describing the UWEC of 1993, she saw the university had a new administrative leadership full of "energy . . . as well as a much broader experience." Fourth, the university had once again begun new curricular initiatives, confounding "the notion that nothing can be done without new monies." She was especially proud of the Honors Program launched in 1983.

Hindsight from 2016, if not 1993, confirms the accuracy of many of Hannah's envisioned major changes. Perhaps the most apparent was her promise to transform UWEC by hiring and empowering a new generation of academic and student affairs leaders. That pledge came with an open criticism of past practices of promoting from within, especially those who had spent their entire careers at the university. To staff top academic and student affairs jobs, Hannah relied on her network of contacts in the Minnesota State University System. As mentioned previously, she hired Lee Grugel, a department chair from Moorhead State University, to fill the dean's job in the School of Arts and Sciences; to fill the vacant position of assistant chancellor for student affairs after Ormsby Harry retired in 1983, she chose another candidate from Moorhead, Elliott Garb. Also, in 1983, she picked yet another Minnesotan, Robert Frost, to be the new full-time director of international education. Before Frost arrived from St. Cloud State University, Steve R. Marquardt had left that campus to come to Eau Claire to serve as director of libraries.

Faculty grumbled about a "Minnesota Mafia" taking over UWEC, but not all the new deans and directors came from that state. Hannah hired a new graduate dean, Ronald N. Satz, from the University of Tennessee System and a new School of Nursing dean in Patricia Ostmoe from the University of Iowa. Her last important hire came in academic year 1983–84 when she finally got to hire an academic vice chancellor, Norman Doorenbos from Southern Illinois University. In her same looking-backward report from the supposed vantage point of 1993, Hannah acidly commented that "except for Dean Ostmoe, all are white males, in accordance with Wisconsin tradition and standards of acceptance."

Hannah could also point to the change in the UWEC faculty from merely a "family of teachers" to a "community of scholars." This was not so much in a rise in scholarly production by the faculty in peer-reviewed publications, but rather in bringing the practice of peer reviewing into more and more of university life. This began in the university research office which organized faculty panels to review and rank proposals for sabbaticals, for time reassignments for research, and for internal grants for equipment and travel to conferences. The practice of peer review also became part of university life in other areas, such as the implementation of regular rotations of audit-and-review reports.

The university as a whole and its academic programs were already subjects of external reviews for accreditation (chapter six). In 1982, Hannah's Task Force on Student Services programs recommended the initiation of regular audits and reviews by faculty of academic support units. All academic departments also had to undergo reviews by faculty peers at least once every five years. Hannah wrote O'Neil in the same looking-backward letter that although she regarded long-range planning by the Faculty Senate as a waste of time, she had a high

Graduate Studies Office Staff, c. 1990

Left to right: Vicki Lord Larson, Ronald N. Satz, and Cheryl Barrows. Lord Larson would later serve as interim chancellor from 2005 to 2006 (chapter ten) and Satz would serve as provost and vice chancellor for academic affairs from 1999 to 2006 (chapter ten). Barrows managed day-to-day affairs in the graduate office for over thirty years before her retirement in 2006.

CONFLICTING PATHS TO EXCELLENCE 201

regard for the work faculty panels performed in audits and reviews. Without articulating her views in the language of the engineer and business consultant W. Edward Deming, Hannah advocated for using peer review on campus as means of total quality management. Data gathering, self-study, criticism, and response became the UWEC way in the 1980s.

A New Chancellor and Old Problems

In May 1984, Chancellor Hannah announced her resignation to take a staff job in the Pennsylvania State System for Higher Education, a position similar to the one she had held in Minnesota. President O'Neil and the board of regents reached down below Vice Chancellor Doorenbos, the next in line, to ask Larry Schnack, the long-time assistant vice chancellor for academic affairs, to serve as interim chancellor. The campus readied itself for another chancellor's search and screen process, the second in just four years. Schnack took care in public neither to commit himself to apply for the chancellor's vacancy or to declare himself out of the running. However, he received considerable encouragement on campus and around the state to make his application, which was endorsed by a faculty petition to the regents organized by John Morris. The campus was genuinely pleased when the regents named him the permanent chancellor in the summer of 1985.

The faculty may have thought they were getting a restoration of the Leonard Haas and John Morris years, if only because Haas and Morris had hired Schnack and promoted him within the administration. However, Schnack continued many of the initiatives Emily Hannah had started and pressed several of them even further. He, too, followed Deming's ideas for improving the efficiency of an organization through total quality management, and he, too, believed in faculty peer review of instructional and even non-instructional activities.

Schnack wanted to examine UW–Eau Claire as outsiders saw it. Recalling an early initiative of President Davies, one of his first acts as interim chancellor was to convene an ad hoc study group with the charge to survey state opinion leaders about their views of UWEC. Schnack appointed Graduate Dean and Director of University Research Ronald Satz to chair this group. The Satz group sent out 1,600 questionnaires to three audiences: high school guidance counselors; high school teachers; and professionals such as attorneys, dentists, architects, and physicians. Each group had a different set of questions to answer. The response rates alone told a story of UWEC's comparative unimportance. Although half of the guidance counselors returned the survey, barely a quarter of teachers did and only an eighth of professionals bothered to reply, despite follow-up requests.

The survey findings revealed none of the three audiences thought of UWEC as excellent in any way. High school counselors and high school teachers regarded the university as a solid institution, but not much different than its peers. When asked if they thought the university should emphasize faculty research, neither high school counselors nor high school teachers answered in the affirmative. The replies from architects and other professionals were even more revealing. Those few who took the time to respond knew little about UWEC, did not see a faculty research mission as being of any value to the state, and could not associate the university with excellence in any regard. The 1985 survey results showed the university could no longer coast on a reputation for excellence earned in earlier decades. Again, in the 1980s, as it had in the 1970s, the university would have to generate new sources of excellence from within, all the while encountering external constraints in the form of policy and budget limits.

It was not merely the statewide audience of education and other professionals who did not automatically connect the words UWEC and excellence. Even before President Haas's retirement, outside evaluators had looked at specific academic programs at UWEC and found them wanting. The new bachelor's degree program in social work, first provisionally accredited in 1974 by the Council on Social Work's Commission on Education Accrediting, ran afoul of that same agency four years later and wound up on probation. The council charged Eau Claire's faculty in the program was stretched too thin and found other problems as well. The university had to scramble to find resources to address the external criticisms.

The next year the accrediting agency for the School of Business, the American Association of Collegiate Schools of Business (AACSB), began its review of the undergraduate BBA program. The AACSB gave the program its imprimatur in 1980, causing much celebration on campus, given how few colleges and universities could claim an AACSB-accredited undergraduate business program. Still, the 1980 AACSB report warned the school had to make improvements before the next visitation. AACSB specifically said too many faculty members in the Departments of Accountancy and Business Administration did not have an earned doctorate degree. Too many of the School of Business faculty taught overloads, stretching them too thin and not leaving them with enough time, AACSB observed, to publish peer-reviewed research. This was an ominous warning as the university had launched a master's in business administration (MBA) degree program in 1976. Without significantly more faculty positions and more faculty research, UWEC stood in danger of not having its MBA degree accredited and perhaps even having the hard-earned BBA accreditation imperiled.

To some extent, the School of Business fell victim to its own success with students, as its majors had grown dramatically in popularity in the 1970s and early 1980s. About 1,500 students selected a business major in 1973, and thirty-eight faculty members taught them. Eight years later, more than 2,500 declared a major in the school. Fully half of the incoming first-year class in 1981 indicated they intended to pursue a business major. When the dean of the School of Business asked John Morris for more faculty positions after the first AACSB report, to handle the crush of students, the university's chief academic officer had none to give, thanks to the tenure management plan imposed in 1976 (chapter seven). Instead, Morris instructed the school to limit enrollment by instituting a minimum grade point average requirement. Admission to the school therefore became competitive after 1981, but limiting growth of the student body did not solve the problem of too few faculty and too little research to satisfy the AACSB.

Predictably, when the AACSB came to visit the School of Business in 1983 to review the MBA degree for accreditation, it found little change from the problems of 1979–80. The AACSB's words stung: it said UWEC lacked the faculty of an "overall high quality" to offer the MBA degree. Too many of the faculty stayed briefly, then left. Among those who stayed, too few conducted research that resulted in peer-reviewed publications. Only nine of forty-four faculty members had published any peer-reviewed research since the 1980 AACSB report. Consequently, AACSB denied accreditation of the MBA, although it did not withdraw its 1980 accreditation of the BBA. The School of Business faculty and administrative leadership got to work after 1984 in addressing faculty workloads, research, and publications. The school suspended its MBA program until a future date when it could offer the degree at the level of quality called for by the AACSB.

During the 1980s, almost every externally accredited academic program on campus faced challenges in meeting review standards. The Department of Chemistry, when faced with reviews of its MS program by the American Chemical Society, decided to suspend and then eliminate its degree programs at the graduate level. Other programs, however, certainly did meet the national standards of excellence. The School of Nursing effectively managed to meet rising expectations for faculty with earned doctorates and faculty scholarship, so much so its MSN in nursing program—started in 1976—met with enthusiastic reviews from the National League of Nursing accreditors. The same held true for the Department of Communication Disorders, which won praise from the American Speech and Hearing Association for its master's degree program in speech pathology. UWEC learned the hard way maintaining excellent programs that started in the growth era cost money and needed continual attention.

Should UWEC Emphasize Quality or Accessibility?

On the occasion of the tenth anniversary of the UW–WSU merger, in October 1981, President O'Neil told an audience that the UW System "has come increasingly to be viewed as that of federation." Faculty and staff at UWEC might have wished to amend that phrase to read "autonomous federation," one in which the university was left alone by system administration and the regents. The 1980s, however, was a

What the Kids were listening to in the '80s

The limited seating capacity at the arena continued to hinder efforts by student groups to bring big-name popular music groups to campus. The Student Senate abolished the Social Commission in favor of a more wide-ranging University Activities Commission. The UAC sponsored films, live entertainment at the Cabin in the Davies Center, and the occasional rock concert in the arena. In 1977, Gary Wright ("Dreamweaver") filled the arena and in 1979, Johnny Cash returned to campus for a sell-out concert. Other groups promoted by the UAC, however, drew few students to their performances. The Kingston Trio ("Scotch and Soda" and "Tom Dooley") drew only 250 paying fans in 1979; Helen Reddy ("I am Woman") performed that same year in the arena before what one student critic called "an older crowd." Student dissatisfaction grew in the fall of 1980 when the UAC sought and failed to book a concert by the Police ("Message in a Bottle"), not because of money or schedule, but because an official in the dean of students office stated that group "are a punk band . . . not conducive to the educational atmosphere of the University." The dean of students office also canceled a planned screening of the John Waters film *Pink Flamingos* for similar protective reasons about the educational atmosphere at UWEC.

For several years after the failure to book the Police, the UAC did not even try to get groups to campus that students wanted to hear. Instead, outside promoters, such as radio station WAXX, rented the arena for performers such as Conway Twitty, who sang at two sold-out shows in 1982. Students flocked to the show of the punk star Wendy O and her band the Plasmatics ("Butcher Baby"), but at the Old Mill Center at the edge of the city, not on campus. One exception to what students called the "drought" of on-campus popular music events was the performance of the alternative group the Violent Femmes ("Blister in the Sun") on campus in the Council Fire Room in 1983. The next year, the UAC booked—and the administration allowed—a genuine big-name group, the Thompson Twins ("Hold Me Now"), for the arena. The drought was over as a packed arena of students, some dressed in what the *Periscope* reported as "long trench coats and ankle boots . . . in the punk style." The *Periscope* went on to note, "Girls weren't the only ones wearing makeup." Thousands of students danced and sang on a warm spring night near the end of the semester, with the arena once again at the cutting edge of popular music.

decade when the system president and the regents repeatedly directed UWEC and other campuses to focus on the questions of who should be admitted to college, at what cost, and who should pay that cost.

These officials read the many national reports proclaiming a crisis in US public education; they also read budgets and saw governors and legislators of both political parties were of a mind to spend fewer dollars, adjusted for inflation, on higher education in the 1970s and the 1980s. The political shift in Washington following the 1980 national election also signaled the federal government would spend less on higher education, or at least curb the rate of increase of support. Indeed, newly elected President Reagan pledged to abolish the US Department of Education. Many in Madison and Eau Claire believed developments in the forthcoming decade would force the university to confront choices between maintaining excellence in education against continuing openness to students; that choice was soon termed one of "quality vs. access."

The regents decided in favor of quality over access in the early 1980s when they worked with the Department of Public Instruction to raise standards in college preparatory work in high schools. In large part this development was a response to the complaints by faculty and staff at UWEC and other campuses about the large number of first-year students needing remedial work in reading, writing, and mathematics. In 1983, the regents announced to eighth graders and their families, and especially to high school guidance counselors, starting in 1988–89, successful applicants for admission to a UW campus would need to present sixteen units of academic subjects in high school, with at least nine in English, math, science, and history. UWEC decided it would only accept students in the top 50 percent of their high school graduating class; those in the bottom half would have to achieve a score on the American College Test sufficient to show they deserved provisional admission.

UWEC showed an impressive change in the profile of incoming first-year students over the decade. In 1979–80, the entering class scored a composite average of 19.6 on the ACT; a decade later, the ACT average for newcomers topped twenty-three. That same first-year class starting in 1990 also showed a much higher class rank than the university's minimum: more than a fifth of the new students ranked in the top 10 percent of their high school graduating class and fully two-thirds ranked in the top 30 percent. UWEC had moved from something close to open enrollment in the Haas years to an institution that was, in the language of admissions offices, "selective" in the students it offered entrance.

The regents decided in favor of quality over access, quite literally, starting in the 1987–88 academic year when they devised an enrollment management policy. The board called for an overall reduction of seven thousand students across the UW System, the better to match expected revenues with the ability to instruct students. Further, the regents instructed some campuses to grow—notably UW–Green Bay, UW–Parkside, and the thirteen two-year UW Centers (which became UW Colleges in 1997)—and others to shrink. The regents directed UWEC, the second-biggest campus among the regional comprehensive universities, to shrink by more than two hundred students in the first round of enrollment management and to shrink by an additional three hundred students by 1990.

The university did shrink following the regents' directive, and then shrank some more. From about 11,500 students in 1986–87, UWEC reduced its enrollment to a little over 10,600 for 1992–93 and to less than 10,400 in 1995–96, before enrollment began to climb again (overall, system enrollment declined 9.4 percent from 1986 to 1996). The university implemented its enrollment decline by limiting first-year admissions. Fewer than 1,600 first-year students enrolled in the fall of 1990, barely two-thirds the number that began each autumn twenty years earlier. A smaller first-year class also meant the university could select even more carefully among applicants in offering admission. The academic profile of the UWEC student body, as measured by high school class rank and ACT scores, continued at a high level with the implementation of enrollment management in the late 1980s and into the 1990s.

One demographic group defied the pattern of enrollment decline in the period of enrollment management: students matriculating at UWEC from Minnesota. These students took advantage of an interstate tuition reciprocity, a program in which students could attend colleges and universities in one another's state and yet pay their own in-state tuition. Originally signed in 1972, tuition reciprocity was at first limited to institutions immediately adjacent to the St. Croix–Mississippi Rivers boundary line, that is, UW–Superior, UW–River Falls, and UW–La Crosse on the Wisconsin side and UM–Duluth and Minnesota State University, Winona on the Minnesota side. The two states agreed to completely throw open the borders in 1983; the impact on UWEC was a steady increase in enrollment by students from Minnesota. Only a few Minnesotans paid out-of-state tuition before 1983; just three years later in 1986–87—before the onset of enrollment management—about 1,400 students came from Minnesota, over 12 percent of the UWEC student body. In 1995, at the university's enrollment nadir, more than 1,600 students hailed from west of the big rivers, almost 16 percent. By 1997, as enrollment began to increase again, more than two thousand Minnesotans made up about 20 percent of the student body.

The combined effects of increased high school graduation standards and enrollment management had another consequence for UWEC: the percentage of women in the student body continued to increase. It hovered between 55 and 58 percent of UWEC students in the 1970s and up through 1986, yet after the start of enrollment management it surpassed 60 percent. UWEC became a place of three women for every two men, a ratio that persisted into the twenty-first century. UWEC did not stand alone in this trend. The entire country underwent a long-term change as women began to seek post-secondary education in greater proportion than did men—after 1990 women were increasingly more likely to go on from high school to college.

Alumni Homecoming Banquet, October 4, 1986

A brunch and open house had preceded the banquet, and a masquerade dance concluded the evening with music provided by a jazz group, The Hot 19, and a rock group, Ambush. Alumni from the classes of 1946 and 1961 were honored at special dinners. On the football field at Carson Park, the Blugolds dominated UW-Stout by 20-0.

Map 8.1

Tuition reciprocity with Minnesota, on the one hand, and a rise in out-of-state tuition on the other, dramatically shifted the recruiting of UWEC students from outside Wisconsin.

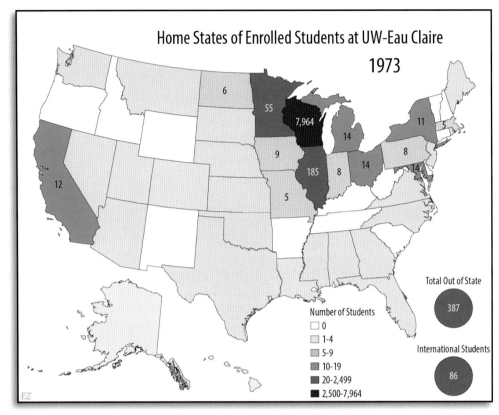

Map 8.2

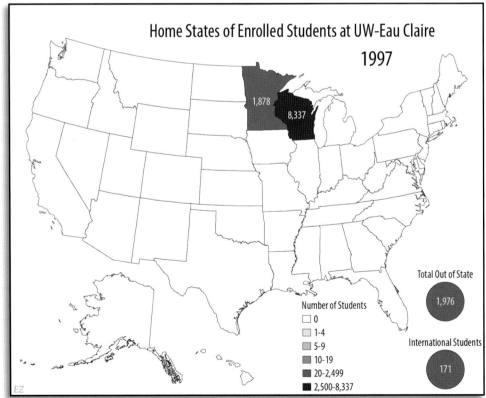

So-called "super seniors," who were in their fifth or even sixth year of study at the university, became more numerous in the 1980s. In the 1960s, the senior class had been the smallest of the four classes, in part because of annual growth in numbers of first-year students and in part because of the high dropout rate (chapter six). By 1973, the number of students with senior status outnumbered the number of juniors, and by 1977 the number of seniors surpassed the number of sophomores. At the start of the 1980s, first-year students (including returning first-years) still outnumbered seniors, but each year the gap narrowed until by 1990 seniors at UWEC outnumbered first-year students.

The increase in the senior class caught the eye of the regents. A new term, "time-to-degree," became both a measure of the phenomenon and a challenge for the university to reduce. Regent Ody Fish complained students averaged 8.6 semesters to earn a degree at UW institutions in the 1970s, but by 1984 they took more than ten semesters on average, and the typical student graduated with more than 140 credits, as much as a semester's worth of extra work beyond the needed minimum for the baccalaureate.

The extended time-to-degree had numerous causes, whose relative weights were hard to specify—students took courses that would not apply to their degrees because of poor advising; academic requirements were too heavy and/or too complex; students dropped courses too freely, necessitating re-enrollment; students changed their minds about their majors and learned courses they had already taken did not apply to their new program; the rising cost of attending the university required students to do more paid labor and take lighter course loads; to enhance their employability, students wanted to earn certificates and competencies beyond the minimum requirements; and so forth. To address the issue, Governor Tommy Thompson, a Republican elected in 1986, proposed in his executive budget for 1987–89 that the board of regents devise policy to levy a tuition surcharge for credits taken past a student's degree requirements. That proposal got the regents' attention, and in turn, the attention of faculty and staff at UWEC. Only 14 percent of matriculates in the fall of 1981 crossed the platform to receive their diploma in Zorn Arena four years later. The rate was much higher when super-seniors were taken into consideration: 40 percent completed the baccalaureate within five years and 46 percent within six years. That rate was still not good enough, and the challenge to the university for the rest of the decade and beyond was to lower time-to-degree (Thompson's idea of a surcharge for excessive credits finally came into effect in 2002).

Commencement Ceremony, Zorn Arena, May 23, 1987

During the 1980s, the university held morning and afternoon commencement ceremonies in December and May, as well as an August ceremony.

CONFLICTING PATHS TO EXCELLENCE

Residence Hall Room, 1980

Lofting of beds was one solution for the space crunch in residence hall rooms, unforeseen in the early 1960s when the halls were designed. The overcrowding was particularly caused by students' increasing possession of microwave ovens, refrigerators, and consumer electronics items.

Who Was a Blugold in the 1980s?

The 1980s was a decade in which university administrators turned to survey research data to understand how people on and off the campus understood UWEC, as the example of the Satz study group shows. The office of student affairs contracted with the American College Testing program to conduct an opinion survey among incoming UWEC first-year students on a rolling three-year basis, starting in 1984 and continuing through 1993. Students answered multiple-choice questions about academics and student life but also had a chance to write short replies to open-ended questions.

Replies from non-traditional age students were striking on the 1984 survey. They indicated how much these students appreciated what the university offered them in the way of support, notably the Children's Center as a safe, high-quality daycare facility for their youngsters, and the adult opportunity office for its mentoring and advice. On the other hand, this student group found frustrating the lack of courses available at times more convenient for working adults, such as in late afternoons and evenings.

The ACT survey asked students if they worked at the same time they attended college. Respondents were instructed to mark yes if they were full-time students and yet worked at campus jobs funded by work-student monies or off-campus jobs unrelated to the university. The 1984 survey showed more than half of the first-year students, 55 percent, did not work when they began at UWEC. Those who did work were sub-divided into three equal categories: those who worked fewer than ten hours per week, those who worked between ten and twenty hours, and those who worked more than twenty-one hours per week. The ACT survey findings suggested more than half of the students could devote themselves to full-time study at UWEC because of a combination of parental support and financial aid.

Students, faculty, and staff paid close attention in the 1980s to the question of how to pay for college and who did the paying. At the start of the decade, the Department of Economics hosted a debate between two economists on the question of who benefited from a college degree. UW–Madison professor Eugene Smolensky took the position the main beneficiary, by far, was the individual degree holder, not some amorphous entity called "society" or even the "State of Wisconsin." Smolensky argued that "rich college students" stood to recoup much higher income in their earning years by completing a bachelor's degree, at taxpayers' expense, even as they postponed entry into the workforce. He maintained public higher education was a misguided subsidy of the already prosperous by the State of Wisconsin and the individual who stood to gain higher lifetime earnings should pay for college.

Smolensky acknowledged that some poorer students attended college, and for them, he favored extending more loans so they could pay their tuition and then repay their lenders from their expected higher earnings. The professor articulated the growing belief in the United States that college should be priced based on true costs of instruction, on the one hand, and expected future earnings on the other. Smolensky advocated what came to be called a "high tuition, high aid" formula where college remained open to those academically qualified, but students and their families had to pay a much greater share, whether immediately in the form of tuition or long term in the form of loan repayments.

Arguing against Smolensky was UWEC professor of economics Edward G. Young, who argued that public higher education in Wisconsin was an investment in the future of the state in two senses. The first investment was economic in that UWEC graduates earned more and paid more in taxes to the state. In Young's view, state support for higher education was economically rational because of expected higher future tax payments. But Young also argued for an older, civic sense of the value of investment in public higher education: an educated citizenry was better able to make Wisconsin democracy work and to discover solutions to old and new problems.

The Smolensky-Young debate UWEC hosted played out in the state and national politics of the 1980s and beyond. After supervising the *Nation at Risk* report and leaving the US Department of Education to return to the University of Utah, Terrel Bell took on the task of leading a study group on the future of regional comprehensive colleges and universities. The American Association of State Colleges and Universities (AASCU), the group Leonard Haas helped found at Bemidji State University in 1961 (chapter six), asked Bell to offer some direction for the role of these institutions. The 1986 Bell report, *To Secure the Blessings of Liberty*, took up some of the themes of *A Nation at Risk* about the achievement gap between American students and their competitors overseas. However, the AASCU-commissioned study found the achievement gap between white students and minority students even more alarming. That gap led directly to the formation and continuation of an "underclass" in the United States, a social outcome that threatened American democracy, the authors of the report believed.

UW Regent Ruth Clusen, a UWEC alumna, served as a co-author with Bell on *To Secure the Blessings of Liberty*. The authors called for a "Marshall Plan" of new spending on public higher education, mainly from the states but also from the federal government, directed mainly to the more than four hundred regional comprehensive colleges and universities across the nation. The Bell report called for a renewed emphasis on teacher education at institutions such as UWEC and urged faculty at regional comprehensive universities to begin work on assessment of student learning in the public schools.

To Secure the Blessings of Liberty strongly argued for keeping tuition low at regional comprehensive colleges and universities. The report directly engaged those individuals like Smolensky who viewed education as chiefly a benefit to the individual graduate. Bell and his group argued, as had Ed Young, that financing college education was akin to financing social security: those working paid taxes to support public colleges and universities and those in college would become future taxpayers and pay to support future students. Their study went so far as to advocate that those who took up as a career teaching in kindergarten through twelfth grade public education in under-achieving school districts should attend college tuition free.

Whoever had the better policy argument, Smolensky or Young, the political decisions in Madison and Washington in the 1980s came down more on Smolensky's side. The 1970s standard that the State of Wisconsin should pay 75 percent of the cost of UW instruction fell to about 70 percent in the 1985, but then held steadily near that level until the end of the 1990s. The financial aid office reported in the 1986–87 academic year, almost three-quarters of the undergraduate student body received some sort of financial aid, either in the form of a scholarship or grant, a loan, or work-study employment funds. The financial aid office stated, "It is conservatively estimated that at least thirty percent of students could not attend the university without financial aid."

The first part of Smolensky's preference for the high-tuition, high-aid funding formula was raising tuition, which happened regularly in the 1980s. At the start of the decade, tuition and fees for one semester at UWEC cost $455 for an in-state student; by 1989, the same tuition and fees had more than doubled in nominal dollars to $950. One member of the board of regents during that decade, Frank Nikolay, an Abbotsford attorney and former member of the state assembly, objected to any tuition and fee increase on the grounds that raising tuition denied access to those able to make use of a UW education. The other side of the equation, the amount of state and federal money available in the form of grants, whether merit-based scholarships or income-based grants, also did not keep pace with the rising cost of instruction. Only the volume of loans, mainly from the federal government in the form of private loan guarantees, kept expanding for UWEC students.

To Secure the Blessings of Liberty did not use the words "achievement gap" or "equity gap" to describe different school outcomes for white and non-white students; that phrase had not yet come into existence. However, the report made the point that a gap existed and needed to be addressed. Non-white America was at risk of becoming a permanent "underclass," in Bell's view, and in the language of the 1980s, that meant a permanent criminal class, indeed a threat to American democracy itself.

Bell had not made this case in his earlier *A Nation at Risk*; his change in position was perhaps an indication of the changes in the country between President Reagan's first and second terms. At the start of the Reagan presidency, UW President Robert O'Neil observed the United States, in the form of the Justice Department, did not care about enforcing affirmative action. He contrasted that with the previous decade, "when the goal was compliance." Therefore, in January 1981, O'Neil proclaimed, "The fate of affirmative action programs in colleges and universities will thus depend greatly on our inner resolve to go beyond the external mandate."

O'Neil put this idea on the back burner for the UW System, and it remained a peripheral concern at UWEC. The affirmative action office duly collected statistics on the recruitment and enrollment of minority students, and for most of the 1970s and 1980s, minority students at the university made up between 1 and 2 percent of the student body.

UWEC began in the 1980s a more thoughtful approach to recruiting minority students. Following the recommendations from the 1981 task force on support program organization, Chancellor Hannah combined the American Indian Program coordinator's office and the Black Students Organization coordinator into a new "American Ethnic Coordinating Office." That office asked psychology professor Kenneth Heilman to survey white and minority students about why they chose to attend UWEC. His results confirmed that minority students often faced a lonely time at the university; whereas white students chose Eau Claire because friends and family attended, convenience, or its overall reputation, minority students selected the university because of specific excellent academic programs. When minority students arrived on campus, they had fewer social resources on which to draw to make their college experience more meaningful. The American Ethnic Coordinating Office became a combined academic, social, and cultural center on campus for minority students.

Chancellor Schnack expressed his concern for the impact the 1983 changes in UW System admission standards might have on minority students coming to study at UWEC. He asked his staff in 1986 to study the effects of the adoption of more stringent high school subject requirements for admission. What he learned was American Indian and African American enrollment had dropped somewhat, from an already modest level, but Southeast Asian enrollment had surged. A deeper probe into the numbers showed applications and admissions to the university by the first two groups had not changed, yet what was new was a sharp decline in the number of those who were admitted but chose to attend elsewhere. One conclusion from the study was more and more universities were competing to enroll qualified minority students, and Eau Claire would have to work harder in recruiting, enrolling, and retaining qualified African American and American Indian students.

The percentage of minority persons on the faculty and academic staff was at a similar low level, below 2 percent in the 1970s and early 1980s. The North Central Association had called attention to this figure, which it saw as a shortfall, in its 1980 report on reaccreditation of the university. The Wisconsin Department of Employment Relations summoned UWEC and other campuses in 1981 to report on

Native American Honoring Education Powwow, April 1983

minority hiring and found Eau Claire wanting. Employment Relations suggested UWEC work harder at increasing the pool of minority applicants by advertising in specialized publications. UWEC countered by saying the strict tenure management plan set in place in 1976 limited the ability of the university to make new hires.

O'Neil's successor as UW System president, Kenneth Shaw, and the regents decided in 1988 to push all UW campuses to promote greater minority student enrollment and greater minority faculty and staff employment. The regents called their plan "Design for Diversity" and they set specific numerical goals for the percentage of minority students and faculty by 1993, and then again by 1998. The regents told UWEC and other campuses to double the number of minority students enrolled by 1998 and to increase minority faculty and staff by 75 percent over the 1988 level. The regents defined a minority as belonging to one of four groups: African Americans; American Indians; Hispanic Americans; and Southeast Asian migrants, the last-named group a reference to the wave of Vietnamese, Cambodian, and especially Laotian refugees who settled in Wisconsin after 1975.

If, as former President O'Neil said in 1981, affirmative action in the 1970s was about legal compliance, by 1988 Design for Diversity aimed for a larger transformation in UW campuses such as Eau Claire. The regents' policy went beyond affirmative action as a means of making amends for past discrimination and made diversity a goal that benefited everyone, including white students and faculty. They instructed the faculty at each system campus to devise coursework in the history and culture of the four ethnic minority groups; starting in 1989, therefore, Eau Claire students had to take at least three credits of classwork related to at least one of the four groups. Pointedly, the regents also tied the performance evaluation of each chancellor, including Larry Schnack, to meeting the goals they set in Design for Diversity.

In part demography, not the achievement gap, underlaid Design for Diversity: the regents read reports such as the Hudson Institute's 1987 *Workforce 2000* forecasting a rising non-white population in the United States, one in which all students at UW campuses would have to work and live. Students who graduated from UWEC without meeting and understanding people different from themselves would fare poorly in a future multicultural world, especially in the labor force. In effect, Design for Diversity promised to benefit white students by giving them so-called cultural competence.

Another reason the regents moved to promote racial and ethnic diversity on campuses, and the study of different minorities, was the open racism displayed against Chippewa Indians who exercised court-protected off-reservation walleye spearfishing under treaties signed in 1837 and 1842. Starting in the spring of 1985, the annual April Chippewa spearing season on northern Wisconsin lakes brought forth white protesters who became increasingly disruptive and confrontational in trying to prevent tribal spearers from access to lakeside boat landings. Sheriff's deputies arrested numerous whites for disorderly conduct during the April 1987 season, and a year later—the same month the regents proclaimed Design for Diversity—nearly two hundred whites were arrested at boat landings. UWEC Graduate Dean Ronald Satz became the leading public academic in Wisconsin in explaining Chippewa treaty rights, but even he acknowledged the depth of ignorance and hatred shown in what he called "the white backlash." An opinion survey conducted by the UW Population Laboratory in April 1988 showed the white population had little understanding of the legal basis of Chippewa Indian treaty rights. Perhaps the UW could lead the state away from racial confrontation with its new Design for Diversity.

Governor Thompson supported Design for Diversity by proposing additional scholarship money for minority students. This touched a nerve with some students at UWEC and other campuses across the state. A 1989 *Spectator* cartoon titled "Minority-in-a-Minute" mocked scholarships reserved for minority students, perhaps inspired by the 1986 Hollywood comedy *Soul Man*, in which a white student darkens his skin to earn a scholarship reserved for African Americans. Nobody found any humor in the *Spectator* cartoon; indeed, its publication caused an uproar on campus. The cartoon showed there was a white backlash among some students against Design for Diversity, and clearly some white students did not believe the program proposed by Governor Thompson would help them.

The Great Catch-up Debate

In 1986, relations fell to a low point between UWEC faculty and staff on the one hand and the president of the UW System and the board of regents on the other. The Eau Claire faculty and academic staff had their own separate reasons for disillusionment with their work-lives. The faculty reacted negatively to the first draft of a regents' report on the "Future of the UW System." Eau Claire's Faculty Senate objected to the regents' plan to require four-year campuses such as UWEC to accept all general education credits that transfer students brought with them from the UW Centers and Wisconsin technical schools. The Faculty Senate denounced this policy as an infringement on the faculty's statutory right of "primary responsibility" for the curriculum. Moreover, the Faculty Senate decried the regents' decision that some credits from the centers and technical schools had to be acceptable at all UW four-year campuses: "[This] is the beginning of the trend toward uniformity among the universities of the UW System. Nowhere in the report do we find affirmation of the characteristic of the System . . . as a federation of relatively autonomous universities, each with a somewhat different mission."

The UW president and board of regents also antagonized UWEC's faculty in the way they sought to distribute so-called catch-up salary monies appropriated by the legislature. One study after another had found UW campuses falling behind their peers in compensation. A study group Governor Anthony Earl appointed in 1983 reported in the summer of 1984 the salary gap was widening and if Wisconsin wished to retain its faculty, and recruit new faculty, it would have to pay more. Specifically, the report said a one-time "catch-up" pay raise was needed to supplement whatever pay plan the legislature decided for 1985–87.

However, the governor's study group report angered UWEC and the other comprehensive UW campuses by emphasizing the pay gap between UW–Madison and its peers, rather than between UWEC and its peers. The study group recommended a pay raise of 15 percent for UW–Madison and 11 percent for UW–Milwaukee faculty, but only 6 percent for UWEC and the comprehensive campuses. These recommendations brought back the bad feelings about "equal work for equal pay" from the time of the merger.

In response to the report, President O'Neil advocated for more money for UWEC faculty salary catch-up: 9 percent. The UWEC Faculty Senate requested 12 percent. TAUWF, more militant on behalf of UWEC faculty, demanded a 14 percent raise, while supporting 15 percent for UW–Madison. In addition, TAUWF pointed to the plight of underpaid academic staff, a group left out of the governor's study commission.

The subsequent "great catch-up debate," as Acting President Lyall called it, occupied the legislature for much of the spring 1985 session. In the end, the legislature bent a bit toward UWEC's position, setting a 10 percent catch-up raise. In addition, TAUWF won a raise of 5 percent for instructional academic staff and a commitment to investigate and redefine the job titles and work performed by all academic staff.

Centers of Excellence at UWEC

In contrast to the problems with catch-up, the regents seemed to speak UWEC's language, when, in 1987, they invited UW campuses to submit proposals for academic "centers of excellence." The regents promised to support projects of up to one million dollars provided that campuses supply one-third of the project costs through internal reallocations. The regents also tied funding to the centers of excellence to revised mission statements: the board very much expected campuses would look to their mission statements and submit proposals designed to support their core missions. What amounted to an intra-system one-time grant agency resulted in a great many discussions, rounds of proposals and reviews, and intense conversations about the future at UW–Eau Claire.

The regents asked campuses to screen proposals and submit ones that had the backing of campus governance structures regarding the one-third funding match. The University Senate (the successor in 1985 to the Faculty Senate) assigned the University Planning Committee the task of screening proposals in the spring term of 1988. Ideas for twenty proposals came forth, ranging from naming the Children's Center an academic center of excellence to endowing McIntyre Library as an academic center of excellence in bibliographical instruction across the curriculum. Hundreds of faculty and staff threw themselves into the tasks of dreaming about a new initiative, working budgets, and then writing and submitting a proposal. The Planning Committee selected seven of the proposals for further development and provided money to contract with external reviewers who would make campus visits and write letters of support.

By the end of the spring semester, the University Senate and Chancellor Schnack selected four proposals for submission to the regents: the Honors Program, the general education program, teacher education, and faculty-undergraduate student research. Each proposal offered a vision of its relation to the university mission, and how, if funded, it would create or enhance academic excellence at UWEC.

The Honors Program, for instance, which had only started in 1983, proposed to expand to six hundred students, all of whom with a high school class rank in the top 5 percent and recruited with special scholarships and the chance to study in small classes with leading faculty. The proposal told the regents the excellent core of Honors Program students would serve as mentors and tutors to the rest of the student body. It was a novel and thoughtful proposal to raise UWEC's academic standing through enhancing a special program within the university.

The proposal for making general education an academic center of excellence originated from the deans and faculty in the School of Arts and Sciences. The proposal asked for funds to hire more faculty to teach introductory courses, as well as money to convene regular groups of faculty to examine and refine general education. The external consultant hired by the university to look at the proposal wrote of the faculty at UWEC: "Everyone in Arts and Sciences teaches general education courses there. And almost no one regards this as an unwanted chore, interfering with their desire to teach upper-division courses to majors. During my visit to campus, I did not once hear the expression 'service courses,' which so often reveals a level of contempt for general education, elsewhere."

The third UWEC proposal to the regents named teacher education as an academic center of excellence. This proposal took up the ideas included in the two reports submitted by Terrel Bell, *A Nation at Risk* and *To Secure these Blessings*. UWEC's Center of Excellence in Teacher Education promised to be a research center that would work with the public schools to investigate teaching, assess learning, and disseminate findings about best practices.

Finally, UWEC proposed a fourth center of excellence: a new idea called faculty-undergraduate student collaborative research. This proposal was somewhat different from Emily Hannah's idea that Eau Claire faculty members should publish more in peer-reviewed outlets. Instead, the thought behind the center was on the research process nearer its start: funding proposals should be written with students as explicit participants without so much concern for the end result of publishing peer-reviewed writings. This idea also drew on an existing tradition at UWEC in the Departments of Chemistry and Biology of undergraduates working as associates in labs with their faculty as mentors. UWEC's Center for Faculty-Undergraduate Research Collaboration aimed to extend this model from the physical sciences to all departments and disciplines.

The regents received more than one hundred proposals for centers of excellence from the UW campuses. The Screening Committee selected the top forty-nine proposals for approval. UWEC was disappointed only one of what it regarded as four fine proposals received the nod from the regents, the Center for Excellence in Faculty-Undergraduate Research Collaboration. Most of the other UW campuses in the University Cluster (the old WSU schools plus UW–Green Bay and UW–Parkside) garnered approval for two centers, and UW–Stevens Point had three proposals approved.

However, after so much work by so many people around the UW System, the legislature chose not to fund the forty-nine centers in its biennial 1989–91 budget. Instead, campuses were told to find the funds in their own local budgets to pursue their excellence initiatives. UWEC did this, not only for the Center for Excellence in Faculty-Undergraduate Research Collaboration, but for some of the other excellence proposals. The reason had much to do with the "community of scholars" that former Chancellor Hannah envisioned emerging on campus, or more precisely, with the culture of honoring the results of faculty peer review of campus programs.

Students Crossing Footbridge

A 2010 student-faculty collaborative research project found the footbridge was indeed the coldest spot on the UWEC campus. In 2014 Niche.com identified the campus as the fifth coldest in the United States (MSU-Moorhead was coldest).

At the same time the university sought state funding to support collaborative faculty-student research, the Chemistry Department earned the first of many significant grants from the Research Corporation for Science Advancement to underwrite faculty development, especially in preparing undergraduates for careers as chemists. In 1988, professor Warren Gallagher wrote the first UWEC grant funded by the Research Corporation, a modest one to help him engage students in ongoing research projects. The program officers at the Research Corporation encouraged the department to think bigger and apply for a half-million dollar development grant. In preparing this proposal, the department researched its own history and estimated more than five hundred students had a BS degree in chemistry from the university between 1957 and 1990. Three of them who had become distinguished academicians—George Rossman (California Institute of Technology), Richard Saykally (University of California, Berkeley), and Steven Burke (UW–Madison)—had received the Alumni Distinguished Service Award in 1987. With funds from the Research Corporation, the Chemistry Department set out to diversify its faculty with new hires in 1991, including one of the first Hmong Americans with a chemistry PhD, Thao Yang, and a woman chemist, Dr. Cheryl Muller.

Transforming the University: UWEC Online

Twice a year, the entire student body gathered in the newly named Zorn Arena for a college ritual: not only for commencement, not only for a Forum lecture or an Artist Series performance, and not to cheer on men's basketball on winter nights, but instead, for fall and spring registration week. For four days in August and five again in January, two thousand students each day stood in long lines, moving from table to table attempting to find open classes for their schedules. When a student found such a class, he or she received a punch card indicating a space reserved, and then it was off to another table until the student obtained a full load of classes. Next came stops at the financial aid table and the cashier's table for payment of tuition and fees. Seniors went first and first-year students went last; the latter found themselves frustrated to find class after class was closed. Faculty from every department staffed the tables offering informal academic advising over the shouting din of the arena. Overseeing the semi-annual frenzy was the staff of the registrar's office.

Registration in Zorn Arena, c. 1983

There had to be a better way. UWEC was not alone in struggling to improve registration, as every other UW campus faced the same problems. Laura Patterson, who became registrar in 1986, committed her office to finding that better way. She investigated the solution adopted at Brigham Young University—telephone registration by touchtone. BYU engineered a dial-in menu of choices, allowing students to register from anywhere. The BYU system, in essence, used computers to translate what students tapped into the keypad. Why not skip that step entirely, Patterson and her colleagues in the registrar's office asked, and go directly to student-inputted online registration?

The spring term of 1988 marked the last time students registered *en masse* in Zorn Arena. For the fall term, students went to the Old Library where registrar's staff members used the SOLAR (Student Online Advising and Registration) system to input student course choices into hard-wired computer terminals. With registration now spaced out over weeks, rather than the few days it had been in the arena, students had more opportunities to meet with their advisors and plan their programs. A few semesters later, the students themselves began registering directly by computer.

CONFLICTING PATHS TO EXCELLENCE   215

This move to online registration represented a huge computer programming challenge to the registrar's staff and to the staff in the office of administrative computing, a challenge which continued to grow as faculty and students came to expect more and more from SOLAR. Starting in the 1988–89 academic year, students and their advisers had access to SOLAR for a new feature, the degree audit. This computer program allowed students and their advisers to check what requirements a student had met and what ones remained unfinished. SOLAR's degree audit laid the basis for students and faculty taking a more active role in planning paths to degrees.

One immediate effect of student online registration for classes was students could now register for more classes than they expected to keep. In the days of registering in person at Zorn, a student had been fortunate to get five separate punch cards from five open classes, sufficient to make a full-time student load of fifteen or sixteen credits. With the advent of SOLAR, students could easily sign up for eighteen credits (six or more courses) at no extra cost, and then drop one of the courses before the end of the second week of the semester. This drop-add period became more frequently used, so much so that Assistant Registrar Connie Russell called it one of the three certainties of life along with death and taxes. Its effect was first-year and sophomore students had to continually scramble to find open classes.

McIntyre Library sought to computerize its catalogue into an OPAC (online public access catalogue) by using academic staff, as the registrar's office had done for SOLAR. Newly hired Library Director Steve R. Marquardt put that task as his first priority when he joined the university in 1981. By 1982, McIntyre Library had its first OPAC and all new acquisitions were entered through that system. At first, most of McIntyre's book collection remained accessible only through the paper card catalogue. What was called retrospective conversion began in 1983 with a UW System library automation project, and by 1984, nine-tenths of the library's half-million volume collection was accessible via the OPAC. That same year, McIntyre's Reference Department librarians began offering online searching of remote databases to students and faculty.

At the start of the decade, a large portion of the first floor of McIntyre had been devoted to bound volume print indexes of resources in the sciences, humanities, business, social sciences, and the fine arts. Beside these index-book tables stood the many rows of wooden drawers of cardstock index cards. By the end of the decade, the Reference Department had removed both catalog drawers and many of the print indexes, freeing up space for study tables and especially for computer terminals that gave access to the new OPAC and remote databases. The OPAC also accommodated acquisitions, circulation, and cataloguing—the technical services behind student and faculty access to the library's collections. Computerization of the resources of McIntyre Library represented one of the benefits of membership in the UW System.

McIntyre Library, First Floor, May 1989

By the end of the 1980s, the card catalog had long since been removed, and access to the library's collections was through the computer terminals shown in this photograph. As seen in the background, however, the library's reference collection was still in bound format, and its removal was not complete until the middle of the following decade.

By 1986, the OPAC was linked to all other UW System campus libraries via the Internet. In addition, in the early 1980s, faculty members could receive Internet email accounts from the university. By the end of the decade, students had email as well. Of more significance was the proliferation of microcomputers on campus, especially for word processing and spreadsheet analysis. The microcomputer revolution promised to change the way students, faculty, and staff did their work in almost every facet of the university, as will be seen in the following chapter.

Council Oak after It Was Downed by a Wind Storm, May 29, 1987

The tree already was diseased when what the Campus Police characterized as a "small tornado" blew it down. In 2016, a bench made from its wood is located beneath a large window at the southwest corner of the first floor of McIntyre Library, overlooking the replacement Council Oak tree. The University Mace, reintroduced at the 2016 commencement, was also carved from a surviving piece of the Council Oak.

Assessing the Eighties: NCA's View of a Decade of Change

In the fall of 1987, the university began its preparations for the coming decadal evaluation by the North Central Association. The university's self-study for the NCA addressed some of the issues from the previous 1980 accreditation report, notably the changes in administering the graduate program, a coordination of the support-program proliferation of student services, and a new commitment to recruiting more minority students and faculty as part of the UW System's Design for Diversity. UW–Eau Claire could claim at the end of the 1980s it was meeting the challenges of excellence better than it had at the start of the decade.

The response of the NCA study team that came to campus to inspect UWEC in 1989 was simple: prove it. The NCA in 1989 repeatedly used the word "assessment" in its call for Eau Claire to measure how well it fulfilled its mission. For the accreditors, it was no longer enough to offer academic and extracurricular programs and meet targets of inputs. The NCA called for a new way of thinking at UWEC, to assess what were called outcomes of student learning. Grades given by faculty to students did not, according to the NCA, measure outcomes. The university had to ask of its students, not just what *should* they know as educated persons, but what *did* they know and to prove they knew it. Assessment, among other issues, became the new challenge for the university in the following decade.

Redefining Excellence at the End of the Century

> Acting University of Wisconsin System President Katherine Lyall reflected on twenty years of the merged UW System at the board of regents meeting in October 1991.

She acknowledged the merger had not been without controversy in 1971, but from the vantage point of twenty years, she proclaimed it a success. The system had become more centralized, and in some respects it had achieved greater efficiency, Lyall believed, but she regarded campuses as still having "unique strengths and curricula." If not the autonomous federation of campuses the UW–Eau Claire faculty had wanted, the system in 1991 still left room for "individual institutional character and identity." UW–Eau Claire's challenge was to develop its strengths and curricula and strive to make the institution unique, but do so within the now-familiar budget restraints of a mature university system and changing state and regional economies.

Rhythms of Academic Life

By 1990, UWEC had learned to deal with the rhythms of academic life set by outsiders as well as by campus administration, faculty, and staff. Some of those rhythms were annual, some biennial, some varied from quadrennial through septennial, and perhaps the most important one was decennial.

The shift to a fall semester schedule ending before Christmas (begun in 1971) meant instruction began late in August, but effective in 1986 the legislature required classes never begin before September 2. Legislators argued Wisconsin's seasonal employers needed to retain college-age employees through the Labor Day weekend. The university preferred to start classes the last week in August so as to finish final exam week and hold fall commencement well in advance of Christmas Eve. Instead, given the structure of the calendar, in 1995 and again in 2000 final exams lasted until Friday, December 22 and commencement was not held until December 23. Faculty members were unhappy with grading final exams during the Christmas holiday and felt student performance on exams suffered from the rush to leave campus, but they had no choice but to follow the legislature's direction.

The legislature also set the biennial rhythm for the university by means of the state budget. The process started as much as a year before the budget's adoption, which was supposed to occur by June 30 of odd-numbered years, when the governor's office gave budget targets to each state agency, including the UW System. Spending proposals then worked their way through system administration and the regents during the fall, back to the governor's office which prepared the executive budget for presentation in late January, then to the legislature's Joint Committee on Finance for revision, next to each legislative chamber for passage, and then finally back to the governor for signature (or sometimes creative line-item vetoes). As seen in chapter five, the June 30 budget deadline was often missed, disrupting UWEC's planning; the 2001–03 budget, for example, was not adopted until August 31, 2001, after the academic year had begun. Divided government encouraged this practice: Republican Tommy G. Thompson was governor from 1987 until 2001, but Republicans never controlled both chambers of the legislature for an entire session until 2003, by which time Democrat James Doyle was governor. Even worse, mid-biennial adjustments known as "lapses," as occurred in 2002 (which were the consequence of the deliberate absence of a rainy-day fund in the state's fiscal planning), meant the university often had to find ways to quickly reduce spending when cutting back courses, labs, library resources, and other activities in the middle of an academic year.

Another dimension of the rhythm of academic life was the round of internal program reviews. These began in the 1970s, accelerated in the 1980s, and became more regularized in the 1990s. Under Chancellor Emily Hannah, academic departments underwent an internal audit and review every four years. Starting under Chancellor Larry Schnack, academic support units underwent the same type of audit and review, also every four years. Departments and programs with external accrediting bodies had to adjust to a more idiosyncratic calendar, rarely coinciding with the year in which an internal review was due. In the 1990s, the university slowed the frequency of reviews to one every six, then one every seven, years and coordinated them with external departmental or degree reviews.

Once a decade, the North Central Association conducted its accrediting review of the university. In 1987, two years into Schnack's chancellorship, the university began preparing a self-study for the NCA listing how it had addressed the 1980 evaluation concerns (chapters seven and eight), and how it had positioned itself in other ways. The university submitted its self-study in the spring of 1989, and the following fall an NCA review team of seven, including one college president, two college provosts, three deans, and a professor, came to visit. They found the university in improved condition compared to when their predecessors visited in 1979. Graduate studies was in much better shape, with a centralized office including university research; the university had addressed support-program proliferation; and international education was improved. The external reviewers noted with approval the efforts in implementing Design for Diversity and the Center for Excellence in Faculty-Undergraduate Collaborative Research (chapter eight), even if they did not quite understand how the concept of doing research with undergraduate students would work in practice.

Yet the NCA external reviewers found a "sense of complacency" at UW–Eau Claire: they found the university felt it was enough to be regarded as the best of the eleven cluster campuses in the UW System, without having any "aspirations beyond state borders." After reading many volumes of Eau Claire-generated reports and statistics, the outside reviewers tired of encountering the word "excellence" and left unimpressed with the university's slogan of "Accepting the Challenge of Excellence." To the contrary, the NCA reviewers wrote, "'Excellence' seemed to be interpreted quite conservatively in some fields, with less innovation than might have been the case."

The NCA expressed concern about two areas it felt the university had not sufficiently addressed in the 1980s: assessment, broadly defined as measuring the outcomes of student learning and the effectiveness of academic programs; and the state of the undergraduate curriculum, particularly the relationship of general education to the professional and pre-professional programs. The two concerns came wrapped in a basic question about the mission of the institution. Was UWEC primarily a new type of state university, a regional comprehensive university? Or, was UWEC "primarily a center for undergraduate excellence in the arts and sciences." Put differently, was UWEC—despite its size—mainly the liberal arts college Leonard Haas envisioned in 1960? Or, was it primarily the university it had officially become in 1964? For a quarter century, it had been both. In 1989, the NCA said the university did not have the resources to be both (given the pattern of decreasing state financial support) and would have to "choose its priorities, [and] focus its resources more narrowly."

This was a question UWEC had never squarely faced. To concentrate in the 1990s on improving the pre-professional and professional degree programs that had been launched in response to needs in the

Chippewa Valley would require new resources, or perhaps the reallocation of existing ones, likely by reducing the commitment to the liberal arts. Alternatively, the NCA report said, UWEC could cut back on professional programs of regional service and instead become a leader in liberal arts undergraduate education across the state.

What Kind of Institution Should UWEC Be?

The category introduced in the 1960s, "state colleges and universities" (chapter six), had captured the evolution of former state teachers colleges but did not distinguish in the public mind the difference between the land-grant campus (called by the naval metaphor as the "flagship campus," which in Wisconsin was the UW–Madison) and other public institutions. The Carnegie Foundation for the Advancement of Teaching provided some clarification by its 1973 classification of all US institutions of higher learning into four broad categories based on the number and kinds of degrees they granted: doctoral, master's, baccalaureate, and associate. Although more than 90 percent of the students at UWEC pursued a bachelor's degree, the fact Eau Claire granted master's degrees meant it was a "master's level" institution. The Carnegie classification had many subdivisions, based on enrollments and number of degrees granted, but broadly speaking, the UW System's 1971 separation of campuses into "doctoral," "cluster," and "college" anticipated the Carnegie classification of the twenty-six UW System campuses as doctoral (Madison and Milwaukee), master's (the eight original normal schools, Stout, and the UW campuses at Green Bay and Parkside established in the 1960s), and associate (the system of two-year UW Center colleges). By the late 1980s, it became standard in the language of higher education to refer to the larger master's institutions in the United States, such as UWEC, as "regional comprehensive universities."

What the Kids were not listening to—WUEC 89.7 FM

Campus radio began in the 1960s as a closed-circuit, non-broadcast station available only in the residence halls. Students could find it on the AM dial only by having their radios plugged into a residence hall outlet; students with transistor, battery-powered radios were out of luck if they wanted to listen to WUEC. The station went on the FM band in 1975, licensed to the regents for "educational" purposes, and broadcast a few hours each day with news and student selections of pop music.

In 1989, WUEC 89.7 FM became affiliated with Wisconsin Public Radio (WPR), a service of UW Extension, another example of how the university experienced life differently as part of a bigger state system. By the 1990s, WPR broadcast its NPR News and Classical service on WUEC weekdays for thirteen hours—8:00 am to 9:00 pm. It also maintained a station at UW–Stout, WHWC 88.3 FM, with studios in Eau Claire, as part of its Ideas Network. For WUEC, student programming took up the three hours from 9:00 pm until midnight and the entire weekend, with a spotlight on alternative music, especially music created by local artists. A member of the band Venison thanked WUEC as the only broadcast radio outlet interested in playing the work of local musicians in the Chippewa Valley.

Unquestionably, WUEC presented a split personality to listeners. On the one hand, the weekday feed from WPR's classical music service, and on the other, the weekend and late-evening alternative music programming by UWEC students. In the early 1990s, the newly hired director of WUEC, professor of communication and journalism Ken Loomis, decided to address the difference in programming in an unusual way. In the summer of 1994, Loomis told student workers at WUEC to prepare for a format shift in weekend and late-evening programming from student-chosen alternative music to light jazz. Loomis told the *Spectator* that WUEC "will have a consistent sound, and this will give the station an image that is readily accessible to people. We have to sell a product. Our station is a product for the community." Loomis told his faculty colleagues and the university administration that the community—meaning the off-campus listening area of WUEC—had complained about the student-chosen weekend alternative music format. The community, Loomis insisted, wanted something other than new music students selected. In other words, the WUEC listening community excluded UWEC students, yet Loomis wanted students to work on-air and off-mike producing light jazz programming on WUEC.

Students reacted unhappily to the decision. A group circulated a petition signed by 1,700 students protesting the removal of student choice in music. That same petition asked students what they wanted in music programming. More than one thousand said they wanted alternative music returned to the air, another five hundred asked for '90s variety music, and a scattered few students asked for classic rock or country music. No students said they wanted light jazz.

The protesters went to the Student Senate and asked them to defund the $18,000 in student-paid segregated fees given to WUEC each year. Loomis convinced the Student Senate not to withdraw funding, if only so students could keep valuable internship opportunities at the station. The Senate agreed, even as it voted to condemn the programming format change.

Students learned from the WUEC fiasco that if they wanted their own music, they would need their own station, independent of the UW System and WPR. Rather than seek an over-the-air broadcast outlet, students in 1998 decided to launch an Internet radio station, known by the initials SRI for Student Radio Initiative. As for WUEC, light jazz on the weekends and late evenings failed to win many listeners from the community it sought to attract. Instead, WPR took over almost all the programming, eventually leaving only a three-hour slot on Sunday evening for locally produced shows.

UWEC was one of almost two hundred former public teachers colleges that had to decide how to position themselves as regional state colleges or universities. One issue these institutions had to confront was the choice posed by the NCA—should their emphasis be on pre-professional and professional programs or liberal arts undergraduate education?

Another issue was identifying the kind of student the university should serve. State colleges and universities had offered students—especially first-generation college students—access and affordability, both in comparison to private colleges and to flagship state university campuses. UW–Eau Claire's history in the 1980s pitted rising costs against open access at a reasonable cost to students and their families. In decisions about enrollment management and establishing centers of excellence (chapter eight), however, UWEC had chosen quality of education over access and affordability. Indeed, one almost immediate benefit of Enrollment Management I and II was the academic profile of incoming first-year students to the university improved. The median composite American College Testing score reached twenty-three among students entering in the fall of 1989. More than two-thirds of that first-year class achieved a rank in the top 30 percent of their high school graduating class. In the years before enrollment management, UWEC had admitted most of those who chose to apply. For example, just over four thousand students applied for a place in the entering class in the fall of 1985, with the university admitting 3,700 of them and 1,900 students accepting admission and matriculating at Eau Claire.

In the 1990s, as the university began to shrink its incoming class size, it became more selective in admissions. When the demographic echo of the baby boom began to be felt at the end of the decade, more than nine thousand students applied for first-year admission to UWEC, even as the size of that entering class had not changed. The UW System multiple applications and admissions database, introduced in 1996 to help potential students gain admission to some campuses, even if not their first choice, and to balance the demand for admission among system institutions, found UWEC was the second most popular choice within the system. Eau Claire was second only to UW–Madison and was ahead of UW–Milwaukee and every other four-year campus.

UWEC and the Changing Chippewa Valley

Engaging the issue of the university's identity came at a time in the economic history of the Eau Claire region that might be termed the second great dislocation. The first dislocation occurred around the beginning of the twentieth century, following the end of the lumber industry, when Eau Claire remade itself into a manufacturing and assembly center with numerous factories (chapter one). The second dislocation, in the late 1980s and early 1990s, came when many of those manufacturing plants closed. For seventy years, the largest employer in the city of Eau Claire had been the tire plant operated by the corporation known since 1961 as Uniroyal. Uniroyal changed ownership several times in corporate restructurings during the 1980s, piling up hundreds of millions of dollars in debt in junk bonds and was sold to the Michelin Group in 1990. In 1992 Michelin closed the Eau Claire plant, which comprised 1.9 million square feet of manufacturing space and employed 1,350 workers. About the same time, the city lost other old-line manufacturing plants, including a large Armour Meat Packing plant which had been established during Eau Claire's first transformation by David Drummond, the purveyor in 1910 of the land for the site of the Eau Claire Normal School (chapter one).

Suddenly, UW–Eau Claire became the largest employer in the city. The combined spending effect of salary and wage income for more than 1,100 faculty, academic staff, and classified employees and the expenditures by 11,000 students made the university a leading economic force in the region after 1992. UWEC had to look carefully at its role in supporting new economic development in the Chippewa Valley.

Chancellor Schnack was cognizant of the leadership roles in the community that had been taken by Leonard Haas and Richard Hibbard during the 1950s and 1960s, when each had served on the Eau Claire City Council (chapter five). Rather than seek elective office, however, Schnack put time and effort into chairing the Eau Claire Area Economic Development Association (ECAEDA). This group sought to grow local businesses and attract external ones with creative tax and financing support, as well as tangible benefits from associating with the university. An example of its efforts came at the end of the 1980s when computer engineer Steve Chen established Supercomputer Systems in Eau Claire. Schnack's leadership helped convince Chen to locate in the Chippewa Valley rather than in its alternative site, Urbana-Champaign, Illinois. Supercomputer Systems successfully built the world's fastest supercomputer, but burned through its startup costs before it could market the machine successfully. Subsequently, after the closure of Uniroyal, Schnack and the ECAEDA pursued a Minnesota computer hardware manufacturer, Hutchinson Technologies, to open a manufacturing plant in Eau Claire which eventually grew to employ more than one thousand persons. "I think [that Haas and Hibbard] would have been proud of the degree in which I got involved," Schnack later stated. "I think I extended [their work] even some."

The university positively impacted the community in other ways. Academic departments, for instance, sponsored programs that brought talented pre-collegiate students to campus. High school and middle school bands competed as part of the annual Jazz Festival. Beginning in 1982, the Department of Mathematics sponsored an annual Math Meet, with trophies and scholarships for high-scoring high school and middle school students. Early in the twenty-first century, the Department of History partnered with the Wisconsin Historical Society to organize regional History Day competitions from which top-placing students could advance to state and national competitions.

Chemistry is Fun Day, January 1992

The Chemistry is Fun Day was one of UWEC departmental efforts to engage with elementary and secondary pupils.

Students also made a difference in the community through their volunteer activities. In the 1990s, service organizations increasingly joined the array of Greek chapters, departmental and professional clubs, honor societies, and religious groups discussed as student organizations in previous chapters (altogether, there were over two hundred student organizations by the beginning of the twenty-first century). The Student Homeless Awareness Chapter, for instance, was organized in 1998 to support Beacon House and Sojourner House, homeless shelters in Eau Claire, and the Community Table, which had begun in 1992 to offer free daily meals initially at the Unitarian Universalist Congregation building in downtown Eau Claire.

Changes in Campus Leadership

One by one, Chancellor Schnack eventually replaced most of the leaders Chancellor Hannah brought to the university. Some left of their own choosing, as did Norman Doorenboos, Hannah's selection as vice chancellor, in 1986. Schnack asked other administrators to leave. Administrators served at the pleasure of the chancellor, as the language of their contracts made clear. In addition, because of the conflicts which had occurred between Hannah and the faculty, the University Senate had instituted a mandatory personnel review of administrators in their third year of service. A negative review did not necessarily result in termination, but it did provide a referendum on administrators' performance. Suzanne Fleming, Schnack's choice as Doorenboos's replacement, left the university soon after her third-year review found her wanting. Not until Schnack hired Marjorie Smelstor in 1990 did he find a chief academic officer who could bring both leadership and stability to the position (the designation of provost was added to Smelstor's title in 1995).

The most controversial departure from Hannah's team of administrators was that of Elliot Garb, the assistant chancellor for student affairs. Schnack replaced Garb in 1994 after the latter had served eleven years at the university, although Schnack later explained he had not gotten along with Garb for several years before sacking him. When Schnack made a reorganization proposal to the University Senate in 1993, one element included transferring some advising and counseling units from Garb's supervision in student affairs to Smelstor's domain in academic affairs. The breaking point finally came when Garb forced out long-time Director of Housing Douglas Hallatt, whom Leonard Haas had hired in 1969. Unit directors in student affairs under Garb's supervision made a series of missteps, notably when Hallatt's successor spent excessively on redecorating his personal office. In May 1994, Schnack fired Garb and his director of housing, Thomas Kane.

Meanwhile, Schnack and Smelstor had digested the 1990 NCA report that had told the university it could pursue excellence as a regional comprehensive university concentrating on the professional schools, or it could emphasize its 1960s face as a large liberal arts undergraduate college. They decided UWEC should emphasize the liberal arts/undergraduate side, and by the end of the decade, the university had made strides in that direction by building on its strengths and finding ways to pay for it.

This decision was based on the results of a 1993 survey of two thousand alumni who had graduated between 1952 and 1992, 35 percent of whom returned the questionnaire. About a third of the respondents had followed careers in business, about a quarter in education, a sixth in health sciences, and the rest in "other" occupations. Seventy-eight percent reported they worked at a career "highly" or at least "somewhat" related to their major field of study at Eau Claire. The top four skills they thought they learned in college were verbal communication, written communication, problem solving, and working cooperatively as a team member. Specific or even general knowledge of the fine points of a field of study, the respondents thought, were not among the top skills they had learned. Schnack and Smelstor concluded the alumni survey results showed a liberal arts-based education at UWEC prepared a graduate for both the first job in a career as well as the last job.

They also felt a UWEC education provided graduates with "the knowledge and abilities needed for lifelong learning," as the university's updated 1995 statement of academic goals explained. A 1999 exchange between an area assemblywoman, Republican Kitty Rhoades, and UWEC Career Services Director Jeanne Sinz highlighted the challenge in making the public understand the value of educating students to be lifelong learners. Rhoades complained liberal arts graduates from UW institutions, including UWEC, "lacked marketable skills." In reply, Sinz pointed to the 1993 alumni survey and said that "communication skills rank first among the personal characteristics employers seek in job candidates. Communication skills are the hallmark of a liberal arts education." Sinz forecast the "skills and characteristics of our liberal arts graduates . . . will become even more vital as organizations struggle to meet the demands of an increasingly fast-paced, competitive and knowledge-based global economy."

Building the Networked Campus

The last new building constructed on campus as part of the growth era opened in 1981. The Department of Communicative Disorders and the Division of Allied Health Professions found a home in the new Allied Health and Clinical Services Building on Water Street on the parcel adjacent to the Fine Arts Center. Thereafter through the 1980s and 1990s, UWEC built no new buildings. Alumni from the class of 1980 felt largely at home on campus thirty years later, as the architectural horizon looked

Aerial View of Campus, 1989

To a remarkable extent for an institution of its size, the exterior appearance of UWEC changed very little between 1981 and 2012.

the same. There were remodelings and expansions of McIntyre Library and Phillips Science Hall, to be sure, but for decades the physical face of the campus remained largely unchanged, with the exception of the limitation of traffic on Garfield Avenue by removal of the long-time parking lot east of Schofield Hall. Not until Chancellors Hall opened in 2000 did UWEC add a new structure, which at the western edge of upper campus hardly altered the face of the university. And yet, beneath the surface, the 1980s and especially the 1990s was a time of tremendous internal construction. In the 1980s, UW–Eau Claire became a computerized campus. In the 1990s, it became a networked campus.

By the late 1980s, the big demand was for individual stand-alone desktop microcomputers to supplement UW–Eau Claire's two mainframe computers. The university struggled to keep up with requests by faculty and students for microcomputers for the tasks of word processing and numerical data analysis. Faculty wanted desktop microcomputers in their offices to replace typewriters and calculators, and students wanted seats at computer terminals on short notice, say right before a paper was due.

As of 1984, the university had established only five microcomputer labs. A 1987 ad hoc task force, led by history professor Ronald Warloski, identified a target of satisfying student demand with 1,200 microcomputers spread across every academic and administrative building on campus. Soon enough, Housing and Residence Life began converting residence hall spaces into computer labs and by 1995 had purchased one hundred computers so students would have round-the-clock access to a computer and printer.

The cost of providing enough desktop microcomputers for students and faculty was estimated in 1987 at almost $9 million. The Warloski task force recommended the university charge all students a new "technology fee" to pay for the costs of providing microcomputers. The proposers made the analogy to the existing practice in science courses where students paid a breakage fee to cover the cost of test tubes, beakers, and other laboratory equipment: if every student needed access to a microcomputer to succeed at the university, then every student should help pay the costs. The technology fee, first set at $20 per student per semester, brought in $400,000 of revenue each year. Levying this fee also set a precedent for the university in that it showed students would pay, largely without protest, for enhancements to their education. This was a lesson UWEC learned well and came back to repeatedly over the following quarter century.

Chancellor Schnack, Governor Thompson, Professor Susan McIntyre, 1996

The governor visited UWEC in October 1996 for an update on the latest technology initiatives on campus.

The information technology task force could not have been expected in 1987 to see the day of the stand-alone desktop microcomputer was coming to an end. Both academic and administrative computing was about to enter an era when networking from servers to clients would come to define the essence of information technology, but at enormous financial cost. Computing and networking services called the task the "University Wiring Project" and began by connecting every office and lab in Phillips Science Hall to the campus ethernet network and then adding each of the other academic buildings. Next came connecting Davies Center, Hilltop Center, and the residence halls. By 1996, the campus had a functioning integrated network, ready to take advantage of the new Internet resources such as telnet, file transfer protocol, Gopher, and starting in 1995, a homepage on the new World Wide Web.

To its credit, the task force's report did call for changes beyond merely providing more seats behind more stand-alone computer screens. It advocated installing computers and digital projectors in every classroom so instructors could share-and-show computer files directly to students. The report also called for investment in new forms of what was called distance education. Ever since the 1930s, UW Extension had offered classes for college credit to students interested in pursuing degrees. Its methods of delivering distance education ranged from classes by mail, to classes over radio station WHA, to classes delivered over a special telephone conference system—Wisconsin's Educational Teleconference Network. The Warloski task force proposed UWEC become a leader in providing courses for credit over a future statewide multi-way interactive video conferencing system.

The 1987 task force made one other recommendation about what was coming to be called information technology management. Specifically, it advocated for the creation of a director of computers and information technology. William Hogue accepted the newly created position of assistant chancellor for information and technology management in 1990. Not only did the units of academic computing and administrative computing report to him, so too did voice communications, the Media Development Center, and most notably, McIntyre Library. The unification of all support units into one IT division remade the university administration into something of a quadrilateral: academic affairs, student affairs, business services, and now IT affairs.

Using Networked Services for Teaching and Learning

In the 1990s, the School of Nursing proved to be the academic unit that made the most of the new networked campus by introducing an undergraduate program in conjunction with St. Joseph's Hospital in Marshfield, Wisconsin. Thanks to the presence of the Marshfield Clinic, central Wisconsin was an area of the state growing in employment of skilled medical professionals. Rather than make residents of central Wisconsin come to Eau Claire to earn an undergraduate nursing degree, the School of Nursing came to them with a pre-licensure program. Interested applicants completed their pre-nursing curriculum at UW–Marshfield/Wood County or UW–Marathon County, and once admitted to the UWEC School of Nursing they could do all their work for the BN degree at the Marshfield site via two-way interactive video and the Internet. During the next decade, as part of a UW System initiative, the School of Nursing also developed a BSN completion program at the Marshfield site for registered nurses with two-year degrees from Wisconsin technical colleges. For these programs, there were some faculty at the Marshfield site, but most instructors taught classes and led clinical tutorials in Eau Claire by a heretofore unprecedented use of distance education technology.

The School of Business, which became the College of Business in 1995, also began experimenting with distance education in the second half of the 1990s. The college underwent a review from the American Assembly of Collegiate Schools of Business in 1996, and the next year won back accreditation of both its undergraduate BBA degree and its graduate MBA degree. At the end of the decade, the college decided to offer the MBA program entirely over the Internet, primarily to a student body of working adults. In the first class of twenty-nine persons admitted to MBA study, twenty-five pursued it part-time. They worked at full-time employment at area firms such as Luther Midelfort, a large health clinic/hospital affiliated with the Mayo Clinic which was an important part of the emerging second-transformation economy in Eau Claire, and Northern States Power Company, a regional utility company whose roots were in the first economic transformation.

Distance education was slower to come into the curriculum in the College of Education and the College of Arts and Sciences. Students in those colleges in the 1990s, however, learned to use information technology in the numerous computer labs installed on campus, each one tied to the fiber optic network linking UWEC to the Internet. Faculty members, too, had computers installed in their offices. Thanks to a US Department of Education grant, the computers were networked so faculty could communicate with their advisees via email. Academic advising, a sometimes neglected area of the university, received new recognition as an important faculty obligation and one that could be efficiently undertaken using computer technology. For the first time, faculty could access student records on the administrative computing system and offer guidance to their advisees about course selection and degree plans.

Cargill Technology Center, Schneider Hall, 1999

The Cargill Center provided a state-of-the-art conference-style environment used by College of Business students for strategic planning, collaborative writing, survey design and focus group research, and systems development.

Although the campus looked the same on the outside, every classroom at the university had been wired and connected to the Internet by the end of the 1990s. Students could bring a new-style laptop computer to class and use it to take notes and work on problems. From the front of the classroom, instructors could call upon Internet resources, and by the end of the decade, files and programs were stored on campus servers. The transformation of the classroom into a networked learning space also changed the nature of instruction. Thomas Dock, the dean of the College of Business and a professor of information management, summed up the new expectations for classroom instruction: "Faculty must shift from being knowledge repositories to facilitators of knowledge acquisition."

The networked campus also changed another UWEC institution in fundamental ways: McIntyre Library. In the 1970s and early 1980s, as many as 1.5 million students and faculty passed through the turnstiles into the library each year. That number fell by one-half to 721,000 visits to the library in 1998–99. Yet, use of the library's online resources soared, each year setting new records. Librarians collected user statistics and found almost half of the users accessed library databases from computers outside the physical confines of the library. Fully 30 percent of the faculty reported in a survey that they no longer visited McIntyre Library because they could access everything they wanted from the library via remote links.

First Floor, McIntyre Library, 1999

McIntyre Library benefited from membership in the Council of UW Libraries and continually updated its online catalog (chapter eight), giving UWEC users access to library catalogues of all UW institutions. More than perhaps any other part of the campus, McIntyre Library was fully integrated into the UW System. The drawback, from the library faculty's point of view, was as foot traffic and on-site use of the library plummeted, so too did its relative importance in the minds of users. Library Director Steve Marquardt lamented in 1998, "Library Services has become increasingly isolated from Academic Affairs and the central UWEC administration." Marquardt further bemoaned the effects of the administrative reorganization on the library, noting that "over the past five years, the Director has spent a total of 15 minutes meeting with the academic deans as a group."

Paying for College—The New Reality

The board of regents had adopted its enrollment management plan (chapter eight) with the goal of balancing student enrollment at UWEC and other UW campuses with expected state budget appropriations and tuition revenues. The hope was the state would invest more money in the UW System. Instead, it had a renewed budget crisis in 1990–91 as a result of falling revenues caused by the national recession. As a consequence, Governor Thompson ordered a mid-biennial hiring freeze and budget rescissions (givebacks) in December 1990. For their part, the regents ordered a more drastic round of enrollment management, this time lasting through the 1994–95 academic year. UWEC shrank to fewer than 10,400 students in 1995, the lowest number it had enrolled since 1976. In August 1991, Acting System President Lyall told the university to plan to use the savings from its reduced size to put dollars into other priorities, notably faculty and staff catch-up compensation, information technology, and services and supplies. The regents named this directive the "Quality Reinvestment Program."

However, in inflation-adjusted real terms, Wisconsin did not put more dollars into the UW System in the 1990s. Rather, the biggest change in state budgeting was the decision to fund more elementary and secondary education through the state income tax. In doing so, the legislature addressed the clamor of voters to reduce local property taxes, the traditional source of elementary/secondary funding. In 1993, it appropriated $200 million to local governments so the property tax could be frozen. In the 1994 elections, the voters approved a referendum advising the legislature to fund two-thirds of the cost of elementary/secondary education from state appropriations, up from the earlier level of 47 percent.

The immediate consequence of the 1994 referendum was the state had to find an extra $900 million each year in the next biennium to fund property tax relief. Unlike past budget crises linked to the national economy, where UWEC could tell itself the shortfall was temporary, the 1995–97 state biennial budget marked the beginning of a permanent de-emphasis on state funding of higher education. From that biennium forward, every state budget had a line item for "Shared Revenue and Tax Relief," starting with at least $3 billion to meet the state's pledge of covering two-thirds of the cost of public elementary/secondary education. Furthermore, Governor Thompson and the legislature identified the Department of Corrections as the second priority for state spending. That agency saw its budget increase more than 25 percent in the 1995–97 biennium, even as UW System support from the state dropped more than 3 percent and spending on health and social services dropped more than 15 percent. The 1995–97 budget marked the end for the UW System of the Quality Reinvestment Program.

UWEC continued to do what it could during the 1990s to hire nationally recruited faculty members. It did so with the money it saved from the salaries it recouped from retirements of professors hired by Leonard Haas and Richard Hibbard during the university's growth era. In May 1997, twenty-five persons, about 6 percent of the faculty, retired; they had a median of twenty-nine years of service. As the dean of the College of Arts and Sciences put it in 1996, "The number of outstanding faculty on the market is extraordinary. We are making plans to hire as many as possible with the retirements that are being submitted."

With declining state support from the legislature, the regents turned to the other obvious source of increased revenue for all campuses: tuition. At the beginning of the 1990s, tuition and fees for one semester for in-state undergraduates totaled $950. For the 1999–2000 academic year, the cost of tuition and fees had risen to $1,626 per semester, a more than 70 percent increase over the course of the decade and at a rate more than twice the increase in the US Department of Labor's Consumer Price Index.

Students and their families experienced the 1990s as a time of increasing reliance on federally backed loans as the means for paying for a UWEC education. In the last year of the decade, Blugold students borrowed almost $20 million to pay for their expenses. Eau Claire students showed themselves highly responsible customers in borrowing and repaying student loans. In the recession years of 1990–91, about one in five ex-students nationwide defaulted on their student loan payments. By contrast, during these same years not even one in fifty former UWEC students defaulted. UWEC default rates stayed far below national rates, as national economic growth returned after 1992.

In contrast to loans, federal Pell Grants, state-supported grants, and scholarships from the UW–Eau Claire Foundation amounted to less than $10 million in 1990–91. Federally supported work-study employment money, which had been so important in the 1970s, did not keep pace with the cost of attending college, and tighter eligibility rules reduced the number of Eau Claire students eligible. Still, in 1999–2000, UWEC students earned $4 million employed at projects supported by federal work-study funds.

As federally supported work-study money fell in real terms, UWEC students turned increasingly to private sector, part-time, and even full-time employment. The second economic transformation of the Chippewa Valley economy in the 1980s that shed so many manufacturing jobs also resulted in more part-time employment, especially in retail and services. UWEC students filled more and more such jobs. The triennial American College Testing Program survey of UWEC students showed the change from 1984 to 1993. In the former year, 45 percent of Blugold students reported part-time employment, with equal portions working one to ten hours a week, eleven to twenty hours a week, and more than twenty-one hours. Put another way, more than half of UWEC students in 1984 attended college full-time without working during the school year. By 1993, the same ACT survey found 66 percent of UWEC students worked during the school year, almost half of whom worked for at least twenty-one hours a week.

Music at Eau Claire in the 1980s and 1990s

Leonard Haas was a strong supporter of UW–Eau Claire's music program (chapter five) and was proud of its growth when he led the university: Caldwell Johnson (chapter four) took the Concert Choir on European tours in 1964 and 1966, the bachelor of music degree was introduced in 1968, and the National Association of Schools of Music accredited the program in 1970—the same year it moved into the new Fine Arts Center (chapter six). Music continued to be one of the areas of excellence in the university in the 1980s and 1990s. It prepared students for careers, connected the campus to the community, brought recognition to the university by its accomplishments, and provided activities that engaged students in campus life.

By the late 1970s, students needed to audition to earn admission to music degree programs, and during the 1980s and 1990s there were usually about 250-350 students with music majors. Viennese Ball scholarships (chapter seven) increasingly supported their studies. About thirty-five faculty members taught these students. Preparing elementary/secondary teachers continued to be important: about thirty-five to forty-five music education majors graduated each year. In addition, other music students chose majors in vocal or instrumental performance, in theory, in composition, or in music therapy. By the 1980s, students, faculty, and guest artists performed over one hundred public concerts on campus each year.

Morris Hayes succeeded Johnson as director of choral activities in 1966 and immediately developed a highly successful male chorus, the Singing Statesmen. The Statesmen brought recognition to the university by, among other activities, extensive touring—seven international tours by 2016. The Statesmen became a focus of life on campus for its members, about half of whom usually were not music majors. "The big thing is the camaraderie and fun we have in the group," the Statesmen's president told the 1980 *Periscope*. Gary R. Schwartzhoff took over the direction of the Statesmen in 1991, and in 2010 he received the Morris Hayes Award for lifetime achievement from the Wisconsin Choral Directors Association.

Nobuyoshi Yasuda became conductor of the University Symphony Orchestra in 1991. Continuing the practices established by Robert Gantner (chapter four), Yasuda also helped to connect the university with the community by serving as music director of the Chippewa Valley Symphony beginning in 1993. The Symphony Orchestra often performed in conjunction with the Symphonic Choir, which included singers from the community among its members. The community also enjoyed the university's annual Holiday Concert, when the Symphony Orchestra and Symphonic Choir and other music groups, including the Concert Choir, the Women's Concert Chorale, the Women's Chorus, and the Wind Symphony, gave two performances to a capacity audience in Zorn Arena on a Sunday afternoon in mid-December.

Another dimension of the music program was jazz studies, with over one hundred students annually enrolled in coursework during the 1990s. Ronald W. Keezer, who taught percussion from 1969 to 2001, guided the development of the program in the 1970s and continued as director of Jazz Ensemble II until his retirement. Robert J. Baca joined the faculty in 1986 and became director of jazz studies. In 1991, he took Jazz Ensemble I on a path-breaking tour to China, where jazz had been proscribed as bourgeois decadence since the Communist revolution. The annual Eau Claire Jazz Festival brought well-known jazz musicians to campus for performances and master classes.

During the 1980s, when Donald George was director of bands, about 250 students participated in the band program. George, who taught from 1968 to 1995, conducted the Symphony Band and trombonist Rodney Hudson, a faculty member from 1971 to 2003, led the Concert Bands. During the late 1990s, two additional bands, which became popular with students, joined the program: the Blugold Marching Band (chapter ten) and the University Band, which was open to all student players without audition.

Members of the music faculty also distinguished themselves as performers and composers. For example, cellist Paul R. Kosower, who taught at the university from 1970 to 2007, was a soloist with the Milwaukee Symphony Orchestra. When he played at Town Hall in New York in 1973, John Rockwell in the *New York Times* identified his "appealing musicality" and concluded that "musical life" at UW–Eau Claire "must be flourishing." Kosower's colleague from 1968 to 2003, oboist Ivar Lunde Jr., won a 1990 Milwaukee Symphony competition for fanfares for his composition *OVATION*. Throughout the 1980s and 1990s both Kosower and Lunde performed frequently on the *Sunday Afternoon Live from the Elvehjem* series broadcast on Wisconsin Public Radio.

At a Music Department meeting in 1969, a member of the faculty told his colleagues it was "heartwarming" that President Haas "frequently" attended concerts. The quality and accomplishments of the university's music program provided good reasons for Dorellen and Leonard Haas, and faculty, students, and community members during the following decades, to show interest in music.

The Singing Statesmen in Performance, Gantner Concert Hall, November 2008

University students emerged by the 1990s as a key part of the Chippewa Valley labor force, even as their main task was to study for a college degree. One consequence was working students in the 1990s took fewer classes each semester and took longer to complete their degrees than did students in prior decades. The average student credit load per semester dropped to fourteen credits by 1995. With 128 credits required for graduation, students had to average sixteen per semester to complete their studies in four years. Most did not: in 1995, only 16 percent of graduates had finished their degree in four years. UWEC began reporting data on students who graduated within five years (47.5 percent in 1995) and six years (52.5 percent in 1995). A college education at UWEC in the 1990s cost more, took longer to complete, and asked more of students than in earlier decades.

The UW System began demanding reports showing improvements in retention and graduation rates for all its campuses. UWEC administrators, faculty, and staff had worked hard in the late 1980s to improve the first-year student retention rate from 72 percent of entering in 1985 to 82 percent by 1990. Then, the first-year retention rate turned back downward, dropping to 76 percent of students entering in 1993. Even with the return of national prosperity in the mid-1990s, UWEC's first-year retention rates stayed below their peak 1990 level. As a result, Chancellor Schnack organized a task force in 1995–96 to improve first-year retention. The task force reminded faculty to give first-year students graded assignments or exams within the first four weeks of the semester and to report mid-semester grades for them. Above all, the task force urged faculty and advisers to reach out to individual students who appeared to be struggling academically. Their recommendations, when implemented, seemed to make a difference. The retention rate of students admitted in 2001 rebounded to 81 percent, and 60 percent of them completed their baccalaureate degree within six years.

To replace declining state support, during the 1990s UW System institutions turned to an idea Emily Hannah had been told was premature when she had advanced it in the early 1980s: student-approved tuition surcharges. UW–Madison was the first campus to receive the approval from the regents to enact such a surcharge and UW–Eau Claire soon followed. Chancellor Schnack, in an oral history, recalled he started as a determined foe of tuition surcharges because of their effect in limiting college access to students, but given the change in public sentiment about state spending priorities, he came to believe a surcharge was needed.

Schnack first made the case to the Student Senate that an extra million dollars a year in revenue, beyond the tuition set by the regents, could be used to hire more instructors and thereby address a shortage of class offerings, which created a roadblock to timely graduation. The Student Senate had heard repeatedly from students about their frustration at not being able to get the required classes they needed at times when they wanted them. The tuition surcharge, if dedicated to hiring faculty and academic staff to teach the courses with high demand and a backlog of waiting students, promised to solve a pressing problem. The Student Senate voted its approval to direct the university to ask the regents to approve surcharge-levying authority. Schnack made the case before the regents in December 1996, and starting in the fall of 1997 Eau Claire students began paying a "differential tuition" of $50 per semester, yielding about a million dollars in extra revenue.

By 1997–98, the Student Senate and the academic affairs office had identified five priorities for differential tuition dollars, with more than a third of the funds going to underwrite faculty-student collaborative research. Additional fractions went to support senior capstone courses (such as those in which students wrote senior theses), special sections of courses just for first-year students, internships, and the new Service Learning program the university started. The Faculty-Student Collaborative Research Center, first identified a decade earlier as fruit of the regents' competition, had proved its importance to UWEC. Provost Smelstor compared differential tuition to receiving a private donation of $20 million, since such a gift to the UW–Eau Claire Foundation would generate $1 million per year in income to spend on instruction.

Who Was a Blugold? The Student Body of the 1990s

UW–Eau Claire in 1990 had a student body made up of about 60 percent women. The ratio of women to men reflected both particular characteristics of UWEC and characteristics of US higher education in general during the 1990s. The specific mix of academic programs at UWEC included two programs that continued to attract mainly women students: elementary education and nursing. Each of these professional programs enrolled more than 90 percent women and together they accounted for more than 1,200 students at UWEC. Other major programs were more gender balanced, especially in the School of Business and among the liberal arts majors. At its inception in the mid-1960s, the School of Business had largely consisted of male students. Three decades later, the enrollment was almost equal between men and women, as part of a national trend toward women enrolling in business degree programs. UWEC was not alone among UW campuses in having an increasingly feminized study body: others, such as UW–Oshkosh with a similar program array, had comparable ratios of women to men. Nationwide, the gender ratio of all students enrolled in higher education degree programs increased from 55 percent female in 1990 to 56 percent a decade later.

The academic profile of the successive incoming first-year classes showed an upward trend over the course of the 1990s. Some of this improvement was due to the shift in the UW System due to the enrollment management policy. One outcome was UWEC became a more selective institution. Student scores on the American College Testing readiness assessment improved from around 19.6 in 1980 to 23.6 by 2000 (the national average was around 21.0 during the 1990s). On a related measure, by 1990, fully two-thirds of entering students ranked in the top 30 percent of their high school graduating class. In the academic quality of its student body, UWEC was changing from open access to increasingly selective.

The ACT surveyed two thousand UWEC students in 1993, asking them their feelings about an Eau Claire education. Asked to rate the university overall, on a scale from 0 to 5, students scored UWEC at 4.10. If not an excellent rating, this score showed students considered the university very good. Students showed more variation in rating non-academic services than classroom education: they voted the recreation and intermural facilities in McPhee Physical Education Center as the highest-valued services;

CUBEFest, September 1999

The housing and residential life office originated CUBEFest in 1993 as a program to welcome first-year students to campus.

at the same time, they rated parking services (or, more accurately, the lack of parking spaces) and dining services near the bottom. In the area reserved for written comments on the survey, one Blugold demanded, "All faculty and staff have to eat at one of the cafeterias once or twice a week so they can experience having their intestines feel like they are tied in knots."

A 1995 survey for the admissions office returned to the issues of the Satz task force of the 1980s on the university's image. The researcher, Ohio University graduate student Joey Gibbons, sent questionnaires to five hundred high school principals and guidance counselors. Gibbons divided respondents into those from "feeder" high schools, such as Eau Claire Memorial and Chippewa Falls (which sent at least twenty graduates per year to UWEC), and "non-feeder" schools. She also divided them by geography into local schools in Eau Claire and Chippewa Falls, other schools within a fifty-mile radius, and schools more than fifty miles away. Gibbons found a split in perceptions about the university that mirrored the split between the old mission of Eau Claire State and its newer mission as a comprehensive university. Local high schools and those within a fifty-mile radius valued most highly the university's "proximity," while those farther away saw the strength of its academic programs, particularly in nursing and business, as its main attraction. Gibbons showed those who saw the university as their regional home did not always care for its pursuit of excellence. "Stop being a mini-Madison," commented one counselor, and another complained, "[Our] excellent students can't get into Eau Claire," even as a third oddly chided the university as "too involved in academics." The North Central Association's 1989 report had told UWEC it could be an excellent regional comprehensive university or an excellent liberal arts university for Wisconsin and Minnesota, but it did not have the resources to be both; half a decade later, the university found it was disappointing some people in the Chippewa Valley for neglecting local high schools in favor of its wider bi-state mission.

From "Design for Diversity" to "Plan 2008"

The UW System had announced its Design for Diversity with much energy in 1988, and each year campuses duly reported to Van Hise Hall their numbers regarding minority student and faculty recruitment. UWEC was more than meeting its target in recruiting both students and faculty from the four groups the regents had designated for special effort: American Indians, African Americans, Hispanic Americans, and Asian Americans who came to the United States after 1975. The problem at UWEC and elsewhere around the system was retaining the people recruited. For example, when in 1992 the university looked at the twenty-three minority faculty members it had hired between 1987 and 1990, it found it had managed to keep only ten of them.

UWEC had a public parting of the ways with a young African American professor in the Psychology Department. Richard Majors came to Eau Claire in 1990 as an untenured assistant professor and the university featured his presence on campus as a welcome addition to the faculty. He published a book which gained national attention, and he promptly asked to be promoted and tenured. Majors, however, made this request several years before he had completed the standard probationary term as an assistant professor. He reasoned he performed at a level deserving of early tenure and promotion; his colleagues on the department Personnel Committee disagreed and voted to deny him early tenure and promotion. Majors expressed outrage at this action and announced his intention to boycott teaching classes in the 1993–94 academic year and to sue the university in federal court for racial discrimination. He lost on all fronts, and the regents fired him in August 1994 for non-performance of his contract.

While the Majors case divided opinion on campus, it made clear the problem UWEC had in keeping its newly recruited minority faculty. The same held true for minority students, who often felt out of place on an overwhelmingly white campus. In the midst of the Majors case, Chancellor Schnack hired an external consultant, Reginald Wilson of the American Council on Education, to come to Eau Claire and study the climate for minority faculty and students. Wilson read internal reports and then made a pair of visits to campus in January and February 1993 before he submitted his report in March. The report pulled no punches, finding fault with top administrators. The Eau Claire way, Wilson reported, had been to hire a "czar" to take care of problems, such as "minorities" now seemed to be. Instead, what the university needed, he argued, was an institution-wide commitment to recruit and retain minority faculty, staff, and students. He recommend Schnack appoint a task force outside the University Senate to prepare recommendations for change and urged senior leadership hold departments and units accountable for including diversity in their long-range staffing plans.

The timing of Wilson's visits and his report coincided with an important decision by Chancellor Schnack to reorganize the university administration. In a February presentation to the faculty, Schnack proposed to eliminate two of the five dean positions and also consolidate the Schools of Nursing, Education, and some departments from Arts and Sciences into a new College of Human Services. The Schnack proposal redesignated the reduced School of Arts and Sciences as the College of Arts and Sciences; the School of Business was unchanged except for a name change from School to College. The former deans of the School of Education and School of Nursing were demoted to associate deans in the new College of Human Services. The graduate dean's position was eliminated, but its occupant, Ronald Satz, was made the new dean of the College of Health and Human Services, even though his faculty appointment was in Arts and Sciences.

The most obvious loser in the reorganization was the School of Nursing, which lost its dean and also its autonomy. "I have to admit I kind of forced that merger down their throats," Schnack later acknowledged. "If I had to do it over again, honestly, I wouldn't do it." When it was implemented in the spring of 1995, the reorganization eliminated the lone woman dean, Patricia Ostmoe in the School of Nursing, and left only white males still standing among the three surviving deans. Ostmoe said in public that she understood the need for administrative efficiency and consolidation, but not at the cost of the School of Nursing. She floated a counterproposal in which a department from Arts and Sciences, such as Communication Disorders, joined Nursing, but Schnack was not persuaded. The campus Commission on the Status of Women protested the elimination of Ostmoe as the sole woman dean at UWEC, to which Schnack answered in defense of his reorganization plan, "I wasn't looking for a female dean to fire."

The reduction of women employees was not just at the higher end in the form of Dean Ostmoe's position; at the lower end, a number of adjunct instructors lost their jobs. They had labored for long periods on year-to-year "no-intent-to-renew" contracts; they were often hired at the last minute to teach courses, such as Introduction to College Writing in the Department of English. That department for years had been unable to meet the student demand for this course, which was required of all students, with its regular faculty. Instead, it relied on a group of adjunct instructors who had come to expect job security, even though they worked under semester-to-semester contracts. In the spring of 1993 Vice Chancellor Smelstor decided to eliminate the student backlog in Introduction to College Writing by assigning more faculty to teach it and also by increasing the section size from twenty-nine students to thirty-three. Five of the adjunct instructors, four of whom were women, did not receive any further contracts. Out of work, one of the women, Laurel Johnson, filed an unsuccessful sex discrimination lawsuit against the university.

The 1993 turmoil on campus came almost two decades after the system had directed every campus to begin affirmative action hiring for women faculty and staff, but in which little had been accomplished at UWEC. In 1975 the university had a ratio of male to female faculty of 79–21, which because of limited new hiring was unchanged at the end of the decade. A dozen years later, the ratio was 72–28, mainly because of women hired as assistant professors. At the rank of full professor, the ratio of men to women was 88–12.

Sentiment against Schnack's administration boiled over in mid-April 1993 as a group called "Friends of Diversity," consisting of faculty, academic staff, and students, denounced his university reorganization and the non-renewal of the contracts of the women adjunct instructors. Friends of Diversity issued a set of "non-negotiable demands" related to hiring and the curriculum and then escalated the tension by occupying the chancellor's office with a sit-in. Schnack calmly met with the protesters; he did not

Admissions Office and American Ethnic Coordinating Office Staff, July 1996

Front row, left to right: Terry Scott, Susanne Felber, Joey Gibbon (Bohl), Shoua Lily Lo. Back row: Roger L. Groenewold, Damian J. O'Brien, Jesse L. Dixon, Barbara Fortin, and James Vance. Admissions worked closely with the American ethnic coordinating office to recruit a diverse incoming class of Blugolds for the fall of 1996.

call University Police or outside agencies to force the eviction of the occupiers. On the merits of the demands of Friends of Diversity, Schnack responded by announcing the appointment of a task force to examine the state of diversity on campus, much as Reginald Wilson had urged him earlier in the spring. The charge to this task force was to report back to the chancellor with recommendations about how the university could do a better job of recruiting and retaining minority faculty, staff, and students.

Schnack's diversity task force, co-chaired by Joe Hisrich and Joan Rohr Myers, academic staff members who had worked in the educational opportunity and affirmative action offices, respectively, began where Wilson's report left off. Recruiting and retaining minority faculty and minority students to UWEC, the task force argued, had to be more than a job for a lone diversity director. This was different from what Wilson had called the Eau Claire Way of hiring a czar to fix a problem. Instead, all faculty and staff had to make an effort at recruiting and retention, the task force recommended, and academic departments had to produce plans for recruiting faculty and then retaining them. The affirmative action office had its staff increased and became more active in reviewing searches for faculty positions to ensure minority candidates were included. For minority students, the university began to work harder at recruiting and retention.

The Hisrich and Rohr Myers task force set more ambitious recruiting and retention goals for UWEC than those the UW System had planned back in 1988 when it launched Design for Diversity. Under Design for Diversity, the university had quietly reported its flagging numbers on minority retention. After the uproar in 1993, the reports received much more scrutiny (see Table 9.1). The university increased its efforts at recruiting minority students, and as a result nearly doubled the number of students from the four regents-denominated minority groups. UWEC recruited more students by 1995 in all four groups, with the largest gains coming from Southeast Asian students.

UWEC faculty, staff, and students were sometimes confused in the 1990s about the language of diversity. With their Design for Diversity plan, the regents had narrowly defined diversity as pertaining to one of four Wisconsin racial or ethnic minority groups. Yet the constellation of civil and human rights statutes the US Congress had passed in the 1960s and the 1970s produced the notion of a protected class of persons beyond the four groups acknowledged by the regents. Congress and federal rule-making agencies extended protection in college admissions and employment to persons with disabilities,

Table 9.1
Minority Student Enrollment at UWEC 1989-1995

Year	African American	American Indian	SE Asian	Hispanic	Total
1989	54	43	84	28	209
1990	60	42	88	41	231
1991	56	50	100	38	242
1992	53	49	121	47	270
1993	54	58	138	63	313
1994	59	85	176	85	407
1995	67	96	173	92	428

women, the aged, military veterans, and other groups. UWEC's affirmative action office struggled to educate departments and administrators making hiring and retention decisions about the new laws and regulations. In so doing, the definition of diversity on campus began to extend in the 1990s beyond the four groups listed by the regents.

Regarding the most visible newly protected class of persons, the Commission on the Status of Women conducted a "campus climate" study in 1993, asking women faculty and staff about their experiences at the university. The survey results included a finding that the climate for women faculty and academic staff was chilly, if not downright cold. The survey authors stated they found "a sense of cynicism and hopelessness" among women instructors. Few reported outright discrimination against them by male colleagues, but instead, respondents complained about a power imbalance in their departments and colleges. Most important, the survey revealed women faculty respondents felt disrespected by male students in the classroom. Schnack did not agree with the survey results, however, pointing out it had a response rate of only 10 percent. Nonetheless, campus leaders had more data to consider in deciding how to make diversity work.

Data and money, or the lack of money, drove Schnack to make one of the most difficult decisions of his time in office, the 1995 elimination of baseball as a varsity sport—a decision that became entangled with women's issues. By 1993–94, more than $500,000 was spent on varsity athletics, in which 519 students participated. The spending on men's and women's programs was in rough proportion to the greater numbers of men than women participating in athletics, about 60–40. Budget tightening caused the men's and women's athletic directors to look for savings. They dismissed the idea of across-the-board cuts and instead recommended dropping baseball to save $30,000, a decision men's director Mel Lewis called "the most difficult thing I have ever done in my athletic career." The faculty of the Kinesiology Department and the university's Athletics Commission supported the recommendation. The academic affairs office pointed to the solid academic record of most varsity athletes, except baseball players who in the spring semester missed numerous classes to complete a league schedule constrained by Wisconsin's "Spring" weather.

Schnack met with the players and their families on July 19 to inform them of his decision to eliminate varsity baseball at UW–Eau Claire. Angry letters to the local newspaper had decried the decision as a politically correct concession, favoring women's sports over men's, a charge Schnack denied. He instead insisted the decision was driven by the funding environment and by the data on academic achievement of varsity athletes.

If women were the most visible protected class of employees among the faculty and academic staff, the most invisible group continued to be gays and lesbians. In the 1990s, they did not represent a protected class in a legal sense. Nonetheless, in the 1990s, the campus slowly moved to become more accepting of differing sexual orientation as another valued form of cultural diversity. One painful episode reverberated across the campus and into the lower west side student neighborhood: in September 1992, a lesbian student reported an assault with her attackers targeting her for her sexual orientation. The student group GLOBE (Gay, Lesbian, Or Bi, for Equality) led marches on campus and on Water Street demanding protection for those with different sexual orientations. The eventual recantation of the assault accusation by the student did not diminish the growing awareness on campus that cultural diversity included sexual orientation.

The decade ended with the UW System concluding Design for Diversity and changing to a new diversity program called Plan 2008. The new program called for continued recruiting of minority students and faculty to all UW campuses, but unlike the earlier 1988 initiative, Plan 2008 addressed a concern not evident in Design for Diversity: the elimination of an achievement gap between minority students and majority students. For the UW System, the achievement gap was quite simple: minority students had a much lower graduation rate than did their white peers. UW–Eau Claire was no exception. The challenge in the next decade was retention and graduation of minority students, a challenge that soon enough extended to all students.

History Class, late 1980s

University Archivist Richard Pifer is shown providing bibliographic instruction in HIST 401: Historical Methodology. At his left is the course instructor, professor Maxwell P. Schoenfeld, who taught at UWEC from 1964 to 1976 and 1978 to 1996. As part of the Redefined Baccalaureate, other departments adopted "capstone" courses, like HIST 401 and 402, for their majors.

What Did a Blugold Know— The Redefined Baccalaureate

In 1984, UW System Vice President Katherine Lyall had called upon each system campus to form a "Commission on the Meaning of the Baccalaureate" and to think about the worth and significance of its undergraduate offerings. UWEC did not immediately take up the challenge, but when the regents established centers of excellence in 1988, the university had proposed its general education program for such a designation (chapter eight). Although its general education program did not become a center of excellence, UWEC did commit to rethinking what it wanted all its students to learn. The University Planning Committee in 1990 listed what it saw as the value of an Eau Claire degree. An Eau Claire graduate, the committee wrote, would be known for critical thinking skills; communication skills in speaking, writing, and calculating; and, in line with Design for Diversity, an ability to work and live in an intercultural nation and world.

Determining the meaning of the UWEC undergraduate degree was a task Marjorie Smelstor took on as the newly appointed vice chancellor in 1990. Smelstor paraphrased Virginia Woolf in frequently stating, "The unexamined curriculum is not worth teaching." She appointed a twenty-four-person task force called the Commission on the Redefinition of the Baccalaureate. The commission began with the document prepared by the University Planning Committee and agreed a college graduate from Eau Claire had to demonstrate high-level skills in reading, writing, speaking, and numerical analysis. General education remained the foundation every student in every college had to complete, the commission believed, and it updated the required distribution of general education credits from what had been set by the last revision in 1984. The commission proposed students had to show competencies in the same four broad categories of knowledge as they had before, but they were now encouraged to take more interdisciplinary courses. For their major areas of study, the commission wanted the university to provide special sections limited to first-year students to introduce them to the life of the mind in their chosen discipline. The commission's idea was at the end of a student's career, their major would provide a "capstone" course calling upon them to master and synthesize advanced knowledge in their disciplines.

The commission recommended trimming the number of credits needed for graduation from 128 to 120, and therefore reducing the expected full-time credit load per semester from sixteen to fifteen. At the same time, the commission indicated a preference for limiting to sixty the number of credits students could take in comprehensive majors. That reduction stemmed from a sense that individual disciplines were calling for more and more specialization in their comprehensive majors, thereby keeping students from graduating in a timely manner with a broad foundation of coursework. The reform was consciously intended to emphasize breadth of learning over depth of learning. Schnack told the *Chronicle of Higher Education*, "Students 40 years ago had a broader education than students 20 years ago, who had a broader education than students 10 years ago. It doesn't take a genius to figure out why. The curriculum has been largely in the hands of the disciplines."

In other areas, however, the commission proposed new requirements for a bachelor's degree. For example, the previous physical education requirement was changed to a "Wellness" obligation. Wellness included both physical activity and instruction in nutrition and health. Leonard Haas's old wish that all UWEC students study a foreign language returned, in a modified way, with a choice between a foreign language or a "foreign culture" requirement for all degrees. A student had to show competence in a foreign language comparable to mastering two semesters of college study or take nine credits of coursework emphasizing foreign cultures.

The most unusual change in the curriculum was an innovation called service learning. To earn a bachelor's degree, all Eau Claire students had to perform thirty hours of volunteer service, preferably in an area related to their academic major. The benefits to Chippewa Valley non-profit associations were almost immediate, as thousands of students began volunteering tens of thousands of hours per year.

Schnack and Smelstor convinced the University Senate to approve the redefined baccalaureate and it took effect in 1995 at the same time the Student Senate approved differential tuition. This pair of reforms earned the university plaudits in the *Chronicle of Higher Education* and in the influential annual rankings of American colleges, which had been initiated by *U.S. News & World Report* in 1985. When *U.S. News* published its evaluations of public master's-level universities in the Midwest, UWEC surpassed all other UW System comprehensive campuses and rivaled the best regional master's-level universities in neighboring states.

The success of the new curriculum and getting the money to pay for it from students was part of the reason for the public awareness of renewed excellence at UWEC. In addition, the university made good its promises to fund the center of excellence in faculty-student collaborative research. In fact, with more than $300,000 allocated to support faculty-student research collaboration in 1997–98, that activity— rather than the older model of faculty research and publication in peer-reviewed publications—became increasingly the definition of what scholarship meant at UWEC. Regarding the new curriculum and its emphasis on faculty-student collaborative research, Schnack recalled, "Many of the comments we got from visitors were that we were leaders in these developments."

The question remained, however, of how UWEC knew what a Blugold had learned. The North Central Association had told the university in 1989 that traditional answers—scores on assignments, course grades, grade point averages—were insufficient, and what was needed was assessment of student learning in relation to what the university had defined as its learning goals. The next year, the regents told every UW System campus the same thing: devise a plan of assessing undergraduate student learning, one part of what the regents called "Issues for the Nineties." The regents wanted a new, more intentional UW System that "must also be accountable to the public by demonstrating effectiveness." Some of the regents wanted a standardized test administered at the end of the sophomore year to measure student ability in verbal and quantitative reasoning, but the board did not go so far as to require that of every campus. Instead, the regents settled for a directive requiring campuses to demonstrate their effectiveness by stating "educational goals and assess[ing] student learning."

The UWEC faculty decided it would assess students based on eleven learning goals that had been identified in the Redefined Baccalaureate. In 1995, the provost appointed a University Assessment Committee to consider the daunting challenge of assessing if 11,000 Blugolds were on track in meeting these goals. Faculty members felt they had enough work in their regular teaching, advising, scholarship, and service activities. The Assessment Committee, therefore, tried student surveys, so-called "exit interviews" with graduating seniors, and alumni surveys of opinions about what they had learned. In the end, the committee decided surveying student and alumni opinions was not the same as evaluating what students actually produced. The only way to do that was to have faculty and staff read papers from students, not for a grade this time, but to see if the students showed mastery of the learning goals. After much discussion, the students were called upon to prepare portfolios of their work, at first in print but later in online folders, and their chosen work provided examples of how they had mastered the learning goals.

Donald J. Mash

Mash was chancellor from 1998 to 2005. In 2015, he received an honorary DHL degree from his alma mater, Indiana University of Pennsylvania.

Leadership Transition at the End of the Decade

At the beginning of the fall 1998 semester, Chancellor Schnack announced his plan to retire effective at the end of the semester. He told the university community that his health was good and he enjoyed the job of leading UWEC, yet it was time for a new chancellor to lead the university into the next century. "I felt a great deal of pride to see what we accomplished together," Schnack related to the University Senate.

In the process of selecting Schnack's successor, there were echoes of previous searches. The UW System president and regents appointed the provost, Marjorie Smelstor, as interim chancellor. When asked, Schnack voiced his opinion that Smelstor should be hired as chancellor on a permanent basis. However, it was not his choice. As they had in 1980, the regents instead chose an outsider, Donald J. Mash, to replace a campus insider. There were some significant differences, though, in the type of outsider represented by Emily Hannah in 1980 and by Donald Mash in 1999. Mash reflected in an oral history that he was the rare sitting university president who sought to make a lateral move from one campus to another, in his case from Wayne State College in Nebraska to UWEC. Most newly appointed university chancellors within the UW System, Mash observed, came from the ranks of vice presidents and deans. Instead, he came to UWEC with a decade's worth of experience in leading a public regional comprehensive university.

Mash suggested an additional reason for why the regents chose him, an outsider, at a time when the existing leadership of Schnack and Smelstor could point to many successes in improving the university. Mash related that President Lyall sought a new chancellor for the Eau Claire campus with experience in leading a capital fundraising campaign, not only to help lead UWEC in raising private funds, but in helping tutor fellow chancellors in the tasks of friend-raising and fundraising. "We need to do a comprehensive campaign and we're going to plan one and we'll do one," Mash told the regents at his final interview. "It's not a matter of whether, just when."

In sum, UW–Eau Claire weathered the budget difficulties of the 1990s and emerged from enrollment management leaner but also with a higher-achieving student body. The demographic transition extended to the faculty and academic staff as UWEC replaced the generation of faculty recruited by Leonard Haas, Richard Hibbard, and Lester Emans with a new cohort of instructors. The university made another, largely invisible, change in embracing the information technology revolution and becoming a truly networked campus. The transformation of teaching and learning extended to every discipline and class, as well as the way the university did its business outside the classroom. UWEC decided to emphasize its liberal arts heritage with its newly redefined curriculum, even as it accepted the redefinition of faculty scholarship to consist, in large measure, of collaborative work with undergraduate students. In both the collective work behind the Redefinition of the Baccalaureate and in the collective work behind Design for Diversity, UWEC learned a lesson the chancellor and provost could lead, but also needed the cooperative help and work of all faculty and staff. Academic leadership consisted of conversation and motivation of talented people in support of agreed-upon goals.

Measured Excellence in the New Century

New buildings, changing leadership, and increased external recognition for its achievements characterized the first fifteen years of the twenty-first century at UW–Eau Claire.

At the same time, the campus struggled with difficult problems, some of which had occurred regularly since 1916 and some of which emerged from the transformation of the university in the 1950s and 1960s. Public financial support for UWEC declined sharply, as it also had at points in the past, but now the administration turned to students to fill the gap from lost state appropriations. Critics continued to be concerned about student behavior and academic commitment, but in the context of the student freedoms gained in the 1960s and 1970s the administration now had to use suasion more than the authority of *in loco parentis* to address these issues. Off-campus events had fearful implications, as there had been previously with the flu epidemic of 1918, World War II, and the war in Southeast Asia, but now the campus was much larger, more diverse, and less of the cohesive community it had been at the time of these previous threats. Despite—or perhaps because of—these challenges, UW–Eau Claire ended its first century with an enhanced commitment to excellence.

Years of Living Fearfully, 2001–04
On the second day of the second week of classes at UW–Eau Claire in 2001, hijacked airplanes hit the World Trade Center in New York City and the Pentagon in Arlington, Virginia, and crashed into a field in western Pennsylvania. News spread rapidly on campus about the horrors unleashed by these attacks. Some instructors suspended classes; others used their networked classrooms with their students to follow events via television and the Internet. The most visible person on campus that day was Chancellor Donald Mash. He walked around the campus, talking and listening to students and giving them comfort. Later that week, Mash led a memorial service on the footbridge in which students, faculty, staff, and community members dropped roses into the Chippewa River in memory of those killed.

A sense of shock and then unity on campus soon gave way to feelings of uncertainty, edginess, and even fear. Just days after the 9/11 attacks, the Federal Bureau of Investigation took an interest in the Eau Claire campus when it learned seventy-four Kuwaiti men had come to the university in the summer of 2001. While enrolled in an English language program, some took flight-training lessons at the Chippewa Valley Regional Airport. Were these men still in the United States, waiting to launch a second strike of terrorist attacks? UWEC did its own investigation and learned the Kuwaiti students were not enrolled at UWEC, but rather were students of a language program run by a Massachusetts for-profit school.

To augment revenue, the university had rented Horan Hall to the school, much as it did other facilities to similar enterprises. That practice ended after 9/11. The FBI never developed any information the Kuwaitis were anything other than students seeking to learn English.

The 9/11 attacks represented only the most bloody and deadly of strikes by the terrorist group Al-Qaeda on Western targets. During the next few years, bombings in Bali, Indonesia, the London Underground, and especially the Madrid commuter railway system killed hundreds of innocent people. UWEC students studying abroad could be at risk from terrorist attacks. Spanish majors and minors studying at Eau Claire's exchange campus in Valladolid, Spain, directly experienced the March 11, 2004, bombings. None of them were harmed in the attacks, but students regularly took the same commuter trains into Madrid on expeditions. As exchange student Anna Jackson commented, "You feel like it could have been you on that train."

Later in the fall of 2001, a seemingly random group of journalists and elected officials around the United States received a spate of envelopes and packages which contained the deadly bacteria anthrax. On campus, the chancellor's office unexpectedly received a suspicious package from an unrecognized return address in Iran. University and Eau Claire Police removed the package, opened it remotely, and observed a white powder, but soon identified it as harmless and definitely not weaponized anthrax. Still, the anthrax scare in Schofield Hall brought home, once again, the nearness of UWEC to what US President George W. Bush called the war on terror.

As part of this effort, in the fall of 2002, the Bush administration began active preparations for war in Iraq. Subsequently, for most of the next decade UWEC students served in Iraq and Afghanistan, many with reserve and National Guard units called to active duty for one-year deployments. One consequence of this pattern was that by 2014 about three hundred students were military veterans. Students also began to participate in the Reserve Officer Training Corps program. Beginning in 2005 they could enroll in UW–Stout's program and starting in 2009 they had their own unit, which quickly expanded from seventeen cadets initially to forty-five by 2011. By the middle of the following decade, about four graduating seniors per year earned army commissions. Although Staff and Faculty for Peace and Justice grumbled about the army's "don't-ask don't-tell" policy regarding sexual orientation, in contrast to the controversy in the early 1970s (chapter six) ROTC was quietly accepted on campus; by the 2000s regent policy and federal statutes precluded UW–Eau Claire faculty or administration from having any say about hosting ROTC.

Another scare proved all too deadly for students living on and off campus: meningitis. In November 2001, UWEC senior Amber Krenz complained of aches and a fever and was dead of meningitis by the evening of the following day. In April 2002, first-year student Sean Coleman felt the same symptoms, left his Horan Hall room to check in at nearby Sacred Heart Hospital, and died that same evening of meningitis. Coleman's death prompted sixty-five residents of Horan Hall to get the antibiotic Cipro as a preventive measure. The next fall, Sutherland Hall first-year student Adam Griggel contracted meningitis and had only minutes to live before his roommate rushed him to Sacred Heart, where quick treatment by medical staff saved his life.

Perhaps the saddest element of fear to sweep over the Eau Claire campus and other colleges and universities in the upper Midwest was the unexplained disappearance of a number of students, mainly men. Students from the University of Minnesota and Saint John's University, as well as UWEC's own Michael Noll, disappeared without a trace around Halloween in 2002, leading some people to fear a serial killer was stalking students in Wisconsin and Minnesota. Friends reported seeing Noll leave a Water Street tavern on his twenty-second birthday, but thereafter, nobody could identify his whereabouts. The mystery of what became of Michael Noll lasted the entire winter. At the end of March, police found his body in Half Moon Lake. He had likely consumed too much alcohol on his birthday and stumbled and died of drowning, not foul play.

First-year Student Orientation, June 1996

The Phase I portion of new student orientation, jointly sponsored by the dean of students and academic and career services offices, was held in June and July and included a session encouraging alcohol awareness, which took the form of a skit performed by continuing students. Phase II of the orientation, when first-year students arrived on campus in the fall, was held in conjunction with CUBEfest (chapter nine).

Encouraging Alcohol Awareness

Fear and sadness about Michael Noll gave way to a renewed determination on the part of university officials to directly address the problem of alcohol abuse by UWEC students. University Police made a point of taking intoxicated students from residence halls to Sacred Heart's detoxification unit for treatment. Upon awakening and discharge from the hospital, students received a bill for services of $1,500. The dean of students office also began "Alcohol Awareness Week" in October, before Homecoming, in an attempt to educate students about the dangers of excessive alcohol consumption.

Most students were unimpressed with attempts to curb drinking. The annual Halloween gathering on State Street in Madison attracted tens of thousands of students from every UW campus, prompting system officials to begin a half-million dollar education campaign to teach responsibility in using alcohol. A *Spectator* editorial rebuked the regents, maintaining, "By enacting such a program at Eau Claire, the university very likely would squander money, on a hopeless cause . . . on top of the fact that a program like this would be an infringement on the rights of responsible adults." Here was one legacy of the 1960s student revolt against *in loco parentis*: no one was going to tell students, at least those twenty-one years and older, how to behave or how much to drink. The *Spectator* quoted students who said instructors told them the first day of class, "You are adults now and will be treated accordingly in this class." Many students believed adulthood included the right to "get hammered, get wasted" whenever they wanted.

The first step in addressing a problem with alcohol, say twelve-step program advocates, is to admit there is a problem. Survey research data compiled in the early 2000s showed UWEC had a problem with drinking. The university participated in the national "Core Alcohol and Drug Survey" of both legal and underage student alcohol use. Almost nine out of ten UWEC students of all ages responded they consumed alcohol at least once a month; 78 percent reported they had experienced a hangover after drinking while at college. More than three in five Blugolds surveyed reported they had engaged in binge drinking during the school year, so much so that a significant percentage of the binge drinkers were so incapacitated they missed class the next day, indicating that problem drinking at Eau Claire was not limited to Friday or Saturday nights.

The university decided to address problem drinking among students with a mix of advocacy, education, and enforcement. Student Senate President Adrian Klenz saw part of the problem as drink specials offered by Water Street taverns. Klenz made the round of taverns and asked for two changes. First, he asked tavern-keepers not to offer twenty-first birthday specials with free drinks to those coming of age. UWEC had already mourned one student in 1994 who died with a blood alcohol content of 0.34 on the night he turned twenty-one after consuming free birthday drinks at several Water Street locations.

Klenz also asked Water Street taverns to stop the Tuesday night "all you can drink" specials. The owners of the Brothers Tavern on Water Street agreed and asked their fellow barkeeps to follow suit. The Water Street Merchants Association and Student Senate cooperated on another measure. They put together a fund of almost $14,000 to pay for late-night bus transportation from Water Street and elsewhere in the city to campus, a service intended for students incapacitated by drink who might otherwise attempt to walk back to the residence halls and possibly stumble into the river.

Another area of concern was student (and alumni) drinking during Homecoming. For years, the Water Street Homecoming Parade had been marred by public drunkenness (chapter five). By the 1990s, Carson Park drew large crowds on Homecoming Saturday, but more for tailgating in the parking lot than for attendance at the football game. Eau Claire police and university officials sought to end the consumption of alcoholic beverages in the park and crack down on underage drinking by raiding house parties and issuing more citations to offenders. Those providing alcohol to minors received a fine of $435 and those underage who were consuming alcohol were fined $298 for a first offense.

The university received a $300,000 grant from the US Department of Education to address the problem of alcohol abuse among students. In return, in 2006 the university pledged to start a new Center for Alcohol Studies and Education (CASE). CASE committed itself to addressing the problem of first-year students drinking, as well as the problem of students driving while under the influence of alcohol. Among other actions, it decided to expand Alcohol Awareness Week in October to Alcohol Awareness Month. In 2011, with financial support from the Wisconsin Department of Transportation and the Student Senate, it facilitated the introduction of the Saturday Night Shuttle, a free bus that took students to entertainment venues around Eau Claire which would provide alternatives to drinking.

University officials and Student Senate leaders tried to address the problem with alcohol abuse, but the student body as a whole did not see itself as having a drinking problem. CASE's 2007 survey of two thousand students showed a comparatively low level of habitual cigarette smokers and marijuana smokers, 20 percent and 15 percent, respectively, but a high level of regular drinkers of alcohol—77 percent. Yet the same respondents denied there was much of a problem on campus. Only 11 percent said alcohol abuse was extreme or even a serious problem at UWEC, while 89 percent said there was either no problem at all, or at most, a moderate problem. Two out of three students reported no effect on their classroom activities from alcohol abuse, either on their own part or on the part of fellow classmates not living up to group responsibilities.

In sum, the survey research from the period after 2000 showed an increasing problem with alcohol abuse among Eau Claire students, yet the same survey research showed the student body did not believe anything needed to change. The older discourse of rights trumped the newer language of addiction, therapy, and treatment. Individual students could not understand what seemed to them to be a witch hunt for alcohol users. An underage student-drinker expressed outrage at receiving a misdemeanor citation in 2004 for drinking alcohol from an open container. "Having an open container is not endangering anybody," he said. "You have a right to have any beverage in your hand."

New Directions in Schofield Hall, 1998–2016

When Donald Mash became chancellor at UW–Eau Claire after a successful ten-year presidency at Wayne State College in Nebraska, he brought with him a trusted business affairs vice president, Andrew Soll. For the most part, however, Mash developed his leadership team from within UWEC. One of the first tasks he faced in 1998–99 was organizing a search for a new provost and vice chancellor of academic affairs. Instead of selecting an external candidate, as every provost had been since John Morris, Mash picked an insider, Ronald Satz, dean of the hybrid College of Professional Studies, which included the Schools of Nursing, Education, and Human Sciences and Services.

Mash and Satz moved to revise Chancellor Larry Schnack's 1995 reorganization of the university which had consolidated the five existing schools into three colleges. Although Mash later reflected, "I didn't come to reverse controversial decisions," he also found Schnack's decision to downgrade the status of nursing was a "gnawing issue . . . that thing never went away." After much study, Mash asked the University Senate to create a College of Nursing with its own dean, and in 2004 the Senate approved the proposal. However, the revision to the reorganization of academic affairs stopped short of bringing back the graduate school as its own college. Instead, Satz took on the responsibilities for graduate studies into his office, delegating supervision to an associate vice chancellor for academic affairs, initially computer science professor Andrew T. Phillips.

Mash's policies also recreated a top position for student affairs, which had been void since Schnack fired Elliott Garb in 1994 (chapter eight). Mash first established within student affairs a new position of associate vice chancellor for student development and diversity, and in the spring of 2003 hired Kimberly Barrett for that post. After Barrett left UWEC in 2007, Mash's successor expanded the responsibilities of the position and in 2008 named Beth A. Hellwig as vice chancellor for student affairs and dean of students.

Mash soon recognized he needed a strong leader as head of university development and president of the UW–Eau Claire Foundation. He eventually found the right person already worked in his office: Carole Halberg, his special assistant and former director of alumni relations. Mash promoted Halberg to be president of the foundation, and more specifically, to oversee the much-anticipated capital campaign, which had a goal of raising $35 million to support initiatives such as student scholarships, smaller focused classes for first-year students, and enhanced faculty-student research collaboration. With the help of a new development director, Kimera K. Way, Halberg brought Mash's capital campaign, dubbed Fulfilling the Promise of Excellence, to a highly successful close, raising over $50 million.

In addition to overseeing the capital campaign, Mash in 2003 supervised the design of a campus facilities master plan which called for $150 million in capital improvements. The plan proposed upgrades to Phillips Hall, especially, and also to Schneider Hall, McPhee Physical Education Center, and Haas Fine Arts Center. The most dramatic change Mash called for was the demolition of Kjer Theater and the adjoining Campus School building and their replacement with a new academic building for the College of Education and Human Services and the Department of Psychology.

The stability of campus leadership that Mash, Satz, and Halberg brought to UWEC came to an end in 2004 and 2005. UW System President Katherine Lyall announced her retirement in January 2004, leading to speculation that Mash would be a candidate to replace her at the head of the system. Local assemblyman Republican Robin Kreibich, chair of the Assembly Higher Education Committee, talked up a Mash presidency, but the chancellor took himself out of the running. Soon enough, Lyall's replacement, Kevin Reilly, asked Mash to join him as system executive vice president. The chance to help Reilly proved too intriguing and Mash announced his departure from UWEC in February 2005. A retired provost from UW–Oshkosh, who was also a one-time faculty member and dean at Eau Claire, Vicki Lord Larson, accepted the interim chancellor's post at UWEC for three semesters until the university could find a permanent chancellor.

Donald Mash and Student Telefund Volunteer, c. 2000

Chancellor Mash tried to have close personal interactions with students, in this instance by working together on the Fulfilling the Promise of Excellence *campaign.*

Late in 2003, Satz developed a life-threatening disease, one he battled until his death in 2006. Beginning in May 2004, Associate Vice Chancellor Steven Tallant oversaw academic affairs on an interim basis. Meanwhile, a chancellor's search in 2005–06 again led to an outside hire, Brian Levin-Stankevich, the interim president at Eastern Washington University. Levin-Stankevich kept Tallant as his interim and then permanent provost, but after a year, the latter left for the presidency at Texas A&M–Kingsville. In 2007 Halberg also left the university for a new challenge, leading the St. Mary's Hospital Foundation in Madison.

When she was system president, Katherine Lyall took pride in hiring chancellors and provosts for UW campuses who stayed for at least a decade. In the twenty-first century, however, UWEC experienced leadership turnover in its chancellors at a more rapid rate, in fact, more often than the national norm of seven years on the job. As chancellors came and went, so too did their key staff in student affairs, academic affairs, business affairs, and development. Starting in 1998, the UW System encouraged all UW campuses to hire national personnel consultants to work with chancellor search committees. Consequently, the same consultants who sought out candidates might, a few years later, come back and tempt the successful candidate with news of another presidential vacancy. That was the experience of Levin-Stankevich. After four years, recruiters sought him out for a private college presidency in Hawaii, which he pursued but did not get; in his sixth year at Eau Claire, he landed such a job at Westminster College in Utah and at nearly triple the salary paid him to head UWEC. After another year of interim leadership by Gilles Bousquet, James C. Schmidt, from Winona State University in Minnesota, succeeded Levin-Stankevich as UWEC chancellor in the summer of 2013.

Chancellor Brian Levin-Stankevich Inauguration, October 2006

MEASURED EXCELLENCE IN THE NEW CENTURY   245

Inauguration of Chancellor James C. Schmidt, November 8, 2013

Chancellor Schmidt is watching a performance of the Blugold Marching Band from the balcony of the new Davies Center. In the foreground is Vice Chancellor for Student Affairs Beth Hellwig.

Faculty and other administrators on campus found the comparatively rapid turnover of chancellors, provosts, and associate vice chancellors "very disruptive," as one faculty member put it. Another said that in a career as a unit head for fifteen years at the university, he had worked for five different chancellors, four provosts, and four associate vice chancellors, some of whom had held only interim appointments. UWEC lost its top leaders for a mix of reasons, including relatively low pay compared to other states and the need to struggle with the budget cutting that was seemingly part of every biennium. To the dismay of long-time UWEC faculty and staff, in the twenty-first century the chancellor's job at UW–Eau Claire seemed to have become a steppingstone for the ambitious, not the capstone of a successful career. "Because they start looking for another, higher-paying position as soon as they arrive on campus, they have no incentive and zero commitment to appreciating the culture of a campus, bonding with the long-term faculty, and understanding an institution's unique place in the wider world," observed Brady Foust, who retired as professor of geography in 2009. Looking back fondly to the era of Haas, Hibbard, Morris, and Schnack, Foust believed, "The best deans, provosts and chancellors come directly from the faculty . . . and return to the teaching faculty."

In contrast to the turnover in Schofield Hall, the university governance body, the University Senate, showed remarkable stability during the Mash and Levin-Stankevich chancellorships. The same person, computer science (and later mathematics) professor Susan Harrison, chaired the Senate from 1998 to 2013 and also served as UWEC faculty representative to the UW System from 1998 to 2005; Andrea Gapko, Senate vice chair and director of the Academic Skills Center, supplemented Harrison's leadership. Psychology professor Barbara Lozar, a Senate chair during the 1980s, subsequently led the Senate's important Academic Policies Committee for many years. Judith A. Blackstone, a psychologist who worked in counselling services, served as academic staff representative to the UW System during the Mash and Levin-Stankevich years, while computer science professor Michael R. Wick (a second-generation faculty member) led the Senate Compensation Committee. The institutional memory and expertise of these long-serving faculty and staff helped new chancellors, provosts, and deans understand what Levin-Stankevich called the student-focused "Eau Claire Way."

Paying for College

Wisconsin's budget for 1999–2001 was the last in which the UW System received a generous increase in appropriations from the state. What followed was one difficult budget after another, sometimes for macro-economic reasons when state revenues dropped due to international economic conditions and sometimes when legislators decided to make other spending choices higher priorities. Republican

Governor Scott McCallum used his line-item veto both to cut the system's budget in the 2001–03 biennium and also to raise tuition on out-of-state students. The McCallum budget pushed funding at UWEC down to a ratio of 60 percent from state revenues to 40 percent from tuition revenues. Matters only got worse in the second year of that biennium as the state faced a billion dollar shortfall. In early March 2002, the governor proposed to cut the system's budget by about $50 million and the legislature threatened to cut another $50 million, with UWEC bearing $5 million of that reduction. The UW System responded with a hiring freeze, and more ominously for high school students, a freeze on new admissions. Students who had expected to attend UWEC but who had not yet completed their applications for the fall term were shut out. Reassured that cuts would not exceed what McCallum had proposed, the regents lifted the freeze on admissions in late March, but maintained a hiring freeze.

The McCallum budget cuts were severe, but not as severe as what followed in the first of Democrat Governor James Doyle's two terms. The new governor-elect learned in late November 2002 that the state faced a projected budget deficit of at least $2.6 billion, a figure which kept rising in the weeks after he took office in January 2003. The governor proposed and the legislature enacted a quarter-billion-dollar cut to the UW System in 2003–05, with UWEC absorbing $12.5 million of the reduction. The university cut faculty and staff positions, extended the hiring freeze, and enacted other cost-saving measures. The doors stayed open and the lights remained on only through the largest pair of tuition increases in the history of the system: 16 percent the first year and 17 percent the second year. Doyle's second biennial budget, for 2005–07, also hit the UW System with more cuts and students with more tuition raises.

In this fiscal atmosphere, UW–Eau Claire increasingly relied on instructional academic staff, rather than faculty, to lead its classrooms, which had become common practice throughout American higher education. In 2008, the university enrolled 3 percent more students than it had in 1998, who were taught by 3 percent fewer teachers. The proportion of the teaching staff which was academic staff, at the same time, had risen from 18 to 28 percent. Academic staff earned lower salaries than faculty and usually taught twelve to fifteen credit hours per semester, in contrast to the nine hours generally taught by faculty members, thereby offsetting the overall loss in teaching positions.

Fiscal austerity also meant there was little opportunity for UWEC to add academic programs. Exceptions were where the programs could be directly linked to regional economic development. The most significant example was materials sciences. A Material Sciences Center was initiated in 2004, a major was introduced in 2008, and a separate program within Arts and Sciences was established in 2012.

Governor Doyle said he did not like to see tuition raised, on the one hand, but on the other hand he argued the state was in crisis. Furthermore, he regarded the UW System's tuition levels as still below those of neighboring states. The old debate about who should pay for college was decisively decided in the Doyle administration: students and their families should pay as they were the main beneficiaries of a UW education. The governor did try to make the tuition raises less harmful to low-income students with an increase in state student aid. Nevertheless, by his second budget, Doyle had pushed the ratio of state dollars to tuition dollars below the 50–50 mark.

In the new language of higher education, UW–Eau Claire was no longer a state university but a state-supported one, or a "public purposes" university, as Chancellor Levin-Stankevich termed it. Yet the university did not get the flexibility it sought to control its spending and revenues. As the legislature expended less and less on UWEC and other UW institutions, it sought to attach more and more strings to their operation.

The recovery in the business cycle during Doyle's second term allowed some increase in state support for the UW System, but not to the extent of restoring the base budget that had existed before 2001. In any event, the recovery was short lived as the state faced yet another multi-billion-dollar shortfall in the wake of the economic crisis of 2008–09. The Republican governor elected in 2010, Scott Walker, responded with a proposed quarter-billion-dollar cut to the UW System in his executive budget submitted in February 2011. UWEC eventually took a hit in the form of an almost $10 million reduction in its state appropriation for 2011–13.

Blugolds—Democrats or Republicans?

In 1971 the adoption of the Twenty-sixth Amendment to the US Constitution empowered eighteen- to twenty-year-olds to vote. Like all young Americans, UW–Eau Claire students subsequently became, in the language of campaign strategists, "persuadables" who were more likely than other voters to swing between Republican and Democratic candidates. The actual choices UWEC students made in presidential elections in the late twentieth century can be identified more precisely, although still imperfectly, than those they made earlier in the century (chapters three through five) because beginning in 1972 at least one voting ward in Eau Claire consisted exclusively of residence hall inhabitants.

In the presidential election of 1972, Democrat George McGovern opposed the war in Southeast Asia and challenged incumbent Republican, President Richard M. Nixon. McGovern had some appeal among UWEC students, but as their overall moderation during the anti-war protests of the late 1960s and early 1970s (chapter six) would suggest, they were not overwhelmingly enthusiastic about the senator from South Dakota. Just over half of UWEC students voted for him, which was better to be sure than the 38 percent he won nationwide, but not as well as he did in the city of Eau Claire as a whole. As at UWEC, nationwide the college student vote split evenly, much to the disappointment of McGovern strategists, who had counted on a wave of newly enfranchised idealistic voters to support their candidate.

Later in the 1970s, UWEC student voting preferences turned sharply to the right. In 1976 the Republican incumbent, President Gerald Ford, captured over two-thirds of the student vote in his race against Jimmy Carter, even as he lost statewide and nationwide. The results of this election showed the largest deviation by the student vote from the statewide vote for any presidential election after World War II. Carter campaigned in Eau Claire on October 11, but perhaps sensing student opinion about him, did not visit the campus. The *Spectator* criticized him for this; the paper also ran a highly negative cartoon representing Carter as a tool of big labor. Were students put off by the moralistic Carter, from the South, who appealed strongly to rural voters, in comparison to an ex-football player from the Midwest with college-aged children who admitted to smoking marijuana?

During the 1980s, UWEC students joined eighteen to twenty-nine year olds nationwide in trending Republican. In the presidential election of 1980, they again rejected Carter, preferring challenger Ronald Reagan. In 1984, ignoring the *Spectator*'s endorsement of his opponent, former vice president Walter Mondale, almost two-thirds of them backed Reagan's reelection, far exceeding his margins statewide and nationwide. Student Michael Lillybald explained he supported Reagan because the president's policies had enabled corporations to expand and "sprinkle money down to the poor through job opportunities," in contrast to Mondale who promised "welfare" programs for the "low-middle class" financed by tax increases. The level of support for Reagan at Eau Claire was similar to what he received in student wards at UW–Oshkosh and UW–Platteville, but Mondale won by a similar landslide among UW–Madison students.

Beginning with the 1988 election, however, UWEC students supported Democratic candidates for president. By growing margins across time, their percentage Democratic exceeded the statewide percentage Democratic, reaching 68 percent for Barack Obama in 2008. Younger voters generally trended Democratic in the early twenty-first century, but the Obama margin among UWEC students exceeded his margin among eighteen to twenty-nine year olds in Wisconsin (64 percent) and nationwide (61 percent). Buoyed by a fiery campaign speech from Vice President Al Gore to a packed audience in Zorn Arena, students supported Obama's reelection in 2012 by a 63–37 percent margin.

Students Registering to Vote, Davies Center, Election Day, November 2, 1976

On the whole, however, by the 2010s UWEC students were not strongly progressive in their politics. Not only did support for Obama drop between 2008 and 2012, but at 63 percent it was about at the level of all unmarried voters (66 percent nationwide, 63 percent in Wisconsin) and eighteen to twenty-nine year olds (62 percent nationwide and 60 percent in Wisconsin). A high level of support for Obama would also have been expected due the fact over 60 percent of UWEC students were women, a group which voted 10 percentage points more for Obama than it did for Republican Mitt Romney. Furthermore, in the 2014 gubernatorial election, in which the budget cuts for the UW System instituted by Governor Scott Walker were a major issue in his reelection campaign, only 53 percent of students supported Democratic challenger Mary Burke, less than the 55 percent level of support she received in the city of Eau Claire. In addition, based on surveys of students, the website Niche.com ranked UWEC as the third-most conservative politically of the twelve UW System campuses and 248th of 880 campuses nationwide.

By the early twenty-first century, Wisconsin had become a "purple" state, in which election results largely depended on the level of turnout. The same pattern held with on-campus elections, which showed conservative and progressive threads competed for student support. For decades, the Student Senate had been dominated by conservatives, who waged an ongoing struggle with the more progressive United Council of University of Wisconsin Students, a statewide umbrella organization initiated in 1960 by Wisconsin State College student governments, which by 2011 represented students on twenty of the twenty-six UW campuses. Following the policy adopted in 1980 by the regents, UWEC students had reaffirmed membership in the United Council by a 2–1 margin in 2011 in a referendum in which almost two thousand voted. The Student Senate, however, elected in a poll in which fewer than five hundred students had voted, took the lead in persuading the legislature, under Republican control following the 2010 election, to override the regents' policy and eliminate referenda as an option in determining campus affiliation with the United Council. The Senate then voted in early 2013 to disassociate UWEC from the United Council. However they voted in state and national elections, UWEC students now had only a conservative voice directly speaking for them.

Barack Obama Rally, Zorn Arena, February 16, 2008

In the key Wisconsin Democratic presidential primary on February 19, Senator Obama defeated former Senator Hillary Clinton by 64 percent to 35 percent in Eau Claire County, far exceeding his statewide margin.

With declining state support for higher education, a seemingly permanent feature of fiscal life, the UW System reached the breaking point in 2011. UW–Madison's chancellor, Carolyn "Biddy" Martin, proposed—ultimately unsuccessfully—dissolving the UW System with the Madison campus going its own way as an independent state-supported institution. UWEC also had to ponder its fate. Perhaps, as Levin-Stankevich mused, the university was better off as a stand-alone, state-supported institution with its own governing board and its own autonomy. Levin-Stankevich saw the problem in stark terms: either Eau Claire would be "allowed to soar and be given the freedom to do that" or it would be beaten down by limits, cuts, and restrictions and become a "McUniversity" indistinguishable from any other public regional comprehensive institution. Reflecting in 2012, he thought the culture of excellence that made UWEC distinctive was at risk from the "broken funding model" of Wisconsin higher education.

The answer to the financial crisis was the university would have to turn even more to its students to pay for excellence. The differential tuition implemented in the 1990s (chapter nine) gradually drifted up in five or ten dollar increments to $100 a semester by 2002. The biggest expenditure of these dollars supported faculty-student collaborative research projects. Early in his administration Mash sought to convince Student Senate leaders to approve an expanded differential tuition. This proved a difficult sell, however.

Shortly after Levin-Stankevich assumed Eau Claire's chancellorship, UW–La Crosse began implementing its part of the UW System's "Growth and Access Agenda" to increase enrollment. Their agenda included a tuition differential of $1,320 per student per year, yielding an expected extra $15 million in revenue. During that same year UW–La Crosse wrapped up its capital campaign to raise $35 million. Observing the success of the competition, Levin-Stankevich decided UWEC had to seek its own differential tuition. First he worked with the faculty and academic staff to produce a strategic centennial plan that emphasized student learning and success. Of its seven goals, the plan's first three focused on "fostering purposeful learning, connected learning, and global learning."

The chancellor next went to the Student Senate and proposed a differential tuition, dubbed the "Blugold Commitment," the proceeds of which were to be spent on more financial aid for needy students, more hiring of faculty to teach more sections of key courses, and more money to support high-impact practices. Levin-Stankevich left the exact amount of the differential tuition rise to the student senators: the more they sought in enhancements, the more they should pay. With a student body of about 11,000, spending on those enhancements would start at $11 million and go as high as $27 million, based on a range of $1,000 to $2,500 per student per year.

The Student Senate debated Levin-Stankevich's differential tuition during the fall of 2009 and decided to ask the student body to vote on the idea via an online referendum. More than three thousand students, a record number, participated and by better than a 2–1 margin rejected the idea. Student referenda at UW–La Crosse and UW–Madison had also resulted in similar rejections, in UW–Madison's case by a 4–1 margin. Nonetheless, student senates voted to accept differential tuition at UWEC by a narrow 17–15 vote in December 2009. The regents quickly accepted the Student Senate vote and the Blugold Commitment went into effect with the fall 2010 semester, starting with a $300 surcharge and building by an additional $300 per year to an expected level of $1,200 in 2013–14. Governor Walker, however, exercised a line-item veto in the 2013–15 budget that froze differential tuition at its 2012–13 level of $900. Still, $900 per student per year produced $10 million in revenue, almost 10 percent of the total the university received from the state and from tuition and academic fees. Among its other purposes, it funded more than thirty faculty positions.

On the eve of UWEC's centennial in the fall term of 2014, an in-state Blugold paid $8,750 in tuition and fees and an estimated $6,986 for room and board in a campus residence hall. Minnesota residents paid a somewhat higher tuition, based on the reciprocity formula their home state and Wisconsin maintained. Tuition for out-of-state residents not from Minnesota was more than double the in-state rate. In addition, the university advised prospective students they should expect to spend another $3,000 a year in transportation and other expenses.

A typical student, whether an in-state Wisconsinite or a Minnesotan, who graduated in four years could expect to spend at least $75,000 for the cost of a UWEC degree—except the student who graduated in four years was not at all typical of the twenty-first-century Blugold. Only about one-fourth of entering first-year students graduated four years later. To be sure, more than two-thirds of those who matriculated in 2007 graduated in six years, but that length of time could push the total costs of attending the university beyond $100,000 per student.

Students and their families increasingly depended on the federal government to finance their UWEC education and more and more from loans rather than from grants or work-study funds. For the 2014–15 academic year, students signed loan agreements to borrow $26 million. The overall student debt owed by Blugolds, those who graduated and those who did not, ran into the hundreds of millions of dollars. UWEC floated, in part, on student debt financed by the national government, which rose from $200 billion in 2000 to more than $1.3 trillion in 2014. One bright spot in funding student education at Eau Claire was in 2014 the UWEC Foundation granted more than $2 million in scholarships, in large part as a result of the highly successful capital campaign Mash launched and Levin-Stankevich completed.

Despite these benefits from the federal government and private largesse, UWEC faced even greater fiscal challenges in the 2015–17 biennium. Governor Walker proposed a budget which reduced the appropriation for the UW System by $300 million, even as all but a handful of other states were increasing spending on higher education. At UWEC, students took the lead in opposing these cuts by creating an on-line petition which attracted over thirty thousand signatures from around the United States. Katie Beaton, a 2014 UW–Eau Claire graduate, told the Joint Finance Committee at a public hearing, "By cutting funding . . . you are cutting life-defining experiences like mine." When finally adopted, the budget reduced general purpose revenue funding to UWEC for 2015–16 by $7.7 million, about 20 percent less than it had been in 2014–15. In contrast to the situation in 2003, furthermore, when there had also been steep cuts in state support, the legislature froze in-state tuition for the 2015–17 biennium. Consequently, due to attrition, buyouts, and layoffs UWEC's workforce had been cut by 15 percent by the fall of 2015. "The university doesn't deserve this cut," said Senator Luther Olsen, dissenting from the work of his fellow Republicans. "We are fools if we go around bashing one of the best things in the state of Wisconsin."

During the spring of 2015 the legislature did not agree to Governor Walker's proposal, which was strongly supported by Chancellor Schmidt and UW System President Ray Cross, to transform the system into an autonomous "public authority." To give the regents more flexibility, however, the legislature repealed the statutory provisions regarding tenure (which had existed for UWEC faculty since 1931) and shared governance (which had been worked out so laboriously at the time of the merger in 1973. "[P]eople who can leave, will," explained Geoff Peterson, political science chair and faculty representative to UW System, referring to his faculty colleagues. "And replacing them will be really challenging," he warned.

In contrast to the self-reinforcing "virtuous spiral" which had existed in Wisconsin in the quarter century after World War II (chapter five), in the first decades of the twenty-first century the Badger state seemed to have entered into a self-reinforcing downward spiral. Support for higher education declined: between 2002 and 2012 Wisconsin cut state higher education appropriations per student at three times the national rate, and the state fell below the national average to thirty-first place. The Pell Institute for the Study of Opportunity in Higher Education reported that, as a percentage of the average household income, state support for higher education in 2013 was one-third what it had been in 1974. Correspondingly, between 1990 and 2009 the proportion of Wisconsin's population aged twenty-five and over who had earned a college degree continued to lag the national average and did not grow as rapidly as it did in neighboring Illinois, Iowa, and—especially—Minnesota. Regarding the proportion of over-twenty-five year olds with an advanced degree, Wisconsin ranked thirty-fourth among the states. Probably in part because of the educational characteristics of its population, Wisconsin could not keep up economically. Median household income in the state fell by almost 15 percent between 2000 and

2015 to below the national average; Wisconsin had the largest decline in the nation in middle-class families (those earning between 67 and 200 percent of the state's median income). Families with declining incomes were understandably reluctant to support taxation to finance the UW System, continuing the downward cycle.

"Ranking" UW–Eau Claire

Chancellor Larry Schnack proudly posed for the photographer in 1996 holding a copy of *U.S. News and World Report*'s college-ranking issue, which named UWEC as among the top three regional public universities in the Midwest. His successor, Donald Mash, dealt annually with the release of the *U.S. News* rankings, as well as those of other organizations such as the *Princeton Review* and *Washington Monthly*. Each of these ranking schemes called upon the university to supply data in the form of admissions, retention, student body, and campus resources. Starting in 1990, Congress also required colleges and universities accepting student federal financial aid to publish statistics on college graduation rates and on-campus crime rates. By the time of the university's centennial, administrators had to begin planning for data submission to the US Department of Education's expected college affordability and effectiveness rankings. "Transparency" became the watchword for the university in measuring and then publicizing its operations.

At least Chancellors Mash or Levin-Stankevich or Schmidt did not have to read in a popular periodical that the university ranked among the top ten national party schools, unlike their counterparts at UW–Madison. Still, every year university officials responded to more and more such rating schemes, emphasizing some and downplaying others. *Princeton Review* hailed UW–Eau Claire as one of its "best value" colleges, a measure combining parsimony and excellence. In the more widely watched *U.S. News* rankings, however, UWEC began to change in position relative to its peers. The fact UW–La Crosse caught and passed UWEC in the rankings during the first decade of the century opened eyes across the state. Other UW comprehensive campuses also showed up on the same lists and on a par with UWEC.

The data on student academic achievement of incoming students at Eau Claire, however, did not show the university was slipping. Entering students in the early twenty-first century topped all previous matriculants in their academic profile. For example, the first-year class entering in the fall of 2003 had the highest median combined ACT score of any matriculating class (24.5), the highest percentage of students in the top 10 percent of their high school graduating class (23 percent), and the highest percentage of students in the top 30 percent of their high school graduating class (69 percent). This upswing came at a time when the university started growing after the experience with enrollment management in the late 1980s and early 1990s. In the fall of 2010, total enrollment was 11,413, 10 percent greater than what it had been in 1995 (enrollment across the system increased 17 percent during this period).

Some of that enrollment growth came because of the demographic echo of the baby boom, that is, the increase in the number of births each year borne by women who themselves were baby boomers.

Students displaying America's Best Colleges in 1998

This new generation, born after 1985, was soon dubbed the Millennial Generation. More and more millennials, like their baby boom parents, chose to attend college each year. As long as the millennials were numerous—the number of births in Wisconsin was stable between 1979 and 1990 and the number of high school graduates increased steadily until 2003—UWEC could be selective in admissions. When the post-Millennial Generation began to decline in numbers—births in Wisconsin fell 8 percent between 1991 and 1997 and the number of high school graduates correspondingly declined about 7 percent between 2008 and 2015—UWEC faced a challenge in continuing to recruit an excellent first-year class. Classes entering the university after 2010 did not quite match the academic background of Blugold millennials.

Adjustments to America in the Early Twenty-first Century

In one national ranking, UW–Eau Claire found itself with egg on its face—and its students in hot water with the law. The root of the problem was the same campus network that allowed faculty and students to access the Internet directly from the classroom also provided high-speed access to residence halls. In their residence hall computer labs students could, for example, access the new web-based online learning system Desire2Learn. Students could also surf the web for non-academic interests. In the spring of 2005, the social networking service called "The Facebook," recently developed by Harvard undergraduates Mark Zuckerberg and Chris Hughes, added UWEC as a participant. The *Spectator* reported more than 2,400 UW–Eau Claire students immediately signed up for accounts, and on campus the verb of the moment was "facebooking."

In addition to facebooking and accessing course materials and library databases, however, students used the Internet to download music files from so called peer-to-peer file-sharing sites. Such sites as Napster gave students access to tens of thousands of copyrighted songs at no price. That the residence halls were part of the campus fiber optic network (chapter nine) meant a student could download rapidly from the high-speed labs in the halls.

The trade group of the music business, the Recording Industry Association of America (RIAA), first went after the file-sharing site companies, but in 2006 and 2007 it began pursuing individuals it tracked from the sites, especially college students. RIAA sent letters to 473 UWEC students demanding they pay fines to settle charges of copyright violation. One stunned student had to pay $3,000 to satisfy RIAA. Students wrongly assumed anything they could access on the Internet was free; many learned the hard, expensive way that the copyright of music owners trumped any imagined student right to take without paying for somebody else's intellectual property. As with alcohol abuse, the university had to begin an educational campaign to teach its students, faculty, and staff to respect copyright.

The university may have been pleased it ranked so high as a "value" institution by the *Princeton Review*, but it was stung when it was sued on the grounds of suppressing "values," indeed constitutional rights, held by its students. The issue arose in the summer of 2005 when a resident hall assistant (RA), Lance Steiger, received a cease-and-desist letter from University Housing, telling him to stop holding Bible study meetings in his room in Horan Hall. University Housing explained that Steiger was both a student and an employee, and in his capacity as the latter, he could not use his place of work as a site to proselytize his religion. University Housing told Steiger he could hold Bible study outside of Horan, say in a Davies Center meeting room, but his doing so in the residence hall where he worked made students vulnerable to pressure to participate because of his supposed power over their lives.

Steiger did not accept University Housing's reasoning, especially when the office could not even provide him with a written policy statement on the matter. He sought help off campus from the Foundation for Individual Rights in Education (FIRE) and from the Alliance Defending Freedom (ADF). FIRE provided the publicity and ADF provided legal assistance to Steiger in filing a Section 440 ("other civil rights") violation complaint in federal district court. The lawsuit came at a particularly bad time for the UW System, more than for UWEC, as the system suffered from several personnel scandals on the UW–Madison campus that summer and fall.

The regents and Chancellor Lord Larson quickly came to terms with Steiger, settling the case by issuing a new written policy allowing RAs such as Steiger to hold Bible study in their dorms, so long as they did not coerce students to attend. That had never been the case with Steiger and he emerged from the contretemps having vindicated his constitutional right to free exercise of religion over the supposed rights of students on his Horan floor to be free of undue pressure from their RA. The individual complaints from RIAA and the institutional one from FIRE and ADF reflected the increased public scrutiny and criticism higher education came under in the twenty-first century, in large part due to the rising costs and to the rising federal expenditures for grants and guaranteed loans.

The Steiger incident reflected another national pattern in the late-twentieth and early-twenty-first centuries: the increasing influence of the Christian Right, whose followers asserted their freedoms were under assault by a secularized America. At UWEC, a growing number of students worshipped and participated in youth activities at conservative churches in the community. St. Mark Lutheran Church, for instance, which was affiliated with the conservative Wisconsin Evangelical Lutheran Church rather than the mainstream Evangelical Lutheran Church in America in which Leonard Haas had been active, organized a weekly Bible study in the Davies Center and provided Sunday morning bus transportation for students to attend its worship services.

On campus, student behavior reflected this shift in American religious practices. The United Campus Ministries, an arm of mainstream Protestant denominations, closed. Following the retirement in 2010 of the Reverend Donald Wisner, after twenty-one years of leadership, and the cessation of financial support from the National Lutheran Campus Ministry, the University Lutheran Church had to make due with a part-time pastor. Students at the Newman Community increasingly came from traditionalist home parishes, as beginning in the 1990s the Catholic hierarchy and younger clergy in Wisconsin reoriented their church in a conservative direction. These students were not always comfortable with the teachings and liturgical practices of long-time pastor Reverend George Szews and its long-time members from the community and university staff, who were committed to continuing in the direction set out by the Second Vatican Council. As an alternative to these long-standing campus religious institutions, students increasingly joined organizations such as the Campus Crusade for Christ, which started in 1999.

Evaluating and Demonstrating Success at UWEC

In the twenty-first century, American higher education came under criticism much in the way elementary and secondary education had in the 1980s (chapter eight). The US Secretary of Education, Margaret Spellings, appointed a commission in 2005 to investigate what she regarded as a failing post-secondary education system. The Spellings Commission report pointed to research findings from the National Assessment of Adult Literacy that showed a drop in the writing, reading, and math abilities of college graduates. The commission felt the completion of a college degree was insufficient: colleges and universities were failing the nation by graduating students not ready for the workforce, which imperiled the United States in global economic competition. A few years later, sociologists Richard Arum and Josipa Roska charged that at least for first-year students and sophomores, students in American colleges and universities learned very little because their instructors asked very little of them. In *Academically Adrift*, Arum and Roska challenged every college and university to examine how well it measured the inputs of student engagement, that is, the time students spent on studying and how much they took advantage of learning opportunities.

Well before the publication of the Spellings Commission report and of *Academically Adrift*, the Pew Charitable Trust established a regular study of what it called student engagement. Pew defined engagement in two ways, first by quantitative measures such as how much time students spent preparing for class and second by how many "enriching educational experiences" in which they partook . UWEC joined Pew's National Survey of Student Engagement in 2000 and every third year thereafter asked a random sample of its first-year and senior student to complete NSSE's questionnaire. UWEC's 2001 results showed two features: first, UWEC seniors both had higher levels of engagement than did respondents from peer institutions in and out of the UW System; second, first-year students in particular did not take advantage of enriching educational experiences such as faculty-student research, study abroad, and career-related internships, at least compared to peer institutions.

One attempt to engage entering students was the freshman seminar program begun under Provost Smelstor in 1996. About one-quarter of the money raised by differential tuition went to pay for these small seminars, capped at an enrollment of twenty so students would have a close relationship with a faculty member early in their careers. As part of its First Year Experience Program, by 2001–02 the university offered one hundred such seminars, reaching 85 percent of the entering class.

Student engagement programs cost money. Differential tuition was a start, but the Blugold Commitment, which went into effect in 2010 after acceptance by the Student Senate, provided many more dollars. These additional millions allowed administrators to hire more faculty in key parts of the curriculum and to fund more of what came to be called "high-impact practices." Provost Patricia Kleine began a competition to receive funding to enhance or develop such practices. Faculty and academic staff submitted more than one hundred proposals and the provost awarded sixty grants. University Research and Sponsored Programs also received almost $1 million per year to underwrite student-faculty collaborative research and creative activity projects. The First Year Experience Program, the Domestic Intercultural Immersion Experience Program, and the Seminar in Critical Reading and Writing also received generous support for their programs to engage students.

The university committed itself to providing every student with such an opportunity. Data from the 2014 NSSE showed almost half of first-year students took part in a high-impact practice. By the time they earned senior status, about 92 percent had taken part in at least one such practice.

For especially academically talented students, the opportunity to take part in high-impact practices made them competitive with graduates from the very best colleges in the country, most notably in receiving Rhodes Scholarships. Established by the estate of colonizer and imperialist Cecil Rhodes in Great Britain, the Rhodes Trust largely cleansed itself of racism and sexism and emerged as perhaps the premier international scholarship for American students. Thirty-two students receive a Rhodes each year, a number unchanged since 1903. For much of the history of the scholarships, Ivy League colleges and the service academies produced a large proportion of the select thirty-two. Over its first century, for example, Harvard graduates averaged more than three awards each year. Only about one-quarter of the scholarships went to graduates of public institutions other than the service academies. During this period, only a handful of Rhodes Scholarships went to graduates of former teachers colleges, and none to those in Wisconsin.

Charles L. Tomkovick, 2002

Tomkovick, a popular instructor, was a professor of marketing and management from 1992 to 2012. This photograph was taken at the dedication of the Hormel Foods Team Project Lab. Following Tomkovick's untimely death in 2013, the Chuck Tomkovick Excellence in Teaching Fund was established to support faculty-student collaborative research.

UWEC, however, cracked the list of Rhodes Scholars twice early in the twenty-first century, first with Chauncy Harris Jr. in 2005 and again in 2014 with Tayo Sanders II. Harris, an Eau Claire native, pursued a double major in geography and history. He attributed his success in gaining a scholarship to "the great relationships I have with faculty helped keep me challenged and allowed me to go beyond the work and experiences that are typical of college." He also had the benefit of mentoring from a namesake great uncle who had won the award in 1934. Harris chose to study Middle Eastern history and geography at Merton College, Oxford University. Sanders was a materials sciences major who continued his studies at Lincoln College, Oxford. A native of Kimberly,

MEASURED EXCELLENCE IN THE NEW CENTURY   255

Research Day, 1995

Left to right are Chancellor Larry Schnack, unidentified, and Provost Marjorie Smelster

he attributed his success to UWEC faculty members whom he said "are the individuals who have dedicated years of their lives to academic pursuits." Sanders called himself an example of the value of the high-impact practice-based curriculum at the university: "UWEC's emphasis on undergraduate research has also developed my ability to draw connections between material learned in my courses and their applications to the real world," he said.

Sanders was also among seven UWEC students who in April 2015 presented the fruits of their student-faculty collaborative research to state legislators and other leaders in the annual "Posters in the Rotunda" showcase at the state capitol in Madison. On campus, other students had the opportunity to share work they had done in collaboration with faculty members through posters and other means of presentation at the annual Celebration of Excellence in Research and Scholarly Activity. Beginning in 1992 as Research Day, over 350 students participated in CERCA in 2015.

Before receiving his Rhodes honor, in 2014 Sanders had won a Barry M. Goldwalter Scholarship, a prestigious national award for college sophomores and juniors majoring in science, mathematics, or engineering. The following year, two UWEC students—material science major Elizabeth Stubbs and geology major Sarah Knutson—were among just 260 nationwide Goldwalter Scholarship winners.

One of the science departments in the forefront of encouraging undergraduate academic success through faculty-student collaborative research was Chemistry. During the decade from 1999 to 2008, faculty members in this department published over 160 peer-reviewed papers or patents with over 125 student coauthors. Well prepared by this experience as undergraduate researchers, chemistry graduates went on to attend graduate or professional schools at high rates—over the forty-five-year period beginning in 1966, the National Science Foundation calculated UWEC had the highest rate of baccalaureate origin of PhD chemists among comprehensive universities in the upper Midwest. The regents recognized the quality of the Chemistry Department's work in 1993 by awarding it the initial UW System Departmental Teaching Award.

At the end of the twentieth and beginning of the twenty-first century, UWEC undergraduates also continued to shine as student-athletes. Lisa Stone took over as head women's basketball coach in 1988 and in some ways replicated Ken Anderson's success with the men's program (chapter eight). Her teams won conference titles in six of the next twelve years. Following the lead of other former Wisconsin state universities, UWEC left the National Association of Intercollegiate Athletics in 1994 and began to compete on the Division III level in the National Collegiate Athletic Association. In 1997, Stone's team was runner-up in the national NCAA Division III tournament. National titles did come to the Blugolds in men's golf in 2001, women's cross-country in 2009, men's hockey in 2013, men's cross-country in 2015, men's indoor track in 2015 and 2016, and—most dramatically—in softball on Jill Janke's walk-off home run in the title game in 2008. The focus of Blugold athletics, however, remained competition with traditional rivals within the exceptionally long-standing and cohesive Wisconsin State University Conference, which was retitled in 1997 as the Wisconsin Intercollegiate Athletic Conference. The WIAC continued to disdain athletic scholarships and in 2016 UWEC student-athletes in twenty-two sports collectively had GPAs well above the campus average.

Who was a Blugold and What Did They Learn?

In some ways, the university student body remained constant in its makeup from the 1990s. UWEC stayed predominantly female, with women students comprising 61 percent to 66 percent of entering classes. At the same time, the university continued to work at recruiting, retaining, and graduating minority students, and the percentage of students of color increased from 4 percent to 8 percent of the student body. The efforts were especially successful in recruiting students of Hispanic and Southeast Asian origin, but less so in attracting African American and American Indian students.

As part of its periodic overhauling of the 1965 Higher Education Act, Congress added a new category of "Title III" grants to strengthen institutions that served minority student populations, such as American Indian tribal colleges, historically black colleges and universities, and colleges with large numbers of students with financial need. UW–Eau Claire took advantage of these new federal programs to increase access by minority students and first-generation college students. Starting in 2000, the university won several US Department of Education "GEAR UP" (Gaining Educational Awareness and Readiness for Undergraduate Programs) grants to work with American Indian youth in middle school and high school to prepare them for college by having them spend time at UWEC. Toward the end of the decade, the university won a $1.75 million Title III grant to reform general education, part of a larger curricular reform initiated by the Centennial Strategic Plan.

Historic Schofield Hall

Since its construction in 1916, Schofield Hall—known as Old Main until 1960—has been at the center of UW–Eau Claire. A handsome Collegiate Gothic-style building designed by Henry Van Ryn and Gerrit Jacob DeGelleke, it earned a place on the National Register of Historic Places in 1983 for its historical significance (one of seventeen Van Ryn and DeGelleke buildings around the state that have been listed). The City of Eau Claire has also designated it as a Local Landmark, which restricts exterior alterations. Although there have been a few exterior changes, most have been sympathetic to its original design and appearance.

With its 650 seats, Schofield Auditorium has been the largest fixed-seating space on campus since 1916. For Eau Claire's first thirty years, the entire student body was able to gather there regularly for assemblies. The balcony served as a between-class study hall and site for mild flirtations. By the late 1950s, however, the auditorium—which had not been redecorated since 1930—began to appear shabby. President Davies wrote to Director McPhee, "We are ashamed to have the public see it." In 1958, Dean Haas proposed to Davies the construction of a new auditorium, encompassing all three levels of Schofield Hall, which would have seated more than 1,500. Perhaps because some of the proposed space was needed for other purposes, this large auditorium was never built, and instead the existing auditorium was redecorated in the early 1960s. Essentially unchanged for over forty years, it again appeared shabby by the first decade of the twenty-first century. Consequently, during 2011 there was a major restoration of the auditorium, provided by a partnership among the Student Senate, the UW–Eau Claire Foundation, University Centers, and the State of Wisconsin. While the basic appearance of the room would still be very familiar to Harvey Schofield, updated electrical and sound and video display systems, as well as new seats and carpeting, again made the auditorium an attractive place for performances by student groups and visiting artists.

Schofield, however, would recognize very little else of the interior of what he knew as Old Main. Indeed, he would probably become lost in it. Most space within the building has been reconstructed or repurposed at least three or four times since 1952. As Haas said in 1985, because of the solidity of its original construction, "It has proved to be a remarkably adaptive building for all purposes." In 2016, the women's room in the east corridor on the first floor is the only room with the same shape and purpose it had in 1952. There are still, however, some historical interior features evident in Schofield Hall. Some original window casings, hallway rails, and stairway woodwork remain. The stairway railing at the south door on the east side, for instance, still contains the small wooden squares Davies ordered installed in 1943 to prevent rambunctious army air force trainees from sliding down the railings. This railing is also inscribed with numerous carved initials of past generations of students. In addition, the terrazzo floor installed in 1921 is still in use in some corridors. The 1916 wood floor in what originally had been second-floor classrooms on the north side of the building was also exposed and refinished as part of the redecoration of the chancellor's personal office in 2012.

After the removal of the original 1959 Davies Center as part of campus reconstruction between 2011 and 2013, Schofield Hall appeared to regain size and dignity when it could be viewed without obstruction from the south and east. The building's relationship to Little Niagara Creek again became apparent. With the removal of the mid-century breezeway between Schofield Hall and the original Davies Center, viewers could now appreciate the stone trim and other features of the south entrance of Schofield Hall. Replacement windows installed in 2015–16 also restored the original look of paned windows. The new appearance of Schofield Hall illustrates the general point that it is possible for new construction, in this case the new Davies Center, if carefully planned, to enhance existing historic structures.

The university also increasingly recognized the differences that existed among its students. Chancellors Mash and Levin-Stankevich expanded the meaning of what came to be known as EDI (equity, diversity, inclusiveness). Mash spent a day on campus confined to a wheelchair to better understand the life of a disabled student, experiencing firsthand the barriers to access to academic buildings. Levin-Stankevich supported the expansion of programming for gay, lesbian, and transgendered students, making UWEC a more GLBTQ-friendly campus. The return of hundreds of student veterans from wars in Iraq and Afghanistan also changed the campus in significant ways. The provost convened a Veterans Advisory Council to listen to the academic needs of returning service personnel. The veterans services office was set up to advise veterans about state and federal programs that could benefit them. The university also provided space in Schofield Hall for a veterans center and supported a veterans club. Overall, shortly before he left UWEC in 2012, Levin-Stankevich observed, "I think the focus we have on diversity and inclusiveness is far more than when I first came."

From the mid-1970s to the mid-1980s, UWEC had the largest enrollment of any of the old Wisconsin State University campuses, and until 2004 it usually trailed only UW–Oshkosh. As a response to cuts in state support, however, and the Growth Agenda for Wisconsin policy adopted by the regents in the early 2000s, other UW campuses began a deliberate policy of increasing their undergraduate enrollment and funding operations through ever-higher tuition. By 2014, UW–Oshkosh reached nearly 14,000 students and UW–Stout, nearby to UWEC, had increased enrollment from less than 8,000 in 2004 to almost 9,300. After peaking above 11,400 in 2010, however, UW–Eau Claire's enrollment slipped back to about 10,600 in 2014. Whereas UWEC had enrolled more than 13 percent of the students in the comprehensive universities in the system in 1996, it enrolled only about 11.5 percent in 2014.

UWEC did not have the physical campus, especially in residence hall space, to serve a student body the size of UW–Oshkosh. Instead, UWEC decided in 2010 to increase the number of students it served, not by significantly increasing the size of the student body, but by retaining more of those who matriculated and by graduating a higher percentage of them in fewer years. In 2014, the university set a goal to increase the percentage of first-year students it retained from around 80 percent to closer to 90 percent. It further vowed to retain its sophomores as juniors at a higher rate, from 75 percent to 80 percent. The biggest planned change was to improve the four-year graduation rate from around 25 percent to 40 percent.

Professor Barbara Meier, 2014

Meier, who was appointed to the faculty in 2013, is shown teaching SPED 400, the course in special education required of all teaching majors. The Department of Special Education also offered graduate and undergraduate major programs and was proud of the near-universal placement rate of its graduates. The students in SPED 400 are sitting at tables, a common arrangement in courses in the College of Education.

Improving the university's four-year graduation rate also meant looking at the curriculum to identify why students took more than 120 credits and more than eight semesters to graduate. General education came under particular scrutiny as more of a roadblock to student success than a building block. Students did not understand the reasons behind the distribution model of GE, which could allow them to select one course from as many as a half-dozen different academic disciplines to meet a requirement. Students called such courses "generals" and mainly regarded them as something to be gotten out of the way before the more serious business of undertaking a major, especially one in the professions or pre-professions.

Chancellor Levin-Stankevich's Centennial Plan identified a need to re-invent general education. The Higher Learning Commission, the new title for the North Central Association, encouraged this work in its report which was part of re-accreditation of the university in 2010. The re-invention began with a new statement about what UWEC understood by the term "liberal education." The faculty defined it as something more than the academic disciplines of the liberal arts. Part of this effort was to educate students, their families, and the wider public that "liberal" was not a dirty word, or at least it was not to be confused with political liberalism. Instead, in 2008 the faculty postulated five goals of a liberally educated person, competencies students needed to demonstrate to earn an Eau Claire bachelor's degree. Students had to show: 1) they understood human culture and the natural world; 2) they engaged in critical and creative thinking; 3) they communicated effectively; 4) they took individual and social responsibility in their lives; and 5) they respected diversity among people.

In 2014, the faculty further refined the university's academic goals for students as knowledge, skills, responsibility, and the ability to integrate the three goals across disciplines. They identified specific outcomes for each goal. For example, regarding knowledge of the social sciences, the outcome of a student who "begins to evaluate basic characteristics of social activity and human behavior" exceeded the expected benchmark.

These newly identified goals and outcomes were the basis for a new set of university-wide liberal education requirements set to go into effect in the centennial year of 2016 and promised both to make progress toward the degree easier and at the same time make it more valuable to students. This new curriculum retained distribution requirements across academic disciplines, but also required students to engage in broad-based interdisciplinary learning and required them to integrate in-class and out-of-class activities.

The university's mission statement in 2016 proclaimed at its core, UWEC offered every student a "rigorous, intentional and experiential undergraduate liberal education for life and livelihood." In the tradition of the Haas and subsequent chancellorships, professional and graduate education would be built on Eau Claire's "proud tradition of liberal education." The question posed by NCA in 1989—was UWEC a liberal arts institution or a regional comprehensive university— was once again answered as first and foremost, a liberal arts university. Students would live and learn in diverse settings, on and off campus, and work at being inclusive. The university promised to supply "academic leadership in transforming liberal education" as part of its overall vision to become the "premier undergraduate learning community in the upper Midwest."

Blugold Marching Band, 2006

Under Director Randal Dickerson, the Blugold Marching Band increased from sixty members in 2000 to over three hundred in 2016.

The New Campus of the New Millennium

The physical plant on campus had changed little since the Allied Health Building (renamed Human Sciences and Services in 1995) opened on Water Street in 1981. Another two decades passed before the university opened Chancellors Hall on the upper campus. Posed on the edge of the bluff above the Chippewa River, on the outside Chancellors fits into the line of sight of Oak Ridge, Bridgeman, Sutherland, Governors, and Horan Halls. On the inside, however, it is a residence hall for a new generation and a new century. Instead of tiny, cramped single or double rooms, Chancellors features suites for four students, each suite having four bedrooms, a bathroom, a kitchen, and a living room. Chancellors offers returning students an attractive on-campus alternative to off-campus student housing.

As the university entered the twenty-first century, it faced major maintenance and renovation costs for buildings erected when William R. Davies and Leonard Haas had been presidents. The most pressing issue Donald Mash and Vice Chancellor Andrew Soll faced was the state of the student center—the inadequate, crumbling-in-places Davies Center. In 2001, Soll obtained an initial estimate of $8.5 million simply to keep Davies Center operating. Students would have to bear the costs through segregated fees. A second estimate in 2003 for upgrading and expanding the center came in at $33 million. Mash and Soll talked with student leaders about an alternative of building an entirely new center, at a cost they estimated at $36 million. Students were unenthusiastic about paying fees for a new building; a March 2003 student referendum went decisively against the idea with 1,435 opposed and just 386 in favor.

After Mash left the university, Interim Chancellor Vicki Lord Larson took up the issue of what to do with the Davies Center. She and Soll asked the Student Senate to call for another referendum on raising student-segregated fees to pay for renovations or to build a new student center. The vote in the fall of 2005 marked a big change: students did favor paying more for a better student union, but they wanted the existing Davies Center renovated and not a new building. In the spring 2006 semester, the new chancellor designate, Brian Levin-Stankevich, expressed his opinion, "We have to say, what do our facilities look like to a prospective student and are they going to select another university?"

Once in office in the summer of 2006, Levin-Stankevich signed off on a plan for a new student center, at a cost of $48 million, citing student support in the December 2005 referendum, as well as the need to change the appearance of the campus for the better. The regents approved his proposal in December. UWEC had joined in the so-called arms race of offering new amenities in student centers, although Eau Claire modestly omitted a climbing wall from the plans for the new center. Campus planners decided to move the site of the new student center about one hundred yards south of the old location and keep the old site as open space.

Last Day of School, May 18, 2012

A farewell for the vacant Campus School building was held in conjunction with the groundbreaking for the Education Building. Echoes of the voices of pupils across sixty years could be heard in rooms like the one shown in this photograph.

In 2003, Mash's Campus Master Planning Committee, chaired by Michael Rindo, a broadcast journalist who joined the university as executive director of communications in 2001, had proposed to knock down Campus School and in its place build a new home for the College of Education and other academic units. Consequently, the Children's Center, displaced from its home in the Campus School, moved to the former St. Bede's Monastery and Center on a 112-acre site three miles south of campus in the town of Washington, which the UWEC Foundation bought in 2011 and leased to the university. Longer-range planning envisioned replacing Brewer Hall and Kjer Theater and finding additional uses for the Priory, as St. Bede's was redesignated. In addition, in 2014 alumni John and Carolyn Sonnentag gave the university twenty-one acres, between Menomonie Street and the Chippewa River across from the entrance to Carson Park, as the site for a multi-purpose event center which would replace Zorn Arena.

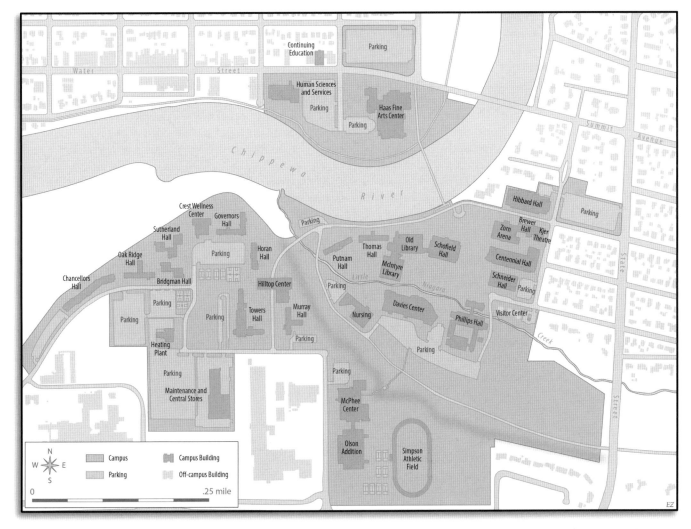

Securing funding for the Education Building took years of lobbying in Madison, in contrast to the student center which was financed with $125/semester in student fees. It was finally included in the 2011–13 biennial budget and opened in the spring of 2014 as Centennial Hall. The new construction gave the lower campus a different look with one quadrangle flanked by Schofield Hall, McIntyre Library, the new student center, Phillips Hall, and Schneider Hall and a second perpendicular quadrangle flanked by Schofield Hall, Schneider Hall, Centennial Hall, Zorn Arena, and the Chippewa River.

Students decided to keep the name Davies Center for the new center and many of the same names for meeting rooms, especially ones honoring American Indian tribes of Wisconsin. At the same time, campus planners decided to cut down the replacement Council Oak, which had been the symbol of the university since 1966 (chapters three and six), in order to accommodate the loading dock for the new center. American Indian students and faculty were outraged by the decision to turn the Council Oak into a few splinters which would be saved as a bench. Levin-Stankevich had to reverse the decision, even as it meant decreasing the size of the new Davies Center. He made the case clearly, "The Council Oak is important historically and culturally and we must treat it accordingly." Unfortunately, the construction of the new building necessitated the destruction of the four trees planted on May 8, 1970, to memorialize the four slain Kent State students (chapter six), but they were replaced in a commemoration ceremony on May 4, 2015, which was attended by about forty persons who had been present at the 1970 strike rally.

Map 10.1

The campus in 2016 included a new Davies Center, with the replanted Council Oak at one end, a new quadrangle with replanted tress in memory of the Kent State Four, and a new academic building for the College of Education and Human Sciences.

The Power of [And] as the Eau Claire Brand

During the spring 2014 semester, the university announced a new motto, or in the language of the day, it underwent a "rebranding," the first one in almost a half-century. Leonard Haas had established "excellence" as a durable motto. When Emily Hannah tried placing "Accepting the Challenge" on university stationery, pressure from the faculty made her modify it to "Accepting the Challenge of Excellence." Larry Schnack did not bother with a branding campaign. Donald Mash thought the public face of the university was of great importance, but more in the way of having a unified look in publications, both print and online. Brian Levin-Stankevich had used distinctive language "Gold Arrows" to implement the new strategic plan and "charrettes" to describe planning reviews. More comprehensively, James Schmidt and his leadership team decided in 2014 on the motto "The Power of [And]." Schmidt explained that students at UWEC could do more than one thing; for example, they could be "a scientist and a poet, a musician and a marketing guru, a nurse and a world traveler."

The Power of [And] motto drew a predictable amount of gentle ribbing and double entendres, but it was neither the chancellor nor a marketing guru who could best explain what it meant, but rather the student commencement speaker who found the words to describe the Power of [And]. Nicholas Schneider, a social work major, gave the Response of the Senior Class at the December 2014 commencement. He explained a UWEC education gave students on the one hand, knowledge, and on the other hand, relationships. Schneider told his graduating classmates, their families, the faculty, and the chancellor that the combination of knowledge and relationships "are the resources, the tools if you will that we have to flourish in our next leg of life's journey."

Seventy-five thousand UWEC graduates over the course of the first hundred years of the university's history could agree with Nicholas Schneider that there was a lot of power in knowledge gained at UWEC [and] relationships made at the university and continued through life.

Centennial Hall, 2014

The appearance of the lower campus changed dramatically between 2012 and 2014 with the construction of Centennial Hall and the reconstruction of the Davies Center. The stature of Schofield Hall could now be appreciated by unobstructed views from the south and east.

Where Are Blugolds Today?

About two-thirds of UW–Eau Claire alumni in 2016 live in Wisconsin. Reflecting the fact that the homes of first-year students increasingly come from beyond the "district" around Eau Claire, as the text discusses, they have chosen to work and live in all parts of the state.

Almost 20 percent of alumni live in Minnesota, a consequence of the growing number of enrollees from that state since the 1980s drawn to UW–Eau Claire by tuition reciprocity, as well as the attraction of job opportunities after graduation in the Twin Cities metropolitan area. Interestingly, perhaps showing their continued state loyalties, the strongest concentration of alumni within the Twin Cities metropolitan area is in St. Croix and Pierce Counties in western Wisconsin.

Map 10.2

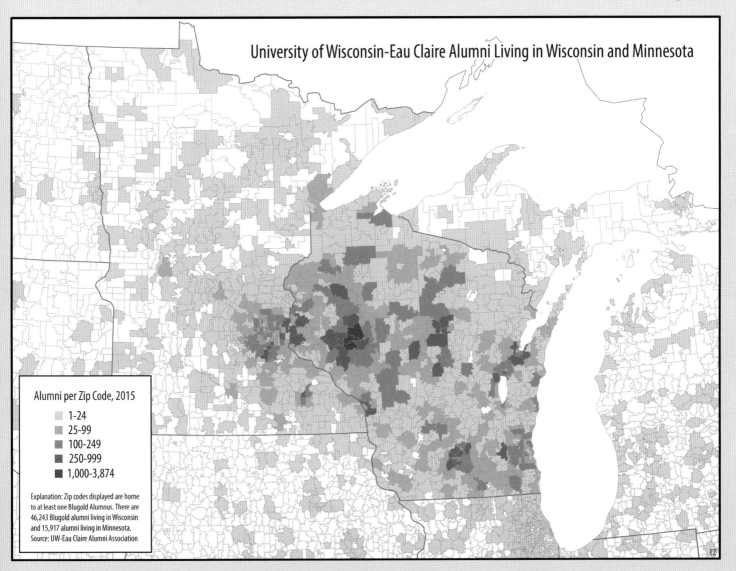

MEASURED EXCELLENCE IN THE NEW CENTURY

Acknowledgments

The University of Wisconsin–Eau Claire Foundation made the most important contribution to this book. Carole S. Halberg, then president of the foundation, conceived the project and her successor, Kimera K. Way, provided generous financial assistance for its execution and publication and gave the authors needed encouragement. Most importantly, neither she nor anyone else in the university administration interfered with its writing.

Director of Libraries John H. Pollitz generously provided accommodations in McIntyre Library for the project. Essential to our work was the assistance of the staff of the University Archives, part of the library's Special Collections and Archives Department. We give our thanks to University Archivist Greg Kocken, Assistant Archivist Lark Keating-Hadlock, and their student assistants, especially Jennifer Barth, who provided us with access to their well-organized collections and suggested profitable ways to use them. By arranging temporary transfers of materials through the Wisconsin Area Research Center network, they also facilitated our access to the collections of the Wisconsin Historical Society in Madison. Greg Kocken also assisted us with the selection and scanning of the photographs used in book. Unless otherwise indicated, all photos are from the University Archives.

Other UW–Eau Claire offices gave vital assistance to the project. The chancellor's office and the Office of Research and Sponsored Programs provided funds for undergraduate research assistants and transcribers. The History Department, led by Kate Lang, furnished services and supplies. Marty J. Wood, dean of the College of Arts and Sciences, arranged reduced teaching assignments for James Oberly to facilitate his research and writing.

Many other individuals also helped us. Emily Hannah and Katharine C. Lyall provided us with detailed email responses to our questions. Archivists at UW–River Falls, UW–Stevens Point, UW–Madison, Winona State University, and Bemidji State University answered our queries. On campus, helpful assistance came from John Bachmeier, Wayne Carroll, Bill Hoepner, Robin Leary, Timothy Peterman, Alex Smith, and the staff in the registrar, facilities management, and academic advising offices. Max Garland allowed us to quote from *For a Dedication by the River*. We are also especially grateful to alumni, faculty, and staff who gave us their oral histories.

Parts of the *Building Excellence: University of Wisconsin–Eau Claire, 1916–2016* have been presented at various forums on campus between 2013 and 2016 and at the 2013 Northern Great Plains History Conference. We are especially thankful to Chancellor James C. Schmidt for sponsoring the Chancellor's Centennial History Series. Jan Sloan and Suzanne Olsen of his office made the arrangements for these presentations. Some of them enabled us to learn from other UW–Eau Claire faculty and staff, including James E. Boulter, Erin K. Devlin, Kate Hale-Wilson, Greg Kocken, Karen Mumford, Gretchen Peters, Timothy A. Petermann, Alice Ridge, and their students who were working on university history-related projects. At all of these public forums, comments and questions helped us to format and sharpen this book's argument.

Ezra J. Zeitler suggested ways our book could be enhanced by cartography and carefully prepared the resulting maps. Martin Goetti and Emily Christenson assisted him.

Parts of the book have been read in typescript by Charles R. Bauer, Mary Canales, Rodd Freitag, Deborah M. Gough, Sarah Harder, Susan Harrison, Greg Kocken, Katharine C. Lyall, John W. W. Mann, Ronald E. Mickel, Joan Rohr Myers, Kathleen M. Mitchell, Teresa E. O'Halloran, Jane Pederson, and Alan J. Rieck. Their editorial and substantive suggestions assisted us greatly. Anne Burns of the Donning Company did yeoman work in editing the typescript into a book. We alone, of course, remain responsible for the factual details and the interpretations presented in our book.

A special word of appreciation goes to the late Richard P. McCormick. He was teaching Robert Gough in a course in the fall of 1966 when he published *Rutgers: A Bicentennial History* (New Brunswick, 1966), which won the biennial book award of the American Association of State and Local History and helped to inspire Gough to become a historian. A half-century later, McCormick's book was one of the authors' models for a university history.

Bibliographical Note

A fully documented version of the *Building Excellence: University of Wisconsin–Eau Claire, 1916–2016*, with footnotes to the printed, oral, and electronic sources on which it is based, is available at the University Archives and Special Collections website. This website also contains other materials including features on some aspects of the university's history not included in this book.

This book builds on previous histories of UW–Eau Claire. Laura Sutherland, a long-time faculty member who retired in 1959, received the assignment to write the university's first history. Sutherland drafted a full-length typescript for publication as part of the university's Golden Jubilee and a chapter-length typescript for publication in a collection of essays which was intended to mark the centennial of Wisconsin normal schools in 1966 (both works are in the University Archives in 2016). Sutherland died before she could revise either of her works for publication. The task of chronicling the university's history fell to Hilda R. Carter, who beginning in 1965 worked in the university's public information office. Relying on Sutherland's work, but based on her own research in the primary sources, Carter's chapter-length history appeared in the belatedly published centennial volume in 1968, and with the assistance of a student, John R. Jenswold, she completed a full-length book, *The University of Wisconsin–Eau Claire: A History, 1916-1976* (Eau Claire, 1976) to mark the sixtieth anniversary of the university (Carter's research notes are part of the Hilda Carter Papers in the University Archives and the book can be found digitally at http://digital.library.wisc.edu/1711.dl/UW.UWECHist).

Sutherland's work was a careful compendium with numerous insights. It was also valuable for us because it has some characteristics of a primary source. For her part, Carter provided useful perspectives as an outsider to the university. She had spent the 1930s as a factotum on the staff of Harvard University as secretary to the Society of Fellows among other assignments, and then observed Eau Claire State for a quarter century as an active member of the Eau Claire community. Both Sutherland and Carter were very close to their subject, of course, and were careful about criticism of the institution and persons associated with it who were still living when they wrote.

Since 1976 there has been further work on the history of UW–Eau Claire. Numerous students in the capstone seminar for history majors chose to write papers on university-related topics. When we taught the seminar in 2011–12, the entire class focused on the history of the university. During 2012–14, several other students investigated university-related topics as independent study projects. Papers written since 2007 are available at Minds@UW (http://minds.wisconsin.edu). Paper versions of earlier ones are in the University Archives.

To put UW–Eau Claire into context, we especially depended on John R. Thelin, *A History of American Higher Education* (Baltimore, 2004) and, for the first half of the university's history, Roger L. Geiger, *The History of American Higher Education: Learning and Culture from the Founding to World War II* (Princeton, 2014). To understand its specific origins as a teacher education institution, we relied on Christine A. Ogren, *The American State Normal School: "An Instrument of Great Good"* (New York, 2005). For comparisons to other institutions in the UW System, the essays in Walker D. Wyman, ed., *History of the Wisconsin State Universities* (River Falls, 1968) were useful. There are also full-length studies of all the thirteen University of Wisconsin institutions other than Eau Claire. Especially important is *The University of Wisconsin—A History*, the first two volumes (Madison, 1949) by Merle Curti and Vernon Carstensen, and the second two (Madison, 1994, 1999) by E. David Cronon and John W. Jenkins. (A frank memoir by a Wisconsin teachers college president is E. H. Kleinspell, *In the Shadow: Reflections of a State College President* [River Falls, 1975]). Helpful on specific topics were two University of Wisconsin–Madison PhD dissertations: Ronald A. Smith, "From Normal School to State University: A History of the Wisconsin State University Conference" (1969), and William Harold Herrmann, "The Rise of the Public Normal School System in Wisconsin" (1953). Two landmark books which influenced our thinking about the history of student life are Helen Lefkowitz Horowitz, *Campus Life: Undergraduate Cultures from the End of the Eighteenth Century to the Present* (Chicago, 1987), and Donald O. Levine, *The American College and the Culture of Aspiration, 1915-1940* (Ithaca, 1987); the number and quality of studies on student life have grown immensely since the publication of these works. We got some ideas about how to write a university history from the essays in Marybeth Gasman, ed., *The History of U.S. Higher Education: Methods for Understanding the Past* (New York, 2010).

The primary-source foundation for this book is the collections in the University Archives, which are held in the Archives and Special Collections Department of McIntyre Library at UW–Eau Claire. The most important collection is the Office of the Chancellor Correspondence and Subject File, 1936–2001, which has 226 archival boxes. A smaller collection, Chancellor Miscellaneous Subject File, has some pre-1936 and other disparate material (one folder is marked "found in Mr. Davies' desk"). Beginning with the Dean of Instruction—Arthur J. Fox Papers, 1939–1948, the University Archives includes the records created by vice chancellors, assistant chancellors, deans, directors, academic departments, and other administrative units. Extremely important collections are the registrar's records, which extend back to 1910 and include pre-1936 reports and correspondence missing from the Chancellor's Correspondence, and enrollment statistics, 1916–63. There are also several collections of papers related to individual faculty members. The Bill Zorn Papers, 1925–1984, are essentially the records of the offices of the dean of men and of the director of athletics. The Sarah Harder Papers, 1970–2000, includes extensive materials related to gender issues during the 1980s and 1990s. The John Schneider Papers, 1928–1954, provide some insight into how Schneider taught history and sociology. The Howard Lutz Papers, 1951–1985, document Lutz's professional activities, such as with the American Association of University Professors. The Grace Walsh Papers, 1931–1988, include the records of the debate program and well as copies of the numerous off-campus public addresses given by Walsh. Some of the efforts of the faculty to organize itself are documented in the Association of University of Wisconsin Professionals Records, 1920–1974, at the Wisconsin Historical Society. From the perspective of student life, the Jeannette Gaffney Miller Collection, 1925–1930, in the University Archives provides rare insights.

More so than Carter and Jenswold, we also relied on archival records of UW–Eau Claire's governing boards and their members. The collection at the Wisconsin Historical Society, Board of Regents of State Universities Administrative Subject File, 1921–1973, has detailed records of the era in which Eugene R. McPhee was executive director. For the post-merger period, the Minutes of the Board of Regents for 1971 through 1991 can be found at www.uwdc.library.wisc.edu/collections/UWBoR and for 1991 through 2016 at www.wisconsin.edu/regents/meetingmaterials/. Especially rich collections for individuals were the Edward J. Dempsey Papers, 1916–1949, and University of Wisconsin System Presidents Records, 1971–2002, particularly for Robert O'Neil. Both are at the Wisconsin Historical Society.

Oral histories made an important contribution to this study. Carter and Jenswold conducted about a dozen oral histories for their book; the tapes of some (and the transcript of Jenswold's interviews with Leonard Haas) are in the University Archives. Since 1976 the number of university-related oral histories has grown substantially. Most useful was *An Oral History of the University of Wisconsin-Eau Claire: A 75th Anniversary Publication,* compiled by Leonard C. Haas and Richard L. Pifer (Eau Claire, 1991). This is a collection of nineteen oral histories by UWEC faculty and administrators, the most important of which is by Haas himself—its transcription is about four hundred typed pages. Haas was obviously reading from carefully prepared notes, more so than responding to questions, so this oral history has many of the characteristics of an autobiography. It is the single-most important source for the history of UW–Eau Claire between 1932 and 1980, but of course it is also a deliberate effort by someone who was a trained historian to construct a history favorable to himself. In 2012, in preparation for *Building Excellence: University of Wisconsin–Eau Claire, 1916–2016*, students under our direction conducted about twenty-five oral histories of faculty and staff to complement the ones in the Haas and Pifer volume. Since 2013, UW–Eau Claire public history students under the supervision of professor Erin K. Devlin have interviewed more than fifty alumni from classes extending back to the 1940s. Between 2012 and 2014 Gough interviewed Chancellors Larry Schnack, Donald Mash, and Brian Levin-Stankevich and Interim Chancellors Vicki Lord-Larson and Gilles Bousquet. Together, transcriptions of these recent oral histories form the Centennial Oral History

Project in the University Archives. The transcript of a detailed oral history by Executive Director McPhee, conducted by Howard R. Fredricks in 1973, is also in the University Archives.

Until the 1960s the *Biennial Reports* and *Proceedings* of the regents of the state normal schools, state colleges, and state universities included extensive data and analytical essays. Since 1993 the UW System has published electronically (with various URLs) a *Legislated Accountability Report,* reporting system-wide information. The biennial, and later annual, *Bulletins, Catalogs,* and *Factbooks* of UW–Eau Claire provide details about admissions requirements, curriculum, academic programs, faculty qualifications, student organizations, and other topics. We found useful data about Wisconsin in general in the biennial *Bluebooks* (http://uwdc.library.wisc.edu/collectins/WI/WIBlueBks). National educational data can be accessed at the US Department of Education's National Center for Educational Statistics (http://nces.ed.gov).

As did Carter and Jenswold, we relied heavily on Eau Claire newspapers. The *Eau Claire Leader* and the *Eau Claire Daily Telegram*, and after 1970 the *Eau Claire Leader–Telegram*, provided both information about events and insight about the community's perspective towards the university. We also found UW–Eau Claire-related items in the *Chippewa Herald–Telegram*, which was surveyed through 1950 by Gough as part of another research project. Unlike Carter and Jenswold, we were also able to search some newspapers electronically through NewspaperArchive.com. This enabled us to find firsthand information about state politics, especially as it related to higher education, in the statewide newspapers, the Madison *Capital Times* and the *Wisconsin State Journal*. We also searched the *Milwaukee Journal Sentinel* and its predecessors, the *New York Times,* and the *Chronicle of Higher Education,* through their own databases. By dipping into the Oshkosh, Stevens Point, La Crosse, Sheboygan, and other newspapers for selected periods we gathered "out-state" views on the state normal schools, especially Eau Claire, and their successors, as well as unexpected information. For example, before the electronic era, even the most-diligent searcher of Wisconsin newspapers for information about UW–Eau Claire would never have found the 1904 *Janesville Daily Gazette* article on the issue of Harvey Schofield's athletic eligibility.

Two campus publications were essential sources for this study. The student newspaper, the *Spectator*, began publication in 1923. The campus yearbook, the *Periscope*, was published from 1917 to 1995. We also made selective use of the campus newspapers published at La Crosse, Stevens Point, and Oshkosh.

The University Archives has an extensive collection of historic photographs. In 2016, over two thousand were available for viewing at https://rescarta.apps.uwec.edu/ResCarta-Web/jsp/RcWebBrowse.jsp?browse_layout=GRID. A selection of them has also been published in Greg Kocken and Jennifer Barth, *Picturing the Past: The University of Wisconsin-Eau Claire, 1916-2016* (Eau Claire: privately printed, 2013). Two interesting short film documentaries about Eau Claire State, made in 1934 and 1942, are also available at the archives' website.

We had an abundance of sources to use in preparing this study. Many will not be available, however, fifty or one hundred years from now, for use by the authors of the next history of UW–Eau Claire. Reflecting the rise of email, the quantity of printed archival material preserved in the University Archives has shrunk dramatically in the past fifteen years (just as few pre-1941 internal memos exist because Harvey Schofield could communicate orally with all his staff). The *Periscope* ceased publication in 1995 as a consequence of declining sales, which no doubt resulted from the erosion of class identity as students increasingly took five or six years to complete their degree programs. Reflecting the nationwide decline of print journalism, by 2016 the *Spectator* has shrunk to a slim bi-weekly publication. The 2015 edition was the last printed *Catalog*.

The authors of the next history of UW–Eau Claire, however, will no doubt have different sources from which to work. The email correspondence of chancellors Mash and Levin-Stankevich, for example, has already been acquired by the University Archives and will soon become available for research. In many ways we cannot anticipate, the bicentennial history of the UW–Eau Claire certainly will be a different sort of book than the present volume.

Index

A
academic advising, 226, 230
academic calendar, 218
academic standards, 24, 70-71, 72, 74, 94, 118, 122-123, 133, 138, 201, 236-238, 252
accreditation, 35, 73-74, 77, 92, 97-98, 104, 146-147, 190-191, 196, 210, 217, 219-221, 223, 232, 238, 259
achievement gap (equity gap), 210, 236
Ackerman, Frank, 35, 82
ad hoc task forces, 196, 199; on campus computing (1987), 224-225; on graduate education (1981), 196-197, 201; on international education (1981), 196-197; on minority student and faculty recruiting and retention (1994), 233-234; on public image of UWEC (1985), 202, 208; on student retention (1995), 230; on student services (1981), 196-197, 201, 210
admissions requirements, 16, 17-18, 71-72, 74, 122, 133, 175, 204-206, 211, 221, 252
admissions office, 204, 231-232, 258
Affirmative Action, 210-212, 232-235
African American students, 87, 126, 149, 151-153, 181, 210-212, 232-235, 257
alumni association, 38, 50, 85, 107, 178
American Association of Colleges and Schools of Business, 203, 226
American Association of State Colleges and Universities, 147, 164, 209
American Association of Teachers Colleges (and successors), 73, 95, 103, 146-147
American Association of University Professors, 95, 104, 121, 128, 166, 168
American College Test (ACT), 125-126, 133, 204, 205, 208, 221, 228, 231, 252
American Ethnic Coordinating Office, 210
American Federation of Teachers (local 917), 95, 121, 166
American Indian students, 149, 182-183, 210-212, 233-235, 257
American Indian Studies program, 183
Ames, Joseph W. T., 15, 18, 30
Anderson, C. J., 30, 36
Anderson, Ken, 198, 256
Andresen, Karl, 112, 155, 158
Area Advisory Committee, 84, 85, 92, 128
Army Air Force Training Program, 44, 78-80
Arts and Sciences, School of, 145, 213
assessment, 217, 219
Association of Wisconsin State Teachers College Faculties (and successors), 94, 103, 128, 166- 167, 168-169, 173, 175, 191, 213
athletics, 28, 35, 47-48, 63, 64, 77, 90, 104, 115, 126, 235, 256

B
Bailey, Norman, 82
Barrett, Kimberly, 244
Barrows, Cheryl, 201
Bauer, Charles, 139
Beaton, Katie, 251
Bell, Terrel, 195, 209-210, 213-214
Beloit Incident (1955), 119
Benning, James, 107, 118
Big Apple (dance step), 54
Bingham, Robert, 95-96
Biology Department, 106, 111, 139, 214
Blugold Marching Band, 229, 259
Blugold Room, 116-117
Bollinger, James, 139
Bousquet, Gilles, appointed interim chancellor (2012), 245
Boyer, Ernest, meetings with UWEC leaders, 194-196
Brewer, Charles J., 32, 41, 57; appointed to the faculty, 21; as director of Teacher Education, 22, 42
Brewer Hall (Education Building), 97-98, 112
Bridgman, Benjamin W., 21, 37, 48, 82
Bridgman Hall, 140-141
Buchholz, Erna, 39, 44
budgets, 44, 208-210; 1923–1925, 30; 1931–1933, 36; 1933–1935, 37; 1939–1941, 40; 1941– 1943, 77; 1943–1945, 86; 1945–1947, 86; 1949–1951, 97; 1953–1955, 126-127; 1963–1965, 128; 1940–1970, 128; 1973–1975, 172; 1979–1981, 192; 1987–1989, 207; 1993–1995, 227; 1995–1997, 227-228; 1999–2001, 246; 2001–2003, 218, 247; 2003–2005, 247; 2009–2011, 247; 2011–2013, 247, 250; 2013–2015, 250; 2015–2017, 251
Burke, Valena, 155-156, 184
business program, 86, 101, 134, 146, 170
Business, School of, 146, 226, 231, 233; faculty, 203; MBA program, 203, 226

C
Camp Fire movement, 39, 60, 61, 66
Campus Players, 82, 113-114
Campus School (and predecessors), 22-23, 29, 42, 46, 77, 97, 173
Carnegie Foundation for the Advancement of Teaching, 194-196, 220
Center for Alcohol Studies and Education (CASE), 243
centers, student, 46, 108-109, 112, 116, 118, 119, 139, 141, 152, 204, 260-261
Chapman, Sara, 191, 197, 199-200
Chemistry Department, 111, 137, 203, 214-215, 256
Chipman, Mabel, 44
Chippewa Falls High School, 14, 21, 195, 232
Chippewa Valley Technical College (and predecessors), 15, 113
Children's Center, 184-185, 208, 213, 260
Chronicle of Higher Education, 237
Chute, Philip A., 197
Clusen, Ruth, 209
Cochrane, William, 94, 103, 104
Commission on the Redefinition of the Baccalaureate, 237
Commission on the Status of Women, 184-186, 233, 235
Communication disorders program, 170; Department, 203, 223
community-university relations, 46-48, 76, 92-93, 112-114, 171, 188-189
Computer Science Department, 170
computers, 216-217, 223-227, 253; administrative, 111
Coordinating Committee for Higher Education, 127, 128, 133, 145, 146, 164
Cooperative Campus Ministry, 144
Corporation for Public Broadcasting, 195
cost of attending UW–Eau Claire, 1916, 26; 1930s, 56; 1964, 100; 1968, 134; 1970s, 176; 1980s, 208-210; 1990s, 227-228, 230; 2000s, 246-247, 250
Council Oak, 66, 108, 148, 261
county normal schools, 14, 35
Creutz, Lester R., 21, 23, 29
curriculum, changes during World War II, 86; college course, 24, 26, 31; junior college in 1937, 40; 1916, 17-18; late 1920s, 33; 1935, 35; 1959, 102-103, 136-137; 1972, 178-179; 1978, 179; 1981, 196-197; 1990s, 236-238; 2000s, 254-255, 257-259

D
Dahle, Jo, 131, 156
Davenport, Samuel, 59, 80, 81
Davidson, J. Kenneth Sr., 169
Davies, Delpha (Mrs. William), 104, 107
Davies, William R., 39, 44, 79, 82, 93, 94, 97, 99, 104, 118, 122, 123, 126; appointed president, 50; as internationalist, 81, 121, 183; background, 50-51; building program, 76-77, 86, 91, 96- 97, 108-112; builds administrative team, 107-109; campus expansion, 112-114; consolidation with University of Wisconsin, 92, 99, 126, 127; death, 125; directs wartime programs, 77-78; educational philosophy, 75, 78; leadership style, 84, 95, 128; 1941 commencement, 74-75; opposes alcohol consumption, 119, 187;

plans for 1952–1962, 99; politics, 120-121; relations with community, 76, 113; relations with students, 118-119; religious beliefs, 119-120, 144; retirement, 124; solicits faculty opinion, 121-122; surveys reputation of Eau Claire State, 74, 76

Dempsey, Edward J., 31, 36, 37, 49, 50, 57, 77, 86, 89

Devroy, Ann, 150

Dick, R. Dale, 147, 197

differential tuition, 230, 250-251, 255

distance education, 225, 226

Dock, Thomas, 226

Doorenbos, Norman, appointed vice chancellor for academic affairs (1983), 201-202; resigns (1986), 222-223

Doudna, Edgar, 21, 36; appointed secretary to the regents, 33; appointed to the faculty, 19; denounces NCA, 73-74; influences appointed of Davies as president, 50; reaction to salary cuts in 1930s, 37, 40; reports on visit to Germany, 59, 68; resigns in protest, 89; threatens budget cuts, 77

Doyle, James E. Jr., 219

Dreyfuss, Lee Sherman, 149, 165, 177, 192, 199

E

Earl, Anthony, 212

Eau Claire Area Economic Development Association, 222

Eau Claire (Senior) High School, 11, 19, 39, 48, 63, 65, 82

Eau Claire Memorial High School, 195, 232

Eau Claire North High School, 195

Economics Department, 146

Ecumenical Religious Center, 113, 143-144, 254

Education, School of, 145, 195, 233

Emans, Lester, 97, 104, 111, 146; appointed dean of education and graduate studies, 107; appointed director of teacher education, 89; appointed vice president, 107; retirement, 145

English Department, 95, 103, 121, 123, 136, 143, 162, 233

enrollment, 24, 28-29, 31-32, 36, 40, 48, 77, 88, 100, 132-133, 164, 172, 173-174, 252, 258

environmental awareness on campus, 159, 170-172

Evans, Marie, 184

F

Faculty, academic freedom, 92, 95-96; awards for excellence, 148; community service, 106; growth in numbers, 136, 138; increased responsibilities, 76, 84, 104; lack of authority, 41, 43, 104; layoffs in early 1950s, 88; layoffs in 1970s, 172-173; opinion on merger, 166-167; original selection, 18, 21-23; qualifications, 43, 59, 73, 81-82, 92, 93, 94, 99, 103, 147; rejects ROTC program, 161; research and publication, 105, 147, 191; retention, 103-104, 138, 169; salaries, 36-37, 40, 93, 99, 103-104, 128, 166-167, 175, 192, 199, 212-213, 228; scholarship and publication, 200-201; shared governance, 168-169; student course evaluations, 179; teaching load, 31, 104, 105, 138, 147; teaching practices, 68-70, 137, 178; tenure rights, 36, 168; undergraduate research collaboration, 214, 219, 237; World War II, 81-84

Family Educational Rights and Privacy Act (1974), 176

Farmer, A. N., 1914 report on Wisconsin normal schools, 17, 69, 74

Fay, Mark, 94, 111

financial aid, 38-40, 93-94, 99, 100, 121, 176, 208-210, 228, 251

First-year Experience Program, 255

Fish, Ody, 207

Flager, Lyla, 60, 94

Fleming, Suzanne, 223

footbridge (across Chippewa River), 140, 187

Forum Series, 81, 116, 121, 126, 151, 215

Foust, Brady, 246

Fox, Arthur J., 35, 36, 50, 70, 85; appointed registrar, 42; appointed to the faculty, 19; retires, 89; teaching philosophy, 68; unpopular with students, 84; fraternities and sororities, 60, 81, 115, 117, 177, 188-189

Freshman Forum, 156, 157

Frost, Robert, 201

"Fulfilling the Promise of Excellence" (capital campaign), 244

G

Gallagher, Warren, 215

Garb, Elliot, 223

GLOBE (Gay, Lesbian, or Bi for Equality), 236

Golden Jubilee, 147-148

Goodland, Walter, 86

Governors Hall, 113

Graduate Studies program, 144-145, 146, 170, 233

graduation and retention rates, 72, 88-89, 112, 133-134, 207, 230

Grambling College, 153

Great Depression, 36-40

Groenewold, Roger, 135, 175

Grover, Herbert Jr. "Bert," 195

Grugel, Lee, 197, 201

H

Haas, Dorellen (Mrs. Leonard), 104, 147, 162, 163, 189, 190

Haas Fine Arts Center, 144, 187, 189, 190, 223

Haas, Leonard, 39, 41, 44, 46, 50, 74, 79, 82, 84, 85, 89, 90, 95, 99, 103, 104, 112, 136, 146, 147, 178; appointed dean of instruction, 89-90; appointed executive vice president of UW System, 167-168; appointed president, 124-125; appointed to the faculty, 82; as dean of instruction, 94, 107, 111, 118, 123; as executive vice president, 170, 184; building program, 139-143, 171; deflects protests after Kent State shootings, 160, 163; does not recognize SDS, 158-159, 163; educational philosophy, 101, 102, 108, 125, 128, 130-132; elimination of rural course, 126; encourages diversity, 149-150, 153; eulogizes Davies, 125; evaluation of leadership, 161-163, 193; "excellence," 128, 131; gives Golden Jubilee address, 148; leadership in community, 105-106, 112; merger, 165-166; obtains donation from L. E. Phillips, 140; opposes renaming WSU-EC, 164; promotes construction of fine arts center, 111,114, 142; rejects censorship of student publications, 105, 161; relations with students, 124, 154, 157; religious beliefs, 119; retirement, 189; returns to UWEC as chancellor, 172; service on ad hoc task force on international education, 196; shared governance with faculty, 131, 161; supports reappointment of Davidson, 169; teaching style, 70

Halberg, Carole, 244

Hallatt, Douglas, 223

Hannah, M. Emily, 190-202, 214, 218, 221; ad hoc task forces appointed (1981), 196-197; background, 191; conflict with faculty, 197-201; inauguration, 192; meetings with Carnegie Foundation leaders, 194-196; selected as chancellor, 190

Harder, Sarah, 184

Harris, Chauncey Jr., 255

Harry, Orsmby, 139, 152, 154, 177, 181, 201

Haug, Frederick Jr., 191-192, 199

Hellwig, Beth A., 244

Heil, Julius P., 40, 75, 77

Heilman, Ken, 210

Hibbard Hall, 137, 138, 143, 170-171, 192

Hibbard, Richard, 193; appointed dean of instruction, 107; appointed interim president, 167; appointed vice president, 145; as student, 59; as vice president, 146, 153, 162; background, 106-107; city council member, 106; death, 173

Hibbard, Sarah, 115, 126

Higher Education Act (1965), 136, 176

Higher Education Act Amendments (Title IX, 1972), 184, 186

Hispanic American students, 210-212, 233-235, 257

Hisrich, Joseph, 234

History Department, 106, 121, 123

Hoff, Roma, 177, 183

Homecoming, 63, 65, 90, 115-116, 152, 173, 180, 189, 205, 242, 243

honors societies, 60, 61, 81, 118, 177

Honors Day/Week, 118, 177

Honors Program, 213

Horan, Emmett, 12, 13

Horan Hall, 113

Hoot, The (dance club), 116, 152, 187

Hruza, Thelma, 81, 82

Hudson Institute, 211

INDEX 269

I

in loco parentis, 53-54, 118-119, 154-157, 241
instructional academic staff, 247
international education, 81, 87, 99, 183-184
isolationism, 1930s, 59-60

J

Johnson, Rodney, 195
Junior Prom (and successors), 48, 60, 65, 66, 75

K

Katherine Putnam Hall (men's residence hall), 108-109, 112, 116
Katherine Thomas Hall (women's residence hall), 108-109, 112, 154
Karwand, Elwood C., 199-200
Kearney, John, 107, 134
Kennedy, John F., 124, 131
Kent State shootings, 144, 160-161, 261
Kinsman, Delos, 14, 18
Kittle, George, 31, 33, 72
Kleine, Patricia, 255
Kohler, Walter, 126-127
Kjer, Earl, 81-82, 86, 94, 104, 114
Krause, Floyd, 82, 104, 139-140
Kronshage, Theodore, 18, 22, 26-27
Ku Klux Klan, 57

L

L. E. Phillips Science Hall, 137, 139-140, 147, 149
LaFollette, Robert M., 24, 28, 57
Larson, Charles O., 195
Lavine, John, 165, 191
Legislative Scholarships, 40, 94, 100, 122
Levin-Stankevich, Brian, 246-252, 258, 261; appointed chancellor (2006), 245
libraries, 39, 110-111, 213, 216, 224, 227
liberal arts, emphasis by Haas in 1940s, 85; formally added to curriculum, 97; growth in 1950s, 101, 102; in original curriculum, 17; liberal education program, 259; 1930s, 40; 1960s, 134, 145; 1990s, 213
Little Theater, 97, 113, 114
Loomis, Orland, 75, 86
Lord Larson, Vicki, 201, 254, 260, 266; appointed interim chancellor, 244
Lucey, Patrick J., 165, 166, 172, 173
Lyall, Katherine, 196, 213, 218, 227, 236, 244-245

M

Majors, Richard, 232
Marquardt, Steve R., 201, 216, 227
Mash, Donald J., 238-245, 252, 258, 261; appointed chancellor (1998) 238; budget, 240; mood on campus after attacks of September 11, 2001, 240-241; resignation (2004), 244
McCarthy, Joseph R., 120-121
McIntyre, William D., 99, 110, 154; appointed regent, 85; arranges land acquisitions, 112-113; city council member, 106; influence with legislature, 89, 126, 128; supports consolidation, 127
McPhee, Eugene, 19, 39, 48, 53, 54, 88, 90, 97, 103, 106, 124, 125, 126, 128; appointed director of teacher education, 42-43; appointed secretary to the regents, 89; backs dismissal of Bingham, 95-96; defends *in loco parentis*, 154, 156; leave of absence, 77; library dedication speech, 111; opposes elimination of rural course, 126; projects enrollments, 133; retirement, 167; supports merger, 165; stops construction of chapel, 119; warns Davies about termination, 93; Wilson Purchase, 113
McPhee Physical Education Center, 141
Medical Technology program, 101, 106, 145
Memorial Hall, 49, 96, 108, 113
Merger Implementation Study Committee, 168-170
merger, of Wisconsin higher education systems, 92, 99, 126-127, 164-170, 218, 250-251
Miller, Vine, 42, 43, 94, 120
Milliren, Monroe, 42, 50
Minnesota, tuition reciprocity with, 205-206, 250
mission statements, 17, 169, 170, 259
Morris, John, 122, 179, 200; appointed dean of arts and sciences, 145; appointed interim vice president, 167; appointed vice chancellor, 173; as dean of arts and sciences, 146, 162; as interim vice president, 169, 172, 173, 181; as vice chancellor, 191; community service, 167; not appointed chancellor, 190; resignation as vice chancellor, 197
Murray, Arthur L., 43, 84
Murray Hall, 141, 155
Music program, 43, 46, 60, 83-84, 86, 111, 115, 142, 229
Myers, Joan Rohr, 234

N

National Association of Intercollegiate Athletics (NAIA), 198
National Commission for the Accreditation of Teacher Education (NCATE), 147, 195
National Defense Education Act (1958), 121, 136
National Survey of Student Engagement (NSSE), 254-255
National Youth Administration, 38-39
Nelson, Gaylord, 128
New Deal, 38-39, 58
Newman Center, 143, 254
Nix, Edmund A., 124, 126
Nixon, Richard M., 124, 159, 160
normal schools, 10-19, 21-22, 25, 26-27, 28, 30-33, 36, 39, 46, 48, 54, 57, 60, 64, 65, 69, 71, 72, 74, 147, 166, 220, 265, 267
North Central Association of Colleges and Secondary Schools (and successors), 35, 73-74, 77, 97-99, 146-147, 190, 196, 210, 217, 219-221, 223, 232, 238, 259
Nursing Building, 143
Nursing program, 86, 101, 113, 134, 145, 170
Nursing, School of, 145-146, 203, 225, 233, 243-244; Marshfield Program, 225

O

Oak Ridge Hall, 141
Olson, Ade, 90
O'Neil, Robert, 189, 190, 194, 195, 203; dealings with Emily Hannah and with UWEC Faculty Senate, 199-202, 211, 213
O'Neill, Wallace, 199
orientation program, 73, 125, 181
Ostmoe, Patricia, 201, 233
Oxby, Hilda Belle, 22, 44, 49, 59, 67, 72, 81, 94, 95

P

Patterson, Laura, 215-216
Periscope, 60, 66, 78
Petersen, Stella, 90, 107, 111
Philipp, Emanuel, 17, 27, 57
Progressive Movement in Wisconsin, 13, 14-15, 24, 27
Putnam Park, 12, 49, 96-97, 104, 112-113, 171-172

Q

Quality Reinvestment Program, 227

R

regents, board of, normal schools, 12, 17, 31, 32, 48, 166; state colleges, 125, 128; state teachers colleges, 89, 96, 97; state universities, 146, 153, 159, 164, 165-168; University of Wisconsin System, 167-168, 172, 176, 179, 190, 204-207, 211-214, 233
registrar, 215-216
Reilly, Kevin, 244
Rennebohm, Oscar, 92, 97
residence halls, 138-141, 154-156, 208
Reserve Officers Training Corps, 59, 95, 159, 161, 163, 241
Resnikoff, Neal and Betty, 162
Reynolds, John, 127-128
Rhodes Scholars, 255-256
Russell, Connie, 216
Ryan, Bo, 198

S

St. Olaf College, 101, 111, 131
St. Louis, Nadine, 186, 197
Sacred Heart Hospital, 112-113, 145-146, 241
Sampson, Helen, 133, 134, 184
Sanders, Tayo II, 255-256
Satz, Ronald S., 201, 211, 243-244
Schlattman, Ronald, 199
Schmidt, James, appointed chancellor (2013), 245
Schnack, Larry, 202, 213, 218, 221, 223, 231-238, 251; appointed chancellor (1985), 202; appointed interim chancellor (1984), 202; Design for Diversity, 210; retires (1997), 238
Schneider, John, 67, 68, 95; AWSTCF leader, 94; critiques racism, 59; death, 126; politics, 121; teaching style, 68-69

Schneider, Josephine (Mrs. John), 48-49, 69
Schneider, Nicholas, 262
Schneider Hall, 137, 138, 143
Schofield, Dorothy (Mrs. Harvey), 44
Schofield, Frances Jagoditsh (Mrs. Harvey), 44
Schofield Hall (Old Main), 13-14, 30, 34, 38, 49, 67, 112, 139, 257
Schofield, Harvey A., 22, 23, 26, 29, 30, 35, 40, 43, 44, 46, 57, 73, 74, 99; appointed president, 18; athletics, 20-21; background, 18-19; building program, 49; death, 75, 82; educational philosophy, 50, 71; leadership style, 41-42; relations with community, 46-48; relations with students, 45-46, 54, 67, 118; retirement, 50
Schofield, John, 54, 65
Service Learning Requirement, 237
Serviceman's Readjustment Act (1944), 86-89
Shaw, Kenneth, 211
Simpson, George, 19, 25, 26, 28, 50, 65, 67, 68, 77
Singing Statesmen, 229
Sinz, Jeanne, 223
Smelstor, Marjorie, 223, 237-238
Smith, Peter J., 30, 47, 50, 89
Smolensky, Eugene, 208-210
Social Work, Department of, 202
Sociology Department, 169, 170
Southeast Asian students, 210-212, 233-235, 257
Spellings Commission, 254
Sports Illustrated, coverage of UWEC Men's Basketball (1971), 198
Steiger, Lance, 253-254
Stone, Veda, 149, 183
Student Health Service, 73, 99, 185-186, 241
Student Homeless Awareness Chapter, 222
Student Radio Initiative, 220
Student Senate, 203, 220, 230, 250-251; University Activities Commission, 203
Students, alcohol consumption, 54, 116, 118, 119, 123, 187-189, 242-243; assemblies, 58-59, 118, 156; beanies, 66, 118, 156-157; disabilities, 40, 117; free speech, 156, 158; geographical origins, 24, 53, 89, 100, 175; government, 46, 92, 93, 99, 117, 119, 125, 176, 179, 185, 189; graduation rates, 207, 230, 259; marriage, 101, 117, 155; off-campus employment, 208, 228, 230; off-campus residences, 53, 80, 154-155; organizations, 60-64, 65, 115; opinion on merger, 167; parents' socio-economic status, 55-56, 100; political voting behavior, 57-58, 83, 121, 124, 126, 127-128, 248-249; popular music, 54, 152, 180; ratio of women to men, 205, 231; religious activities, 57, 119-120, 125, 143-144; retention, 230; sexual behavior, 54, 65, 115, 119, 186; sexual orientation, 117, 235-236, 258; singing, 66, 73, 229
Students for a Democratic Society, 149, 158, 162
summer session, 40, 78, 103-104

Sutherland Hall, 140-141
Sutherland, Laura, 18, 43, 46, 48, 50, 58, 60, 94, 198; appointed dean of women, 42; as dean of women, 80, 81, 90; death, 147; politics, 121; teaching style, 69; writes UWEC history, 147
Symphonic Choir, 229

T

Tallant, Steven, 245
Teacher education program, 17-18, 32-33, 122, 134, 145, 194-195, 213-214
textbooks, 23-24, 69
Thomas, Katherine, 22, 57, 89
Thompson, Tommy, 207, 212, 219
Tornado Watch, 188-189
Towers Residence Hall, 141

U

United Council of Students, 167
University Assessment Committee, 238
University Forum, 131, 153, 156, 158, 171, 189
University Lutheran Church, 254
university mottos, "Accepting the Challenge," 199, 219; "Accepting the Challenge of Excellence," 219; "Excellence," 148, 199; "The Power of And," 262
University Research Office (Office of Research and Sponsored Programs), 201, 255-256
university seal, 148
University Senate, 136, 156, 159, 178, 197, 199, 201, 212-213, 236-238, 244, 246
University Symphony Orchestra, 229
University Wiring Project (Ethernet), 224-227
University of Wisconsin System, 167-168, 170, 186, 194, 196, 245, 250; Centers of Excellence, 213-215; Design for Diversity (1980s), 211-213, 217, 219, 232-236; Enrollment Management (1980s and 1990s), 204-207, 221, 227; "Future of the UW System" (1980s), 212; "Plan 2008," 232, 236
University of Wisconsin–Extension, 15, 78, 92, 127
University of Wisconsin–Green Bay, 172
University of Wisconsin–La Crosse (and predecessors), 14, 49, 73, 158, 162, 170, 250
University of Wisconsin–Madison (and predecessors), 15, 17, 23, 26, 28, 31, 32, 36, 37, 38, 44, 58, 71, 88, 92, 126, 127, 128, 145, 146, 158, 165, 170, 172, 175, 187
University of Wisconsin–Milwaukee (and predecessors), 33, 48, 58, 73, 78, 86, 92, 127, 158, 165, 172, 175
University of Wisconsin–Oshkosh (and predecessors), 16, 44, 58, 73, 141, 149, 153, 162, 163, 173, 258
University of Wisconsin–Parkside, 172
University of Wisconsin–Platteville (and predecessors), 91, 125, 127, 155, 162
University of Wisconsin–River Falls (and predecessors), 14, 16, 42, 170, 183
University of Wisconsin–Stout (and predecessors), 13, 63, 115-116, 127, 170, 258

University of Wisconsin–Superior (and predecessors), 16, 86, 92, 128, 168, 170
University of Wisconsin–Stevens Points (and predecessors), 45, 143, 149, 158
University of Wisconsin–Whitewater (and predecessors), 14, 16, 91, 101, 153, 158, 162, 167, 172
upper campus, development, 96-97, 112-113, 141

V

Van Hise, Charles R., 15, 16, 23
Van Ort, Suzanne, 197
veterans, 29, 86-89, 116, 117, 159, 241
Viennese Ball, 177-179, 184
Vietnam War, 149, 159-161

W

Walker, Scott, 247, 250-251
Wallin, James R., 42, 77, 93, 95
Walsh, Grace, 82-83, 86
Ward, Clara May, 43, 57, 83
Way, Kimera K., 244
Weaver, John, 167-168, 170, 172, 184
West Central Wisconsin Consortium, 170
Wick, Marshall, 69, 168, 172
Wilcox, Frances, 81, 113
Wilson Purchase, 113
Wilson, Reginald, 232-234
Wing, Geraldine, 41, 69, 80, 84
Winter Carnival, 115, 152
Wisconsin Bureau of Capital Development, 170-171
Wisconsin Department of Public Instruction, 36, 204
Wisconsin Intercollegiate Athletic Association, 198
women, athletics, 63, 186-187; faculty, 22, 103; gender roles, 1930s, 64-65; 1950s, 123-124; panty raids, 116; proportion of students, 9, 64, 89, 101, 135, 181; second-wave feminism, 184- 187
Women's Chorus, 229
Women's Concert Chorale, 229
Woodson, Charles B. Jr., 87
World War I, 28-29
World War II, impact on Eau Claire State, 77-81; postwar adjustments, 86-89; student attitudes toward in 1930s, 59-60
WUEC, 89.7 FM, 220

Y

YWCA, 39, 60, 61, 62, 65
Young, Edward G., 208-210

Z

Zorn Arena (and previous names), 97, 125, 126, 158, 180, 185, 204
Zorn, Willis, 35, 43, 78, 79-80, 97; appointed dean of men, 82; appointed to the faculty, 63; as dean of men, 111, 116, 118-119, 139, 149, 157, 198

About the Authors

Robert J. Gough is a professor emeritus of history at the University of Wisconsin–Eau Claire and was the Maxwell P. Schoenfeld Distinguished Professor in the Humanities for 2009–10. He earned a BA degree from Rutgers University and MA and PhD degrees from the University of Pennsylvania. His published scholarship has been in the areas of early American history, twentieth-century Wisconsin history, and the history of education.

James W. Oberly is a professor of history and American Indian studies at the University of Wisconsin–Eau Claire. He earned a BA degree from Columbia University and MA and PhD degrees from the University of Rochester. His published scholarship has been in the areas of nineteenth-century American public land policy, Wisconsin American Indian history, and Hungarian immigration to the United States. In 1997 he received the University of Wisconsin System Board of Regents Excellence in Teaching Award and at present he is a member of the Organization of American Historians Executive Board.

Professors Gough and Oberly share an academic genealogy which traces back to Wisconsin's Frederick Jackson Turner, originator of the "frontier thesis" explanation of American history. Gough was a graduate student at Penn of Lee Benson and Oberly was a graduate student at Rochester of Mary Young. Benson and Young had been students at Cornell University of Paul W. Gates (in whose book *The Wisconsin Pine Lands of Cornell University* [1943] Eau Claire's Henry C. Putnam plays a major role). Gates in turn had been a graduate student at Harvard University of Frederick Merk, who was Wisconsin-born and a graduate of the University of Wisconsin. Merk was a graduate student of Turner's after Turner was called to Harvard from the University of Wisconsin in 1910.